A Collection of Ranter Writings

A Collection of Ranter Writings

Spiritual Liberty and Sexual Freedom in the English Revolution

Edited by

Nigel Smith

www.plutobooks.com

First published 2014 by Pluto Press
345 Archway Road, London N6 5AA

www.plutobooks.com

British Library Cataloguing in Publication Data
A catalogue record for this book is available from the British Library

ISBN 978 0 7453 3360 1 Paperback
ISBN 978 0 7453 3361 8 Hardback
ISBN 978 1 7837 1010 2 PDF

Library of Congress Cataloging in Publication Data applied for

10 9 8 7 6 5 4 3 2 1

Typeset by Andrew Miller
Printed and bound by CPI Group (UK) Ltd, Croydon, CR0 4YY

for the Ranters of Hull,
the Raunters of Oxford, and
the Rockers of New Jersey

'ther's a most glorious designe in it:
and equality, community and universall love'

in memoriam amicorum pretiosorum

Bill Readings (1960–1994)
Jeremy Maule (1952–1998)

'Together both, ere the high lawns appeared
Under the opening eye-lids of the morn,
We drove a-field'

Contents

Foreword

Many forms of protest necessarily foreground the cause for which they fight: better social justice, better political representation, ending gender, sexual or racial discrimination (or exploitation), protecting the environment and the climate, and of late, protecting and promoting a faith, or a version of a faith. This usually means commitment to some kind of revised social order, and along the way, protest may be linked with a utopian vision of the future.

But there are other kinds of protest that refuse the above. Their force arises from such deep unhappiness with the present predicament that it is driven by a need for immediate, forceful rejection of the customs and ways of prevailing conditions because those old ways are merely a compromised way of getting by. They won't do, and there must be an immediate noise of refusal. Ordinary life, they claim, is lived as a betrayal of another truth that is being ignored or, what's worse, suppressed and even cruelly denied. So the Sex Pistols and the punk revolution that they spearheaded were understood as a necessary angry deformation of the polite conventions in 1970s Britain and elsewhere that were the carapace of class oppression. For many people life in 1976 was not fun and had NO FUTURE. It had to be rejected by the brusque, grotesque denunciation of English manners and institutions that was the punk song. That's how Greil Marcus saw matters in his widely revered *Lipstick Traces: A Secret History of the Twentieth Century* (1989), 1–15, and he regarded the Ranters, notably Abiezer Coppe, as seventeenth-century predecessors of Johnny Rotten (p. 27).

This was rebellion by means of a vulgar, foul-mouthed aesthetic of protest, one that has not left our culture. Punk's exuberant anger was directed at the shallow hypocrisy of the establishment, an attitude that was bitterly sharpened by the sanctimonious politics that followed in the 1980s and 1990s. It was the stiletto moment of punk protest when, early on, the four-letter F word was unsheathed on early evening TV, at a time when no one had dared do that. Quite sensational, reducing a live interview to anarchy, this infamous 'hit' was probably well-planned and very effective. Swearing has always been a direct way to expose moral hypocrisy. Think it no longer matters? Think Pussy Riot, and its imprisoned members, two of whom were whipped publicly in Sochi, Russia, the day before this foreword was written.

Such moments were not silly pranks during those quaint days before the latest age of terror. They are in fact part of a larger, much longer history of agit-prop-style protest against the profound inadequacy of the conventional ways of doing things. Sometimes politeness is just not good enough. It may be necessary to invent an art movement in order to escape into a frame of being where life becomes more authentic and more just, and this has certainly been part of the mission of the earlier twentiety-century *avant garde*, or indeed the visionary poetry of Blake and Shelley in the late eighteenth and early nineteenth centuries. Post-punk anti-authoritarianism, witnessed in the acid house gatherings of the late 1980s and early 1990s, has a literary component in the form of poetic declamation, a new expression of freedom that aims to perpetuate the moment of protest. As Peter H. Marshall writes, 'It fuses fact and fiction, history and myth, and opposes the primitive to the civilized. Rather than resorting to agit-prop, it tries to politicize culture and transform it from the inside' (*Demanding the Impossible: A History of Anarchism* (2010), 494). Such a move seems like deploying a creative anarchism within the heartland of mass popular culture.

The Situationist movement of the mid-twentieth century believed that individual expression through directly lived experiences and the fulfillment of authentic desires had been denigrated by commodity capitalism. The solution was to use art to make moments of life deliberately constructed for the purpose of reawakening and pursuing authentic desires; everyday life was to be made liberating. Turning his attention to history, the Situationist philosopher Raoul Vaneigem regarded the 'Free Spirit' mysticism of the Middle Ages as an attempt by pious lay people in the past to assert a genuinely creative devotion, over and against the repressive powers of national (or international) churches and the state, powers that were at least disciplinary and at worst violent. For Vaneigem the 'orthodox,' sexually sterilized mysticism of the famous medieval mystics of the monastery — Meister Eckhart, Suso, Tauler, van Ruysbroeck, Groote — was 'revenge of the spirit for attempts to emancipate the body' by the 'Free Spirit' lay mystics (*The Movement of the Free Spirit* (1994), 91). The Ranters, he thought, seemed to have brought this sense of liberation to bear on the rigors of Calvinist discipline in mid-seventeeth-century England.

The Ranters.

Who flourished briefly in the middle of the seventeenth century, shortly after the execution of King Charles I, the abolition of the House of Lords and the proclamation of a republic. For a short time a number of unusual individuals loudly expressed their spiritual liberty in the name of God: they swore, allegedly practiced free love, and their writings were remarkable for their candid and daring originality. God was in them, surging through them and giving their every action life and meaning. The most prominent Ranter, Abiezer Coppe, saw this way as the ultimate just fellowship: sharing everything as the Bible tells us to. Coppe's example reminds Marcus of the wasted, noisy down and outs of Berkeley, CA (*Lipstick Traces*, 434–35). For a while Laurence Clarkson developed a personal cosmology that justified unbounded free love, and, although their writings seem less startling, both Joseph Salmon and Jacob Bauthumley let that God within them banish sin. They reconnected with the idea of a sustaining natural world, which is where God also lived and to which they would return at death. They re-imagined themselves as untainted, beautiful and wholly at one with their redeemer, Jesus, with whom they enjoyed a fulfilling mystical marriage. Other Ranter writings contain a theology embodied and celebrated by sexual intercourse. Orthodox theology and the social structure denied this and said people had to suffer in sin and subjection, but the Ranters had other ideas.

Whatever the Ranters learned from their brief moment (they were all punished, most recanted, and moved on), those who wrote each did something extraordinary with the resources of the English language and the cultural reservoir that it had become by the mid-seventeeth century. They invert, jest, make new certainties, new rhythms (sometimes falteringly, sometimes with impressive struggle), swear, channel God, see God's hand in the events of their world, voice angels, and speak with the freshness of people who have finally, at long, long last, come to terms with themselves. Sin is gone: I can be who I am. It is altogether a remarkable verbal architecture and why they are worth reading.

The literature that is still read today from the seventeenth century is incredibly rich in its originality and its enduring value: the later Shakespeare, Ben Jonson, Donne, Descartes, Thomas Hobbes, Milton, Marvell, Margaret Cavendish to name just a few. The Ranter writings, in their outrageous way, are right up there with them.

Nigel Smith
21 February, 2014

Foreword to First Edition, 1983

Why read the Ranters? Two different kinds of answer could be given to that question, depending on whether your main interest is in English history or English literature. (A third kind of answer would apply if your main concern were the development of English Christianity — but then you would inevitably be interested in both literature and history as well.)

The historian's answers are the most obvious. The surviving Ranter writings tell us things we could not otherwise know about how the English imagination — or some English imaginations — structured the world, politically and metaphysically, in the critical years of the mid-seventeenth century, about the extremes of English Antinomianism and millenarianism, and about their possible connections with the reaction to social injustice (specifically in the period following the suppression of the Levellers, when the hopes of those capable of advanced social thinking seemed finally to be deprived of any practical outcome).

The historian is also likely to be intrigued by authority's antagonism to the Ranters, and by the persecution to which, with the convenient warrant of religious orthodoxy, they were subjected. Are we to read this as an index of the danger the Ranters were believed to represent, and hence as an intimation that their ideas and attitudes were not, as the governing class successfully made it appear, monstrous and eccentric, but typical of a fairly widespread scepticism among the common people?

That we do not know more about such issues, and about the Ranters themselves, testifies to the success of official censorship and intimidation. One of the most difficult and challenging aspects of Ranter study is the disentangling of what these remarkable individuals actually thought and felt, not only from the misrepresentations of their enemies, but also from the confusion of their own writing. This confusion can probably be attributed at times to hopes of evading the attention of the censor. But at a deeper level it sprang from the newness and strangeness of their intellectual and spiritual enterprise, which (though certainly some parallels can be found in the writings of earlier visionaries) lacked any conventional forms and any inherited language that could adequately encompass it.

This brings us to the literary significance of the Ranters — or rather to the question of whether they have any at all; for a certain kind of literary sensibility would find it hard to concede that they have. From traditional histories of English literature, and even from more specialised accounts of seventeenth-century English prose, they have been wholly excluded. No mention will be found of Coppe, of Clarkson, of Salmon, or of Bauthumley in Douglas Bush's *Oxford History of English Literature in the Earlier Seventeenth Century*, even in its revised edition (1962); nor do they appear in the *Cambridge History of English Literature*. Their rediscovery has been the work of historians, notably Christopher Hill, who has the advantage of being a historian who understands literature and has earned the confidence of literary critics. Hill's *The World Turned Upside Down* (1972), and most recently his 1982 Bateson Lecture (printed in *Essays in Criticism*, Vol. XXXII, April 1982), have made it clear that assessments of seventeenth-century literature can no longer ignore the Ranters.

But what kind of literature did the Ranters produce? How can we accommodate their writings within our notions of what literature constitutes, and the pleasures it provides? Sometimes, of course, this presents no difficulty: a work such as Bauthumley's *The Light and Dark Sides of God* is immediately recognisable as a neglected masterpiece of seventeenth-century devotional prose. But more often it is the very difficulty of answering these questions that forces us to acknowledge the importance of the Ranters. Their failure to fit into our accepted categories confirms our need to revise those categories. For it is clear that Ranter writing is more serious, engaged and impassioned and, from the viewpoint of expression, more adventurous, than any of the conventionally accredited 'literature' that emanated from the Civil War years (than, say, the Cavalier lyrics, which students are still encouraged to think of as one of the war's chief cultural achievements). Intensity is the vital factor in Ranter prose, and this intensity not only precludes routine modes of expression, it also impels the Ranters towards, or beyond, the limits of coherence. Yet paradoxically, though it is destructive in this sense of literary effect, it obliges us to widen our concept of literature in order to embrace it — for an idea of literature that could not find a place for such intensity would be unduly shrunken and enfeebled.

The charge of madness, which some critics have used as an expedient for dismissing the Ranters, cannot be taken seriously. For even if insanity and literary significance were obviously incompatible, which they are not, it would still remain true that what the modern mind diagnoses as mental unbalance in the Ranters was common among seventeenth-century Christians. In the tradition of the spiritual autobiography, to which Ranter prose partly belongs, accounts of visions and paranormal revelations are frequent, as Owen Watkins's survey of the genre, *The Puritan Experience* (1972), shows. When Bunyan in *Grace Abounding* tells us how he fled from a church steeple, lest God should topple it upon his head as a punishment for his delight in bell-ringing, we may find it painfully deluded, but only ignorance of history will allow us to pronounce it mad.

Besides, though Ranter beliefs may seem initially surprising, we can identify features in them that relate them to other and potent areas of our literary experience. The godhead of man, as promulgated by the Ranters, is one of the dynamic ideas behind Traherne's *Centuries of Meditation*, though Traherne derived it from the writings of Alexandrian neo-Platonists. The question of God's putative responsibility for evil exercised many minds in the seventeenth century, including Milton's, and is the central issue in *Paradise Lost*. As a historical phenomenon Ranterism seems to have notable affinities with Romanticism. Both coincided with revolutionary political upheavals; both replace authority, and outmoded academicism, with personal illumination; both develop pantheism; both demand a new and compassionate attention to the outcast and oppressed — beggars, rogues, thieves — and both couple this with antagonism towards the great ones of the earth. Both are combatively irrational and anti-intellectual movements, and seek unorthodox means of expression — so that, for example, Blake's prophetic books are, like Ranter utterances, difficult to contain within usual notions of the literary or the intelligible.

Reading the Ranters also brings vividly to mind the pronouncements of a late Romantic, D.H. Lawrence. The sense of a new age, released from old bondages, the shameless celebration of sexuality, the trust in impulse and instinct, and the belief that any act may be good if it is done with passion and conviction, however it may square with the moral codes of the tame and the law-abiding — these are common properties in Lawrence and the Ranters, and in the twentieth century, as in the seventeenth, they have seemed life-affirming to some and hideous to others, and have attracted persecution and censorship.

Some aspects of Ranter thought, such as the rejection of the literal truth of the Bible, disbelief in the actuality of heaven and hell, and incredulity about personal immortality, may strike us as singularly modern. But ultimately the justification for reading Ranter literature (as for reading any literature from the past) must be that it can widen our understanding of human potential by showing us what it was like to be alive in another age. At times Ranter literature can do this more fully, and more startlingly, than any other literary artefacts that have survived from the mid-seventeenth century. As an example, we might cite Abiezer Coppe's encounter with the beggar in his *A Fiery Flying Roll* (see pp. 93–95). Christopher Hill calls this 'experimental prose,' which is surely right, in that Coppe has found a medium that conveys with unprecedented dramatic force the simultaneous pressure of internal and external stimuli. The raw poetic power of the passage derives from the way in which it brings the ungainly splendour of its Biblical echoes into conjunction with the mundane (as in 'And behold, the plague of God fell into my pocket'). This conjunction is not, as it at first seems, merely artless and intemperate. Rather, it is a stylistic correlative to the situation which the Ranters postulate. For it is Coppe's contention that you are in heaven, or hell, on earth. This apparently squalid little encounter is a focus for mighty influences. It is not a moral incident, nor a psychological one (a conflict, as a post-Freudian might see it, between the ego and the superego): rather it is, in Coppe's eyes, as spiritual as a Bible narrative, and his style signals this. Where else, we may ask, in mid-seventeenth-century literature could we find a piece of writing which so aggressively conveys the dominance of the inner world over the outer, which simultaneously enacts and analyses a vivid and recognisable psychological situation, and which also exhibits such practical compassion?

A knowledge of Ranter literature which, for these various reasons, seems desirable, is difficult to acquire. Ranter tracts are among the rarest of rare books. Even a great library like the Bodleian lacks copies of several of the texts Nigel Smith presents here. In these circumstances his collection is extremely opportune.

John Carey

Preface

In the preface to the first edition of this anthology I wrote this opening sentence: 'Many books on seventeenth-century literature, culture and society mention the Ranters, often as the absolute end to which liberty of belief could go, but often in elusive, ill-defined terms.' I wrote that in 1982, during the summer after the Falklands War; the book was published the following spring.

Unlike the other extreme Puritan sects and radical groups of the English Civil War and Interregnum years, the Ranters had received very little attention until an obvious analogy appeared between them and the sexually libertine 'underground' movement of the later 1960s. There had been Norman Cohn's *The Pursuit of the Millennium* (1957), concerned mostly with mystical anarchism and communism in the Middle Ages, but with its important appendix of Ranter pamphlet extracts. Then came the valuable A.L. Morton's *The World of the Ranters* (1970) and Christopher Hill's magisterial, highly influential account of mid-seventeenth-century radicalism, *The World Turned Upside Down* (1972), probably his greatest work. There was also J.F. McGregor's important thesis of 1968, the findings of which remained unpublished in 1983, but which had informed Hill's views. These were works by historians; Abiezer Coppe and Laurence Clarkson had also been noted very occasionally in literary studies, as very minor figures in the history of autobiography.

In the space of thirty years much more has become known about the Ranters, and thanks largely to Cohn and Hill, awareness of them is now well-embedded in popular culture, where they are revered by many as the ancestors of outrageous but righteous protest against not merely social injustice but moral hypocrisy. The eminent authority on popular music, Greil Marcus, saw an obvious connection between the extravagance of the Ranters and that of the punk movement of the later 1970s and early 1980s. That long line of dissent, Morton's community of the 'everlasting gospel,' holds that the strict moral norms of orthodox western Christianity are nothing more than a cruel means of social control: humans are not inherently sinful and may find their true and innocent relationship with God in a liberated present: heaven on earth.

Inside academe the Ranter phenomenon was subject to a severe test in J.C. Davis's *Fear, Myth and History: The Ranters and the Historians* (1986). Davis argued that the Ranter movement was mostly the invention of a hostile press, so that Hill and others had believed what was merely an invented chimera. There were, he claimed, very few if any genuine holy, swearing sexual libertines, and moreover, historians had largely misunderstood the actual theology of those called 'Ranters,' which was usually far less subversive than was in fact the case. Historians like Morton and Hill had been misled, he averred, by their own left-wing bias. The right wing intelligentsia in Britain loved it: in the aftermath of the Thatcher government's victories over organized labour in the mid-1980s, the Secretary of State for Education, Kenneth Baker, championed a book (he chose *Fear, Myth and History* as his book of the year in *The Observer*, 29 November 1987) that undermined the history of popular movements.

Davis was certainly challenged, not least for his stringent insistence on definitions, so as to make each Ranter fail to fit his required identikit picture, and his use of evidence, which was almost exclusively printed books: a very different picture of the Ranters emerged from manuscript evidence in archives, not least the existence of the milieu he was at pains to deny, and before the hostile pamphlets and newsbooks had been printed. Nonetheless, he did importantly focus attention on the complexity and sometimes contradictory nature of Ranter ideas. This perspective connected fruitfully with an older tradition of scholarship on radical Puritans represented by Hill's contemporary G.F. Nuttall. If the Ranters (and by association the other radical groups) were seen to be less numerous than they had been imagined to be, the debate triggered by Davis also led to a new wave of detailed research on Civil War radicalism in which a far more finely-grained view was assembled in the 1990s and 2000s; thankfully one constructed beyond partisan politics. Most of the major radical figures and groups became the subjects of even more highly exacting research, using hitherto unknown or unused evidence, and their writings have been examined in exciting and valuable new commentaries and editions in literary studies (and not forgotten, as they are sometimes imagined to be): since 1996 the Levellers, Diggers and Ranters have all been substantially reborn through new accounts in the work of, among others, David Como, John Gurney, James Holstun, Nicholas McDowell, Ariel Hessayon, B.J. Gibbons, Ann Hughes, Thomas N. Corns, David Loewenstein, Rachel Foxley and Clement Hawes. The introduction and necessarily brief commentary in this edition is both informed by this work and in places adds to its findings. The Ranters certainly existed and they did say and sometimes act that for which they are notorious, but also much more; now we can understand them and take what we will from them with a clarity unimaginable in 1983. By turns I personally find them both uplifting and distinctly terrifying. I can quite understand why they met with such a hostile response, and that seems like a good reason to guard their memory now.

In 1982 I was a first year graduate student in Oxford, and inexperienced in the business of editing. In this edition all the texts have been thoroughly checked: the spelling and punctuation is as in the originals, except where very occasionally emended to correct obvious errors, and represented by placing the emendations inside diagonal brackets, or in a very few instances of incorrect punctuation, silently emended. Two errors in the compositing of Hebrew text have also been silently emended. The two instances of a pamphlet that went into a second edition are discussed in the notes. The first edition of this anthology included Coppe's printed recantations; these are now omitted in order to make space for the anonymous *A Jvstjfjcatjon of the Mad Crew* (1650) and Joseph Salmon's *Divinity Anatomized* (1649), of which no copy was known to have survived in 1983.

Many readers, especially in universities, can now read nearly all the original Ranter tracts on the Early English Books Online website, and there are several online texts. However, many other readers will not have such access, and the point of this edition is to provide a reliable edition of the original texts along with explanations of unfamiliar or difficult words and ideas, a historical and critical introductory account that is indebted to the best scholarship, and that points to questions for the future. The first edition, published by Junction Books, certainly had an impact: it was widely reviewed in the UK press, and is frequently cited, despite its growing rarity over the years. It was particularly pleasing to see Coppe being included, albeit temporarily, in the Norton Anthology of English Literature. Now this little book in transformed form (as Coppe would have said) can enjoy a second life.

I would like to acknowledge the facilities and staff of the following libraries: The Bodleian Library, Oxford; the British Library; the Library of Worcester College, Oxford; the William Andrews Clark Memorial Library, University of California, Los Angeles; Princeton Theological Seminary Library. I must thank Lesley Montgomery, Mr. L.E. Weeks and Dr. J.H. Parker at Worcester College for their prompt attention. The Committee for Research in the Humanities and Social Sciences at Princeton University generously helped fund the production of camera-ready copy. I am very grateful to John Barton for translating Hebrew vocabulary, to Leon Grek for help with Latin, and to Will Poole for checking Latin, Hebrew and Greek. Michael Mason and Judy Bennett proved sympathetic and perceptive editors in 1983, as Anne Beech and Robert Webb have in 2012–13; Sally Mapstone helped much with editorial and general advice in 1982. I owe much gratitude to Christopher Hill and Geoffrey Nuttall for encouragement, but my biggest debts are to my two teachers: John Hoyles in Hull introduced me to Antinomianism with a remarkable insider's perspective; John Carey, peerless, inspiring, exacting Merton Professor of English Literature recognized and encouraged my interest and was good enough to provide the fine galvanizing and probing foreword in 1983 that is reproduced in this edition. My graduate student Andrew Miller patiently digitized the original edition and then learned new software so that we could produce camera-ready copy for Pluto Press. His efforts have been truly extraordinary and his advice often crucial, as the reader will see in some of the notes (see below, pp. 67, 204, 210, 213, 214; there is much more). Antoinette Sutto and Joe Moshenska also helped at earlier stages of preparation. Someone told me that doing a doctorate in Oxford was a good way to make a mark, and shortly afterwards Christopher Hill told me to edit the Ranters, so I did. While the Ranters might be inspiration for anyone to turn orthodoxy and oppresiveness on its head with intense creative energy, I dedicate this volume to all my graduate students past and present in Oxford and Princeton: go and make your mark, and when you need to, rant!

Nigel Smith,
Princeton, NJ,
21 February, 2014

Abbreviations

BDBRSC	Richard L. Greaves and Robert Zaller, eds., *A Biographical Dictionary of British Radicals in the Seventeenth Century*, 3 vols. (Brighton: Harvester Press, 1982–84).
CJ	*Journal of the House of Commons*, 34 vols. (1742–92).
CRW	Nigel Smith, ed., *A Collection of Ranter Writings from the 17th Century* (London: Junction Books, 1983).
CSPD	*Calendar of State Papers Domestic.*
EHR	*English Historical Review.*
ERI	Nicholas McDowell, *The English Radical Imagination: Culture, Religion, and Revolution, 1630–1660* (Oxford: Clarendon Press, 2003).
HJ	*Historical Journal.*
HMC	*Publications of the Historical Manuscripts Commission.*
JEH	*Journal of Ecclesiastical History.*
JFHS	*Journal of the Friends Historical Society.*
JHI	*Journal of the History of Ideas.*
N & Q	*Notes and Queries.*
ODNB	*Oxford Dictionary of National Biography* (online edn., 2005–).
OED	*Oxford English Dictionary.*
RES	*Review of English Studies.*
SCen	*The Seventeenth Century.*
TRHS	*Transactions of the Royal Historical Society.*

Introduction

I

The family of love is meeting
For the enjoyment of their fellow creatures
An Ocean of beings with no sin in them
I hear the demon
Can't fight the demon
Oooh! The demon in me
In the middle of the winter.

This stanza sounds like the something from a Ranter pamphlet, most probably Abiezer Coppe in the first line, turning into Laurence Clarkson in the second. I wonder what the demon can mean? It is not the Ranters but the Mekons, the (originally) Leeds punk-folk-art-rock band with a strong social conscience and a visionary imagination, hotwired into history. The song is 'Winter' from the album *Oooh! (Out of our heads)* (Quarterstick Records, 2002). Snapshots of imagined popular experience of the English Civil War and the revolution that followed run through the lyrics, and they are completely present in the first track, a Mekons live favourite: 'Thee Olde Trip to Jerusalem,' which leaps from the 17th to the 19th and 20th centuries and into the present, with the Bible interpolating class war throughout, as the thunderous stomp in the song rises into the listener's awareness:

The seed of the devil lives on in men
Verses 4 5 6 chapters 8 9 10
The Landlords and the rulers with their foot on
Your neck
Oh I love the Union and Glory Hallelujah!

There's a nice piece of Ranter pastiche in a pre-chorus, which echoes Abiezer Coppe's habit of fusing national and highly personal symbols: 'Heart of the Lion/The plunder & the killing/ Over and over/We just tried to stay sober.' (I wonder if this is in some sense an allegory of the Mekons' own career.) Then the rousing last chorus that names the 'radical tradition,' and you realize that probably the Mekons, especially songwriter and guitarist Jon Langford, have read left-wing historians A.L. Morton and Christopher Hill:

The sword is sharp the arrows swift the
Witnesses all seeing
So shake & shake for all your worth from
Innocence to experience
The Queen of Holland went to meet Red Ken

> With the Ranters and the Quakers and the
> Fabians
> William Blake, William Morris, Tony Benn
> The Levellers and the Diggers and the
> Muggletonians

To sing the names again is to make them live again (and one is yet alive!). The Mekons may be the darlings of the arty and elite *New Yorker*, but they also know their art is part of a long protest tradition, just as Abiezer Coppe's printed prophetic mode, which he saw as in continuity with the time of the Old Testament, was used as a model for some of the printed protest in the recent Occupy movement in the United States.[1]

With good reason. To encounter Abiezer Coppe on the page is to witness quite literally the voice of God, or rather God and Coppe sharing a voice (after all Abiezer in Hebrew means 'the father is help'), denouncing inequality, poverty, lack of charity and the kind of selfish and shallow Puritan piety that causes these abuses:

> *For lo I come (saith the Lord) with a vengeance, to levell also your Honour, Riches, &c. to staine the pride of all your glory, and to bring into contempt all the Honourable (both persons and things) upon the earth,* Isa. 23.9.
>   12 For this Honour, Nobility, Gentility, Propriety, Superfluity, &c. hath (without contradiction) been the Father of hellish horrid pride, arrogance, haughtinesse, loftinesse, murder, malice, of all manner of wickednesse and impiety ...
>   13 I see the root of it all *The Axe is laid to the root of the Tree* (by the Eternall God, *My Self,* saith the Lord) *I will hew it down.* And as I live, I will plague your Honour, Pompe, Greatnesse, Superfluity, and confound it into parity, equality, community; that the neck of horrid pride, murder, malice, and tyranny, &c. may be chopt off at one blow. And that my selfe, the Eternall God, who am Universall Love, may fill the Earth with universall love, universall peace, and perfect freedome; which can never be by humane sword or strength accomplished.   (pp. 80–81)

Coppe had a visionary experience lasting four days and nights, in which, after being abandoned by his family, and, so he apprehended, being in complete isolation, he returned to a womb-like state of primal innocence to confront hell, and then an elevating vision of divinity in the form of three brilliantly glowing hearts, with voices giving him his prophetic mission: 'Go up to London, to London, that great City, write, write, write' (p. 74). The experience of being visited and possessed by God is represented as both extremely violent and virtually beyond expression: much of the interest in Coppe as a writer comes from his ability to map out these details thoroughly.

---

1   See http://afieryflyingroule.tumblr.com/post/16324449342/the-first-second-decades-a-handful (accessed 5 August, 2013) and Eirik Steinhoff, *A Fiery Flying Roule (1–25)* (Barrytown, NY: Station Hill of Barrytown, 2013).

He went to London and proclaimed universal love in a kind of agit-prop prophetic acting, replicated on the printed page, and where the community that must arrive in the world is embodied in the sharing of money, in kissing and hugging male and female beggars, and in swearing, which is a means of casting off the hold of oppressive, greed-inducing, sanctimonious religion. Coppe imitates and extends the language and gestural behaviour of Old Testament prophets, especially Ezekiel, even as he denounces in the voice and name of God. It must have seemed noisily outrageous and transgressive ('i'th open streets, with his hand fiercely stretcht out, his hat cockt up, his eyes set as if they would sparkle out'), and on the page it is obviously an imitation of the appearance of printed Bibles even as it is a wild poetry of passionate and angry condemnation, neither entirely prose nor verse. The voice of the prophet is heard in the land:

> What have I engaged my goods, my life, &c. forsooke my dearest relations, and all for liberty and true freedome, for freedome from oppression, and more laid on my back, &c.
>
> 2 Mine eares are filled brim full with confused noise, cries, and outcries; O the innumerable complaints and groanes that pierce my heart (thorow and thorow) O astonishing complaints.
>
> Was ever the like ingratitude heard of since the world stood? what! best friends, surest friends, slighted, scorned, and that which cometh from them (in the basest manner) contemned, and some rewarded with prisons, some with death?
>
> O the abominable perfidiousnesse, falseheartednesse; self-seeking, self-inriching, and Kingdome-depopulating, and devastating, &c.
>
> These, and divers of the same nature, are the cries of *England*.
>
> And can I any longer forbeare?
>
> I have heard, I have heard, the groaning of my people. And now I come to deliver them, saith the Lord.
>
> Woe be to *Pharaoh* King of *Egypt*.
>
> You Great Ones that are not tackt nor tainted, you may laugh and sing, whom this hitteth it hitteth. And it shall hit home.   (pp. 85–86)

This is intriguingly dialogical: Coppe gives us the voice of the family and friends who object to his conversion, a quality that is an important, distinguishing aspect of his work. His tracts are a source of many voices, his proper humanist education in Warwick and Oxford giving him a facility to make prophetic drama out of these encounters. We hear the 'plaguey holiness' and adultery-fearing mainline Puritanism not least as a cautious inner feminine voice known as the 'wel-favoured Harlot,' the Levellers whose mistake was thinking that they could prevail in an armed rebellion, deformed village idiots, a highwayman, groups of ill-clad, obsessively cursing Londoners, and, mostly in splendid marginal glosses, humanist literary authority replete with Latin puns and the startled, bathetic voice of a young Warwick scholar who cannot quite understand what has happened to him. There are other personalities so sharply described we nearly hear them speak: the 'little childe' of a self who understands that moral laws no longer matter, that nakedness and being dressed are the same; the prophet re-describing himself as a pregnant woman. Coppe is one of the great holy fools in English literature and his pamphlets are directly in line with Erasmus's startling and era-defining work of moral and educational reform *In Praise of Folly* (1ˢᵗ edn., 1511), where the righteous Christian looks like a madman in the eyes of the corrupted world. Earlier, in a no less Erasmian spirit, Coppe had sent up the entire education system in a parody of grammar learning as he showed how the Holy Spirit was really at work in his community of inspired believers, and later prophesied another fiery visitation of the Lord who would quite literally burn the flesh of prostitutes and heavily made up courtly women, pitting holy against profane sexuality (pp. 53–55, 112).[2]

Laurence Clarkson was a far less flamboyant customer than Coppe, matching his quest for true faith with a careful eye for lucrative preaching jobs: a 'have a care for the main chance' that so disenchanted Coppe. The details contained in his autobiography *The Lost Sheep Found* (1660) give us much insight into the working of urban ranting groups. Since Clarkson was no longer a Ranter when he wrote it, we must treat the narrative with caution; nonetheless it is largely believable when put in context with other pieces of evidence. Yet Clarkson's adulterous tales are only one part of the story: his struggle to articulate a metaphysic that escapes from the binary logic of good and evil makes him no less compelling reading than Coppe. The poem that opens *A Single Eye* claims that orthodox conceptions of a remote God in a physical location beyond the earth '*shall dy truly*' before what he says is the truth (that heaven is '*in our present peace*') can be apprehended:

> *look not above the Skies*
> *For God, or Heaven; for here your Treasure lies*
> *Even in these Forms, Eternall Will will reigne,*
> *Through him are all things, onely One, not Twain:*
> *Sure he's the Fountain from which every thing*
> *Both good and ill (so term'd) appears to spring.* (p. 115)

It is one shocking thing to be shown that good and evil, light and dark, do not in the end amount to opposites (for if God is in all, all acts are as one to God), but quite another and substantially more shocking to be led to realize that if God is in all creatures, then holy communion is free love, God making love to God.[3] Clarkson knows well that his 'Reason' is deep heresy, making God part of the sublunary universe: '*God is passionate, God is affectionate, and if either,*

---

2   See Nicholas McDowell, *The English Radical Imagination: Culture, Religion, and Revolution, 1630–1660* (Oxford: Clarendon Press, 2003), ch. 4.

3   On Clarkson's fusion of light and dark see Nigel Smith, *Perfection Proclaimed: Language and Literature in English Radical Religion, 1640–1660* (Oxford: Clarendon Press, 1989), 249–57. On the collapse of the distance between God and man in the Ranters and Clarkson in particular, see Paul C.H. Lim, *Mystery Unvailed: The Crisis of the Trinity in Early Modern England* (Oxford: Oxford University Press, 2012), 109–12, 115.

then changeable' (p. 116). The world is also an *ex Deo* creation, another unorthodox view: the things in the world being made of God are God. Sin is in fact all in your mind: 'sin hath its conception only in the imagination' (p. 121). If you do not think about it as sin it will not be. Sin is just a word and damnation nothing more than coming to an awareness of how things really are. Hence the Ranter embrace of the term:

> Now it is damm'd, and ramm'd into its only Center, there to dwell eternal in the bosom of its only Father: This, and only this, is the damnation so much terrifying the Creature in its dark apprehension, that it shall be robbed and carried it knows not whither, cryeth out I am damned, I am damned, being carried out of its former knowledge, now knoweth not where it is. (p. 124)

The tract becomes more worrying and more challenging as it goes on: if heaven and hell are estates in this life, there can be no afterlife save a merging through decomposition of the dead body with glorious nature. So then what about resurrection? Turns out it means being aware that dualities are properly singularities, and the 'second resurrection,' the acting of 'sin' now reconceived as holiness is in short holy sex and a final escape from guilt: 'till acted that so called Sin, thou art not delivered from the power of sin, but ready upon all Alarums to tremble and fear the reproach of thy body' (p. 125).

Clarkson speaks with the 'divine majesty' just like Coppe, but he stumbles expressively when articulating tricky concepts: it lends an interesting if awkward dimension to his prose. That is not the case with the one anonymous tract in this collection, *A Jvstifjcatjon of the Mad Crew*, sometimes attributed to Andrew Wyke. Whoever wrote it certainly understood Coppe and Joseph Salmon's vocabulary, and had probably read Clarkson. It is so assured you might not unreasonably think it was a spoof Ranter tract, a plot to imitate and presumably embarrass them in public. The preface signed by 'Jesus the Son of God' eloquently affirms, *pace* Clarkson, that God has neither affections nor passions but nonetheless is in and through all creation:

> *he loves all sweetly, powring out himself in and upon all, making all at Peace with him, bowing and serving him, that the devil and he are one, that the devil is but a part of Gods back sides, which terrifies because of the curtain, that he sports and feasts himself in swearing, drinking, whoring, as when he is holy, just and good: that the holliness of man and unholiness of man are both one to him.* (p. 142)

> He sees dancing, lying with one another, kissing pure and perfect in him. (p. 148)

Like Clarkson the *Jvstifjcatjon* author thinks that people usually end up worshiping many gods rather than one god, and that this polytheism is really a product of greed. Ranting is the true monotheism (!): 'to these there is but one God, who feeds and cloths the wicked, causing his Sun to shine, and his rain to fall upon them; nay more, he that only leads them up, and takes them by the hand, and carries them up to the life of drinking, whoring, cursing, swearing, damning' (p. 146). The tract delights in the inversion of moral categories that comes with its revelations, and the banishment of concepts that are no longer needed: sorrow, sin, repentance, shame, marriage, property. Immortality is this life.

With Joseph Salmon we enter the territory of the mystical visionary, a sophisticated Gnostic, sometimes a holy fool, one who fuses allegory with historical narrative. God is within in that he is the animating force within the events of history: the surprising, sometimes violent shapes that phenomenal reality takes. Salmon thus distils his experiences on the battlefield in *A Rout, A Rout*: 'few can behold his beautiful presence under the power of the Sword. The Lord here besmears himself with blood and vengeance, deforms his own beauty, hides his aimable presence under a hideous and wrathful form' (p. 163). Salmon's ranting insights are fully revealed in the recently discovered (all copies of this notorious pamphlet were once thought lost) *Divinity Anatomized*, where God is certainly essentially of spirit, but where his coming to be with man in Christ means being in the flesh of all people all the time. Salmon is ponderous but effective as he lays open the startling new revelation, which is that we are in an ongoing union with God, described astonishingly as a purification of two oppositely-poled women grinding together between millstones in order to remove the chaff (p. 174). 'To grind in the mill of a undelighted and servil copulation' was John Milton's spectacularly unpleasant image of an incompatible marriage: not even D.H. Lawrence in his most mawkish Chatterley moments could have bettered it. Like the very early Coppe, Salmon's description of spiritual illumination is offered in extensive allegorical terms derived from the Bible, here the Song of Solomon, that are very rarified and hard to follow:

> Because (saith she) of the savour of thy good ointments, thy name is as ointment poured forth, therefore the Virgins love thee: She here compares the name (or nature of Christ, for so the word here imports) to ointment.
> Secondly, to ointment poured forth.
> First, to oyntment, which heales, and refreshes: this ointment is the Spirit flowing out, and expending it selfe, upon the soule, in which dispensation, all the sores, wounds, and breaches of the creature are salved and cured. (p. 185)

It is not hard to see how this could be seen as sexual even when it was not. Salmon describes an equally worrying proposition—an outright deification of man in this life:

> The spirituall unction, or fulnesse of God, although poured upon the head; yet centers not only in the head, but it hath a sweet influence upon the rest of the members; it ran downe upon the beard, and descended to the skirts of the garment: the fulnesse of God dwelling in the Sonne, is no more but a patterne or figure of the same fulnesse in us. (p. 187)

Salmon might insist that his meaning was metaphorical but the eroticism of his language is overbearing and would have signaled danger to any remotely orthodox Christian: 'The soul now is possessed with a spiritual passion: and (as men in passion are most vigorous and ardent) so the soul in the heat and fervor of the Spirit spends it self upon God' (p. 190). Yes, right. I hear you say: the soul, with the help of the Holy Spirit, experiences an orgasm in the presence of God and because of it. 'It is a Metaphoricall espression, borrowed from the naturall delight, which we usually take to weare sweet flowers in our breasts, or bosomes, delighting in them for their sweet smell and savour' (p. 191). Sure. As in Clarkson, the explicit sense of God making love to God would have been seen as outrageously flagrant: 'when God lies downe in the sweet embraces, and refreshing bosome of his own love!' By now the heresies are dropping off the pen: '*Adams* fall was no more but Gods weakness' (p. 193); sin is an invention of human moral laws and to God all is good. Abiezer Coppe's presence also surfaces: 'The true Libertine,[4] is one that walks in the Spirit, is led by the Spirit, and so from under these carnal laws of bondage; he is free in all his actions, and in every performance' (p. 197).

To move to Jacob Bauthumley is to find the sweetest spirited autodidact setting out a nature mysticism, indeed a pantheism in terms that put the reader into a trance of focused attention:

> Nay, I see that God is in all Creatures, Man and Beast, Fish and Fowle, and every green thing, from the highest Cedar to the Ivey on the wall; and that God is the life and being of them all, and that God doth really dwell, and if you will personally; if he may admit so low an expression in them all, and hath his Being no where else out of the Creatures. (p. 227)

It has been called a work of 'high seriousness and patient, eloquent expression' operating at 'the leading edge of theological speculation,' espousing anti-trinitarianism, the view that God exists only in his creatures, denial of personal immortality, and 'disregard for Christ's redemptive acts.'[5] A surviving 1655 handwritten copy of the tract is bound up with a Hermetic, Neoplatonic treatise.[6] For which beautifully expressed blasphemies Bauthumley was bored through the tongue with a hot iron.

Enough, or Too much!

What are we dealing with? Put prosaically the Ranters were a group of religious libertines who flourished in the three years following the execution of Charles I in January 1649.

---

4   For the history of this term, imported from France, and referring either to spiritualist Puritans, like the Seekers, or hedonists, see Jean-Pierre Cavaillé, 'Libertine and Libertinism: Polemic Uses of the Terms in Sixteenth- and Seventeenth-Century English and Scottish Literature,' *Journal for Early Modern Cultural Studies*, 12 (2012), 12–36.

5   See Thomas N. Corns, 'Radical Pamphleteering,' in N.H. Keeble, ed., *The Cambridge Companion to Writing of the English Revolution* (Cambridge: Cambridge University Press, 2001), 81; Daniel P. Jaeckle, 'The Realised Eschatology and Sweet Style of Jacob Bauthumley,' *Journal of Religious History*, 35 (2011), 321–36.

6   BL, MS Sloane 2544, fols. 1^r–53^r. The copy is signed by the Quaker Benjamin Antrobus.

They represented one extreme response to the religious and social problems that had come to a head in the conflict between King and Parliament in the 1640s. Ranters believed that God dwelt inside them, as an inner presence whose authority was above all laws, and any organized church. Salvation existed here on earth, and any act was justifiable so long as it was performed under the working of the spirit. Sin was thus made to disappear. The consequence was, for some Ranters, sexual licence, and for others, blasphemy and swearing. The Ranters did not call themselves so, and the term itself, in its variant forms, 'Rantipoler,' 'Rantizer,' 'Rantism,' was loosely applied to anyone of extreme opinions. They were often confused with the hard-drinking, hard-living young gentlemen in the capital who also went by the name of 'Raunter.' There is further confusion in that some of the Ranters' expectations, such as the sharing of wealth, and some of their expressions, were used by other radical and religious groups of the period; to some degree these groups parodied each other's private languages. Nevertheless, it seems that there was an identifiable body of interconnected individuals sharing a common heterodox religious language between 1649 and 1651 that was subject to a thorough persecution by the government.[7] The breakdown of royal and Episcopal authority at the start of the 1640s, especially the collapse of censorship, resulted in an intensification of radical Puritan activity, and undoubtedly rendered it more visible. It has become customary to think of the Civil War and Interregnum years giving rise to a milieu in which a heightened popular consciousness fostered many different religious and political ideas and practices. It was this milieu that spawned Ranterism, and through which the Ranter spokesmen, Coppe, Clarkson, Salmon and Bauthumley passed, on their way to their own millennial and egalitarian solutions. Why there appear to be no Ranter pamphlets by women is something to which we will come.

New research has shown us that this milieu existed before 1640. Here views were developed and exchanged in the very different circumstances that then prevailed.[8] There were notorious instances of extravagant Protestant prophecy before 1600, even to the extent of an attempted coup in church and state.[9] Neither was sex outside marriage and in the name of religion invented in 1648: it was a phenomenon that had been alarmingly observed in early separatist communities and had a longer history in Europe.[10] The force of the critique of 'left wing' history has been to argue that the sects and other civil war radicals were not nearly

---

7   For a robust summary of those who owned up to the title or the practices, or who were labeled as such, see Ariel Hessayon, 'Abiezer Coppe and the Ranters,' in Laura Lunger Knoppers, ed., *The Oxford Handbook of Literature and Revolution* (Oxford: Oxford University Press, 2012), 355; see also J.F. McGregor, 'Seekers and Ranters' in J.F. McGregor and B. Reay, eds., *Radical Religion in the English Revolution* (Oxford: Oxford University Press, 1984), 121–39.

8   David R. Como, *Blown by the Spirit: Puritanism and the Emergence of an Antinomian Underground in pre-Civil-War England* (Stanford, CA: Stanford University Press, 2004); Ariel Hessayon, *'Gold tried in the fire': the prophet TheaurauJohn Tany and the English Revolution* (Aldershot and Burlington, VT: Ashgate, 2007).

9   Alexandra Walsham, '"Frantick Hacket": Prophecy, Sorcery, Insanity, and the Elizabethan Puritan Movement,' *HJ*, 41 (1998), 27–66.

10   As in the case of the bigamous Colchester prophet Richard Farnham and his associate John Bull in 1636: Thomas Heywood, *A true discourse of the two infamous upstart prophets* (1636); see also Naomi Baker, ed., *Scripture Women* (Nottingham: Trent Editions, 2005).

as numerous as had been claimed, and that affrighted hostile depictions greatly exaggerated and misrepresented the truth of numbers and ideas. It is also entirely fair to say that many less extravagant reformers were busy propounding new ideas of liberty from within the boundaries of the Puritan churches, and their voice was drowned by the furore concerning the Ranters in the 1970s and 1980s.[11] Nonetheless we cannot avoid the presence of a number of individuals who cannot be consigned to oblivion by these critiques, and some of whom left behind some remarkable pieces of writing, together with related evidence of their activities. It is their writing that this anthology discloses, celebrates and invites you to explore. You may wish to turn to the pamphlets themselves now, but for a fuller historical, theological, social and literary account of the Ranter phenomenon, read on.

II

The victory secured by the Parliamentary forces by 1648 did not satisfy all of its supporters. No small degree of religious toleration was established, and the continuity of all but the most extreme Puritan sects seemed assured in the early years of the Commonwealth. However, in London and the New Model Army in particular, interests arose demanding more than the Parliamentary gentry were prepared to give. The Levellers called for legal reforms, more religious toleration and a considerable extension of the franchise, while Gerrard Winstanley and his True Levellers, or Diggers, cultivated common land in Surrey as a commune so that all might share God's bounty equally. It was in the aftermath of the brutal defeat of the Leveller movement that the Ranters acquired their notoriety. This was also a period of some economic hardship, and it appears that Ranterism appealed to a distressed urban artisan class. Their use of ritual and narcotics might therefore be seen as a form of social escape. Indeed, the Ranters possessed no organisation or programme as such, and a careful distinction must be made between the many people who were arrested in taverns as Ranters, then released immediately on a promise of good behaviour, and the Ranter prophets who published and were felt to be far more dangerous as well as more sophisticated. For the Ranter, Christ had returned to inspire man directly through the spirit within. This attitude did lead to striking social outrage, but its spiritual aspect afforded the potential for quietism. Many Ranters turned to the spiritual withdrawal and rectitude offered by some Quakers and other groups as the 1650s progressed, howsoever the Quakers offended contemporaries with their symbolic testimonies (such as going naked for a sign).

The Ranters believed that Christ's atonement on behalf of mankind, as witnessed in the Gospels, was sufficient to save believers in such a way that they, the believers, lived on earth in a state of grace. This is known as the Antinomian heresy, where such 'free grace' is asserted over and against the Law of Moses embodied in the Ten Commandments. There were many Antinomians during the middle years of seventeenth-century England, and some earlier. The heresy's assurance of election acted as an antidote to the harsh strictures of Calvinism, which

---

11   John Coffey, *John Goodwin and the Puritan Revolution: Religion and Intellectual Change in Seventeenth-Century England* (Woodbridge and Rochester, NY: Boydell Press, 2006).

emphasized salvation through predestination, making eventual grace beyond the control of the individual. Being sure that you were saved and that no sin could endanger your salvation lifted the psychological burden of predestination theology. Nevertheless, Antinomianism was an ultimate extension of Luther's call for justification by faith, and the first modern Antinomian was Luther's follower, Johannes Agricola (1494–1566).

English Puritanism itself came to place an emphasis upon the immanence of Christ in the hearts of all believers. This was so in the enormously popular sermons of the Puritan patriarch Richard Sibbes. The first Antinomian statement in England came with John Eaton's (1574/5–1630/1) distinction between Gospel and Law. Eaton's claim that God could see no sin in those who were justified was readily identified as Antinomianism and attacked in print while Eaton, his wife and his followers were disciplined by local church synods and the Court of High Commission. But not before Eaton was having considerable influence by preaching, through discussion and through the circulation of manuscripts. All of this happened between 1612 and 1631; only after Eaton had been dead for 11 or 12 years, after the collapse of the licensing system, was it possible to print his writings.[12] Also in the second decade of the century John Traske and his follower Returne Hebdon preached a fusion of antinomianism, perfectionism, Saturday sabbatarianism, and resistance to formal church organization, with egalitarian and communistic hues. The mathematician and alchemist Edward Howes imagined in visions and esoteric symbols a community of perfected saints who would populate New England. He has been seen as an Antinomian and indebted to Familist literature.[13] Tobias Crisp (1600–43) went further than Eaton, and though anxious to avoid the charge of Antinomianism because he foresaw the claims it made against the social order, his insistence upon free grace is unremitting:

> So, beloved, your hearts are dry things, there is no sap, no moisture, no life in them. Christ must first be poured in, before you can get any thing out. Wherefore then stand you labouring and lugging in vain? Oh stay no longer, goe to Christ; It is he that must break thy rocky heart before the plough can come over it, or at least enter into it. As I told you before, so I tell you again, you must consider Christ as freely given unto you by the Father, even before you can believe.[14]

Significantly, both Eaton and Crisp were published posthumously (Crisp's writings in particular were widely read), while Archbishop Laud's Court of Ecclesiastical Commission clamped down hard on cases of popular Antinomianism in the 1630s. Other Antinomians included the mystical Roger Brereley, the 'Grindletonian,' and John Webster. The tendency passed into the Parliamentary army to the chaplains John Saltmarsh, William Dell and Henry Denne. The great majority of Antinomians did not take the doctrine to its extreme. Most were more interested in questioning church covenants and ordinances, and there were also universal salvationists, like the Baptists Paul Hobson and Thomas Lambe, and Seekers, like

---

12   *ODNB*.
13   See David Como, *Blown by the Spirit*, 57–62, 388, 415–31, 468–71.
14   Tobias Crisp, *Christ Alone Exalted* (1643), 214.

William Erbery, who concentrated upon experiencing the inner revelation over and above the 'forms' of church organization and visible worship. Several of the Ranter authors, especially Joseph Salmon and Abiezer Coppe in his earlier works, espoused largely Seeker views, but it was in the Ranters that critics of Antinomianism were able to see their fears of individual licentiousness, of moral and social anarchy, fulfilled: '*in our outward dancing and sporting, there thou kissest us and there thou dandlest us on thy knees. When we go in to a Whore-house we meet thee*' (p. 143).

The Ranters were millenarians in the sense that they believed that Christ would return to earth to rule a kingdom of perfect saints, and they held that this would occur in a violent apocalypse in which all would be reduced to a 'base' material and spiritual level. The prediction of the second coming of Christ had been appropriated for the Reformation by several divines in the sixteenth and seventeenth centuries including Johann Heinrich Alsted and Joseph Mede. Precise dates were given, as opposed to St. Augustine's metaphorical interpretation of Revelation, which had indefinitely postponed the return. Millenarianism intensified as the events of the 1640s and the upheavals in Europe convinced many that the millennium was imminent. Many shared Joseph Salmon's view that the New Model Army was God's first instrument in bringing on the Last Days (pp. 162–67). The Fifth Monarchist movement of the mid-1650s assumed that Christ would appear again in bodily form, but the Ranters believed that Christ would return in the spirit, and that the inspiration they felt was the first manifestation of the new age. Eventually, the spirit would return to live in all mankind, destroying all earthly institutions and material possessions, so that man would live by direct inspiration of and in perfect union with God.

Most millenarians believed that Christ's kingdom would last for one thousand years, after which the Last Judgment would be made. That final day of reckoning was denied by the Ranters. Their eschatology accorded with the projection of the twelfth-century thinker Joachim of Fiore, who saw history in three stages. Firstly, there was the Age or Dispensation of the Father, recorded in the Old Testament, succeeded by the Age of the Son, related in the New Testament, and finally the third Age of the Spirit, in which perfection would be reached on earth by man. Joachism occurred in the thought of several radicals, including the army chaplain John Saltmarsh, Erbery, Winstanley and Lodowick Muggleton, who with John Reeve founded his own clandestine sect dedicated to experiencing and prophesying the dawning of the third and final dispensation. It was in the Ranters, however, that the claims for inspiration were most flamboyantly presented. There were other prophet figures working under self-proclaimed divine inspiration, such as the silversmith Thomas Tany, who claimed to be the reborn Kings of the Jews and possessor of the Adamic language. At least you can understand the Ranters; Tany's fusion of different tongues and self-made terms tests the greatest polyglot. There were also those who claimed to be 'God and father of Christ,' like John Robins, and a risen Christ, like William Franklin with his Mary Magdalene, Mary Gadbury. However, these latter two did not articulate their beliefs in writing, and made no attempt to explore the ramifications of their ecstasy beyond a simple assertion of their privileged status. Robins's associate Joshua Garment did publish a pamphlet in which he revealed messianic plans of the two to gather the Jews and take them to Jerusalem. Is Garment in fact mentioned punningly in Salmon's letter to Thomas Webbe?[15]

The collapsing of the distance between God and man, so that the believer can be said in some way to embody God, has been seen as a particular interpretation of medieval mystical writings, such of those Nicholas of Cusa, which were circulating in translation in radical circles. To this extent the Ranters have been seen to be related not only to predecessors like the Familists but also in some respects early English Antitrinitarians or Socinians.[16]

<h3 style="text-align:center">III</h3>

Separatist religious activity, that is, activity outside the Established Church, had been known in England since the Lollards of the fourteenth century, and commentators in the late sixteenth and early seventeenth centuries warned of the threat to order posed by pre-Civil-War sects like the Brownists and Familists. The onset of toleration permitted what had previously been underground to flourish in the open. Apart from the staunch Calvinism exhibited in Presbyterianism, there lay to the 'left' of this mainstream several alternatives. Independency was the next stop, with self-governing congregations, still if not always Calvinist, followed by the Baptist congregations, featuring adult baptism, 'dipping,' for members. It was from the Baptist movement that most of the Ranters came, although they had usually experienced every form of religion, including Anglicanism, genuinely seeking the most personally satisfying belief. The extent and variety of sectarian opinion is most famously recorded in the Presbyterian minister Thomas Edwards's *Gangraena* (1646), which, if sometimes exaggerated, provides much evidence for the 1640s.[17] Separatism may be associated with particular areas, and the continuity between Lollard and later sectarian occurrence is notable in Coventry, Kent and East Anglia. Coventry happened to be where the Ranters made their greatest mark, although it was only events in London that stirred the Rump Parliament into action, and reports of Ranters came from East Anglia, the Midlands, Wiltshire and, more dubiously, Yorkshire.

Edwards detected the first man to engage in Ranter activity at least three years before the main outbreak. Thomas Webbe, a Southwark feltmaker and hatmaker, appeared before the House of Lords on the charge of professing Christ to be formed inside man, and that the deity was limited with humanity.[18] He toured Sussex and Essex, to be ejected eventually from a living at Milton, Kent for seditious preaching. Then Webbe acquired the living of Langley Burrell in Wiltshire, where he gathered together a community, including his patron's wife, and at one point a 'man wife' with the appropriate name of John Organ, that practiced sexually licentious rites, featuring music and dancing, under the alleged dictum 'there's no heaven but women, nor no hell save marriage.'[19] Webbe defended himself against *Gangraena*

---

15   Joshua Garment, *The Hebrews deliverance at hand* (1651). See below, p. 199.
16   Nigel Smith, *Perfection Proclaimed*, ch. 3; Paul C.H. Lim, *Mystery Unvailed*, 103.
17   See now Ann Hughes, *Gangraena and the Struggle for the English Revolution* (Oxford: Oxford University Press, 2004).
18   Edwards, *Gangraena* (1646, 3rd edn.), ii.113–15; iii.111.
19   See Christopher Hill, *The World Turned Upside Down* (1972), 226–27; J.F. McGregor in *ODNB*.

in his *Mr. Edwards Pen No Slander* (1646), which reveals little about his activities, but Webbe, who was pro-Leveller, and who corresponded with other Ranters, was tried in 1650 under the Adultery Act of May that year after complaints from his own followers. He was acquitted, but was finally ejected by the Committee for Plundered Ministers in September 1651.

Abiezer Coppe, perhaps the most notorious Ranter, certainly their most notable author, was born at Warwick on 30 May 1619, the son of Walter, a taylor. After an obsessively godly youth, and an education in the free school at Warwick where he learned to recite Homer as well as contemporary sacred poetry in Latin, Coppe went to Oxford in 1636, first to All Souls and then a year later Merton, where he showed Presbyterian leanings, and left without a degree at the beginning of the war probably because he was too poor to remain in residence. In 1641 he was given limited preaching rights even though he was probably unlicensed. Anthony Wood provides some colourful anecdotes concerning Coppe's career as a loose-living seducer in Oxford, but this can be discounted in light of the respect with which Coppe's teachers regarded him.[20] Through his schoolmaster and patron Thomas Dugard he met the Platonist Puritan Peter Sterry and had been taught in Merton College by Ralph Button, an academic whose library would have given Coppe access to some of the texts from which he appears to take direction. By 1646, Coppe had turned Baptist and was preacher to an army garrison at Compton House in Warwickshire. It seems that he had a sizeable following with many converts in Warwickshire, Oxfordshire and Berkshire. He was capable of 'admirable good oratory,' and recommended the necessity of rebaptism, separatism and of reproaching the ministry in defiance of ordinances, for which he was imprisoned, so he claimed, for fourteen weeks. He was associated at this time with the Baptist leaders William Kiffin and Hanserd Knollys, both of whom were by now maintaining an Antinomian position influenced by the sermons of Tobias Crisp. During the next two years Coppe met the itinerant preacher Richard Coppin, whose influence set him on the road to a position beyond the Baptist conventicles, even as Coppe played the mentor in writing a preface for Coppin's works. Coppin was often confused with the Ranters because he knew many of them, and because his religion was egalitarian. In fact he had a distinctive theology that included belief in universal salvation. Although he was imprisoned in 1655, he took no part in the most demonstrative Ranter activities.[21]

In 1648, Coppe provided the preface to the anti-clerical *John the Divine's Divinity*, attributed by a contemporary to John File, and a year later, another preface for Coppin's *Divine Teachings*.[22] The latter is important for its 'hieroglyphical' representation of the Trinity as a unity, which establishes the symbolic code elaborated in Coppe's later works, and provides evidence that Coppe was reading the German mystic Jakob Böhme.[23] 1649 also saw the publication of *Some Sweet Sips, of some Spiritual Wine*, as fiercely critical of formalized religion as the two prefaces, and excitedly Antinomian, but also stressing the

---

20   Ariel Hessayon, 'The Making of Abiezer Coppe,' *JEH*, 62 (2011), 38–58.

21   See Nigel Smith, *ODNB*; Davis, *Fear, Myth and History*, 36–40.

22   Michael Hunter, et al., eds., *A Radical's Books: The Library Catalogue of Samuel Jeake of Rye, 1623–90* (Woodbridge and Rochester, NY: D.S. Brewer, 1999), 168.

23   Hessayon, 'Abiezer Coppe and the Ranters,' 365.

sublimity of God in man and in nature. The pamphlet seems to have circulated mainly in the south Midlands: George Thomason did not acquire it for the collection he was assembling in London, while John Osborn, an Oxfordshire minister, cited it in 1651 as one of the most dangerous exponents of 'Sensual Liberty.'[24] Hilariously the tract both affirms and ridicules the most influential grammar book at the time, written by William Lily and John Colet in consultation with Erasmus, and authorized by Henry VIII. The spirit speaks through but then out and beyond the working of the grammar in an ecstatic rebellion against the entire education system: 'Coppe deforms an icon of institutional learning, and of ecclesiastical and political power,' revealing his 'scorn for the humanist philosophy that a classical education instills Christian virtue.'[25]

Some time towards the end of 1649, Coppe experienced his true awakening (p. 73) when, in Baxter's words, 'God gave him over to a spirit of delusion, that he fell into a Trance, and professeth himself that he continued in it three or four dayes, and that he was in Hell.'[26] This was described as an extreme form of melancholy that Baxter felt was 'worse then mad in his delusion.' But Coppe's subsequent recourse to swearing, the claimed language of God in him, attracted some support, and received printed expression in late 1649 with the publication of *A Fiery Flying Roll*, bound together with *A Second Fiery Flying Roule*, so adding a crushing denunciation of the rich to Coppe's apocalyptic hopes. Parliament was sufficiently worried to respond with an order condemning the *Roll*'s 'horrid blasphemies, and damnable and detestable opinions,' and authorizing the collection and burning of all the copies of the tract, while those responsible for it were to be investigated. The broadsheet carrying the order is dated 1 February 1650, but Coppe himself had already been arrested in Warwick on 8 January, and transferred to Coventry jail on the 10th.[27]

During the second week of March, Joseph Salmon arrived in Coventry with the intention of visiting the imprisoned Coppe. Salmon had been in the army and had preached in London. His first pamphlet, *Anti-Christ in Man* (1647), written from a Seeker position, looked forward to the birth of the spirit in man:

> This *Mother of Harlots*, thy fleshly wisdom wil propose herself to be all to thee, that so She may draw thy affections after her; Shee will tell thee that she can supply all thy wants and relieve al thy necessities, and therfore thou needst not to be beholden to God for any thing, She will tell thee with *Adam*, that She can give thee the knowledge of good & evill; and she can open thy eyes, & She it is that gives thee any thing.[28]

Perhaps Salmon's 'Mother of Harlots' was the origin of Coppe's 'well-favoured Harlot' (p. 103). This type of allegory, structured around the Three Dispensations, and applied to the events of the 1640s, the war and the execution of the King, formed Salmon's next work, *A Rout, A Rout*, of February 1649. Soon after this Salmon embraced Ranterism fully: 'His Hour spent

24   John Osborn, *The World to Come* (1651), Sig. A2ʳ.
25   McDowell, *ERI*, 109.
26   Richard Baxter, *Plain Scripture Proof of infants church-membership and baptism* (1651), 148.
27   See the newspaper *Mercurius Pragmaticus*, 5–12, Feb. 1650.
28   Joseph Salmon, *Anti-Christ in Man* (1647), 19; there are three separate editions of this work.

with us to the admiration of Honest Men, ... but soone after found a disciple in Coppe ... and heard him swear many sad oaths.'[29] Salmon seems to have known most of the figures in the Ranter milieu, not only Coppe and Wyke, but also Coppin, possibly Bauthumley, and certainly Webbe, with whom he corresponded (p. 199). Salmon began to preach in Coventry, and Bulstrode Whitelocke reports of his 'wicked Swearing, and uncleaness, which he justified and others of his way, *That it was God which did swear in them, and that it was their Liberty to keep company with Women, for their Lust.*'[30] Arrest for Salmon followed quickly.

Nevertheless, another Ranter arrived to preach. This was Andrew Wyke, who had come with a kinswoman, Mrs. Wallis, to visit the imprisoned Coppe, probably with financial support from Baptist churches to the east. Wyke travelled from Colchester, where he had been active, according to *Gangraena*, as a preacher and a rebaptizer, refusing to answer questions put by the Assembly of Divines in 1646. Wyke was held in custody, during which time he is reported to have written his first work, *The Innocent in Prison Complaining.*[31] Wyke's behaviour in Coventry was as astonishing as Salmon's, as he 'kissed a Souldier three times, and said, *I breath the Spirit of God into thee*, and many the like abominable Blasphemies.'[32] He was attempting to leave Coventry when he was arrested and imprisoned with the others; both he and Salmon were able to attract a considerable audience by preaching through the grates of the prison on Sundays.[33]

Salmon and Wyke were originally fined two shillings each for common blasphemy by Coventry Corporation, but their connection with Coppe caused their cases to be referred to Westminster. In jail, Wyke wrote letters protesting his imprisonment. Salmon also wrote to friends outside. Like Coppe, he was prepared to make a protest of belief even in captivity.

The government was not particularly worried by the events in a provincial city, but it was concerned when it became apparent that Ranters were active in the capital. Coppe had, in fact, been acquainted with the London Antinomian group that used nakedness in its rituals, My One Flesh, through the publisher and bookseller, Giles Calvert. Calvert was instrumental in the publication of Ranter literature, as well as much other sectarian material, including Winstanley, Saltmarsh, new editions of some Familist writings, and later on, many Quaker tracts. Calvert acted as an important link between individuals.[34] He was not unsympathetic to any one group, and it was also through him that Laurence Clarkson was able to contact My One Flesh (p. 133).

Clarkson, or Claxton, was born at Preston in 1615, and drifted from Anglicanism to Presbyterianism, Independency and Antinomianism. He served as an army chaplain under Paul Hobson until 1644, and was paid to preach at Pulham Market, Norfolk. In November 1644 he was rebaptized by Thomas Patient and in 1645 was arrested with the Baptist Hanserd Knollys and charged in Suffolk with dipping. The following year, he had turned Seeker, and

---

29   Bulstrode Whitelocke, *Memorials* (1682), 430.
30   Whitelocke, *Memorials*, 430.
31   Edwards, *Gangraena*, iii.169–70.
32   Whitelocke, *Memorials*, 430.
33   Leybourne-Popham MS. (HMC), 59.
34   See Mario Caricchio, *Religione, politica e commercio di libri nella rivoluzione inglese: gli autori di Giles Calvert 1645–1653* (Ferioli di Baveno: Name, 2003).

was unofficial preacher to the troop of Cornet Nicholas Lockyer, soon to become a Leveller agitator. He preached universal redemption under the influence of William Erbery and William Sedgwick. This story comes largely from Clarkson's account of his religious career published in 1660, *The Lost Sheep Found*. He goes on to relate how he was paid £14 for penning a Leveller piece, *A Generall Charge or Impeachment of High Treason, in the name of Justice Equity, against the Communality of England*, in 1647. It argued that Parliament derived its power from the people, and crudely imitated the dialogue form developed by the Leveller Richard Overton, but it also criticized those like the Levellers who sought radical solutions in constitutional reform. During 1649 Clarkson joined My One Flesh, publishing *A Single Eye All Light, no Darkness* in June 1650, in which he justified adultery by means of a close extrapolation of the phrase from Isaiah 42.16; 'I will make darkness light before them.' It is the work that may well have singlehandedly kick-started the government's clampdown on religious libertinism.[35] Clarkson at least knew of Winstanley, and accused him of being a self-seeking tithe-gatherer in disguise. It would be nice to think that Clarkson was one of the Ranters the Diggers ejected from their commune, and whom Winstanley felt had sacrificed inner Reason to outward lustings, but we cannot be sure.[36] Another pamphlet appeared in the summer of 1650: Thomason dates his acquisition of the anonymous *A Jvstifjcatjon of the Mad Crew* as 21 August.

The Rump Parliament was more worried by the threat to social order than by shades of theological opinion, and it established a committee on 14 June to investigate the Ranters, and to find a means of dealing with them. Nonetheless, there had been serious concern among mainstream Puritans (the vast majority) at the emergence of heretical and blasphemous opinions in the 1640s, associated with the radicals. A Blasphemy Ordinance with stiff penalties had entered the statute books in 1648 after a long and discontinuous debate between Presbyterians and Independents in Parliament. The context of the Second Civil War had enabled the Presbyterians to gain the upper hand, and these new controls of opinion went hand in hand with the attempt to produce a unified national church in a Presbyterian shape. John Weaver was nominated chairman of the investigative committee, authorized to interrogate and hold offenders. On 21 June, Weaver reported back to Parliament, having questioned several people.[37] *A Single Eye* had come to his attention, and an order was given for the searching out of its author, while the committee was charged with the responsibility of drawing up a Bill that would quell Ranterism. What emerged was the Blasphemy Act of 9 August 1650. It outlawed the essential opinions held by Ranters, and enforced this with severe penalties.[38] An 'Atheistical, Blasphemous and Execrable' opinion consisted, it was decided, of denying 'the necessity of Civil and Moral Righteousness amongst Men,' of affirming that man or any creature was God, and of affirming that God lived inside living

---

35   Davis, *Fear, Myth and History*, 77.
36   *A Vindication of those, whose endeavors is only to make the earth a common treasury, called Diggers* and *Englands Spirit Unfoulding*, Gerrard Winstanley, *Complete Works*, ed. Thomas N. Corns et al., eds., 2 vols. (Oxford: Oxford University Press, 2009), II.235–42, 167.
37   *CJ*, vi.423, 427, 437, 440, 443.
38   *CJ*, vi.474–75.

beings. To this last was added the qualifier, 'and nowhere else,' whereas most of the Ranters who wrote, particularly the moderate ones like Salmon and Bauthumley, believed that God lived everywhere in all of creation.

The Act also outlawed 'Uncleanness, prophane Swearing, Drunkenness, Filthiness, Brutishness, ... Stealing, Cozening and Defrauding others, ... Murther, Adultery, Incest, Fornication, Sodomie,' and professing that 'Heaven and Happiness consisteth in the acting of these or such things.' These later sections meant that the Act compounded the intentions of the Adultery Act of 10 May 1650, as Coppe pointed out.[39] Parliament may have aimed at precise terminology, or it may be that some of the blasphemies identified by the committee were too close to beliefs held by members, for the House voted out a clause which made illegal the attribution of sins 'only through the Darkness that is in Men.'[40] The debates over the penalties are equally interesting. The Act finally instituted six months' imprisonment for a first offence, with banishment for a second, and death if the offender returned. Parliament voted out clauses that would authorize the punishment of publicans who harboured Ranter meetings, and officers of the law who were lax in their investigations, as well as vetoing the adoption of the army's punishment for blasphemy: as already noted, being bored through the tongue.

As it turned out, the authorities were content just to keep Ranters locked up until satisfied with their recantations. Many were quickly released on a promise of future good behaviour. One pamphlet, entitled *Strange News from Newgate and the Old-Baily* (1650), described the interrogation and confessions of one J. Collins and one T. Reeve, both of whom were given six months imprisonment. Though the ringleaders and pamphleteers did present a more serious problem, the administration of the Act was again inconsistent. Wyke was released on bail on 5 July, giving surety that he would appear before the Council of State when required.[41] Salmon was interrogated by Robert Beake, the officer supervising the captured Ranters in Coventry, and the staunch Puritan soldier and politician William Purefoy. As he recalls in *Heights in Depths* (p. 202) he was able both to satisfy his integrity and return to conformity, although he had been held for six months.

At the command of Parliament, Coppe had been transferred from Coventry to Newgate prison in London early in April.[42] Purefoy was ordered to bring Coppe to trial on 19 July; Parliament was still pressing for the completion of the case of *A Fiery Flying Roll*'s author on 27 September.[43] Coppe actually held up his interrogation by a parliamentary committee by throwing 'apples, pears and nutshells' around the court room from the dock, and by feigning madness (at one point he appeared to speak to himself). Perhaps then he played the holy fool in court. He was returned to Newgate, and remained there for the first half of 1651, being finally released after 28 June.[44] Early in January of that year he published his

---

39 *CRW,* 119.
40 *CJ,* vi.453–54.
41 *CSPD* (1650), 133.
42 See p. 108.
43 *CJ,* vi.474–75.
44 *ODNB.*

first 'recantation,' *A Remonstrance of the Sincere and Zealous Protestation*, which is more of a protest, expressing indignation at being imprisoned for opinions he had never held, and for acts which he had never committed. In May, Coppe wrote *Copp's Return to the wayes of Truth*, which did deny the tenets levelled at the Ranters in the Act, though Coppe's language is as ambiguous here as Salmon's was in his own recantation. John Dury, the ecumenicist, was impressed by Coppe's apparent reformation but John Tickell was far from convinced when he witnessed one of Coppe's recantation sermons at Burford later in 1651.[45]

The committee had examined *A Single Eye* towards the end of July 1650. Clarkson describes his arrest at a meeting in Bishopsgate soon after this in *The Lost Sheep Found* (p. 136); he had displayed his gift of the gab in resisting arrest, for which he became famous: 'he framed an excuse to return back into the house, pretending he had left something of great use behind him, and so escaped away at a back door; but is re-taken, and at this day in prison.'[46] On 27 September, Parliament published a broadsheet condemning *A Single Eye*, and authorizing its collection and burning. The same publication announced the outcome of Clarkson's trial. At his interrogation before the committee on 27 September, we know that Clarkson had stood on his right to refuse to answer questions that might incriminate him, but his persecutors were convinced of his guilt, and sentenced him to three months imprisonment, with labour, to be followed by banishment. Clarkson's connection with Major William Rainborowe, brother of the murdered Leveller Thomas, had interested the committee who suspected that Rainborowe had financed the publication of *A Single Eye*. Consequently, Rainborowe lost his right to sit as a judge on the Middlesex Bench. As for Clarkson himself, he was released from New Bridewell prison after a month, was not banished, and returned to see his long-suffering wife in East Anglia (p. 138).

Jacob Bauthumley or Bothumley has no connection with either Coppe or Clarkson, although Salmon had heard of him (p. 199). He was born in Leicester in 1613, the son of a separatist shoemaker who was excommunicated and forced to leave the county.[47] Bauthumley was given redress against Laud by the Long Parliament, and joined the army early in the war. He stayed in for a long time, eventually being promoted to Quartermaster in Colonel Cox's regiment. He published *The Light and Dark Sides of God* in late 1650; Thomason acquired a copy on 20 November. It is probably fair to see Bauthumley as the most moderate of the Ranters. His denial of the Trinity is clear, but he did not reach the extreme conclusion regarding sin to which Clarkson came (pp. 236–40). Nevertheless, the pamphlet was published by the Leveller William Larner, emphasising the possibility of a connection between Ranters and disaffected Levellers. Most important though is how Bauthumley was perceived by the authorities. His pamphlet did worry them, and Bauthumley was tried under military law for spreading blasphemous doctrines, cashiered, and, as we have seen, pierced through the tongue.[48] Bauthumley was not the only Ranter in the army. Salmon, who had been both soldier and chaplain in the regiment of Commissary-General Henry Ireton, had already left

45   John Tickell, *The Bottomless Pit Smoking in Familism*, 2nd edn. (1652), *passim*.
46   Anon., *The Routing of the Ranters* (1650), 3.
47   See *ODNB*.
48   *A Perfect Diurnall*, 11–18 March 1650.

service by the time of Coventry, but there was also the case of Captain Francis Freeman, whose defense, *Light Vanquishing Darkness* (1650), reveals a belief in a pantheistic Antinomianism. God was inside table-boards and candlesticks, and 'every Scripture is a mystery, untill it be made known to us, or revealed in us: and so it comes to be above that Scripture without us; for, it is said to be a hidden mystery.'[49] Freeman, a man popular with his troops, was accused of singing bawdy songs on the march and in private meetings, and his superiors tried to be rid of him. His case came before Cromwell before he lost his commission. It seems, then, that the army was marginally more consistent in punishing offenders than were justices, although the force of Bauthumley's pamphlet, and its coincidence with the events in Coventry, singled him out for exemplary punishment.

Ranter gatherings occurred sporadically throughout the 1650s, although without the intensity of the second year of the Commonwealth. The subsequent history of each of the major Ranters shows a return to separatist activity, although with a quietistic emphasis in most cases. Bauthumley became a publican, guardedly preached at Leicester and managed to be a corporation official after the Restoration, publishing an abridged version of Foxe's *Book of Martyrs* entitled *A Brief Historical Relation* in 1676.[50] Coppe and Wyke returned to the Baptist community. Wyke preached vigorously in Ireland, and was imprisoned there as a nonconformist in 1663, while Coppe continued to preach in Baptist conventicles, although he thought it prudent to change his name to Higham (of course playing on his earlier assumption of a name of God, spoken by God: 'I am that I am' (Ex. 3.14)), under which he earned his living as a physician.[51] An anonymous broadsheet of 1657, *Divine Fire-Works*, has been attributed to Coppe.[52] In stylistic terms this would seem to be just, and the millennial element is still there, with prophecies directed against female manners and cosmetics, envisaging a fiery and violent judgment on sinners. Coppe was amongst the Ranters who visited George Fox in prison in 1655, where their behaviour was not compromised as, according to his testimony, they invoked 'universal majesty' with beer and some smokes. Fox said (but he *would* say this) he managed to shame them:

> they began to call for drink and tobacco: and I desired them to forbear it in my room, if they had for a mind of it they might go into another room.
> And one of them cried, 'All is ours', and another said, 'All was well': but I replied, 'How is all well when thou art so peevish and envious and crabbed': for I saw he was of a peevish nature. And I spake to their conditions, and they knew it and looked at one another wondering.[53]

---

49   Francis Freeman, *Light Vanquishing Darkness* (1650), 4–5.
50   Hessayon, 'Abiezer Coppe and the Ranters,' 368.
51   For Wyke, see *ODNB*. Anthony Wood, *Athenae Oxonienses* (Oxford, 1721), Vol. 2, Col. 500.
52   Owen C. Watkins, *The Puritan Experience* (1972), 147; Abiezer Coppe, *Selected Writings*,
      ed. Andrew Hopton (London: Aporia Press, 1987); Nigel Smith, '"Making fire":
      conflagration and religious controversy in seventeenth-century London,' in J.F. Merritt, ed.,
      *Imagining Early Modern London: Perceptions and Portrayals of the City from Stow to Strype
      1598-1720* (Cambridge: Cambridge University Press, 2001), 284–86.
53   George Fox, *Journal*, ed. Nigel Smith (Harmondsworth: Penguin Books, 1999), 149–50.

In 1680, eight years after Coppe's death, there appeared a broadsheet poem called 'The Character of a True Christian,' signed A. C., which asserted salvation and blessedness for all on earth in the same ambiguous manner as his second recantation. The attribution to Coppe may reasonably be doubted.

Salmon returned to Kent and became popular in the locality of Rochester, there laying the seeds for what became a Quaker community.[54] He preached on Sundays in the Cathedral, and recommended his successor, Richard Coppin. It appears that Salmon then emigrated to Barbados, where he may have been in trouble for organizing separatist meetings.

Clarkson claimed to have had livings in Norfolk after his release, and to have practiced white magic as a cunning man, but left, so he claims, to rant once more in East Anglia (p. 139). In February 1658 he claims he met the Muggletonian prophet John Reeve, and was converted, but other sources point to his conversion in mid-1656. In his Muggletonian affirmation, *Look About You, or the Right Devil Discovered* (1659), he rebuked any who regarded sin, including lying with women, as justifiable as he had done previously. These were 'white ranting devils' who sinned under the pretence of religious liberty. The Muggletonians were Joachites and believed in the Doctrine of the Two Seeds, where all the rich and wicked descended from Cain, and all the poor, oppressed and devout, from Abel, so Clarkson retained his egalitarian outlook. He tried and failed to challenge Muggleton's authority in the movement in 1660, and died a debtor in Ludgate prison in 1667, having lent £100 for the reconstruction of London after the Great Fire; the money was not returned.[55] The year before several Ranters — Coppe, Salmon, Rawlinson, Mary Lake — were named among a greater community of illuminated 'Friends of the Bridegroom,' including Sir Henry Vane, Erbery, Sedgwick, and even (most unlikely) Thomas Hobbes, and encouraged to join together in a 'Unity of Love.' For some at least the sometime Ranters were worthy members of a larger group of the spiritually inspired.[56]

IV

The Ranters provoked a mass of hostile pamphlets. The great fear in men's minds was the anarchy and slaughter experienced when the Anabaptist communities controlled Munster in the earlier sixteenth century. Many saw Ranting as simply the antithesis of their idea of any form of proper devotion. Some pamphlets were extremely crude and exaggerated, confusing the Ranters with the underworld of bawdy, libidinous revellers and false prophets, the tavern community of which they were certainly a part. The way in which the tracts were used to generate stereotypes of the Ranter and widely used in a sensational literature campaign designed to induce alarm and exert a mainstream godly orthodoxy in the fledgling English

---

54   *ODNB*; see also Douglas Gwyn, 'Joseph Salmon: From Seeker to Ranter — And Almost to Quaker,' *JFHS*, 58 (1998), 114–31.

55   Barry Reay, 'Laurence Clarkson: An Artisan and the English Revolution,' in C. Hill, B. Reay and W. Lamont, eds., *The World of the Muggletonians* (London: Temple Smith, 1983), 162–87; *ODNB*.

56   See Robert Rich, *Love without Dissimulation* (1666), 6–7; Caricchio, *Religione, Politica e Commercio*, 309.

republic has been documented in further detail by J.C. Davis and Ariel Hessayon. The former also argues that some modern historical accounts have compromised themselves by believing the stereotypes, a charge that has been vigorously debated.[57]

Fear-mongering aside, a few tracts, like John Holland's *The Smoke of the Bottomless Pit* (1650), give fairly accurate accounts of what was in Ranter writing itself. Holland accuses Ranters of holding that God is in man and in every creature, and that there is one spirit in the world: good and bad spirits are imaginary, while there is no sin since God has made it. Thus, the Devil is the left hand of God, and there is no heaven and hell but what is in man. The Scriptures and Biblical commandments are rejected as contradictory, and church ordinances are denied. Christ is a form or shadow only of a transcendent truth, and what he did in the flesh is now inside men in the spirit. Marriage is seen as a curse, and there should be a complete liberty for all to choose sexual partners. Holland grasps the characteristic Ranter language, where God is defined as 'Being,' 'Fulnesse,' a 'Great Notion,' 'Reason' and 'Immensity,' while 'when men dye their spirits go into God, as the small rivers go into the sea.' There are also some examples of a kind of free-thinking logic at work. For instance, the world must surely pre-date the Biblical creation since Cain went off to build a city, implying that there was more than just Adam's family alive, a view made infamous in Europe by the French thinker Isaac de la Peyrère (1594–1676).

Some pamphlets divide Ranterism into several sects, like Shelomites, Clements, Athians and Adamites, though there is no other evidence for this. The important point is that the Ranters are being identified with earlier forms of heresy, and the words 'Gnostick,' 'Donatist' and 'Nicolaitan' are used. Indeed, Coppe attacks the last of these in *Copp's Return* because their beliefs set them against the law, while the Gnostics had a theory of the soul similar to the Ranters, that the body must ascend from its earthly shell into its divine, ecstatic and spiritual truth. Another telling distinction, made by Samuel Fisher, was between 'Rantizers' who were flamboyant sprinklers of water at baptism ceremonies, and were too 'formal,' and Ranters, who had dispensed with religion altogether.[58]

Most of the pamphlets which aim to lambast Ranting are obsessed with sexual licence, which accusation is then linked with the denial of heaven and hell, good and evil:

> *They taught, that they could neither see* Evil, *know* Evil, *nor Act* Evil, *and that whatever they did was* Good, *and not* Evil, *there being no such thing as sin in the World. Whereupon Mistress* E.B. *striking fire at a* Tinder-box, *lights up a Candle, seeks under the Bed, Table, and stools, and at last coming to one of the men, shee offers to unbutton his Cod-piece; who demanding of her what she sought for? She answeth,* For sin: *whereupon he blows out her Candle, leads her to the Bed, where in the sight of all the rest, they commit Fornication.*[59]

God in man paradoxically results in the levelling of all to the beastly. Nakedness (Adamitism) is familiar, together with the parody of the Christian sacrament in buttock kissing, orgies and

57   Davis, *Fear, Myth and History*, chs. 4–6; Hessayon, 'Abiezer Coppe and the Ranters,' 357–63.
58   Samuel Fisher, *Christianismus Redivivus* (1655), 307–9.
59   J.M., *The Ranters Last Sermon* (1654), 3–4.

even coprophagia. Eating becomes a similar bestial ritual. Ranters were 'sitting at table, eating of a piece of Beef, one of them took it in his hand, tearing it a sunder, said to the other *This is the flesh of Christ*, take and eat,'[60] and the desire for mystical union is seen as an excuse for the physical.

In some accounts of Ranterism, the work of the Devil is detected. Samuel Sheppard's *The Joviall-Crew, or the Devill turn'd Ranter* (1650) is a condensed twelve-page pamphlet drama, probably never intended for performance since it was so short. The play mediates charges of drunkenness and wife-sharing by means of a comic confusion, where the Devil controls Ranters through the 'mask of religion,' and where drugs, the ironic agent of illusion, are the means by which licence is obtained. The play shares part of its title with Richard Brome's *The Jovial Crew, or the Merry Beggars* (first performed 1641–42), and clearly belongs to the satiric tradition previously dominated by Ben Jonson. Sheppard's characters are as much roysters as Ranters, with the emphasis on sexual performance:

> *Wriggle.* I thank you fellow-creatures, I'le serve either of you soul and body.   *They all drink lustily, while*
>
> *Robustio.* Lovely Mrs *All-prate*, in this I *celebrate the creatures health*, who now is plowing on the angry main, whose saddle I supply, hee'l thank me for't. ——   *Apostatus whispers Dose, and he goes off.*
>
> *Mrs. All prate.* He were a divel else: Here's to thee dear *Violentus*, this will inable thee 'gainst next performance, you were faultringly feeble in the last.[61]   *she drinks.*

However, Sheppard is also concerned with the danger of the spread of Ranter ideas and their consequences, especially violence. Elsewhere, the Ranters, like the Familists, are alleged to create their own institutions and organisations,[62] but it is hard to see this in the impromptu gatherings of My One Flesh.

V

It would be a mistake to divorce the visionary aspect of Ranter literature from its context in the forum of polemical exchange. After all, the Ranters, like most other pamphleteers of the time, were seeking to impose their vision upon the world, to assert a universal, essential truth over all others. Anyone who published very extreme material during the Interregnum was liable to severe and violent censure, and the Ranters' close awareness of the conditions of publication and censorship is revealed in various and complex ways. This has an axiomatic effect upon the way in which the pamphlets would have appealed to readers. They show the inevitable clash between subversive critique and the necessity of avoiding persecution in order to maintain uninhibited speech. This is the case even when there is no extensive programme

---

60   Anon., *Strange News from Newgate* (1651), 2.
61   [Samuel Sheppard], *The Joviall Crew, or, The Devill turn'd Ranter* (1651), 6.
62   Gilbert Roulston, *The Ranters Bible* (1650), and Reading, *The Ranters Ranting* (1650), *passim*.

for change. The basis for Coppe's rant at the beginning of *A Second Fiery Flying Roule* is a warning to those in power that they will go the same way as the dead King Charles if they do not give their money to the poor. This is not so much Cohn's alleged 'wary and clandestine propaganda' but rather a blatant confrontation: 'wherein the worst and foulest of villanies, are discovered, under the best and fairest outsides' (p. 72).

By contrast Salmon's last known pamphlet recommends a simple maxim to the reader, 'give it entertainment, ... it will return thee satisfaction' (p. 201), which matches William Erbery's apparently incidental concern for the reader, ''tis well if truth rise in them that read.' This reflects the growing quietism of the sects as the 1650s progressed. *Heights in Depths* is, in fact, Salmon's recantatory tract, though it reads more as an assertion of anti-rationalism by means of a withdrawal into silence. Salmon claims to have gained a new enlightenment from being imprisoned, but ambiguity is fostered in the suggestion that it is 'vanity' to engage in any positive activity whatsoever. Salmon's apparent indifference to the public is as much an incitement to read, since he claims no desire to impose his opinions upon the reader. The rant is therefore merely disengaged: 'I am quite a weary of popular applause, and I little value a vulgar censure; the benefit of the one cannot at all affect me, nor the prejudice of the other much molest me' (pp. 212–13).

The most interesting case of enforced recantation, possible deferred compliance and assumption of quiet conformity is that of Coppe.[63] For the Ranters, recantation is, to say the least, ambiguous. They do not pursue dogmatism, of which Coppe accuses the Anabaptists (p. 88). If their truth did not operate as a dogma it would be entirely possible for them to act in conformity with an orthodoxy, but secretly so to retain their own principles. As far as theology went, this was certainly what John Tickell thought, and he compares the Ranters with the 'double tongues' of the Familists. Familist and Ranter rhetoric (Tickell does not make a distinction) operates thus:

> they will first insinuate an interest in your affections, and then corrupt your judgments. They will smile upon you, and cut your throate: use melting words, *Honey-sweet*, smooth as oyle, but full of poyson. A Christ would they exalt Christ *within*, ... but friends, their Christ *within*, is to crucifie that Christ without.

Furthermore:

> they will put themselves on all expressions, wayes & windings, to keep themselves from being *known*, but to their *owne*: you shall not know where to find them, so as to fasten on them, but their own shall know their meaning, and so may you when you have once got their *Key*.[64]

If Tickell's indignation is anything to go by, authority was further mocked here.

---

63   *CRW*, 118–57.
64   John Tickell, *The Bottomless Pit*, Sig. A6ᵛ, 39–41.

It is clear that the Ranters were involved in complex modes of address. Unlike the writings of other radical groups, the Levellers and the Diggers, and the pamphlets of Royalists and Parliamentarians, there is no narrator figure of apparent common sense and good will, an impartial observer of events. Nevertheless, there is a characteristic speaking subject, an 'I' in each pamphlet, who speaks with the vast emotional depth and force of Coppe, or the self-assured enthusiasm of Salmon or Bauthumley. It is not so much a question of flying a colour of political or religious identity, as might a polemicist, but a strategy of driving home the locus and consequence of the Antinomian experience: 'But I tell you … whiles you are embracing this body of self-safety and outward Liberty, he is dying and departing from it, though you see it not' (p. 164). Going further the speaker in *The Light and Dark Sides of God* attempts to obliterate the distinction between himself and the reader: the reader is assumed to be engrossed in following the discourse. Simultaneously, the speaker makes his presence omnipotent by admitting that he has no objection to any opinion, but then couches this inside the governing explanation. The speaker here is an honest 'I,' alone with the 'reason of that commanding power which is God in me' (p. 252).

The Ranters were concerned with the status assigned to language in its capacity as a bearer of divine truths, and its ability to communicate Ranter ideas to the illuminated and to other people. Special code words were used, which embodied shared ideas and intentions: 'Welcome Fellow Creature!' like the Lollard 'Brother in Christ'; not all of these were the invention of hostile pamphleteers. The 'Ranting mood' was certainly anti-Baconian in spirit, as Salmon realised: 'the form, method and language invites not the curious and nice spirit of anie man' (p. 169). The essence of Ranter experience is beyond language; the naming process becomes hollow, void of meaning. To 'arise into the Letter of these letters,' without realising what is behind them, what is truly signified, is to outstep oneself.

Total illumination would result in the ability to understand all tongues. Babel would be comprehended, but Thomas Tany maintains that most are unable to cope with the stupendously powerful intimations of Adamic Hebrew (this is true: I have tried this out by reading Tany to many undergraduate lecture audiences).[65] John Everard tried to preserve some 'vestigia' of this energy when he produced his translation of Hermes Trismegistus, which had already been translated from Arabic to Latin, and thence to Dutch.[66] Here, Ranterism is in tune with the search of various language reformers in the period for a language that would exactly describe the divine nature of the objects it names.[67] Coppe seems to realise the problems which his readers face with a solipsistic language. Since each utterance is determined by God dwelling within him, the speaking subject has no control over what he says: it can only be hoped that the statement is eventually understood: 'If I here speak in an unknown tongue, I pray that I may interpret when I may' (p. 42). This authorizes the private vocabulary and irregular phrasing, the sense of God's imprint evading regular grammar, which is exactly the point of the prophetic repetitions in Coppe.

---

65   Thomas Tany (or Totney), *Theauraujohn his Theous ori apokolipikal* (1651), 9. For a rich account
     of Totney's career, see now Ariel Hessayon, *'Gold tried in the fire.'*
66   *Hermes Trismegistus his Divine Pymander*, trans. J. Everard (1650).
67   See Rhodri Lewis, *Language, Mind and Nature: Artificial Languages in England from Bacon to
     Locke* (Cambridge and New York: Cambridge University Press, 2007).

The Elizabethan separatist Robert Browne urged the clergy not only to 'preache' but also to 'teache' the Word to the people, to instill truth in the flock.[68] At another extreme, to endow individual utterance with the autonomy of the Ranters is to divorce oneself from the authority of the Scriptures as understood by educated ministers, as well as the conventions of understanding fostered by ordinary language. In the Puritan Platonist, Peter Sterry, there is an essential link between divine authority and individual experience: '*He, that defaceth the Prints, and Image of the Eternal Word in his Natural Man, Crucifies his Saviour in the Flesh, a Second Time.*'[69] Robert Beake, writing of the imprisoned Ranters in his keeping, claimed that his captives had 'acute wits and voluble tongues,' and regarded the Bible as no more than a ballad.[70] Others were held to refer only to the Bible when it suited them, as if 'it were *Gesta Romanorum.*' However, none of the Ranters explicitly states, despite their opponents' accusations, that the Scriptures are a 'bundle of contradictions.'[71] What happens is that the distinction between individual utterance and Scriptural authority disappears in the Ranter imagination: '*there is nothing in the Treatise then the very Language, and correspondency of Scripture in the Letter of it*' (p. 224). The Bible is the 'History' which the 'Mystery' in the spirit comes to bear upon. For the Ranters divine inspiration goes hand in hand with the stricture that in Biblical time, figures of speech were understood literally. Ranter language is rooted in a divine signifying act in the individual, which has a totally free interpretative value: 'you must take it in these tearmes, for it is infinitely beyond expression' (p. 74). This clearly contradicts the projects of both Hobbes and Wilkins, who were searching for a precise one-to-one relationship between signifier and signified. Coppe's theory of language is closely related to his epistemology of forms. His utterances attempt to preserve the inner within the outer form of language. The inner disrupts the outer form, but Coppe has no final control over his public discourse. As Winstanley sees the connection between language and property, where the Church appropriates 'strange tongues' to rule the masses through doctrine, so Coppe's 'great ones' in 'outward declarations ... professe me' but miss their mark. To have a title is to be someone's property. However, since God owns us all, his propensity to name stands above that of the rich and clergy. Coppe shows how appearances switch when the truth is revealed, so that angels turn out to be Ranters, for 'what God hath cleansed, call not thou uncleane' (p. 84).

The Ranter writers' propensity for cursing and swearing is well documented. It has been identified as a form of ritual that parallels other Ranter rites. By parodying orthodox kinds of discourse, such as preaching (they had all been preachers and many would largely return to preaching), the Ranters were able to find an escape from oppressive social restraints, as well as bolster their spirits against threats of persecution. But swearing is also a manifestation of a privileged knowledge. After all, in their view it is God who is swearing in the individual. Coppe would rather attend to the angelic knowledge in swearing than to a preacher, and his pamphlets are punctuated by subversive, game-like motives which match inspired utterance

---

68   Robert Browne, *A Treatise of reformation without tarying for anie* (1582), Sig. A2ᵛ.
69   Peter Sterry, *The Comings Forth of Christ* (1650), Sig. aa4ᵛ.
70   Leybourne-Popham MS., (HMC), 39.
71   Tickell, *The Bottomless Pit*, 39.

with 'posture.' Ezekiel, that 'son of contempt,' is admired for his transgressive 'pranks,' while Coppe is 'confounding plaguing, tormenting nice, demure, barren *Mical*, with *Davids* unseemly carriage' (p. 97). Riddle also functions as part of the secret key: 'Neither can they understand what pure honour is wrapt up in the Kings motto, *Honi Soit qui Mal.y.pense*: Evill to him that evill thinks' (p. 83). Astrological elements are involved here: 'Queene Wisdome' descends to rule Coppe's exposition, and every time the 'Dominicall letter' G occurs (G being the letter which astrologers calculated to represent each Sunday in 1649), it is seen to have supernatural powers, signifying and assuring the presence of the supreme will (p. 93).[72]

It would come as a great surprise if Ranter pamphlets were seen to follow the five-part pattern of Aristotelian rhetoric, or the exegetical methods of preaching. Coppe, Clarkson and Salmon deliberately react against the forms of exhortative and disputative reason, which are seen by them to be a means of imposing religious hegemony. Coppe intricately parodies the art of preaching and the language of scholarly exegesis.[73] The impulse is anti-rational and non-aesthetic, so that the typical Renaissance figure of Apollo, sitting inside his 'O,' the perfect source of knowledge, virtue and grace, is replaced by a circle which is evasive and deceptive, a 'womb of Wind ... an airy notion, even while it appears to be something, it proves nothing' (p. 204).

The roots of Puritan preaching style were embedded in William Perkins's *The Art of Prophecying* of 1592, which demanded plain and methodical procedures. The 'grammaticall, rhetorical and logicall Arts' were to be used in analysing the Scriptures 'whereby teaching is used for the reformation of the mind from error.' This reflected the increasing influence of Ramism, which had enhanced the restrictiveness of logic by divorcing it from its traditional connection with stylistic and oral presentation.[74] Hence 'Interpretation is the *Opening* of words and sentences of the Scripture, that one entire and naturall sense may appeare.'[75] Such intense 'division' led to an expression which was precise and tightly enthymemic. Puritanism itself displayed an intense distrust of the imagination, emphasizing the Word as pure Logos, devoid of all sacramentalism, and this distrust extended to the use of the imagination in secondary procedures of devotional exploration.

The Ranter drive at singularity, so to speak the union of light and dark in God, does not allow such a discriminating movement, but its opposite. Each pamphlet attempts to merge reason, logic or 'formality' with the totalizing moment of illumination, but the tensions between the two impulses are revealing. Since they are using language, semantic categories are necessary for the generation of verbal sense, and the organization of larger arguments does result in some Ranters relying upon some form of disputative order. There is a risk of sell-out to conformity here, and the successive argument by points, together with Biblical

---

72   For instance, see John Booker, *Uranoscopia, or an Almanack and Prognostication, Being a Prospective Glasse, for the yeare of Christ* (1649).
73   McDowell, *ERI*, 109–18.
74   For a full exploration of the rhetorical background, see now Peter Mack, *A History of Renaissance Rhetoric, 1380–1620* (Oxford: Oxford University Press, 2012).
75   William Perkins, *The Arte of Prophecying* (1607), 30.

references, occurs in both of Coppe's recantations, while the lengthy contents descriptions in his pamphlets parody the convention. There is a sense of acute embarrassment, revealed again in self-parody, when Salmon uses an exordium (p. 161). Bauthumley's meditation dispenses with citation: 'and so rather then I would loose, or let pass what was spiritually discovered inside me, I was willing to omit the outward viewing of them in a chapter or verse' (p. 224).

The conflict between literalism and freer interpretation is exemplified in a debate between the Presbyterian John Osborn, and Richard Coppin:

> *Cop. That he shall see God was true but the place and the time was not true: he spake not aright according to the time and place, only as to the thing, that he should see God was true, but that it should be after he had laid down his body, that was not true: and accordingly he did see him, but in his natural life, before he died.*
> *Osb.* That the sight expected *ch.* 19 was accomplished before his death, you onely affirm, without one reason or Scripture to demonstrate it; your bare assertion must be of no weight or consideration with me, so long as I have the text so plainly and fully speaking the contrary: let me hear what you say to this, that *Jobs* sight of his Redeemer was not expected to be accomplished until his skin and bones were destroyed with worms. What say you to this?[76]

Coppe begins *A Second Fiery Flying Roule* with an attack on the 'Formalists' who would tie religious expression down to such tight forms. While Salmon does answer his opponents point by point, the arguments themselves are based not upon the Biblical reference but upon the suggestive trigger in the phrase. Analogous meanings rebound off one another as the sense of spiritual death in the outer body grows paradoxically into rebirth and essence with the inner arrival of God (pp. 209–13).

Ranter literature has more to do with another tradition in Protestant discourse; the individual meditation upon personal religious experience. Coppe renders a fine conversion narrative. The habit of recounting personal experience as part of a conversion to a position of faith provides a clear link between the Ranters and other dissenting groups. Bauthumley claims his work is 'meditational,' while the confessional nature of *A Second Fiery Flying Roule* balances the prophetic drive of the first one. Salmon talks of the space necessary to 'ponder' his condition, but the intention is not pastoral, as if the godly writer should provide an example to others. Instead, the recollection of the inner arrival of God, and the consequent change in the individual's perception and behaviour serves to enhance the authority of the speaking subject. Yet the moment of ranting, the reiteration of the inner light in words, is obviously in opposition to any considered meditation.

Coppe's imagination is emblematic: the image of the hearts being blasted by God (p. 74) perfectly matches Cramer's well known picture in form and intensity, and the Ranter description of the arrival of inner light and grace recalls the woodcuts that accompanied some

---

76   John Osborn, *The World to Come*, 61.

of the Familist treatises.[77] The Puritan emphasis upon plain style is most famously stated in
Bunyan's Preface to *Grace Abounding*:

> *I could ... have stepped into a stile much higher then this ... but I dare not:* God *did not play in
> convincing of me; the* Devil *did not play in tempting of me: neither did I play when I sunk as
> into a bottomless pit, when the pangs of hell caught hold upon me: wherefore I may not play in
> my relating of them, but be plain and simple, and lay down the thing as it was.*[78]

Ranter prose style follows a similar link between moral impulse and expression, fulfilling St
Paul's imperative, 'not with enticing words of man's wisdom, but in demonstration of the
spirit and power' (1 Cor. 2.4). As with the reaction to rhetorical and devotional conventions,
the construction of sentences for the Ranter is both an escape from and a dependence upon
what already exists. Coppe parodies the staid measure of the spoken sermon, deliberately
sprinkling his discourse with the conversational, comic apostrophe, 'Well!' and his Latin and
Hebrew phrases have a part to play in conveying his enthusiasm, but in doing so, they parody
themselves, and the liturgical patterns which they represent (pp. 54–55, 60–63). Coppe's
exegetical technique has been seen in this respect as a 'quasi-midrashic' act, combining and
encountering difficulty in the scriptural original to create something both imitative and
entirely new, 'conflicted and disturbing as it makes great claims that ultimately remain
couched in mystery and strangeness.'[79] The ranting speech act does not sustain grammatical
organization in the final instance, and there is a sense of trying to make words say more than
they possibly can. The frequent repetition of adjectives, though it has a Biblical root here
in Ezekiel, intimates a feeling of frustration with the language, a 'strange new way new new
new,' while a hurried breathlessness is evoked with the use of parentheses, as if the normal
sentence structure cannot hold the full extent of the illumination. The compassion in this
expression has been adduced in a critique of literary approaches indebted to a 'top-down'
model of early modern authority.[80]

   The appearance of the tracts is also unusual and not merely concerned with imitating
printed Bibles. We have no authorial manuscripts of any Ranter text, from which a printed
pamphlet was derived, so it is hard to tell just how far some of this is due to poor compositing

---

77   See Smith, *Perfection Proclaimed*, 155, 160, 163, 165–67.
78   John Bunyan, *Grace Abounding to the Chief of Sinners*, ed. R. Sharrock (Oxford: Clarendon Press,
     1962), 5–6.
79   Noam Flinker, 'The Poetics of Biblical Prophecy: Abiezer Coppe's Late Converted Midrash,' in
     Ariel Hessayon and David Finnegan, eds., *Varieties of Seventeenth- and Early Eighteenth-Century
     English Radicalism in Context* (Farnham and Burlington, VT: Ashgate, 2011), 113–27 (127). The
     precision of Ranter imitation of Hebrew prophets is explored by Achsah Guibbory, 'England's
     "Biblical" Prophets, 1642–60,' in Roger D. Sell and Anthony W. Johnson, eds., *Writing and
     Religion in England, 1558–1689: Studies in Community-Making and Cultural Memory* (Farnham;
     Ashgate; 2009), 305–25.
80   See James Holstun, 'Ranting at the New Historicism,' *ELR*, 19 (1989), 189–225. For further
     extensive readings of Coppe, see David Loewenstein, *Representing Revolution in Milton and his
     Contemporaries: Religion, Politics, and Polemics in Radical Puritanism* (Cambridge and New York:
     Cambridge University Press, 2001), 93–115.

and compromised print resources. In *A Fiery Flying Roll, A Single Eye* and *Heights in Depths* in particular, the punctuation is in places grammatically nonsensical, 'Nor the Beast (without you) what do you call 'em?' (p. 80), and the normalisation of this leads, in some cases, to a different reading. It may be that the compositors simply misunderstood the copy, or that the copy was punctuated in this way in order to foster ambiguity. This would leave a large measure of flexibility if the pamphlet was to be delivered orally. Sentences often remain unfinished, degenerating into an 'etc.,' as if the reader is expected to know what is coming next. In Salmon, colloquial interruptions halt the general fluidity of the discourse, while the exchange of sound between phonic similars in the same sentence serves to confuse meanings, just as Coppe causes extravagant echoes, where the phonetically and semantically similar follow one another, 'Omnipotent,' 'Omnipresent.' All of these features have been called the 'manic style' and seen as a consequence of marginal social positions and therefore the difficulty of making a protest statement in conventional controversial or petitionary terms.[81]

If there is a consistent denial of the verbally rational, there seems also to be a considerable degree of ratiocination, and a design to inculcate enlightenment in the reader. Clarkson names a category of 'reason,' rejected as any kind of unconfused thinking by one modern reader.[82] Like Biblical poetry, Coppe's poems and poetic organisation stand as the most economic and precise expression of Antinomianism. The result is a dramatic intensity as the wrangling syntax is interrupted by the sparse simplicity of Coppe's renunciation of possession. There is an intimation of an intelligence of impeccable authority in the orderly distribution of vowels, as the hurriedness of 'But we brethren are perswaded better things of you &c./Her's some *Gold* and Silver' is cut short by the pious 'But that is none of mine./The drosse I owne' (p. 41). There are rhyming phrases which function as *leitmotifs* of Antinomian experience, of the free grace dwelling in Christ, 'my love, my dove' being repeated throughout Coppe and Salmon, as well as the more ferocious 'Rod of God' in Salmon alone (pp. 44, 160).

There is a sense of playfulness, as the rhymes border on doggerel, which is another familiar characteristic of Familist writing: '*Each Begger that you meet/Fall down before him, kisse him in the street*' (p. 82). Music can also reveal the light of God's grace, the immanence of which is felt in Coppe's ascending grammatical 'scale' towards the optative (pp. 54–55). It is as if, having gone beyond Biblical literalism, the Ranters search for some form of symbolic representation of what is beyond the Word, also instanced in Coppe's love of the sacred signifying powers of Hebrew and Roman letters. In Sheppard's satire, dance is also a divine signifier, though the song that accompanies it is quite wrongly Bacchanalian:

> Viole. By Pluto's Crown, *Proserpine's* hair
> Rob. *Cerberus* yell, *Alecto's* chair,
> Pig. By Epicurus' happy life.
> Dose. And *Messalina, Claudius'* Wife.[83]

---

81 Clement Hawes, *Mania and Literary Style: The Rhetoric of Enthusiasm from the Ranters to Christopher Smart* (Cambridge and New York: Cambridge University Press, 1996), Part I.

82 Thomas N. Corns, *Uncloistered Virtue: English Political Literature, 1640–1660* (Oxford: Clarendon Press, 1992), 183–84: 'for all that it echoes the idiom of Christ's parables, ... passages ... are simply incomprehensible ... This hardly approximates to reason.'

83 [Sheppard], *The Joviall Crew*, 10.

The simple rhyming couplets of the poem prefacing *A Single Eye* (p. 115), or the complex imagery of the two poems discovered in the Clarke papers, are much closer to the movement's sentiments.[84] On the other hand, Coppe and Francis Freeman are supposed to have sung blasphemous songs to the tune of metrical psalms in taverns, and one pamphlet cites a Ranter prayer that works upon similar lines. This biting materialistic pantheism aspect is captured in the Ranter's 'Christmas Carol':

> *They prate of God; believe it, Fellow-Creature,*
> *There's no such Bug-bear, all was made by Nature:*
> *We know all came of nothing, and shall passe*
> *Into the same condition once it was,*
> *By Natures power: and that they grossely lie,*
> *That say there's hope of immortality:*
> *Let them but tell us what a soul is, then*
> *We will adhere to these madbrain sick men.*[85]

VI

By way of conclusion we should note that in their own voices, the Ranters found ways of incorporating sexual performance into their theology. In some accounts, like Clarkson's, they treated sex as prelapsarian and hence devoid of sin, and communal, escaping from the bondage that came with monogamous marriage. Holy sex beyond wedlock was as innocent as swearing in the name of the Lord. Creeping into Clarkson and Salmon's *Divinity Anatomized* is the even more transgressive sense that the sex act (Salmon thinks of its human terms as heterosexual penetration but with no sense of any order of earthly marriage) is the time and place where God's presence is fulfilled in man, and where God is expressing love for mankind. It is also the case that such spiritual liberation appears to free orthodox gender identity and divisions. Coppe speaks of himself sometimes as an impregnated woman, filled by the Holy Spirit, while the Puritan spirit of propriety is conceived of pejoratively as a woman, the 'holy Scripturian WHORE.'[86] Outrageously Coppe offers social equity through promiscuous sex. Some of the more extreme Quakers also experienced such a liberation through the spirit or the inner light into a state where they could claim to be both man and woman at once, messianic androgynes, as was the case with John Perrot. Clarkson's communal sexual mysticism, fusing sense and spirit, suggests a restitution of all things in one harmonious cosmic unity, which is the heaven of the present for those who understand it. In *A Jvstjfjcatjon* communal sex is the marriage bed between men, women and Jesus.[87]

---

84   See Ann Laurence, 'Two Ranter Poems,' *RES*, n.s. 31 (1980), 56–59.
85   *The Arraignment and Tryall with a Declaration of the Ranters* (1650), 6.
86   See the extensive analysis in Hawes, *Mania and Literary Style*, Part I.
87   See further, B.J. Gibbons, *Gender in Mystical and Occult Thought: Behmenism and its Development in England* (Cambridge: Cambridge University Press, 1996), 140–41.

But let us think too about how this would be received. If you were a seventeenth-century parent, would you be having your children exposed to these practices, anymore than you would today? One of the contemporary complaints made against Milton's divorce theory was that it exposed vulnerable children to all the dangers that a modern welfare society tries to avoid: children from broken marriages abandoned to want and open to abuse.[88] In an age when most children lived in extreme proximity to their parents, with many people living largely in one small room, can you imagine how a Ranter meeting might go? You would not in many instances just be able to put the children to bed, set the baby monitor, and proceed with the holy priapics. Such a scenario has been imagined in Thomas Clay's brilliant and visionary forthcoming film about the Ranters and the aftermath of the Civil War. Is it for this reason that we do not hear a single female Ranter voice? The female Ranter is lost to the identity of the 'holy whore,' in which extreme Antinomianism might glory, but absolutely no one else, and there was no public or indeed private way for such an identity to become acceptable in any sustainable way. The vast majority would have regarded this as extremely sinful femininity liable to punishment in the sharpest corporal way. Coppe's companion in Coventry, Mrs. Seney, was 'carted' in London as a prostitute, carried through the streets as an exposure and punishment. The male Ranter comes off more lightly: indeed both Coppe and Clarkson self-present in heroic terms. Coppe even presents himself as a murderous parent willing to kill the 'children' laid at his door, by which he means the false accusations of errors made against him. The choice of this metaphor suggests a residual awareness of the consequences of sex beyond wedlock. Coppe says he is a 'rich Merchant' forced to accept paternity of others' offspring, but he is also using the register of the murderous mother.[89] That Edenic community of all beings envisaged by Thomasine Pendarves in her dream, quoted by Coppe in *Some Sweet Sips, of Some Spiritual Wine*, is not strictly speaking a Ranting voice, but belongs to Seeker spirituality, just before Coppe's Ranter theology developed in full. Both T.P. and Coppe understand that they are interpreting a purely and decidedly spiritual matter; shortly afterwards things would change for Coppe. We do of course find female voices a plenty among the Quakers, and there a theology devoted to the witnessing of the inner light, as opposed to sacred sex or spiritual swearing, prevailed. In that particular messianic configuration the equality of men and women before God was manifest and women's speaking was justified, to echo the title of Margaret Fell's famous tract.[90] Perhaps here we have reached the limits of the appeal of ranting in respect of gender politics. Coppe's last word on women is the terrifying vision of holy wrath wrought upon well-to-do London women who wear make-up, jewelry and perfume: they will be whipped, burned, deformed and raped. The page is literally stomach-turning, appearing to wreak with the smell of burning flesh: 'And instead of sweet smelling there shall be a stink; and BURNING instead of Beauty. ... The Lord wil discover her SECRET parts' (p. 112).

---

88   See Diane Purkiss, 'The Rhetoric of Milton's Divorce Tracts,' in Nicholas McDowell and Nigel Smith, eds., *The Oxford Handbook of Milton* (Oxford and New York: Oxford University Press, 2009), 194–99.

89   Abiezer Coppe, *Copp's Return to the wayes of Truth* (1651), Sig. B1ᵛ–2ʳ.

90   See Margaret Fell, *Womens Speaking Justified* (1667); Phyllis Mack, *Visionary Women: Ecstatic Prophecy in Seventeenth-Century England* (Berkeley, CA: University of California Press, 1992).

Further Reading

Brod, Manfred, 'A Radical Network in the English Revolution: John Pordage and His Circle, 1646–54,' *EHR*, 119 (2004), 1230–53.

——————, 'Doctrinal Deviance in Abingdon: Thomasine Pendarves and her Circle,' *Baptist Quarterly*, 41 (2005), 92–102.

Caricchio, Mario, *Religione, politica e commercio di libri nella rivoluzione inglese: gli autori di Giles Calvert 1645–1653* (Ferioli di Baveno: Name, 2003).

Cohn, Norman, *The Pursuit of the Millennium; Revolutionary Millenarians and Mystical Anarchists of the Middle Ages* (London: Secker and Warburg, 1957; rev. and expanded, London: Paladin, 1970).

Como, David R., *Blown by the Spirit: Puritanism and the Emergence of an Antinomian Underground in pre-Civil-War England* (Stanford, CA: Stanford University Press, 2004).

Corns, Thomas N., *Uncloistered Virtue: English Political Literature, 1640–1660* (Oxford: Clarendon Press, 1992).

——————, 'Radical Pamphleteering' in N.H. Keeble, ed., *The Cambridge Companion to Writing of the English Revolution* (Cambridge: Cambridge University Press, 2001), 71–86.

Davis, J.C., *Fear, Myth and History: The Ranters and the Historians* (Cambridge and New York: Cambridge University Press, 1986). A debate on the claims of this book ensued in the pages of the journal *Past and Present*, 129 (1990), 79–103; 140 (1993), 155–210.

——————, 'Against Formality: One Aspect of the English Revolution,' *TRHS*, 3 (1993), 265–288.

Flinker, Noam, 'Milton and the Ranters on Canticles,' in Mary A. Maleski and Russell A. Peck, eds., *A Fine Tuning: Studies of the Religious Poetry of Herbert and Milton* (Binghamton, NY; Medieval and Renaissance Texts & Studies, 1989), 273–90.

——————, 'The Poetics of Biblical Prophecy: Abiezer Coppe's Late Converted Midrash,' in Ariel Hessayon and David Finnegan, eds., *Varieties of Seventeenth- and Early Eighteenth-Century English Radicalism in Context* (Farnham and Burlington, VT : Ashgate, 2011), 113–27.

Friedman, Jerome, *Blasphemy, Immorality, and Anarchy: The Ranters and the English Revolution* (Athens, OH: Ohio University Press, 1987).

Gibbons, B.J., *Gender in Mystical and Occult Thought: Behmenism and its Development in England* (Cambridge: Cambridge University Press, 1996).

Gucer, Kathryn, '"Not Heretofore Extant in Print": Where the Mad Ranters Are,' *JHI*, 61 (2000), 75–95.

Guibbory, Achsah, 'England's "Biblical" Prophets, 1642-60,' in Roger D. Sell and Anthony W. Johnson, eds., *Writing and Religion in England, 1558–1689: Studies in Community-Making and Cultural Memory* (Farnham; Ashgate; 2009), 305–25.

Gwyn, Douglas, 'Joseph Salmon: From Seeker to Ranter — And Almost to Quaker,' *JFHS*, 58 (1998), 114–31.

Hawes, Clement, *Mania and Literary Style: The Rhetoric of Enthusiasm from the Ranters to Christopher Smart* (Cambridge and New York: Cambridge University Press, 1996), Part I.

Hessayon, Ariel, *'Gold tried in the fire': the prophet TheaurauJohn Tany and the English Revolution* (Aldershot and Burlington, VT: Ashgate, 2007).

——————————, 'The Making of Abiezer Coppe,' *JEH*, 62 (2011), 38–58.

——————————, 'Abiezer Coppe and the Ranters,' in Laura Lunger Knoppers, ed., *The Oxford Handbook of Literature and the English Revolution* (Oxford: Oxford University Press, 2012), 346–74.

Hill, Christopher, *The World Turned Upside Down: Radical Ideas during the English Revolution* (London: Temple Smith, 1972).

Holstun, James, 'Ranting at the New Historicism,' *English Literary Renaissance*, 19 (1989), 189–225.

Hughes, Ann, *Gangraena and the Struggle for the English Revolution* (Oxford: Oxford University Press, 2004).

Iannaccaro, Giuliana, *Ombre e Sostanza: La figura e la lettera nella scrittura radicale della Rivolutione inglese* (Milan: Unicopli, 2003).

Jaeckle, Daniel P., 'The Realised Eschatology and Sweet Style of Jacob Bauthumley,' *Journal of Religious History*, 35 (2011), 321–36.

Kenny, Robert, '"In These Last Days": The Strange Work of Abiezer Coppe,' *SCen*, 13 (1998), 156–84.

Laurence, Ann, 'Two Ranter Poems,' *RES*, n.s. 31 (1980), 56–59.

Loewenstein, David, *Representing Revolution in Milton and his Contemporaries: Religion, Politics, and Polemics in Radical Puritanism* (Cambridge and New York: Cambridge University Press, 2001), 93–115.

McDowell, Nicholas, *The English Radical Imagination: Culture, Religion, and Revolution, 1630–1660* (Oxford: Clarendon Press, 2003).

——————————————, 'Abiezer Coppe, Horace and the Dormouse,' *N & Q*, 53 (2006), 166–68.

McGregor, J.F., 'Seekers and Ranters,' in J.F. McGregor and Barry Reay, eds., *Radical Religion in the English Revolution* (Oxford and New York: Oxford University Press, 1984), 121–39.

Mack, Phyllis, *Visionary Women: Ecstatic Prophecy in Seventeenth-Century England* (Berkeley, CA: University of California Press, 1992).

Morton, A.L., *The World of the Ranters: Religious Radicalism in the English Revolution* (London: Lawrence & Wishart, 1970).

Nelson, Byron, 'The Ranters and the Limits of Language,' *Prose Studies*, 14 (1991), 60–75.

Poole, William, *Milton and the Idea of the Fall* (Cambridge: Cambridge University Press, 2005).

Reay, Barry, 'Laurence Clarkson: An Artisan and the English Revolution,' in C. Hill, B. Reay and W. Lamont, eds., *The World of the Muggletonians* (London: Temple Smith, 1983), 162–87.

Smith, Nigel, *Perfection Proclaimed: Language and Literature in English Radical Religion, 1640–1660* (Oxford: Clarendon Press, 1989).

——————————, '"Making fire": conflagration and religious controversy in seventeenth-century London,' in J.F. Merritt, ed., *Imagining Early Modern London: Perceptions and Portrayals of the City from Stow to Strype 1598–1720* (Cambridge University Press, 2001), 284–86.

Turner, James Grantham, *One Flesh: Paradisal Marriage and Sexual Relations in the Age of Milton* (Oxford: Clarendon Press, 1987), esp. 81–95.

Watkins, Owen C., *The Puritan Experience* (London: Routledge and Kegan Paul, 1972), ch. 9.

Abiezer Coppe

Preface to
John the Divine's
Divinity[1]

 His (*modicum bonum*) this little pretty piece, was put into my hands to read: but (for the present) I pocketed it: and lodg'd it there all night: but viewing it in the morning; I concived it was *conceived of the holy Ghost, and born of the Virgin.*[2] The same spirit moved me to transcribe it; and send it abroad to thy view.

I know (by wofull experience) that *the Truth as it is in Jesus* hath been *spet on, buffeted, railed on, incarcerated, intullianated, pen'd up, and imprisoned.* But *truth* being *strength* hath made *the gates of brasse, and bars of iron flie,* and is now at *liberty; and utters her voice in the streets;* which voice is rending the heavens, *shaking terribly the earth, melting the mountains like wax; and making the lame man leap like a Hart. And the hearts of those that know the Lord to dance for joy,*[3] &c.

Something hereof *sparkles* through these papers. And I only let thee know: that I *know* thers *some sweetnes*[4] in them; and that I durst not turn my back upon them, though (seriously) I know not whose they are, or who writ them, though I know the *Authour;*[5] or are rather known of him.

Stranger! use him, me, and these as thou pleasest; or as thou canst.

Maist thou be taught *not to blaspheme the way thou knowest not,* least thou *spit* out *spite* in the *face of the Heir.* Nor to *presse* sore upon the *man,* even *Lot, least two Angels smite thee with blindenesse.*

Lastly, *Be not forgetfull to entertain strangers, because some in so doing have entertained Angels unawares.*[6] Maist thou entertain them, then thou wilt. *Farewell.*

From London Jan.13.1648.
   two or three daies afore   *However, I am thine*
     the eternal God thun-
       dered at great
         S. Ellens.[7]   Abiezar Coppe

---

1   Dated 1649, signed 'I.' and attributed to John File by the well-informed book collector Samuel Jeake the Elder.
2   Taken exactly from the third sentence of the Apostles Creed, as it was printed in the service of Morning Prayer, and repeated in the service of Public and Private Baptism, 1559 *Book of Common Prayer,* ed. B. Cummings (Oxford, 2011), 110, 144, 149.
3   Biblical references in this sentence are Ps. 107.16; Ps. 2.9; Rev. 2.27, 19.5; Isa. 2.19, 21; Ps. 97.5; Isa. 35.6; Ps. 149, 150.4.
4   Ezek. 1.7, 3.3.
5   Coppe's pun on God; see 1 Cor. 14.33; Heb. 5.9, 12.2.
6   The last two sentences draw on 1 Tim. 1.20, Gen. 19.5 and Heb. 13.2.
7   St. Helen's Bishopgate.

SOME

Sweet Sips, of some

Spirituall *Wine*, sweetly and free-
ly dropping from one cluster of
Grapes, brought between two upon a
Staffe from *Spirituall Canaan* (the
Land of the *Living*; the
Living Lord.)

T O

Late *Egyptian*, and now *bewildered Israelites*.

A N D   T O

אביעזר כף[1]   *A late converted J E W.*

Who must (no longer) hunger, or hanker after the *Flesh-pots* of the
Land of *Egypt* (which is the house of *Bondage*) where they durst not minish
ought from their bricks of their *daily taske*) but look for, and hasten to
Spirituall *Canaan* (*the Living Lord*,) which is a land of large *Liberty*, the
house of *Happiness*, where, like the *Lords Lilly*, they toile not, but grow in
the *Land* flowing with such wine, milke, and honey.——

O R,

One of the *Songs* of *Sion*, sung immediatly, occasioned mediatly
by a Prophesie and Vision of one of the Lords *Handmaids*, and *Youngmen*,
M^{rs}. *T.P.*[2] and expressed by her in an Epistle to *A.C.* An extract whereof is
here inserted, with a Revelation, and Interpretation thereof, as from the *Lord*.

——They cut down—a branch with one cluster of grapes, and they beare it
between two upon a staffe, *Num.*13.23.

She that tarried at home devided the spoile, *Psal.*68.12.
The Lord is my strength and *Song*,—*Exod.*15.2.

London, Printed for *Giles Calvert*, at the signe of the
Black-Spread-Eagle, at the West-end of *Pauls*. 1649.

---

1   'Abiezer Cop' named in Hebrew letters.
2   Thomasine Pendarves (1618–c. 1671), influential Abingdon Baptist, and wife of the Particular
    Baptist minister John Pendarves, with whom she sometimes disagreed and embarrassed.

THE
CONTENTS.

The Titularity of the severall little parcels, wrapt up in this little Fardle.[3]

O R,

The severall Titles, of the severall ensuing Epistles here inserted, A S ,

I. *A* *Preambular, and cautionall hint to the Reader concerning the ensuing Epistles.*
    II. *An Epistolar preparatory to the ensuring Epistles of* אביעזר *a late converted* Jew.
    III. *An Apologeticall and additional Word to the Reader, Specially to the Schollars*
of Oxford, *concerning the precedent and subsequent Epistles.*

IV. *An extract of an Epistle sent to A.C. from* M[rs]. *T.P. (another late converted* Jew) *mediately occasioning the precedent Epistles, and the last letter.*

V. *An Epistle responsorie, to the late letter of* M[rs]. *T.P. wherein there is an opening of her Vision, and an interpretation of her Revelation, as from the Lord; together with an* indiciall[4] *hint of some particular passages infolded, and unfolded in the Letters following, and that as followeth, as the* Contents.——

1. *A call, to arise out of Flesh into Spirit, out of Form into Power, out of Type into Truth, out of Signes into the thing signified; and that call Sparkles throughout these Papers.*

2. *The danger of arising into the Notion of Spirituals afore the Lord awaken a soul, and saies, come up hither.*

3. *Christ in the* Spirit, *a stumbling stone, and rock of offence to those that know him (only) after the* Flesh.

4. *They that walk after the Spirit, and live according to God in the* Spirit, *cannot be offended at any thing, and in them there is none occasion of stumbling.*

5. *Few as yet know the Lords voyes from* Elies, *and they are trudging to the old man at every turne, till the Lord be revealed in them.*

6. *The Trumpet often gives an uncertaine sound—till the last seale be opened.*

7. *Some Saints are* within, *and at* home, *others* without, *and* abroad. *Who they are.*

8. *And how they are said to be at* home, *and how* abroad.

9. *They that are at* home, *are kept at a higher rate then those that are* abroad.

10. *The former feeding upon the daintiest of dainties.*

11. *The later wishing and woulding[5] for a belly full of huskes.*

12. *Wherein is feelingly, and experimentally exprest what huskes, and* bran *are. And,*

---

3   A bundle or collection.
4   'Indicative' (*OED* adj.); from Latin *indicium*, a discovery or disclosure.
5   The action or fact of desiring, commonly coupled, as here, with 'wishing.'

13. *What the finest wheate flower is.*

14. *The formall, externall, or outward, and the powerfull, glorious, and inward Death, and Resurrection of Christ, and how men walke in darkness, and know not at what they stumble, till they attaine to the latter.*

15. *The death of Christ at* Jerusalem, *and the Resurrection out of* Josephs *Tombe without us, is nothing to the dying of the* Lord *in us; and the Resurrection of the Day-star in our hearts.*

16. *The Sabboth, which some are entred into, What it is, and how* they *do no manner of* work, *but the Lord does all in them, plowes in them, sowes in them—prayes in them, sings in them, &c.*

17. *The dismall darkness, and sore slavery in the land of* Egypt, *&c.*

18. *What the Holy Land, the Land of* Canaan, *is.*

19. *Some of the great and glorious priviledges of the free-denizens of the land of* Canaan.

20. *What* Man *is, and how* Man *is the* Woman, *and the* Lord *the* Man.

21. *The River of water of Life, What.*

22. *The purity, and clarity thereof, all other Rivers muddy, men muddy, profound men muddy, &c.*

23. *All* Formes *are wilde, and why, and how.*

24. *All Elements shall melt away, what,—— and how.*

25. *Some men bravely, and sweetly besides themselves, and how.*

26. *One of the* true *Religion, is the* Kings, *and the* Queenes, *and the* Princely Progenies, *and the* Bishops, *and the* Priests, *and the* Presbyters, *the* Pastors, Teachers, *&c. and the* Independants, *and the* Anabaptists, *and the* Seekers, *and the* Family of Loves, *and how.*

27. *The* Day-springs *visit, and the* Day-stars *woing.*

28. *A Patheticall call, and a great pounding at the everlasting* doors, *to open to the* King of Glory.

29. *The great glory of those who have the glory of the King of glory risen upon, and in them.*

30. *The Kings Burglary, and the day of the* Lords *plunder; wherein there is declared, how he plunders——as a thiefe in the night——and of what——together with a Seraphicall Prayer of* אביעזר *upon Siginoth, &c.*

31. *How the Cœlestiall* Fire *of love burnes mens houses over their heads, and that out of huge love to them.*

32. *Doomes Day come already upon some* flesh, *and it is falling upon all* flesh—*and how (ere long) no* flesh *shall have* Peace.

33. *How Gods Heritage hath been a speckled, or party-coloured bird, and when it shall be of one colour, and the Saints of one complexion all of them.*

34. *Severall sweet spirituall Songs, and dainty Dances, &c.*

35. *Many Pastors have destroyed Gods vineyard, and how, and what shall become of them.*

36. *The husbandmens, and Vine-keepers hard usage of the Lords Servants, who come from a Strange Countrey; and their spite against the Heire.*

37. *Who this* Heire *is, who the sonne of the Free-woman, and who the sonne of the Bondwoman.*

38. *Every* Forme, *a persecutor, but the spirit free from persecuting any.*

39. *A loving, and Patheticall admonition to the* Husbandmen; *their dismall, and dolefull doome, and downefall foretold; with a word of consolation to them, and a prayer for them in the close.*

40. *A word from the Lord to* Men-Pastors.

41. *Who is Gods peoples true Pastor, Shepheard,* Teacher, &c.

42. *The knowing of men after the* Flesh, *and of Christ (himselfe) after the* Flesh, *out of date, and Christ in Spirit is comming in request, being the sword of the Lord Generall, is devouring from the one end of the Land to the other:——And the point thereof, set at the very heart of* Flesh, *to let out its very heart bloud, and every drop thereof.*

43. *A sweet, gentle, and loving check to poore* Mary, *seeking the* Living *among the* Dead.

With a prayer for, and Prophecie of an unexpected glory fallen upon some already, and flying swiftly to others.

44. *The pure, and powerfull, various, and glorious, the strange, and immediate teachings of* God *at hand, even at the doores, and come into the houses, and hearts of many already.*

45. *The evill, and danger of limiting the holy one of* Israel.

46. *The green, and glorious, sweet, and pleasant pastures,——those are lead, and fed in, that know no other* Pastor *but the Lord.*

47. *No small stirre raised by the Silver Smiths about this way, in that, thereby their craft is in danger to be set at nought.*

48. *Everlasting wisdome is transacting, and doing over those things in Spirit, power, and glory in his Saints, which were in a more literall, and externall way done for his people formerly.*

49. *Brave schollers, who.*

50. *A Caroll, and Anthem sung to the Organs.*

51. *The eternal God is preaching quick and keene, short and sweet Sermons; through bed and bourd, through fire and water, light and darknesse, heaven and earth, day and night.*

Through Carols, Organs, Anthems, any things, all things to some.

Yea, through Tanners, Tent-makers, leathern aprons, as well as through university men, long gownes, cloakes, or cassocks.

52. *They that have learned all that their Pedagogues can teach them, shall goe to schoole no longer, shall be under the lash no longer.*

53. *The strange things that befall them, who are set to the university [of the universall Assembly] and entred into Christ-Church; [the Church of the first borne, &c.] where they fall besides themselves, and* burne *their Bookes before all men.*

54. *Some spirituall touches upon the six Moodes, together with the* Lunatique *Moode.*

55. *The* Deane *of Christ-Church (the Metropolitan of all Christendome, and Arch-Bishop of* All-hallowes) *teaching his pupils the Accidence, a strange new way, new, new, new.*

56. *An admonition——to entertaine* Strangers *joyfully, because some in so doing have entertained Angels unawares.*

57. *The Message of two Angels.*

Sodom *must be burnt.*

Lot *must be saved.*

Flesh must be crucified and dye, And the eternall Spirit——dwell in the Saints everlastingly.

58. *Mans* Day *almost at an end.*

59. *The day of the Lord at hand.*

60. *Some Prophecies, being in part fulfilled, and the glory of them in part enjoyed, are here so farre—opened.*

And many spiritual discoveries (so farre as my hands have handled them) are here inserted.

Cum multis aliis, quae nunc perscribere longum est.[6]

---

6   'With many other matters, which it would now be tedious to write out in full.'

E pist. I.

A

Pre-ambular, and cau-
tionall Hint to the Rea-
der; concerning the ensuing
Epistles here inserted.

Deare Friends,

Eer's something (according to the wisdome given to us) written unto you, in all these ensuing Epistles. In which are some things hard to be understood, which they that are *Unlearned*, and unstable, wrest: as they doe also the other Scriptures, unto their own destruction.

But we brethren are perswaded better things of you &c.

Her's some *Gold* and silver.

But that is none of mine.

The drosse I owne.

The fire will fall upon it, and consume it; yet I my selfe am saved: yet so, as by *Fire*.

Here is Scripture language throughout these lines: yet Book, Chapter, and Verse seldome quoted.

The *Father* would have it so; And I partly know his design in it; And heare him secretly whispering in me the reason thereof. Which I must (yet) burie in silence, till——

Here is a reede shaken with the winde, and the voice of one crying in the wildernesse,

Prepare ye the way of the Lord, &c. The day of the Lord is at hand, is dawned to some.

Here is a great cry, and at mid-night too; Behold, *The Bridgroome* commeth.

Here is a great pounding at the doors,——But it is not I, but the voice of my *Beloved*, that knocketh, saying, Open to me, and let me come *In*.

Here is the voyce of one crying: Arise out of *Flesh*, into *Spirit*; out of *Form*, into *Power*; Out of *Type*, into *Truth*; out of the *Shadow*, into the *Substance*; out of the *Signe*, into the thing *Signified*, &c.

——Take this cautionall hint.

Arise, but rise not till the *Lord* awaken thee. I could wish he would doe it by himselfe, immediately: But if by these, mediately. His will be done. His is the Kingdome, the power, and the glorie; for ever and ever, Amen.

I would (by no meanes, neither indeed can I) pull you out of Bed by head and shoulders. ——May the cords of *Love* draw you out.

If through the heat of love, mixt with zeale, and weaknesse (in these) thou shouldst start out of thy bed naked, into the notion of these——I should be very sorry for thee, Fearing thou mightest be starved these cold winter nights.

If thou shouldest arise into the Letter of these Letters, before the Spirit of life enter into thee, Thou wouldst runne before the Lord, and out-runne thy selfe, and runne upon a rock, For it is set on purpose, as one,——And as a stumbling-stone to some,—even to those who know Christ after the Flesh (only). But happy they, who are in the *Inside* of them, Nothing can harme them. And in them there is no occasion of stumbling.

To the Lord I leave you all, (Deare hearts) and to the word of his grace, which is able to build you up.

The word of the Lord is precious in these dayes,——There is no open vision to many.

Few know the Lords voyce from *Elies*, as yet: we shall trudge (it may be) to the old man, once, twice, thrice: till the word of the Lord be revealed to us. And,

Then we shall heare, and say, *Speake Lord, for thy servant heareth*, reade 1 *Sam*. 3.1. to 15.

There are many voyces in the world. And some know the fathers voyce, in all voyces, and understand him in all tongues.

If the *Trumpet* here give an uncertaine sound, I cannot help it for the present. You will understand by that—the last seale is opened. If the Temple be filled with smoake, you shall not be able to enter into it, till the seven plagues of the seven Angels are fulfilled.

The vision is for an appointed season, but at the end it shall speake, and not lie: though it tarrie, waite for it, because it will surely come, it will not tarrie.

If the leaven be hid in three measures of meale, Queen Wisdome (the woman that hid it there) will make dough, and then you shall taste it in the whole lump.

If the graine of mustard seed here, be buried in the earth, wait for it: because it will surely spring up into a tree, and the fowles of the aire shall lodge in the branches thereof.

If I here speake in an unknown tongue, I pray that I may interpret when I may.

Only take one Clavall[7] hint.

That which is here (mostly) spoken, is inside, and mysterie. And so farre as any one hath the mysterie of God opened to him, *In Him*, can plainly reade every word of the same here.

The rest is sealed up from the rest, and it may be the most,——from some.

One touch more upon one string of this instrument. Some are at *Home*, and within; Some *Abroad*, and without. They that are at *Home*, are such as know their union *in* God, and live upon, and *in*, and not upon any thing below, or beside him.

Some are abroad, and without: that is, are at a distance from God, (in their own apprehensions) and are Strangers to a powerfull and glorious manifestation of their union with God. That their being one in God, and God one in them; that Christ and they are not twaine, but *one*, is to them a Riddle.

These are without, *Abroad*, not at *Home*, and they would fill their bellies with *Husks*, the out-sides of Graine.

That is, they cannot live without Shadows, Signs, Representations;

It is death to them, to heare of living upon a pure & naked God, and upon, and in him alone, without the use of externalls.——

---

7   As in 'key,' from Latin *clavis*.

But the former reape a thousand fold more *In* their living upon, and in the *Living Lord* alone, then when they saw him through a vaile.

For instance,

They live not (now) in the use of the externall Supper, or outward breaking of bread,

But upon the Lord (whom they have not now by hearesay) but clearly see, know, and powerfully feele *Him in them*;

Who is a continuall feast of *fat* things *in* them, their joy, and chear, being (now) a thousand fold more in the enjoyment of a naked God *in them*, and of Christ *in them*, uncloathed of *flesh* and *forme*, then it was when they saw and knew him otherwise, in and through Signes, Vails, Glasses, Formes, Shaddows, &c.

Thus you have one Claval hint; if the Lord come *in*, it may be an instrumentall key to open the rest. But the Spirit alone is the incorruptible Key. And so I must have done with this Point, and with the Epistle too. Only I must let you know, that I long to be utterly undone, and that the pride of my *fleshly* glory is stained: and that I, either am, or would be nothing, and see the Lord all, in all, in me. I am, or would be nothing. But by the grace of God

I am what I am,

and what I am

in I am,

that I am.

So I am

in the *Spirit*

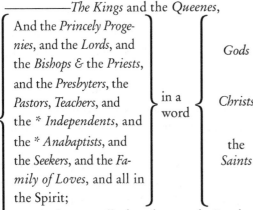

————*The Kings* and the *Queenes*,

And the *Princely Proge-*
nies, and the *Lords*, and
the *Bishops* & the *Priests*,
and the *Presbyters*, the
Pastors, Teachers, and
the * *Independents*, and
the * *Anabaptists*, and
the *Seekers*, and the *Fa-*
mily of Loves, and all in
the Spirit;

in a word

Gods

Christs

the
Saints

And yours; all of ye that are the Lords, by what names or titles soever distinguished, Yours—— אביעזר כף

* The *Key*. * *Christ* was Re-baptized.—The Lord is my *King*, and my Shepheard, or *Pastor, &c.* —The Eternall God, whose *I Am*, is *Independent*,——*&c.*

Epist. II.

An Epistolar—Preparatory to the en-
suing Epistles of— אביעזר *A (late*
Converted) J E W.

TO all the Kings party in *England*, and beyond sea; and to all that *Treate* with *the* King: and to all the Saints in *the upper* and *lower House*;⁸ and to all the *Strangers* (Protestants, Presbyterians, Brownists, Anabaptists, Sectaries, &c. so called by Babels builders, whose language is confounded) To all the Strangers scattered throughout *Pontus, Asia, &c.* And to all the Saints in *Rome, New-England, Amsterdam, London,* especially *Hook-Norton,* & thereabouts in *Oxfordshire,* and at *Esnill,*⁹ *Warwick, Coventry,* and thereabouts in *Warwick-shire.* And to all the Saints, (of all sizes, statures, ages, and complexions, kindreds, nations, languages, fellowships, and *Families,* in all the Earth.

Once intended only, and primely for that precious *Princesse* פ. ת.¹⁰ another late converted *Jew,* and for the Saints at *Abingdon.*

But it being told in darkness, it must (by commission) be spoke in light, and being heard in the *eare,* it must be published upon the house *tops;* to All——

And let him that hath an eare to heare, heare what the Spirit *saith.*

CHAP. I.

DEare hearts*!* Where are you, can you tell? Ho*!* where be you, ho? are you *within?* what, no body at *home?* Where are you? What are you? Are you asleepe? for shame rise, its break aday, the *day* breaks, the *Shaddows* flie away, the *dawning* of the *day* woes you to arise, and let him *into* your *hearts.*

It is the voyce of my beloved that knocketh, saying, Open to me my *Sister,* my *love,* my *dove,* for my head is filled with dew, and my locks with the drops of night. The *day spring* from an high would faine *visit* you, as well as old *Zachary.* Would faine visit you, who sit in *darkness,* and the *shadow* of *death,* as well as those who dwell in the *Hill countrey.*

The day *star* is up, rise up my *love,* my *dove,* my *faire one,* and *come away.* The day *star* woeth you, it is the voice of my beloved that saith open to me— I am *risen indeed,* rise up my love, open to me my faire one. I would faine *shine more* gloriously *in you,* then I did at a *distance* from you, *at Jerusalem without* you. I am risen *indeed;* I (*the day star*) would faine *arise* in your *hearts,* and shine *there.*

---

8 Coppe writes before the King was tried and executed, or the House of Lords abolished. The 'Saints' are the Puritans in both Houses of Parliament.
9 Easenhall, Warwickshire.
10 'T.P.' in Hebrew; see above, n. 2.

Then *arise, shine*, for thy light is come, and the glory of the Lord is risen upon thee, for behold, the darkness shall cover the earth, and gross darkness the *people*; but the Lord shall arise upon thee, and his glory shall be seene upon thee.

And the *Gentiles shall come* to thy *light*, and *Kings* to the brightness of thy *rising, arise, come up hither.*

Then, For brass I will bring gold, and for iron I will bring silver, and for wood brass, and for stones iron. I will also make thine *officers peace*, and thine *exactors righteousness*. Violence shall be no more heard in thy Land; wasting nor destruction within thy borders. The *Sun* shall be *no more* thy *light* by *day*, neither for *brightness* shall the *Moon* give *light* unto thee; but the *Lord* shall be unto thee an *everlasting light*, and thy *God* thy *glory*.—And the days of thy mourning shall be ended, *Isai.* 60.1,2,3,17, *&c.*

Then, Lift up your heads, O ye gates; and be ye lift up ye everlasting doors; and the *King* of *glory* shall come *in.*

Who is the *King of glory?* The *Lord* strong, and mighty, the Lord mighty.

Lift up your heads, O ye gates, even lift them up ye everlasting doors; and the *King of glory* shall come *in.*

Who is the *King of glory?* The *Lord of hosts*, he is the *King of glory. Selah.*[11]

O! Open ye doors, Hearts open; let the *King of glory* come *in*. Open dear hearts.

Dear hearts, I should be loath to be arraigned for Burglary—

The *King* himself (whose houses you all are) who can, and will, and well may break open his own houses; throw the doors off the hinges with his powerfull voyce, which rendeth the heavens, shatter these doors to shivers, and break in upon his people.

CHAP. II.

A Prayer of אביעזר *upon Siginoth.*[12]

OH day of the Lord*!* come upon them unawares, while they are *eating* and *drinking, marrying*, and giving in *marriage*, divorce them from all strange *flesh*; give a bill of divorce to all carnall, fleshly fellowships, betroath them to thy self, (O God,) and to one another in the *Spirit*, marry them to the Spirit, to thine own Son, to thine own Self, O our *Maker*, our *Husband.*

Let them be joyned to the Lord, that they may be *one Spirit*, [if there be any fellowship of the Spirit] sweet fellowship! sweet Spirit*!*

Divorce them from *Forme*, marry them to *power*. Divorce them from Type, marry them

---

11 Occurs frequently at the end of verses in the Psalter. It was supposed to be a musical or liturgical direction, perhaps indicating a pause or rest.

12 From Hab. 3.1, 'Shigionoth.' Coppe is imitating the prophet Habakkuk, and in Hebrew, the word means a kind of psalm. 'Seulah' (see previous note) occurs in Hab. 3.2.

to *Truth* [O the truth, as it is in *Jesus*!]

Fall upon them while they are *Eating* and *drinking without*, Let them eate and drink *within—Bread* in the *Kingdom*—And *drink* wine, *new*, in the *Kingdom*. Even *new*, in the Kingdom. New in the Kingdome, not in the *oldness* of the *Letter*, But in the *newness* of the Spirit.

Fall upon them while they are marrying, and giving in marriage.

Thy *Kingdom come*. Thy will be done on earth as it is in heaven.

For thine is the Kingdome, the power and the glory, for ever and ever, Amen.

O Kingdome come! O day of the Lord come, as a thiefe in the night, suddenly, and unexpectedly, and in the night too, that they may not help themselves.

O come! come Lord Jesus, come quickly, as a thiefe in the night.

Come Lord Jesus, come quickly, these long dark nights, come in the night.

Give the word to the *Moone*, that it may be turned into bloud, and be as black as an hairecloth.[13] Then fall upon them in the dark night, and plunder them of all flesh and *Forme*; that they may henceforth know thee no more after the *flesh*, or in the *forme* of a *Servant*, but in *power* and glory in *them*.

O consuming *Fire!* O God our joy! fall upon them in the night, and burne down *their* houses made with hands, that they may live in a house made *without hands*, for ever and ever, Amen.

The Prayer of אביעזר *is ended*

CHAP. III.

WEll, once more; Where be you, ho? Are you *within*? Where be you? What! sitting upon a *Forme*,[14] without doors, (in the Gentiles *Court*,) as if you had neither life nor soul in you? Rise up, rise up, my Love, my fair one, and *come away*; for lo, the Winter is past, the raine is over and gone, the flowers appear on the earth, the time of the singing of birds is come, and the voice of the Turtle is heard in our land, And [let him that hath an eare to heare, heare what the Spirit saith] the figtree putteth forth her green figges, and the vines with the tender grape give a good smell: *Arise* my love, my fair one, and *come away, Cant.* 2.10,11,12,13.

The day breaks, the *shadowes* flie *away*. *Rise* up, my Love, and come away.

Come with me from *Lebanon*, with me from *Lebanon*, from the top of *Amana*, look from the top of *Shenir*, and *Hermon*, from the Lyons dens, from the mountains of the Leopards. Come with me, *Rise*, let us be going.

Awake, awake, put on thy beautifull garments. Awake thou that sleepest, and arise from

---

13   Cloth made from hair; see Rev. 6.12: 'and the sun became black as sackcloth of hair, and the moon became as blood.'

14   Bench (*OED*, n. II 17).

the dead, and Christ shall give thee *light*.

Awake, awake, thou that sleepest in security, in the cradles of carnality.

Arise from the dead.

From the *Dead*.

From the *Forme* thou sittest on, it is a dead Forme.[15] From the *dead*. From *flesh*, flesh is crucified.

The Cryer crieth. And the voyce said, crie, All *flesh* is grass, and all the goodliness thereof is as the flower of the field; the grass withereth, the flower fadeth, because the *Spirit* of the Lord bloweth upon it. The grass withereth, the flower fadeth, and the glory of the Lord is revealed. *And* [let him that hath an eare to heare, heare what the Spirit saith.]

Thus saith the Lord, Mine heritage is unto me as a speckled, or party-coloured bird, * but it shall be of one colour, and my people of one complexion, all of them.

Jer.12.

They shall not walk after *the flesh*, but in the *Spirit*, where they shall be united; and as a *speckled bird* no longer.

They shall all come in the *unity* of *the faith*, and be party-coloured no longer.

CHAP. IV.

BUt many *Pastors* have destroyed my Vineyard, *Ier.12*. Thus my *Fathers* Vineyard goes to wrack, while it is let out to Husbandmen. But it is yet but a little while, and behold, the Lord of the Vineyard cometh, and will miserably destroy (& that very suddenly) the *Husbandmen*, who now (because Summer is neer, even at the doors) lay about them (especially some grounded men) very lustily, and fall foule upon some of the Lords Servants; (who come from a farr and strange countrey,) for they caught one, entreated him shamefully, sent him away empty, and shamefully handled him; at another they cast stones, and wounded him in the head: another they beate; (at lest) smote with the tongue, and devised evill devises against him, saying, report ye, and we will report it. And another they killed, and so they would all, if they could, and the *Heire* too.

And *Isaac* is the heire, (the son of *the freewoman*, not *Ismael* the son of the *bondwoman*, for he is cast out, and must be no *longer heire with* the son of the *freewoman*()): For *Abraham* had two sons, the one by a *bond maid* [who is persecutor of all that are not *flesh* of his *flesh*, and *forme* of his *forme*;] the other by a *freewoman*, *Jerusalem* which is above, which is free; and the son of the

---

15   Purely physical: without spirit.

freewoman is free indeed, and persecuted of all *flesh* and *forme*, [for * every *forme* is a persecutor] but the son of the *freewoman*, who is free, and very free too—is also free from persecuting any—so: and more then so, the son of the *freewoman* is a Libertine[17]—even he who is of the *freewoman*, who is borne after the Spirit. And [that which is borne of the Spirit, is Spirit,] thats the heire, which is hissed at and hated. And thats the Israel of God, the seed of the Lord, that Spirit, which the whole seede of the flesh, *Ismael* (in the lumpe) and forme (in the bulk) would quench and kill.

And which all those Vine-keepers at *Baall-Haman*, or those (mystically) fleshly husbandmen would slay. But the time is comming, yea now is, that the Lord of the Vineyard will miserably destroy (at least mystically, and that suddenly) these husbandmen.

Take heed then of medling with the *Heire*, Touch not the *Lords anointed*, do his Prophets no harme; Touch not the apple of his eye, His Saints, that are caught up, out of Self, Flesh, Forme, and Type, into the Lord, Spirit, Power and Truth. Into the Truth, as it is in Jesus. That are dis-joyned from carnall combinations, and fleshly fellowships, and are joyned to the Lord, that Spirit, and so are one Spirit: that are *one in* the Father, and *in* the Son; and have fellowship with the Father, and with the Son, and with all Saints; yea, with one another *in* the *Spirit*.

For they are standing before the God of the earth, & if any man wil hurt them, fire proceedeth out of their mouth, & devoureth their enemies; & if any man will hurt them, he must in this *maner* be *killed, Rev*.12. And those Husbandmen that conspire against them shall be miserably (at least mystically) destroyed, [when they heare it, they will say God forbid, *Luke* 20.] But the *Lord* of the Vineyard will say, my Vineyard, which is mine, is *before me, Cant*.8. I will become keeper of it my *Self*,—What will you do for a living then?—He will recover his Vineyard out of your hands, and what will you do in that day? [To *dig* I cannot, and to *beg* I am shamed] will be a hard story, a [*durus sermo*] a hard saying, who can beare it? I could wish this might not be fulfilled (if it might stand with the third Petition)—[*Thy will be done*] in the rigour of the Letter—[for the Letter kills] But in the Spirit, upon, and in you, and then you will be glad of it.

The second Petition—is mine for you, [*Thy kingdome come*] upon them, which will empty you of Self and Flesh, and staine the pride of all externall glory, and make you dance for joy, (before the Lord) with all your might, and sing the conclusion—[*Thine is the kingdome, the power and the glory, for ever and ever, Amen*.]

* Experientia docet;[16] and though one forme persecute another, yet they can joyn hand in hand to persecute the son of the freewoman, and *Herod* and *Pilat* can shake hands, and joyn together in this, to persecute Christ, and can mutually oppose the Spirit; this I have seen, I have looked upon with mine eyes, and my hands have handled.

---

16   'Experience teaches.'
17   Alluding to the original Roman meaning, 'emancipated slave,' but Coppe means someone who believes they are totally taken up by the Holy Spirit and have left all earthly forms behind.

I wish you hugely well, though you have denied the holy One, and the Just,—and desired a murderer to be granted unto you, and killed the *Prince* of *Life.*——

Yet brethren, I wot that through ignorance ye did it, as did also your *Rulers*. And therefore pray—that *Antichrist* in you (for he hath been, and is in us when we knew it not) may be dispossessed, & the strong man cast out, and all his goods spoiled, and the *Man of Sin*, *in* every one of you, may be destroyed, with the brightness of his coming. And that every mans works may be made manifest, and the *day* may declare it, because it shall be revealed by fire, and the fire shall trie every mans work of what sort it is. And that mans works may be burnt, and they suffer loss, but that they themselves may be saved, yet so, as by *fire*, Amen.

Well, to return to my last Theame—Many *Pastors* have destroyed my Vineyard,—*Pastors!* Thus saith the Lord, I will recover my Vineyard out of the hands of all *Husbandmen*, and be *Pastor* my Self, and my people shall know no Arch-Bishop, Bishop, &c. but my Self.

This you will believe and assent to (dear hearts, at first dash;) But they shall know no Pastor (neither) *Teacher, Elder*, or *Presbyter*, but the Lord, that Spirit. You shall see the later, as well as the former swallowed up in——

For, though we have known *men*, after the *flesh, Bishops, Priests, Pastors, Teachers, Elders*, after the *flesh*; yet henceforth know we *them*, know we *no man*, so, after the *flesh* any more: yea, though we have known *Christ* after the *flesh*, yet now henceforth, know we *Him*, so, no more. For the *Sword* of the *Lord Generall*[18]——the *Lord*, that *Spirit* shall *devoure* from the one end of the *Land*, even to the *other* end of the *Land*, And *no flesh* shall have *Peace, Jer.* 12.

CHAP. V.

WHerefore awake, awake, and shake off thy *filthy fleshly* garments; shake off Self; cast off thy carnall clouts, and put on thy beautifull garments. Awake, awake, and watch; Seeke yee *Seekers*, Seeke ye, *Seeke* ye the *Lord*, and *David* your *King*, your *King*; Seeke him in heaven, he is not in the bowells of the earth, seeke him above, he is not *below*. [*He is not here, he is risen—*] And if you be *risen with Christ*, seeke the things which are *above*, and not the things which are *below: He* is not here *below*.

[*He is not here.—*] *Behold* the place where the *Lord lay*; behold the place where *they laid Him*.

[*He is not here, but risen*] *He* is not *below*, in *forme*, in the *forme* of a *servant*; *He* is above in power:—*the Lord*, and *David* your *King.*——

Seeke yee——But, whom seek ye? What seeke ye? What?—crucified *flesh*, took down from a *Cross*, and intombed in the earth? What? the *body*, to anoint it with sweet spices, which you have bought, and brought with you to the grave, to that purpose?

What? Is it Love, Sincerity, and Zeale mixt with weakness that sent thee, (*poor Mary*,) to seeke him in the *Sepulcher?*

---

18   Another pun, diminishing Cromwell and Fairfax in the sight of God.

Why, (sweet *Mary*) why seekest thou the living among the dead? [*He is not here, but risen.*]

O that the love, sincerity, and zeale of true *Maries* indeed might be prevented with unexpected glory, and their weakness swallowed up in strength, death in victory; and their seeking the *living* among the *dead without*, may be prevented with the *power* of the *Resurrection within*, that they being *risen* with *Christ*, may seeke things *above*, may seeke *Spirit* and *Power*, and not *Flesh*, and *Forme*, which was here *below*, while he was here in *our flesh*, ⟨a⟩nd in the *forme* of a servant.

That they may seeke *Truth*. [The *truth* as it is in *Jesus*] That they may seek *Truth*, and not *Type*, which was here *below*, while he was here in the *Vaile*, which is his body. That they may awake, stand upon their legs and walke, and no longer seeke [The *living* among the *dead*.]

——Thine eyes shall see the *King* in his *Glory*, in his *Beauty*.

Yea, they shall behold the *Land* that is very far off——to some as yet, yet neere to others, *Amen, Halelujah.*

Epist. III.

AN

Apologeticall, and additio-
nall word to the Reader, especially to my Cronies,[19] the Schol-
ars of *Oxford*, Concerning the
precedent, and subsequent
Epistles.

Deare hearts!

GOD, who at Sundry times hath spoke to his people, in divers manners; hath spoken mostly, mediately, and muchly, by man formerly.

But now in these last dayes, he is speaking to his people more purely, gloriously, powerfully, and immediately; and that variously, and strangely. More purely, and immediately (I say) and if so (as it is, must, and shall be so) then more powerfully and gloriously. More purely and immediately; for thus saith the *Lord*, I will put my Law in their *Inward* parts, and write it *In* their *Hearts*, And they shall teach *No More* every man his Neighbour, and every man his *Brother*, saying, know the Lord: for they shall all know me, from the least of them to the greatest of them, *Jer*. 31.

Oh thou afflicted, tossed with tempest, &c. I will make thy windowes of Agates, and thy gates of Carbuncles, and all thy borders of pleasant stones. And all thy Children shall be taught of the *Lord*, and great shall be the peace of thy people, reade *Isa*. 54. 11. to the end the Chapter.

It is written in the Prophets; And they shall be all taught of God, *John* 6.45. And,

Ye have an unction from the *Holy One*, and you know all things. And,

The Anoynting which you have received of him, abideth *In You*, And ye need not that any *Man Teach* you; but as the same anoynting teacheth you of all things, and is truth, and is no lie; and even as it hath taught you ye shall abide *In Him*, 1 *John* 2.20.27.

——I neither received it of *Man*, neither was I *Taught* it, But by the *Revelation* of Jesus Christ.

Neither went I up to *Hierusalem*, to them which were Apostles before *me*,——*Gal*. 1. 12. 17. And the Lords hand is not weakned, neither is his arme shortned——

Neither is it good limiting the holy one of Israel; saying, Can God prepare a *Table* in the *Wildernesse?*——

Yea; he can, and will.

Oh God! my God, my *Pastor*, my *Shepheard* can, doth, and will.——

---

19   University slang for friends or associates. Used very specifically by Coppe, it predates the first recorded use in *OED* by 22 years.

And though I have knowne *Men* after the *Flesh, Pastors, Shepheards* after the *Flesh.* Yet *Now, Henceforth* know I them so no more. I now know, that *The Lord* is my *Pastor,* I shall not want; *He* maketh me to lie downe in *Green Pastures.* He *Leadeth* me beside the *Still Waters, He Restoreth* my soule, he leadeth me in the pathes of Righteousnesse, for his names sake: yea, though I walke through the valley of the *Shadow* of *Death,* I will feare no evill: for *Thou* art *with Me,* &c.

Thou *Anoyntest My* head with *Oyle,* my *Cup* runneth over.

Thou preparest *A Table* before me, in the presence of mine enemies, in despite of my foes; And that in the *Wildernesse* too. *He* hath prepared a *Table* in the wildernesse.

This hath been fulfilled in a more literall, externall way, formerly; Is *Now* fulfilling in a spirituall, glorious, and *Inward* way.

He prepares a *Table,* and disheth out dainties to us *Himselfe.* Teaches us *Himselfe, Leads* us *Himselfe.* Feedeth, and foldeth us with *Himselfe,* and *In Himselfe.* And we lye downe in *Green Pastures.*

Oh Lord, our *Bishop, Pastor,* Shepherd!

Surely *Now,* goodnesse and mercy shall follow me all the days of my life; And I will dwell in the *House* of the Lord for ever, and ever, Amen. Amen say I. Amen, Amen, saith the *Lord.*——

——[*Sic volo, sic jubeo, stat pro ratione voluntas.*[20]] even so, *Father,* for so it seemeth good in thy *Sight*; But not in the *Sight* of *Silver Smiths,* Who raise no small stirre about *This Way.* In that, *Hereby,* their *Craft* is in danger to be set at *Nought*; And their great Goddesse *Diana* to be despised, Reade *Acts* 19.23. to the end.

But these things must needs be, but the end shall not be yet.

Yet live according to God *In the Spirit.* The end of all things is at hand, 1 *Pet.* 4. 6,7. For the Lord is teaching his people more gloriously, powerfully, purely, immediately then formerly, and more strangely too.

For everlasting wisdome is doing over those things in Spirit, power, and glory (more invisible to an externall eye) *In Us*: which were in a more literall, externall, and visible way done to, and for his people formerly.

He protected, guided, lead, and lighted his people by a pillar of fire, and cloud formerly. But this glorie and guidance, this light and lustre was a strange one.

It was not Sunne and Moone which *Ægyptians* were acquainted with, and the light they walked by; yea, that mostly, if not altogether that, which Israel was acquainted with, while —— in the Land of *Ægypt*——*The House of Bondage.* But when they were prevented with this unexpected glory (I believe) they were glad of it, and entertained this *Stranger*—joyfully, even this *Stranger, This New Light,* this *Strange* Light; which was trouble and tribulation; Death, and darknesse to the Hoast of the *Ægyptians.*

This thing is *Now* transacted upon, and *In* the true Israel, *Spiritual* Israel, *Israel* in *Spirit*: Is done over againe (I say) and transacted upon them in *Spirit,* Power and glory [*Within* them:] And they that are prevented with such unexpected glorie, dare not be forgetfull of entertaining *Strangers*: because in so doing, they have entertained *Angels* unawares.

---

20   'Thus I wish, thus I command, let my will stand for a reason.' Juvenal, *Satires,* VI.223 reads 'Hoc volo, sic jubeo, sit pro ratione voluntas.'

CHAP. II.

[*Being a Christmas Caroll, or an Anthem,*
sung to the Organs in Christ-Church
at the famous University of——
the melody whereof was made
in the heart, and heard in a
corner of אביעזר *a late*
converted J E W.]

ANd it is neither Paradox, Hetrodox, Riddle, or ridiculous to good Schollars, who know the *Lord in deed*, (though perhaps they know never a letter in the Book) to affirm that God can speak, & gloriously preach to some through Carols, Anthems, Organs; yea, all things else, &c. Through Fishers, Publicans, Tanners, Tent-makers, Leathern-aprons, as well as through University men,—Long-gowns, Cloakes, or Cassocks; O *Strange!*

But what will this babling *Battologist*[21] say? Why *Paul*, the *Athenians* Babler said in this *wise*, the eternall Power and Godhead may be clearly seene by the things that are made; and the eternall God may be seene, felt, heard, and understood in the Book of the *Creatures*, as in the Book of the *Scriptures*, [*alias Bible.*]

Mine eare hast thou opened *indeed*,——may some say; who heare the *Sword*, and him that sent it, even the *Sword* of the *Spirit*, which is quick and powerfull, &c. Who can (I say) heare the *Sword* of the *Spirit* preach plaine and powerfull, quick and keene, sharp, short, and sweete Sermons, through clouds and fire, fire and water, heaven and earth, through light and darkness, day and night.

That can heare [*Verbum Dei, in verbis diei, noctisque sermone*——] the *Word* in the dayes, and nights report. For if we were not pittifull poor Schollers, dunces, dullards, and dull of hearing, we might heare the Lord preach precious pieces to us through the heavens and firmament day and night. For the heavens [מספרים[22] are telling] declare the glory of God, and the firmament sheweth his handy worke. Day unto day uttereth speech, and night unto night sheweth knowledge. There is no speech, nor Language, where their voyce is not heard; Their line is gone out thorow all the earth, and their words to the end of the world.——

To the chief Musician, for the Organist of *Christ-Church*.

Brave Schollers,——they that can heare the eternall God silently and secretly whispering secrets, and sweets into their souls, through bed and board, through food and raiment; that can meet him at every turn, and heare him in all things, that can meet him in this Paper, that can meet him here, and rejoyce in him; that can reade their Lesson in this primer; that can reade him within Book: but better schollers they, that have their lessons without book, and can reade God (not by roate) but plainly and perfectly, on the backside, and outside of the book, as well as in the inside: that can take this Primer in their h⟨a⟩nds; and hold it heeles

---

21　One who needlessly repeats the same thing.
22　Coppe cites the Hebrew from Ps. 19.1, 'The heavens declare the glory of God; and the firmament sheweth his handywork.'

upward, and then reade him there: that can spell every word backwards, and then tell what it is: that can reade him from the left hand to the right, as if they were reading *English*, or from the right to the left, as if they were reading *Hebrew*: that can reade God as plainly in the *Octavo* of a late converted *J E W*, as in a Church Bible in *Folio*: that can reade him within book, and without book, and as well without book, as within book: that can reade him downwards and upwards, upwards and downwards, from left to right, from right to left: that can reade him in the Sun, and in the Clouds, and as well in the Clouds, as in the Sun.

Well, hie you, learne apace, when you have learned all that your *Pedagogues* can teach you, you shall go to Schole no longer, you shall be [*Sub ferula*] no longer, under the *lash* no longer, but be set to the *University* [of the universall Assembly] and entred into *Christs* Church, [the Church of the first born, which are written in heaven,] and when you once come to know that you are *there*, you will heare no Mechanick Preach; (no, not a *Peter*, if he be a Fisher-man) but the learned Apostle, who speaks with tongues more then *they—all*,—and then you will fall upon your books (as if ye were *besides* your *selves*) and bring your books together, and burne them before all men; so mightily will [ὁ λογὸς—] *the word* grow in you, and prevaile upon you, that men shall say you are not only in a Lunatick ——————————————— (1) but quite *besides* your selves; you burne your Books, that is the ——————————— *Indicative* (2)   *Moode.*
and when you are accounted fooles and mad men, and are besides your selves [in good earnest] and your father and mother are troubled at you, grieve for you, and at length forsake you, then the Lord will take you up into himself, and say, Live in me, dwell in me, walk with me;   *Moode.*
there is the ———————————————————— *Imparative*,
and you will sing an *Hebrew* Song, one of the Songs of *Sion*; the Lords Song, when you are lifted up, out of a strange *Land*—[your *selves*] when you are non-entities, walk with God and are not, because the Lord hath took you, then (I say) you will sing one of the songs of *Sion*, an *Hebrew* Song, and say [אבי אתה אלי[23]] thou art my Father, my God, *Psal.* 89.26. Let my Father, my God dwell with me for ever and ever, Amen. Let him there dwell, that is still the ——— *Imparative*.
And it must be so, For you are no more *twaine* but *one*, He is in the *Imparative Moode*, and so are you; For thus saith the Lord, Ask me of things to come concerning my sons, and— *command* ye Me.

And, [*Utinam, si, ô, ô si, utinam.*[24]] I would to God the people of God [*now*] knew their interest *in* God, and *union in Him*, that they knew they were *one*, in the Father, and in the Son, there is the ————— *Optative*[25] (4)   *Moode.*
Some may, can, might, should, would know it: (if they could,) theres the ————————————————— *Potentiall* (5)

---

23   'O Lord thou art my strength.' Ps. 89.26 reads 'He shall cry unto me, Thou art my father, my body, and the rock of my salvation.'

24   *Utinam* ('would that') is the Latin particle of wishing, often replaced in poetry or archaic prose with *o* or *o si*.

25   Expressing wish or desire.

When the Father pleaseth, there is the ————————— *Subjunct.*(6) ⎤ *Moode.*
And by this time I am so far besides my self, as to add an *Interjection*
unto an *Adverb* in the *Optative* line [*now*] ha, ha he,—Thy will be done
on earth as it is in heaven, where we shall live, to sing *Halelujah* to
him, that is the ——————————————————— *Infinitive* (7) ⎦
O *infinite Love!* that Family he is of——who is——Sweet Schollers,

      Your Moody Servant,——— אביעזר

    From *Christ-Church* Colledge——where the *Deane*, his Tutor (who will be, [I meane, will
be known to be] Primate and Metropolitane of all Christendome, and *Archbishop* of *All-
hallows*, and that by *All-hallow-tide*; and it is now *Christ-tide*, for this very day was he borne
of a *Virgin*) is teaching him his *Accidence*,[26] a new way, new new, new; [*Et hoc accidit dum vile
fuit:*——[27]] But no more of this till I come to [*Doctrina magistri*] the learning of the *Master*,
who is teaching me all the parts of Speech, and all the Cases of Nounes, and all the Moodes
and Tenses of Verbs. And there be five Tenses or Times: there is a Time to be merry [*To be
merry in the Lord*] and that is the Present Tense with some, to others the Future.

    There is a Tense or Time to Write, and a Time to give over. It is almost time for me to
knock off here for the present; because I heare *Interjections* of Silence (as *an*, and such others)
sounding in mine eares. Only I must tell my Cronies at *Oxford*, that such schollers who can
speake with tongues more then they all—(and can understand, and interpret all Languages)
know this to be sound and *Orthodox Divinity*.

    But it is not expedient for me doubtless to glory. I will come to Visions and Revelations of
the Lord; and these are looked upon as new Lights too, and *Strangers*.

    But one more, be not forgetfull of entertaining Strangers, for some in so doing have
entertained Angels unawares. Here are two sent to thee, use them as thou pleasest, or as thou
canst: all that they speake, is to this purpose, *Sodome* must be burnt, *Lot* must be saved, *flesh*
must die & be crucified, and the *Spirit* live and dwell in the Saints. Mans day is almost at an
end; and the day of the Lord is at hand; and the day of the Lord shall be upon all mountaines
that are high and lifted up—upon all mountaines, upon mountaines *within* [for there are
mountaines *in us*; upon all mountaines *without*,—on all mountaines, and upon all the oakes of
Basan——upon all the Ships of *Tarshish*, and upon all pleasant *Pictures*,——] and the haughtiness
of man shall be humbled, and the loftiness of men laid low, and the *Lord alone* shall be exalted
in that *day*.

    And they speake out thus much in the words following.
From the Land of *Canaan*,
    the land of *Liberty*——
December 25th. 1648.

                                       Valete.

                                                                   אב

---

26   a) branch of grammar concerned with inflection of words (*OED* n. 2 1) b) fundamentals of a
      subject (*OED* n. 2 2).
27   'And this happened, while it was of little worth.'

E pist . I V.

A N

Extract of an Epistle sent to
A. C. from Mrs. T. P.[28] (another late Converted *Jew*,) mediately oc-casioning the precedent Epistles of the last Letter.

Deare Brother,

M Y true love in the Spirit of one-nesse, presented to your selfe,——with all that call on the name of the Lord; both yours and ours. It hath pleased *The Father* of late, so sweetly to manifest his love to my soule, that I cannot but returne it to you, who are the Image of my *Father*.

I should rejoyce, if the Father pleased also, to see you, and to have some spirituall communion with you, that I might impart those soul-ravishing consolations, which have flowne from the bosome of the Father, to our mutuall comfort. What though we are weaker vessels, women, &c. yet strength shall abound, and we shall mount up with wings as Eagles; we shall walke, and not be weary, run, and not faint, When the *Man-Child Jesus* is brought forth *In Us*. Oh what a tedious, faint way have we been lead about to finde out our rest, and yet when all was done, we were twice more the sonnes of slavery then——But blessed be our God, who hath brought us by a way that we know not, and we are quickly arrived at our *Rest*.

For my part—I have been at the *Holy Land*, and have tasted of the good fruit; not only seen that fruit which the Spies brought, but surely I have tasted, And therefore can say, that *now* I believe, not for any ones word, but because I have seen, and tasted——I have one thing to acquaint you with in especiall: And that is,

That of late the Father teacheth me by visions of the night——It will be too large to communicate by letter, yet because to one is given a revelation; to another an interpretation. I cannot but repeate one, which was thus——I was in a place, where I saw all kinde of Beasts of the field; wilde, and tame together, and all kinde of creeping wormes, and all kinde of Fishes——in a pleasant river, where the water was exceeding cleere,——not very deep——but very pure——and no mud, or setling at the bottome, as ordinarily is in ponds or rivers. And all these beasts, wormes and Fishes, living, and recreateing themselves together, and my selfe with them; yea, we had so free a correspondence together, as I oft-times would take the wildest of them, and put them in my bosome, especially such (which afore) I had exceedingly feared, such that I would not have toucht, or come nigh: as the Snake, and Toade, &c.—And the wildest kinde, and strangest appearances as ever I saw in my life. At last I tooke one of the wildest, as a Tiger, or such like, and brought it in my bosome away, from all the rest, and

---

28   See above, n. 2.

put a Collar about him for mine owne, and when I had thus done, it grew wilde againe, and strove to get from me, And I had great trouble about it. As first; because I had it so neare me, and yet it should strive to get from me, but notwithstanding all my care it ran away. If you can tell the interpretation of it, it might be of great use to the whole body.

Now I must also acquaint you, that I am not altogether without teachings in it. For when I awoke, the vision still remained with me. And I looked up to the Father to know what it should be. And it was shewen me, that my having so free a commerce with all sorts of appearances, was my spirituall libertie,—and certainly, did I know it, it would be a very glorious libertie, and yet a perfect Law too.——There is another Scripture which hath much followed me. And that is, God beheld all things that he made, and loe, they were very good. Now concerning my taking one of them from all the rest (as distinct,) and setting a collar about it——this was my weaknesse, and here comes in all our bondage, and death, by appropriating of things to our selves, and for our selves; for could I have been contented to have enjoyed this little, this one thing in the libertie of the Spirit——I had never been brought to that tedious care in keeping, nor that exceeding griefe in loosing,——waite therefore upon God for a further understanding in this thing, And when you have it, I make no question but I shall partake of it.——

I know you have the *Anoynting*, which sheweth you all things, to which anoynting I now commit you, and rest.

Yours in the Lord, who is that Spirit.

HEre (next) followes an *Epistle* Reponsory, to the late precedent Letter of M^rs. *T. P.* lately sent to *A. C.*

Wherein, there is an interpretation of her Revelation (exprest in the Epistle immediately foregoing;) and an opening of her vision, As from the Lord, and that, as followeth.

Epist. V.

Deare Sister, in the best fel-
lowship, mine intire love, &c.
presupposed——

I Have received your Letter, and the *Fathers* voyce in it, but it came not into our Coast till
the 12. of *November*, which was the Fathers time, since which time, I have scarce been
one whole day at home, but abroad, at my *Meate* and *Drinke.*——so (that if I durst, yet)
I could not so much as plunder an opportunitie,—but now it is freely given me to write.——

I know you are a *Vessel* of the *Lords House*, filled with heavenly liquor, and I see your
love,——The *Fathers* love, in the sweet returnes of your (I meane) his sweets to me. I love
the vessell well, but the *Wine* better, even that Wine, which we are drinking *New*, in the
Kingdome.——

And it is the voyce of my *Beloved*, that saith, drinke oh friends*!* yea, drinke abundantly oh
Beloved*!*

Deare friend, why doest in thy letter say, [what though we be weaker Vessels, women? &c.]
I know that Male and Female are all one in *Christ*, and they are all one to me. I had as live
heare a daughter, as a sonne prophesie. And I know, that women, who *Stay* at *Home*, divide
the spoyle——whilst our younger brethren, who are (as we were) abroad, and not yet arrived
at our *Fathers House*, or are at *Home*, are spending *Their Substance*[29] in riotous liveing, and
would faine fill their bellies with *Huskes*; the outside of the graine. But ere long, no man shall
Give Them unto them, then shall they be hastened *Home*, to the *Inside*, heart, *Graine*. To the
finest wheate-flower, and the pure bloud of the grape; To the fatted calfe, ring, shoes, mirth,
and Musicke, &c. which is the *Lords Supper indeed*.

I am your eccho, in that which followeth in your Letter. (*viz.*) that strength doth abound,
and we walke, and are not weary, &c. when the *Man-childe Jesus* is brought forth *in Us*. Till
then, we walke in darknesse, and know not at what we stumble, while the *True Light* is at a
Distance from us, or we see him not *In Us*, the hope of glory.

For though *The Light* shineth, and shineth alwayes, yet the darknesse comprehendeth it
not, deep darknesse is upon the face of the *Deep*, till the *Spirit* of God move upon it.

And though the *Day-Starre* be up, and up alwayes; yet we are in darknesse, till the *Day-
Spring* from on high visiteth us.

And when *The day* dawneth in *Us*, and the *Day-Starre* ariseth *In* our *Hearts*; then we see
that transacted in us, which formerly was done, in, and upon him; we see him, not only dying
at Jerusalem, but beare about *With Us* daily, *The Dying* of *the Lord in Us*, We see, not only his
death *Without Us*, but clearly see also his *Death in Us*.

I protest, by your rejoyceing which I have in Christ Jesus our Lord. I dye daily, yet not I,
but *Christ*——in *Me*, dying daily to all things below the living God.

---

29 'Estate, means of subsistance' (*OED*, n. III 12a).

I heare a voyce from heaven, saying to me, *write*; *Blessed* are the dead, which thus *die in the Lord, &c.* Thrice happy they, who die to *Formes*, and live in *Power*, who die to *Types*, & live in *Truth.* (O the *Truth*, as it is *in Jesus!*) that die to *huskes*, the *outside*, and live upon, and in the graine, the *inside*; who die to the *bran*, and live upon, and *in the fine wheat flower*, the *true bread*, not formall, but spirituall—which came down from heaven, *the living Lord*, the strength, stay, and staffe of my life.

Princes live, and the *Kings daughter* lives at a higher rate then he who was higher then all the Prophets: yea, more then a Prophet: his meat was *locusts* and *wilde honey.* Theirs, the *fat* of *kidnies*, and *honey* out of the *Rock*, Life *honey*: this is their life; Thou art their life, O *living God!*

How sweet art thou, O *Word*, O *God*, to my taste! yea, sweeter then the *honey*, and the *honey combe*, my *God, sweet God!* Awake Lute, awake Harpe, awake *Deborah*, awake, it is a song, a song; a song of *loves*; one of the *Songs of Sion*, the *Lords song*, I am not in a *strange land* now, though in a strange posture, almost *besides myself—in* the *Lord*—Do I now *walk with God*, and *am not?* hath *God took me?* O it is good to be *here*. Shall we build here a Tabernacle? not *three*—but *one*—one for *thee*, for *thee*, for *thee*, O *God*, my God, my *song!*

One day *here* is better then a thousand *there*, *here within*, then a thousand *without*, in the *fine wheat flower*; then a thousand in the *huske* and *bran*, here in the *inward* Court, then a thousand in the *outward*,—the *Gentiles Court: Here* in the *Power*, then a thousand in the *Forme: Here* in the *Spirit*, then a thousand in *Flesh: Here* in the *Spirit*, O *Spirit!* O Spirit of burning! O *consuming fire!* O God our joy!

Thou hast burnt up the bullock, his *flesh*, his *hide*, his dung without the *Campe*; the *fat* upon the *inwards*, the caule above the liver, and the two *kidnies* and their *fat* is thine and ours; and thine againe, *Halelujah.*

Deare friend, he laieth his *right hand* upon me, saying, I am he that was *dead*, and behold I am *alive* for ever more, Amen.

Thou art *alive* for evermore, O *living God!* This thing is true, and it is true in *Him, and in you*, the *Lord is risen*,—the third day he rose again—out of *Josephs* Tombe,—so much *Papists* say, and see, and boast of ther Creede. This is but the outward Court,—and it is given to the *Gentiles—The Lord is risen indeed*: I see him, not only risen out of *Josephs* Tombe, *without me*, but *risen* out of the bowells of the *earth within me*, and is *alive in me, formed in me*, grows in me: The *Babe springs in my inmost wombe*, leapes for joy *there*, and then I sing, and never but then, O *Lord my song!* to *me a childe is borne, a son is given*, who *lives in me*, O *Immanuel!* O *living Lord!* This *is life eternall*,—its true, both in *him*, and in *you*, because the *darkness is past*, and the *true light* now shineth: thus hath he brought us into a *way* that we *knew not*, and we are arrived at *our rest.*——*The Sabboth of* the *Lord thy God*, in which *thou* shalt not do *any work, thou*, nor thy son, *&c.* thy *manservant*, *&c.* thy *cattle, &c.* Not *thou*,—but the *Lord—in thee*: nor *thy* cattle, *&c.* But the *Lord*—ploweth *in thee*, sowes *in thee*, reapes *in thee, &c.* with *his winde (in thee)* bloweth away the *chaffe* in thee, *&c.* [for *my Father* is the *Husbandman*] grindeth in thee, makes meale of thee, *Searcheth* thee, till thou art the finest wheate flower, doth *all—in thee*, till thou art *all in Him*, [—I *in them*, and they *in me*,—that *they* may be *one* *in us,*—and I *in them.*] And then are we in the *holy Land* (which you mention) *the Land* of the *living*, the *holy Lord*, the *living Lord*. This *land* is far distant from the *land* of *Egypt*, which is the *house of Bondage*.

This, the land of slavery, and sore servitude, *That a large land*, a land of large, (not carnall or licentious; but of pure and *spirituall*) *Liberty*, when we are there, then are we *free indeed.* For the *land* whither thou art gone in to possess it, is not as the *land* of *Egypt*, from whence thou camest out; where *thou* sowest *thy* seed, and waterest it with *thy* foot, &c. but the *land* whither thou art gone in to possess it, is a *land* of hills and valleys, and drinketh water of the *raine* of *heaven;* a *land* which the Lord thy God careth for, the eyes of the Lord thy God are always upon it, from the beginning of the yeare, to the ending of the yeare, *Deut.* 11.10,11.

While we were in the land of *Egypt*, we did toile, moyle, work, and sweat, and groane, &c. while we durst not minish ought from our bricks of our *daily taske.*— But *here*, like the *Lords Lilly*, thou *toilest* not—but growest in the *land*, the *Lord. Here, thou* labourest not, art entred into *thy rest*, ceasest from *thy* labour, as the *Lord* did from his.

Here thou hast *Wells*, which *thou* diggedst not, *houses* which *thou* buildedst not, Vineyards, and Olive yards which *thou* plantedst not, Corne that thou sowedst not, &c. *All is given, freely given* thee. *Here* thou has wine, and milke, and honey without mony, without *price. Here* thou *standest still*, and seest the salvation of God upon thee, *in thee. Here* thou diggest not for a *song*, the Lord (*in thee*) puts a *new song* in thy mouth, O *Lord my song! Here* thou diggest not for gold, nor searchest for fine gold, the Lord is *thy gold in thee*, and thy God thy confidence. *Here* thy garment waxeth not old, for thou art invested with the *best Robe* which shall never be moath-eaten, with the best Robe, O Lord our righteousness! *Here* the morning weede is torne off, and all thy *sackcloath*——[for can the children of the *Bride-Chamber* fast?] *Here* thou art clad with the garments of *Praise*, for the spirit of heavinesse; here is given to thee beauty for ashes, the oyle of joy for mourning: *Here* all *Teares* are *wiped away* from thine eyes; thou shalt not see evill any more. For thou art in *the Holy Land*, the *Holy Lord*, and the Lord thy *God* in the *midst* of *Thee*, who rejoyceth over thee with joy, and *joyeth in*, and over thee with *Singing.* Sing oh Daughter, the *Lord* Sings *In Thee.* Shout oh Daughter, the *Shout* of a *King* is in *Thee.* Take a Timbrell, oh Mirian! the Lord *Danceth in Thee.* Oh *God* My joy! Be merry with all the Heart.

Drink off thy *Cup*, the *Cup* of *Salvation*, its the *Kings Health*, (thy Saving   *Privil.*[28] health, oh God) my God! Drink oh friends; yea drink abundantly oh beloved! it is lively wine, liquor of life, it will make the lame man leap like a Hart, causing the lips of those that are asleep to speak; for it is the *New Wine* in the *Kingdom*—good wine, the best wine, of the *best Vine*. Not of the Vine of *Sodom*, and of the fields of *Gomorrah*, whose grapes are grapes of gall, whose clusters are bitter, whose wine is

---

30   *Privilegiis* — by privilege.

the poyson of Dragons, and the cruell venome of Aspes. But of the *True Vine*, the *Vine indeed* of the sweet grapes; *Sweet God!* grapes indeed, of great worth, and weight——One *cluster borne between two upon a staffe, Numb.* 13. 23. Grapes of life, of *Bloud* of heart bloud, *Drinke indeed*, The *Pure bloud* of the Grape,——Thy Bloud, and Heart, and *Life, Pure God! Oh God! My God.*

Oh Lord, our Lord, how excellent is thy Name——Lord! What is man that thou art thus mindfull of him?

What is man?

Man is the *Woman*, and *thou* art the *Man*, the *Saints* are thy *Spouse*, our *Maker* is our *Husband*; *We* are no more *twaine*, but *One. Halelujah.*

For we are in that pure *River* of water of life, cleere as Christall, and that *River in us*, (which *River* you saw,) which is the *Fountaine* of life, the *Living God, the River*, the streames whereof make glad the City of God.

We are (I say) in that *River*, and that *River in us*, when we are *besides* our selves, undone, nothing, and *Christ* all, in *all, in us.*

The *River* is as cleare as Chrystall, nothing but Christ, all Christ, Chrystall—it is as clear as Chrystall, *Christ-all.* Halelujah.

And all those beasts of all sorts, wilde and tame, Wormes, and all kinde of fishes (which you saw) proceeded out of the *river*, the *Living God*, the *Fountaine* of *Life*. For by him were all things created, that are in heaven, and that are in earth, visible, and invisible, &c. All things were created by *Him*, and for *Him*, and he is before all things, and in *Him* (*the river*) *all things* consist.

The enmity within, and without shall be slaine,——Then shall all channels runne into the Ocean, live in the *river*, returne to the *Fountaine*, from whence they came: *recreating* themselves together there: Reade *Rom.* 8. 19. to 24. The riddle, that riddle is read to me— Then shall the *shaddow* of *Separation* wholy flye away,——those that have been *wilde* and are *tame*, shall play together. The Wolfe shall play with the Lamb, the Lion shall eate straw like an Oxe, &c. A sucking *Childe* shall leade them, &c.

First, Wolves and Lyons——*within*, Then Wolves and Lions *without.*——

The Enmity, the *Serpent*, in all, which is exceeding bad, shall be slaine.

But all that *He* made, which is *exceeding good*, shall returne to the [*summum bonum*] the *chiefest good* to the *River*, shall live there, recreate themselves together there, &c.——But those things are, and shall be first transacted *in us*, are in part, [but the end is not yet.——]

The *Wormes in us* shall give over gnawing, the Tygers, Dragons, Lions *in us* [for my soule hath long dwelt among *Lions*] shall give over roaring, ramping, ravening, devouring, shall *play* with the *Lamb*; Doe they not? A *sucking Childe* shall leade them; Doth he not? They shall not *hurt*, Doe they? *Serpents* stings shall be pulled out, are they not? We shall *beare* them in our *Bosomes*; Doe we not? And they shall not sting us; Doe they?——*Lions in us*,——but they are as *tame*, as if they were dead; Dead they are, and a honey-combe in their carkasse.

The Prophecie is in part fulfilled, in part your vision is opened, not by me, but by him in *me* [who openeth, and no man shutteth,——] And *Sampsons Riddle* is read——

[——Out of the mouth of the Eater came sweet.——] What? a *Honey-combe* out of the carkasse of a wilde, dead, tamed *Lion*; Oh sweet!——*sweet God!*—

We exceedingly feared *them*——Bugbeares frighted us, when we were children, but now we doe not,—now they——cannot. *Halelujah.*

It seemes you can carry them in your bosome, and you saved harmelesse, I am glad of it.

But perhaps I now speak with a stammering tongue, that may be confest; And I expect prejudiciall hearts, eares, and eyes from some; But rejoyce exceedingly that I know *the Fathers voyce*, though I cannot yet speak plaine enough after him, or write that smoothly, which is written fairely in me, in this particular. My poore, sweet, dearely beloved Brethren in the *Land* of *Ægypt*, the *house* of *Bondage*, will say, [*The Lord* hath not appeared to me—*Exod.* 4. 1.]

Oh my Lord, I am not eloquent, neither heretofore, nor since thou hast spoken to thy servant, &c. But *Aaron* my *Brother*, I know he can speake well, he shall be the spokesman, and speake out this plainly in the eares of *Ægyptian Israelites. Halelujah.*

Well, *The River* (which you saw) is exceeding cleare (you say,) no mud, or setling at the bottome,——It is true; All other ponds are usually muddy. Why, then you must not sit by the *Rivers* of *Babylon* (the great, or the lesser, of *Babylon within*, or *Babylon without*) they are muddy men, profound men are Muddy, *Diviners, mad, and muddy.*

The River, the Fountaine of *Life, the living God is* cleere, *pure God*! It is good to be here, to drinke deep draughts *Here*; To wade *Here* up to the ancles,——[it is not very deep] (you say) Neither is it by the bankes-side.

If we were but 2000.cubits off the *Bank*, (drie ground, *Earth*,) in *the River* we should be up to the knees. 3000.off—is to the loynes——And at 4000.——off the Banke,——it is deep enough to swimme in. Oh the *Depth, Breadth*, and *Length*,—how unsearchable, &c.——

We shall ere long *swimme* in the *River*, the *River* of *Pleasures*, for evermore, for evermore, Amen. *Halelujah.*

Then we shall not hug appearances, or *Formes* in our bosome any longer.

It seemes you have tooke some of the *Wildest* appearances, formes, or figures into your bosome.

So have I, but most of them are gone, vanisht in a moment. *They* are all *wilde*, and will *runne away.* [——when the *Day* breakes, the *shaddowes* flie away.] *They* will all turne *wilde*, and runne away, and we shall be *besides* our *selves*, and *Caught* up *into* the *Lord, the Substance*, which swalloweth up his appearances into *Himselfe*, Into *Himself*, Whither our *Fore-runner* is for us entered. *He* was *here*, in *Forme*, or *Flesh*, in *Flesh*, and Forme, [for he took upon him the forme of a servant.]

He is there, (in the bosome of the Father, at the right hand, O my father, *The river of pleasures, pure river, pure God*) in *power* and *glory, &c*—

So, *this corruptible—shall* put on *incorruption*, this mortall shall put on immortality, then shall be brought to passe the saying that is written—*Death* is swallowed *up* in *victory.*—

O dear hearts! let us look for, and hasten to the comming of the *Day* of *God*, wherein the *Heavens* being on *fire* shall be *dissolved*, and the *Elements*, [*Rudiments, first principles*] (Imagine formall *Prayer*, formall *Baptism*, formall *Supper*——&c.) shall *melt away*, with fervent heate, *into God*; and all *Forms*, appearances, *Types, Signes, Shadows, Flesh*, do, and shall *melt away* (with fervent heate) into *power, reallity, Truth, the thing signified, Substance, Spirit.*

This is the *Day, the Lords Day,* the *Sabbath* of the *Lord* thy God, which we look for, and hasten too, and which (in a great measure) some are already entred into.——

O my beloved! Be thou as a Roe, or young Hart——Even so Lord Jesus, Amen, come quickly, Amen.

I see him comming (to some *come*) in the clouds, with great power and glory, Amen, *Halelujah.*

Let us not therefore any longer single out any appearance, and appropriate it to our selves; no—not a *Paul,* an *Apollo,* or a *Cephas,*[31] *&c.*—all is yours, if you will not set a collar upon the neck of any——distinct——or beare it in your bosome, *&c.* For, while one saith I am of *Paul*——(and so single him out—) and another, I am of *Apollo, &c.* are ye not carnall?——But whether *Paul,* or *Apollo,* or *Cephas,* or things present, or things to *come,* or *life,* or *death, &c. all is* yours *(in the Spirit)* for you are *Christs,* and *Christ* is *Gods,* Amen, Amen, *Ho⟨s⟩anna* in the highest.

Blessed is he that commeth in the name of our Lord. Blessed be the *Kingdom* of our Father *David,* that commeth in the name of the *Lord, Hosanna* in the *highest, Halelujah,* Amen.

Thy *Kingdom* is *come*
to *some*
——their joy:
But to others *doome*
It is come
——they cry.——

FINIS.

---

31   1 Cor. 3.22. Coppe inverts the meaning of Paul's explication here.

An Additional and Preambular Hint,
— As a general Epistle written by
A B C.

THus saith the Lord, I am (a) Alpha * and Omega, the beginning and the ending, the first and the last; and now the last is reaching the first, and the end the beginning.

All things are returning to their Original, b where all parables, dark sayings, all languages, and all hidden things, are known, unfolded, and interpreted.

c That God of Peace and Love that eternal and everlasting Being, that eternal Unity, d who is all, and in all, is e reconciling all things into himself.

And in him, who is f the Lyon and the Lamb, g the Branch and Root, the Root and Offspring, h the eternal and everlasting Father, and i the Son of man.

The k Servant, and the l Lord of all, who is m the Prince of Peace, and n a Man of War.

o A jealous God, p and the Father of Mercies; In him (I say) the Lyon and the Lamb, Servant and Lord, Peace and War, Joy and Jealousie, Wrath and Love, &c are reconciled, and all complicated in Unity.

In him, Lyon and Lamb, Branch and Root, Root and Offspring, Father and Son, are all one.

And all those (seemingly cross) Denominations do finely and secretly

*T*He A. Alpha is triangular, Wherein the Trinity (so called) is finely and secretly, certainly and truly seen by the immortal eye, the eye of eternity, the figure only (and perhaps) scearse that is seen into by any mortal eye.

The A. Alpha is the Trinity, viz. Father, Son, and Spirit:

Which A. or Trinity is the Effluence or outspreading of Divinity.

Or out-going of God into ALL THINGS.

The figure is thus;

A —— Father Alpha.
Sonne GOD Spirit

Now, internally, or in the eye of eternity † which is seated in the soft, undone, contrite, i.e. the heart shattered to shivers, grownd down to meal, pounded to dust, and made up a new one, of a humane, a divine one: This A. is a hundred times more clearly seen to be.

Divinity, stepping first out into Rectitude, in figure thus;

———

in name
Father.

2. Into Obliquity, in figure thus;

/

In name,

Sonne

a Revel.

b Prov. 1,

c Phil. 4.
Rom. 15.

d Col. 3.
e Col. 1.20
f Rev. 5.
g Isai. 11.
Rom 15.
Rev 22.
h Isai. 9.
i Matth.
Mark
Luke
John
k John
l Gal.
m Isai 9.
n Exod. 15
o Exod. 20
p 1 Cor.

declare him to be all in all, and one in all, according to the Scriptures.

But he that hath eyes seeth not this, and he that hath ears heareth not this, he that hath his own hard heart understands not this.

This rain from heaven may fall upon that nether milstone, and doth not soak into it, &c.

But he that hath an EAR to hear [a single ear] heareth this.

q Prov.

He that hath an eye to see [a single eye] (and his *q* evil eye picked out, and eaten up by the Ravens of the valleys) sees this.

And he that hath a soft heart, and a soft place in his head, understands this.

r Isai. 57.

He that hath a soft heart, *i.e.* a heart *r* pounded to powder, an old stony heart made new, &c. such a heart that's hinted at in the third colum of the first page at this mark †, whither I refer you.

*A denomination given to fools.
s 2 Cor. 5.

And he that hath [a * soft place in's head] that is out of his wits, and *s* besides himself, besides his own will, knowledg, wisdom and understanding; that is *t* become or made a fool, that he might be made wise, can understand this, and this ensuing Treatise.

t 1 Cor. 3. 18

u Prov.

Wherein are some sweet secrets, and secret sweets, And *u* apples of gold in pictures of silver.

To the (nominal) Author is given *w* the tongue of the learned, though he *x* knoweth not letters.

w Isai. 49.
x Iohn
y 1 Pet. 4. 10 11.

y He speaks as he hath received, and in many things as the Oracles of God, and *z* the Wisdom of God in a mystery.

z 1 Cor. 2. 6. to the end.

3. *Into Obliquity again, in figure thus;*

In name,

(*In which two-fold Obliquity is no pravity, but purity it self.*)

In the middle of the A. (Alpha) there is an overthwart I, *in figure thus;*

———

In name,
God.

Which is eternal Unity; all which, in a word, is God making out himself in various Administrations, as Father, Son, and Spirit; and this is [*Trinity in Unity, and Unity in Trinity.*]

And thus much for A. which no man knows, yet poor, proud man would be called Rabbi, *and pretends he knows the ORIGINAL, when as he hath not learn'd his Primer, nay his A B C, nor yet knows great A.*

———————————

All that the in-being, outspeaks for the present in this way of Hirogliphical Divinity, is this, only a further hint of the A. in another figure, name, and language, (though one and the same in truth, and the inward ground,) which is in the figure thus;

א

In name,
Aleph.

And therein *a* useth great plainness of speech, which I am hugely taken with, because to him it is given, and so it is many times to me, but now it is not (in all these) but I cannot, and must not, but be content, because Everlasting will have it so; and I know his design in it in many particulars, I must not mention all, but something there's in it, That I must yet be a Sign and a Wonder in fleshly *Israel*; and in this (as well as formerly in things of the same nature, and otherwise) I must be comfortable to my forerunner and Pattern, *b* being a stumbling stone, and a rock of offence to both the houses of *Israel*; and for a gin, and a snare to the inhabitants of *Jerusalem* that is below, that many among them may stumble and fall and be broken, and be snared and taken.

That they may stumble and fall (I say) as I have done, before I was raised up; and be broken as I have been, before I was made whole; and be snared and taken, as I have been, before I was set at liberty, where I sing, and shout, and dance before the Lord, because I was stumbled, and broken, and snared:

Which—is none other but the gate of heaven, as mourning is the gate of mirth, and sorrow the gate of joy, &c.

My hearts desire for you, is, That the *c* gates of brass may fly open, & the bars of iron be burst asunder, when they must, that you may enter

Which is ONE — in it self, and yet compounded, or rather branching forth it self into Obliquity, in figure thus;

And a tripple semicircularity, in figure thus;

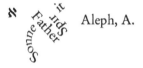

And here's Unity in Trinity, in figure thus;

Aleph, A.

The Unity is complicated in the whole Figure, and clearly seen, and must not (though it might be) clearly decyphered.

This א *Aleph, or A, is* [in lingua sancta] *an aspiration.*

And in its ORIGINAL, and in truth, is the out-breathing, or emmanation of Divinity, into Father, Son and Spirit.

And its circularity maketh out after, and maketh up the Omega, which is in Figure thus,

ω, *or thus,* O

Which is the eye or globe of eternity, where the end makes towards and meets the beginning, and makes up a heart full of love, and all's swallowed up into Unity: And this is Alpha and Omega, the beginning and the end:

ONE, and All, God blessed for evermore. Amen.

a 2 Cor. 3. 12.

b Isai. 8

c Psalm

d Psalm

e Jonah 2.

into d the secret place of the most High, which you are mostly afraid of, and so e withstand your own mercies.

Hoc Scriptum est, est Scriptura, et in Scriptura.¹

f 1 Pet. 3. 16

Well! there are some things in these, somewhat (and in mine muchly) f hard to be understood, which they that are unlearned and unable wrest as they do also the other Scriptures, &c.

g Prov. 8.
h 2 Cor.

But they are all g plain and easie to him that understandeth, though h to the Jew a stumbling block, and to the Greek foolishness: To the Scribe folly; To the Pharisee blasphemy, who hath [ad unguem²] at's fingers ends, He blasphemeth, is a friend of Publicans and Harlots, he is a glutten, and wine bibber; And say we not well, that he hath a devil?

Which Pharisee, in man, is the mother of harlots, and being the worst whore, cries whore first: And the grand blasphemer, cries out, Blasphemy,

i Rev. 17.

blasphemy, which she i is brim full of.

k Prov. 7.

She is also k WITHOUT, ith'streets, abroad, not at HOME.

The Pharisee's not at home, but abroad.

First, He's not at Home in the Lord, but in fleshliness, formality; Abroad, in the streets, in wide, huge, outward zeal, devotion, righteousness, holiness and religion.

Secondly, He is ABROAD, not at home, in his own heart, not looking into his own inside into himself.

l Mat. 23. 13.
to the end.

Who is l a painted Sepulchre, and indeed appears beautiful outward, but WITHIN is full of dead mens bones, putrifaction, and of all uncleanness and filthiness.

Being brim full of worse drunkenness, uncleanness, adultery, theft and murder, then the worst he cries out on.

Being himself in the spirit power and life of those things (and perhaps in the form also of some of them, at least, in some degrees, and in the time of his Publicanism o'r head and ears in them) of which Publicans and Harlots are but in the form and shadow of only; And Christ (whom he most of all hates and traduces) neither in the form or power of what he accuses him of, though he be numbred amongst transgressors, and is indeed a friend of Publicans and Harlots, and open-hearted, and open-handed to them, &c.

m Matth.
Mark
Luke
John.

In a word, he is very zealous against m the form of ungodliness;

But hugging, embracing, living and delighting in the power thereof.

And he is (only) in the form of godliness, hugging, embracing it, and contending for it, vi & armis.³

---

1   'This is written, it is scripture, and in scripture.'
2   Coppe translates literally: unguem means 'fingernail'; the phrase comes from the Carmen de moribus at the end of Lily's Grammar, a code of manners and morals in verse, to be memorized and recited by grammar school boys (ERI, 114).
3   'By force and arms': in Common Law, unlawful violence against persons or property.

But dis relishing, dis owning, denying, blaspheming, persecuting, and mostly opposing the power thereof, *vi & armis*.

But the hour is coming, yea now is, *n* That all his carnal, outward, formal Religion, (yea, of Scripturely cognizance, so far as its fleshly and formal) and all his fleshly holiness, zeal and devotion, shall be, and is, set upon the same account, as outward drunkenness, theft, murther, adultery, &c.

n *A true Prophecy.*

And now the time is come, that *o* He that kills an Ox, is as if he slew a man, &c. And all mans Prayers, Psalms, *p* Fastings (for strife and debate, and to smite with the fist of wickedness, though the very soul be afflicted for a day, and the head hung like a bulrush, &c.) And all mans preachings, hearing, teachings, learnings, holinesses, righteousnesses religions, is as Theft, Murder, and Adultery.

o Isai. 66.

p Isa. 58.

The time is coming, and now is, That no prayer shall be in request but [*Our Father,*] (*He that hath an ear to hear, let him hear.*)

No Psalm shall be sung, but *q* the Lord our Song.

No Holiness,—but the Lord our Holinesse.

No Righteousness—but *r* the Lord our Righteousness.

q Exod 15

r Jerem.

s Reprobate silver shall all other be called, as it is; yea, *t* dung, dross, [σκύβαλα,⁴] dogs-meat.

——*u* Menstruous rags,—worse then the filth of a Jakes house.

s Isaiah.
t Phil. 2.

u Isai.

w Yea, the time is coming, That zealous, holy, devout, righteous, religious men shall (one way) dye, for their Holiness and Religion, as well as Thieves and Murtherers—for their Theft and Murther, &c.

A strange yet true Prophecy.

And shall be punish'd, and put to shame, for their holiness and purity—as well as Drunkards and Adulterers, for their Drunkenness and Whoredom.

But all this while, the righteousness, holiness, purity and zeal of the Lord, is pure, precious, excellent, most beautiful, and glorious; And so is pure Religion and undefiled, as also the Lords preaching, praying, singing &c. And I had rather have my tongue cut out of my mouth, and be stoned to death, then speak against this which is my life and joy.

But once more, the time is coming, that Thieves and Murtherers shall scape, as well as the most zealous and most formal professors; and men shall be put to death, (or be murthered by men) no more for the one, then for the other.

And if this come to pass, say, the Lord hath not spoken by me; and let me dye the death.

But sure I am, there are some, that know me, shall live to see this, and say *Amen* to it: And shall know, that there hath been a Prophet amongst them. Which Prophet is not *Abiezer Coppe*; but *x* the Prophet in him, who is among you all, though, as yet, manifested to few.

x 1 Joh. 2.

---

4   As Coppe says, the Greek means 'dung' or 'shit,' human or animal. The correct New Testament source is Phil. 3.8.

And let him that hath an ear to hear, hear.

To him (only) I commend these, and the ensuing Treatise, knowing that in him *y* there's no occasion of stumbling; and to him, all mine, and these, are plain and easie: And as for others, who cannot but stumble, be offended, and censure, They are to be pathetically and most affectionately told, that our heart akes for them; we have them in our bosom: and the everlasting bowels of eternal love, that dwells in us, yearn over them, are a flame towards them, and towards Publicans and Harlots, (z Considering also our selves) and knowing, that they dwell where we did, and in the remaining part of that *a* old house, which hath been fired about our ears, and over our heads, out of which, in infinite and unspeakable mercy, we were frighted into a house made without hands, the beauty whereof dazelleth the eyes of men and Angels; and at this time the glory thereof amazeth me into silence, and strikes my pen out of my hand, that if I would, yet I cannot now write of its sumptuousness, beauty, and magnificence; onely, as far as we dare, we wish you there, and there you shall be, when you must be.

In the mean while, the charmer cannot charm you thither, charm he never so wisely.

It's but yet a little while, and the *b* dividing of times will be sent packing after time, times; and then there's that in us, knows what shall be.

In the mean while, be not angry if we groan without our selves, waiting for your deliverance out of the Land of Egypt, the house of bondage, (c which Land and house, you cannot beleeve you are in).

Our hearts desire for you is, That *d Jacobs* house (that little spark that lies hid and buried under all your glorious formality) may kindle and flame up from under all your formal prayers, carnal ordinances, fleshly righteousness, holiness, and religion, &c. (which are exceeding glorious in your eyes,) and burn them up, that you may be lifted up into pure Religion, and undefiled; into pure Prayer, Psalms, Righteousness, Holiness, &c.

And that this *e* house of *Jacob* may like fire fall upon the house of *Esau*, (which is as stubble, and now as stubble fully dry,) upon this house of *Esau* (I say) which is rough, hairy, red, fiery, fierce, rugged flesh, hatred, strife, envy, malice, evil surmizing &c. and utterly consume them, that there be not any remaining of the house of *Esau*.

And that the Lord may be exalted in you, and self debased, That the Lord (I say) may be exalted: The Lord, who is love, joy, peace, light, glory, consolation, &c. may be exalted, *i.e.* lifted up above sorrow, trouble, tribulation, fears, doubts, perplexities, wrath, war, darkness, envy, strife, self-ishness.

That the Lord (who is *f* love, and suffereth long, is kinde, envieth not, vaunteth not it self, is not puffed up, beareth all things, thinketh none evil,) may be exalted, or lifted up, (in you) above revenge, malice, unkindness, swelling pride, evil surmizings in you.

y 1 Joh.

z Gal.
a Obad.

b Rev.

c Joh. 8. 32. 33.

d Isa 10. 16. 7. 18

e Obad.

1 Ioh. 4.

f 1 Cor, 13

And that he might ride on prosperously, in glory and renown (in you) conquering, and to conquer, trampling all these (in you) under his feet, as mire in the streets.

To him I leave you, whose heart is larger than you are aware of, and in g *g* Psal.
whose hands are all our times, and remove hence into another coast; whither
I am sent with

The Copy of a Letter written in Heaven——(in the heart of those, whose heart is
    the Lord, who are h *taught of God, and who have their* i *Teacher in them,)*   *h* Ioh. 6.
    By the k *Elder,*   *i* 1 Ioh. 2. 27.
    To l *the Elect Lady.*   k *Christ.*
                                                                                        l *His spouse*

Mine own,
I am thine to all eternity: my joy, my glory, my life, is thine;
all mine is thine: I'l as soon cease to be, as cease to love thee;
for thou wast taken out of me.
I am a jealous God, and that's thy joy.
If thou hast any lovers besides me, I'l not spare——   ** Scriptum*
for it is the day of my vengeance: and I in thee, and thou in me art glad on't. *est.*
If thou hast any delights but my self, I'l crown them all with
discontentments; that thou mightest lie in no bosom, but mine own;
Saith thy Maker thy Husband: In

His and Thine,

ABIEZER COPPE.

The original—was sent by* a friend, which is better then a brother,   ** Prov,*
    To a friend in a corner, with this
                        POST-SCRIPT.

Do not appropriate this to thy self onely; it's a general Epistle: And let this *modicum*[5] suffice thee. For should all the words, things, and thoughts, which I have, do, and will, speak of thee, to thee, in thee; act for thee, in thee, and think towards thee, the whole world would be too narrow to contein them.

Look into a larger volume, thy heart——
    where I am, which I am.

---

5   A small or moderate amount or portion; applied to food or drink, variously a
     quantity intended to stimulate or satisfy appetite (*OED* n. 1 a).

An After-Clap, or second Post-script.

THis is musique, *WITHIN*: The father, the younger brother, and all that are within, in this house, are merry; where this is dainty, and where there are dainties, and dancing, mirth and musique.

But * the serving man—the elder brother, knows not what this meaneth, but is angry, and dogged, puffs and pouts, is sullen, snuffs, swells, and censures *WITHOUT* doors.

* *Serving-brother, the zealous formal professor.* Luk. 1.5

Alias, Or *another of the same, with the former Epistle, Thus;*

a *Script. est*
b Cant. 2.
Ioh. 17.
c Nehe. 13
d Ezek. 16
e Mal. 3.
Heb. 13.
f *Script. est.*

My *a* heart, my blood, my life, is Thine:
It pleases me that *b* thou art mine.
I'l *c* curse thy flesh, and *d* swear th'art fine.
For *e* ever thine I mean to be,
As *f* I am that I am, within *A.C.*

POST-SCRIPT.

Before God, this is one of the Songs O *Zion.*
Before holy man (whose holiness stinks above ground)
It's at least whimsey, if not Blasphemy;
But wisdom is justified of her Children.

A Fiery Flying Roll:

A

Word from the Lord to all the Great Ones
of the Earth, whom this may concerne: Being the
last WARNING PIECE at the dreadfull day of
JUDGEMENT.
For now the LORD is come

to $\left\{ \begin{array}{l} 1\ \textit{Informe} \\ 2\ \textit{Advise and warne} \\ 3\ \textit{Charge} \\ 4\ \textit{Judge and sentence} \end{array} \right\}$ the Great Ones.

As also most compassionately informing, and most lo-
vingly and pathetically advising and warning *London.*

With a terrible Word, and fatall Blow from the LORD,
upon the Gathered CHURCHES.

And all by his Most Excellent MAJESTY, dwelling
in, and shining through
AUXILIUM PATRIS, כף alias, *Coppe.*

With another FLYING ROLL ensuing (to all the Inhabitants of the Earth.) The Contents of both following.

Isa. 23.9, *The Lord of Hosts (is) staining the pride of all glory, and bringing into contempt all
the honourable (persons and things) of the Earth.*
O London, London, how would I gather thee, as a hen gathereth her chickens under her wings, &c.
Know thou (in this thy day) the things that belong to thy Peace——
*I know the blasphemy of them which say they are Jewes, and are not, but are the Synagogue of
Satan,* Rev. 2.9.

Imprinted at *London,* in the beginning of that notable day, wherein the
secrets of all hearts are laid open; and wherein the worst and foulest of
villainies, are discovered, under the best and fairest outsides. 1649.

THE PREFACE.

An inlet into the Land of Promise, the new
Hierusalem, and a gate into the ensuing Discourse,
worthy of serious consideration.

Y Deare One.

All or None.

Every one under the Sunne.

Mine own.

My most Excellent Majesty (in me) hath strangely and variously transformed this forme.

And behold, by mine own Almightinesse (In me) I have been changed in a moment, in the twinkling of an eye, at the sound of the Trump.

And now the Lord is descended from Heaven, with a shout, with the voyce of the Arch-angell, and with the Trump of God.

And the sea, the earth, yea all things are now giving up their dead. And all things that ever were, are, or shall be visible—are the Grave wherein the King of Glory (the eternall, invisible Almightinesse, hath lain as it were) dead and buried.

But behold, behold, he is now risen with a witnesse, to save *Zion* with vengeance, or to confound and plague all things into himself; who by his mighty Angell is proclaiming (with a loud voyce) That Sin and Transgression is finished and ended; and everlasting righteousnesse brought in; and the everlasting Gospell preaching; Which everlasting Gospell is brought in with most terrible earth-quakes, and heaven-quakes, and with signes and wonders following. *Amen.*

And it hath pleased my most Excellent Majesty, (who is universall love, and whose service is perfect freedome) to set this forme (the Writer of this Roll) as no small signe and wonder in fleshly *Israel*; as you may partly see in the ensuing Discourse.

And now (my dear ones!) every one under the Sun, I will onely point at the gate, thorow which I was led into that new City, new *Hierusalem,* and to the Spirits of just men, made perfect, and to God the Judge of all.

First, all my strength, my forces were utterly routed, my house I dwelt in fired, my father and mother forsook me, the wife of my bosome loathed me, mine old name was rotted, perished; and I was utterly plagued, consumed, damned, rammed, and sunke into nothing, into the bowels of the still Eternity (my mothers wombe) out of which I came naked, and whetherto I returned again naked. And lying a while there, rapt up[1] in silence, at length (the body or outward forme being awake all this while) I heard with my outward eare (to my apprehension) a most terrible thunder-clap, and after that a second. And upon the second thunder-clap, which was exceeding terrible, I saw a great body of light, like the light of the Sun, and red as fire, in the forme of a drum (as it were) whereupon with exceeding trembling and amazement on the flesh,[2] and with joy unspeakable in the spirit, I clapt my hands, and cryed out, *Amen, Halelujah, Halelujah, Amen.* And so lay trembling, sweating, and smoking

---

1   a) wrapped up, enclosed b) carried away in spirit, enraptured (*OED* v. 2).
2   i.e., with hairs standing on end; 'goose bumps.'

(for the space of half an houre) at length with a loud voyce (I inwardly) cryed out, Lord, what wilt thou do with me; my most excellent majesty and eternall glory (in me) answered & sayd, Fear not, I will take thee up into mine everlasting Kingdom. But thou shalt (first) drink a bitter cup, a bitter cup, a bitter cup; whereupon (being filled with exceeding amazement) I was throwne into the belly of hell (and take what you can of it in these expressions, though the matter is beyond expression) I was among all the Devils in hell, even in their most hideous hew.

And under all this terrour, and amazement, there was a little spark of transcendent, transplendent, unspeakable glory, which survived, and sustained it self, triumphing, exulting, and exalting it self above all the Fiends. And confounding the very blacknesse of darknesse (you must take it in these tearmes, for it is infinitely beyond expression.) Vpon this the life was taken out of the body (for a season) and it was thus resembled, as if a man with a great brush dipt in whiting, should with one stroke wipe out, or sweep off a picture upon a wall, &c. after a while, breath and life was returned into the form againe; whereupon I saw various streames of light (in the night) which appeared to the outward eye; and immediately I saw three hearts (or three appearances) in the form of hearts, of exceeding brightnesse; and immediately an innumerable company of hearts, filling each corner of the room where I was. And methoughts there was variety and distinction, as if there had been severall hearts, and yet most strangely and unexpressibly complicated or folded up in unity. I clearly saw distinction, diversity, variety, and as clearly saw all swallowed up into unity. And it hath been my song many times since, within and without, unity, universality, universality, unity, Eternall Majesty, &c. And at this vision, a most strong, glorious voyce uttered these words, *The spirits of just men made perfect.* The spirits &c, with whom I had as absolut, cleare, full communion, and in a two fold more familiar way, then ever I had outwardly with my dearest friends, and nearest relations. The visions and revelations of God, and the strong hand of eternall invisible almightinesse, was stretched out upon me, within me, for the space of foure dayes and nights, without intermission.

The time would faile if I would tell you all, but it is not the good will and pleasure of my most excellent Majesty in me, to declare any more (as yet) then thus much further: That amongst those various voyces that were then uttered within, these were some, *Blood, blood, Where, where? upon the hypocriticall holy heart, &c.* Another thus, *Vengeance, vengeance, vengeance, Plagues, plagues, upon the Inhabitants of the earth; Fire, fire, fire, Sword, sword, &c. upon all that bow not down to eternall Majesty, universall love; I'le recover, recover, my wooll, my flax, my money. Declare, declare, feare thou not the faces of any; I am (in thee) a munition of Rocks, &c.*[3]

Go up to *London*, * to *London*, that great City, write, write, write. And

* It not being shewen to me, what I should do, more then preach and print something, &c. very little expecting I should be so strangely acted, as to (my exceeding joy and delight) I have been, though to the utter cracking of my credit, and to the rotting of my old name which is damned, and cast out (as a toad to the dunghill) that I might have a new name, with me, upon me, within me, which is, I am—

---

3   Hos. 2.9.

behold I writ, and lo a hand was sent to me, and a roll of a book was therein, which this fleshly hand would have put wings to, before the time. Whereupon it was snatcht out of my hand, & the Roll thrust into my mouth; and I eat it up, and filled my bowels with it, (*Eze.* 2.8. &c. *cha.* 3.1,2,3.) where it was as bitter as worm-wood; and it lay broiling, and burning in my stomack, till I brought it forth in this forme.

And now I send it flying to thee, with my heart, And all

Per AUXILIUM PATRIS כף[4]

---

4   Coppe renders the sense of his first name in Hebrew ('The [or my] Father is help,' or 'Father of help') in Latin as 'Through the help of the Father' and signs his surname in Hebrew letters.

THE CONTENTS.

The second Flying Roll.

Wholsome advice, with a terrible threat to the Formalists: And how BASE things have confounded base things: And how base things have been a fiery chariot to mount the Author up into divine glory and unspeakable Majestie: and how his wife is, & his life is in that beauty, which maketh visible beauty seem meere deformity.

CHAP. 6.   *Great ones must bow to the poorest peasants, or else they shall rue for it; No material sword or humane power (whatsoever) but the pure spirit of universall love, who is the eternall God, can breake the necke of tyranny, oppression, and abhominable pride and cruell murther, &c. A catologue of severall Judgments recited, as so many warning-pieces to appropriators, impropriators, and anti-free communicants.*

CHAP. 7.   *A further discovery of the subtilty of the well favoured harlot, with a parley between her and the spirit. As also the horrid villany that lies hid under her smooth words, and sweet tongue (in pleading against the letter and history, and for the spirit and mistery, and all for her own ends) detected. Also upon what account the spirit is put, and upon what account the letter, &c. And what the true communion, and what the true breaking of bread is.*

CHAP. 8.   *The wel-favoured harlots cloaths stript off, her nakednesse discovered, her nose slit. Her hunting after the young man void of understanding, from corner to corner, from religion to religion: And the spirit pursuing, overtaking, and destroying her, &c.*

With a terrible thunder-clap i'th close.

A word from the Lord to all the Great Ones
of the Earth (whom this may concerne) being the
last Warning Piece, &c.

---

1 *The word of the Lord came expresly to me, saying, Sonne of man write a Roule,*
 and these words, from my mouth, to the Great ones, saying, thus saith the Lord:
Slight not this Roule, neither laugh at it, least I slight you, and cause all men to
 slight and scorne you; least I destroy you, and laugh at your destruction, &c.
2 *This is, (and with a witnesse, some of you shall finde it, to be) an edg'd toole; and*
 there's no jesting with it, or laughing at it.
It's a sharp sword, sharpned, and also fourbished—
No sleepy Dormouse shall dare to creep up the edge of it.[5]
Thus saith the Lord, You shall finde with a witnesse, that I am now coming

$$to\begin{cases} 1\ Informe \\ 2\ Advise\ and\ warne \\ 3\ Charge \\ 4\ Judge\ and\ sentence \end{cases}\ you,\ O\ ye\ great\ ones.$$

CHAP. I.

Containing severall strange, yet true and seasonable Informations, to the great
 ones. As also an apologeticall hint, of the Authors Principle, standing in the
 front.—

1. Hus saith the Lord, *I inform you, that I overturn, overturn,*
overturn.[6] And as the Bishops, *Charles,* and the Lords, have
had their turn, overturn, so your turn shall be next (ye
surviving great ones⟨,⟩ by what Name or Title soever dignified
or distinguished) who ever you are, that oppose me, the Eternall God, who
am U N I V E R S A L L Love, and whose service is perfect freedome, and pure
Libertinisme.

    2 * But afore I proceed any further, be it known to you, That although that
excellent Majesty, which dwels in the Writer of this Roule, hath reconciled
A L L   T H I N G S to himselfe, yet this hand (which now writes) never drew

* An Apolo-
geticall hint
concering
the Authors
Principle,
the result—is
negative;
hee speaks
little in the
affirmative
because not
one in a
hundred, yea
even of his
former ac-
quaintance,
now know
him, neither
must they
yet.

---

5   Horace, *Ars Poetica,* 139 (McDowell, *N & Q,* 53 (2006), 166-68).
6   Ezek. 21.27.

sword, or shed one drop of any mans blood. [I am free from the blood of all men] though (I say) all things are reconciled to me, the eternall God (I N H I M) yet sword levelling, or digging-levelling, are neither of them his principle.

Both are as farre from his principle, as the East is from the West, or the Heavens from the Earth, (though, I say, reconciled to both, as to all things else) and though he hath more justice, righteousnesse, truth, and sincerity, shining in those low dung-hils, (as they are esteemed) then in the Sunne, Moone, and all the Stars.

3 I come not forth (in him) either with materiall sword, or Mattock, but now (in this my day—) I make him my Sword-bearer, to brandish the Sword of the Spirit, as he hath done severall dayes and nights together, thorow the streets of the great City.

4 And now thus saith the Lord:

Though you can as little endure the word L E V E L L I N G, as could the late slaine or dead *Charles* (your forerunner, who is gone before you—) and had as live heare the Devill named, as heare of the Levellers (Men-Levellers) which is, and who (indeed) are but shadowes of most terrible, yet great and glorious good things to come.

5 Behold, behold, behold, I the eternall God, the Lord of Hosts, who am that mighty Leveller, am comming (yea even at the doores) to Levell in good earnest, to Levell to some purpose, to Levell with a witnesse, to Levell the Hills with the Valleyes, and to lay the Mountaines low.

6 High Mountaines! lofty Cedars! its high time for you to enter into the Rocks, and to hide you in the dust, for feare of the Lord, and for the glory of his Majesty. For the lofty looks of man shall be humbled, and the haughtinesse of men shall be bowed downe, and the Lord A L O N E shall be exalted in that day; For the day of the Lord of Hoasts, shall be upon every one that is proud, and lofty, and upon every one that is lifted up, and he shall be brought low. And upon all the Cedars of *Lebanon*, that are high and lifted up, and upon all the Oaks of *Bashan*; and upon all the high Mountaines; and upon all the Hils that are lifted up, and upon every high Tower, and upon every fenced Wall; and upon all the Ships of *Tarshish*, and upon all pleasant Pictures.

And the L O F T I N E S S E of man shall be bowed down, and the haughtinesse of men shall be laid low. And the Lord A L O N E shall be exalted in that day, and the Idols he shall utterly abolish.

And they shall go into the holes of the Rocks, and into the Caves of the Earth, for feare of the Lord, and for the glory of his Majesty, when he ariseth to shake terribly the earth.

In that day a man shall cast his Idols of Silver, and Idols of Gold—to the bats, and to the Moles. To go into the Clefts of the Rocks and into the tops of the ragged Rocks, for feare of the Lord, and for the glory of his Majesty. For the Lord is now R I S E N to shake terriblly the Earth, *Isa.* 2.10. to the end of the Chapter.

7 Hills! Mountains! Cedars! Mighty men! Your breath is in your nostrils.

Those that have admired, adored, idolized, magnified, set you up, fought for you, ventured goods, and good name; limbe and life for you, shall cease from you.

You shall not (at all be accounted of (not one of you) ye sturdy Oake) who bowe not downe before eternall Majesty: Vniversall Love, whose service is perfect freedome, and who hath put down the mighty (remember, remember your fore-runner) and who is putting down the mighty from their seats; and exalting them of low degree.

8 Oh let not, (for your owne sakes) let not the mother of Harlots in you, who is very subtle of heart.

Nor the Beast (without you) what do you call 'em? The Ministers, fat parsons, Vicars, Lecturers, &c. who (for their owne base ends, to maintaine their pride, and pompe, and to fill their owne paunches, and purses) have been the chiefe instruments of all those horrid abominations, hellish, cruell, devillish persecutions, in this Nation which cry for vengeance. For your owne sakes (I say) let neither the one, nor the other bewitch you, or charme your eares, to heare them say, these things shall not befall you, these Scriptures shall not be fulfilled upon you, but upon the Pope, Turke, and Heathen Princes, &c.

9 Or if any of them should (through subtilty for their owne base ends) creep into the Mystery of that forementioned * Scripture.   Isay 2:

And tell you, Those words are to be taken in the Mystery only; and they onely point out a spirituall, inward levelling (once more, for your for your owne sakes, I say) believe them not.

10 'Tis true, the History, or Letter, (I speake comparatively) is but as it were haire-cloth; the Mystery is fine Flax. My flax, saith the Lord, and the Thief and the Robber will steale from me my flax, to cover his nakednesse, that his filthinesse may not appeare.

But behold, I am (now) recovering my flax out of his hand, and discovering his lewdnesse—*verbum sat*[7]—

11 'Tis true, the Mystery is my joy, my delight, my life.

And the Prime levelling, is laying low the Mountaines, and levelling the Hils in man.

But this is not all.

For lo I come (saith the Lord) with a vengeance, to levell also your Honour, Riches, &c. to staine the pride of all your glory, and to bring into contempt all the Honourable (both persons and things) upon the earth, Isa. 23.9.

12 For this Honour, Nobility, Gentility, Propriety, Superfluity, &c. hath (without contradiction) been the Father of hellish horrid pride, arrogance, haughtinesse, loftinesse, murder, malice, of all manner of wickednesse and impiety; yea the cause of all the blood that ever hath been shed, from the blood of righteous *Abell*, to the blood of the last Levellers that were shot to death. *And now (as I live saith the Lord) I am come to make inquisition for blood; for murder and pride, &c.*[8]

13 I see the root of it all *The Axe is laid to the root of the Tree* (by the Eternall God, *My Self*, saith the Lord) *I will hew it down.*[9] And as I live, I will plague your Honour, Pompe, Greatnesse, Superfluity, and confound it into parity, equality, community;

---

7   'The word sufficeth.'   8   Ps. 9.12.   9   Matt. 3.10; Luke 3.9.

that the neck of horrid pride, murder, malice, and tyranny, &c. may be chopt off at one blow. And that my selfe, the Eternall God, who am Vniversall Love, may fill the Earth with universall love, universall peace, and perfect freedome; which can never be by humane sword or strength accomplished.

14 Wherefore bow downe, bow downe, you sturdy Oakes, and tall Cedars; bow, or by my self Ile break you.

Ile cause some of you (on whom I have compassion) to bow &c. and will terribly plague the rest.

My little finger shall be heavier on them, then my whole loynes were on *Pharaoh* of old.

15 And maugre the subtilty, and sedulity, the craft and cruelty of hell, and earth: this Levelling shall up.

Not by sword; we (holily) scorne to fight for any thing; we had as live be dead drunk every day of the weeke, and lye with whores i'th market place, and account these as good actions as taking the poore abused, enslaved ploughmans money from him (who is almost every where undone, and squeezed to death; and not so much as that plaguy, unsupportable, hellish burden, and oppression, of Tythes taken off his shoulders, notwithstanding all his honesty, fidelity, Taxes, Freequarter, petitioning &c. for the same,) we had rather starve, I say, then take away his money from him, for killing of men.

Nay, if we might have Captains pay, and a good fat Parsonage or two besides, we would scorne to be swordsmen, or fight with those (mostly) carnall weapons, for any thing, or against any one, or for our livings.

16 No, no, wee'l live in despite of our foes; and this levelling (to thy torment, O mighty man) shall up, not by sword, not by might, &c. but by my Spirit, saith the Lord.

For I am risen, for I am risen, for I am risen, to shake terribly the earth, and not the earth onely, but the heavens also, &c.

But here I shall cease informing you.

You may for your further information (if you please) reade my Roule to all the rich Inhabitants of the earth.

Reade it if you be wise, I shall now advice you.

CHAP. II.

Containing severall new, strange, yet seasonable Admonitions, and good advice; as the last warning to the Great Ones of the Earth. from the Lord.

* Sero sapiunt Phryges, sed nunquam Sera est ad Bonos mores via.[10]

1 THus saith the Lord: Be * wise now therefore, O ye Rulers, &c. Be instructed, &c. Kisse the Sunne, &c. Yea, kisse Beggers, Prisoners,

---

10   An amalgam of Sextus Pompeius Festus, *De verborum significatu*, 343M, and Seneca, *Agamemnon*, 242: 'The Trojans understood too late, but it is never too late to follow the way to good' (*ERI*, 116, n. 61).

warme them, feed them, cloathe them, money them, relieve them, release them, take them into your houses, don't serve them as dogs, without doore. &c.

Owne them, they are flesh of your flesh, your owne brethren, your owne Sisters, every whit as good (and if I should stand in competition with you) in some degrees better then your selves.

1 Admonition to great ones.

2 Once more, I say, own them; they are your self, make them one with you, or else go howling into hell; howle for the miseries that are comming upon you, howle.

The very shadow of levelling, sword-levelling, man-levelling, frighted you, (and who, like yourselves, can blame you, because it shook your Kingdome?) but now the substantiality of levelling is coming.

The Eternall God, the mighty Leveller is comming, yea come, even at the doore; and what will you do in that day.

Repent, repent, repent, Bow down, bow down, bow, or howle, resigne, or be damned; Bow downe, bow downe, you sturdy Oakes, and Cedars, bow downe.

Veile too, and kisse the meaner shrubs. Bow, or else (by my self saith the Lord) Ile breake you in pieces (some of you) others I will teare up by the roots; I will suddenly deale with you all, some in one way; some in another. Wherefore

Each Begger that you meet
Fall down before him, kisse him in the street.

Once more, he is thy brother, thy fellow, flesh of thy flesh.

Turne not away thine eyes from thine owne F L E S H, least I pull out thine eyes and throw thee headlong into hell.

3 Mine eares are filled brim full with cryes of poore prisoners, Newgate, Ludgate cryes (of late) are seldome out of mine eares. Those dolefull cryes, Bread, bread, bread for the Lords sake, pierce mine eares, and heart, I can no longer forebeare.

Werefore high you apace to all prisons in the Kingdome,

4 Bow before those poore, nasty, lousie, ragged wretches, say to them, your humble servants, Sirs, (without a complement) we let you go free, and serve you, &c.

2 Admonition to great ones.

Do this (or as I live saith the Lord) thine eyes (at least) shall be boared out, and thou carried captive into a strange Land.

5 Give over, give over, thy odious, nasty, abominable fasting, for strife and debate, and to smite with the fist of wickednesse. And instead thereof, loose the bands of wickednesse, undo the heavy burdens, let the oppressed go free, and breake every yoake. Deale thy bread to the hungry, and bring the poore that are cast out (both of houses and Synagogues) to thy house. Cover the

3 Admonition to great ones.

naked: Hide not thy self from thine owne flesh, from a creeple, a rogue, a beggar, he's thine owne flesh. From a Whoremonger, a thief, &c. he's flesh of thy flesh, and his theft, and whoredome is flesh of thy flesh also, thine owne flesh. Thou maist have ten, times more of each within thee, then he that acts outwardly in either, Remember, turn not away thine eyes from thine O W N FLESH.

6 Give over, give over thy midnight mischief.

Let branding with the letter *B*. alone.

Be no longer so horridly, hellishly, impudently, arrogantly, wicked, as to judge what is sinne, what not, what evill, and what not, what blasphemy, and what not.

For thou and all thy reverend Divines, so called (who Divine for Tythes, hire, and money, and serve the Lord Jesus Christ for their owne bellyes) are ignorant of this one thing.

7 That sinne and transgression is finisht, its a meere riddle, that they, with all their humane learning can never reade.

Neither can they understand what pure honour is wrapt up in the Kings Motto, *Honi Soit qui Mal.y.Pense*. Evill to him that evill thinks.

Some there are (who are accounted the off scouring of all things) who are Noble Knights of the Garter. Since which—they could see no evill, thinke no evill, doe no evill, know no evill.

A L L is Religion that they speak, and honour that they do.

But all you that eat of the Tree of Knowledge of Good and Evill, and have not your Evill eye Pickt out, you call Good Evill, and Evill Good; Light Darknesse, and Darknesse Light; Truth Blasphemy, and Blasphemy Truth.

And you are at this time of your Father the Devill, and of your brother the Pharisee, who still say of Christ (who is now alive) say we not well that he hath a Devill.

9 Take heed, take heed, take heed.

Filthy blinde Sodomites called Angels men, they seeing no further then the formes of men.

10 There are Angels (now) come down from Heaven, in the shapes and formes of men, who are full of the vengeance of the Lord; and are to poure out the plagues of God upon the Earth, and to torment the Inhabitants thereof.

Some of these Angels I have been acquainted withall.

And I have looked upon them as Devils, accounting them Devils incarnate, and have run from place to place, to hide my self from them, shunning their company; and have been utterly ashamed when I have been seen with them.

But for my labour; I have been plagued and tormented beyond expression. So that now I had rather behold one of these Angels * pouring out the plagues of God, cursing; and teaching others to curse bitterly.

4 Admonition to great ones.

* Rev. 15, Judges 5, Revel. 10, Neh. 13.25,

And had rather heare a mighty Angell (in man) swearing a full-mouthed Oath; and see the spirit of *Nehemiah* (in any form of man, or woman) running upon an uncleane Jew (a pretended Saint) and tearing the haire of his head like a mad man, cursing, and making others fall a swearing, then heare a zealous Presbyterian, Independent, or * spirituall Notionist,[11] pray, preach, or exercise.

11 Well! To the pure all things are pure.[12] God hath so cleared cursing, swearing, in some, that that which goes for swearing and cursing in them, is more glorious then praying and preaching in others.

And what God hath cleansed, call not thou uncleane.

And if *Peter* prove a great transgressor of the Law, by doing that which was as odious as killing a man; if he at length (though he be loath at first) eat that which was common and unclean &c. (I give but a hint) blame him not, much lesse lift up a finger against, or plant a hellish Ordinance——against him, least thou be plagued, and damned too, for thy zeale, blinde Religion, and fleshly holinesse, which now stinks above ground, though formerly it had a good savour.

12 But O thou holy, zealous, devout, righteous, religious one (whoever thou art) that seest evill, or any thing uncleane; do thou sweare, if thou darest, if it be but (I'faith) I'le throw thee to Hell for it (saith the Lord) and laugh at thy destruction.

While Angels (in the forme of men) shall sweare, Heart, Blood, Wounds, and by the Eternall God, &c. in profound purity, and in high Honour, and Majesty.

13 Well! one hint more; there's swearing ignorantly, i'th darke, vainely, and there's swearing i'th light, gloriously.

Well! man of the earth! Lord *Esau*! what hast thou to do with those who sweare upon the former account?

Vengeance is mine, Judgement, Hell, Wrath, &c. all is mine (saith the Lord), dare not thou to set thy foot so impudently and arrogantly upon one step of my Throne: I am Judge myself—Be wise, give over, have done—

14 And as for the latter sort of swearing, thou knowest it not when thou hearest it. It's no new thing for thee to call Christ Beel-zebub, and Beel-zebub Christ; to call a holy Angell a Devill, and a Devill an Angell.

15 I charge thee (in the name of the Eternall God) meddle not with either, let the Tares alone, least thou pull up the Wheat also, woe be to thee if thou dost. Let both alone (I say) least thou shouldest happen of a holy swearing Angell; and take a Lion by the paw to thine owne destruction.

Never was there such a time since the world stood, as now is.

* This will come in request with you next; you may remember that Independency, which is now so hug'd, was counted blasphemy, and banishment was too good for it.

---

11   One who holds extravagant opinions (*OED* n. 1; Coppe's usage is the earliest recorded in *OED*).

12   Tit. 1.15.

Thou knowest not the strange appearances of the Lord, now a daies. Take heed, know thou hast been warned.

5 Admonition to great ones.

16 And whatever thou dost, dip not thy little finger in blood any more, thou art up to the elbowes already: Much sope, yea much nitre, cannot cleanse thee, &c.

Much more have I to say to thee (saith the Lord) but I will do it secretly; and dart a quiver full of arrowes into thy heart; and I will now charge thee.

CHAP. III.

Containing severall dismall, dolefull cryes, and outcries. which pierce the eares and heart of his Excellent Majesty, the King of Kings. And how the King of Heaven chargeth the Great Ones of the Earth.

1 THus saith the Lord, Be silent, O all flesh, before the Lord; be silent; O lofty, haughty, great ones of the Earth.

There are so many Bils of Indictment preferred against thee, that both heaven and earth blush thereat.

How long shall I heare the sighs and groanes, and see the teares of poore widowes; and heare curses in every corner; and all sorts of people crying out oppression, oppression, tyranny, tyranny, the worst of tyranny, unheard of, unnaturall tyranny.

—O my back, my shoulders. O Tythes, Excize, Taxes, Pollings, &c. O Lord! O Lord God Almighty!

What, a little finger heavier then former loynes?

What have I engaged my goods, my life, &c. forsooke my dearest relations, and all for liberty and true freedome, for freedome from oppression, and more laid on my back, &c.

2 Mine eares are filled brim full with confused noise, cries, and outcries; O the innumerable complaints and groanes that pierce my heart (thorow and thorow) O astonishing complaints.

Was ever the like ingratitude heard of since the world stood? what! best friends, surest friends, slighted, scorned, and that which cometh from them (in the basest manner) contemned, and some rewarded with prisons, some with death?

O the abominable perfidiousnesse, falseheartednesse; self-seeking, self-inriching, and Kingdome-depopulating, and devastating, &c.

These, and divers of the same nature, are the cries of *England.*

And can I any longer forbeare?

I have heard, I have heard, the groaning of my people. And now I come to deliver them, saith the Lord.

Woe be to *Pharaoh* King of *Egypt*.

You Great Ones that are not tackt[13] nor tainted, you may laugh and sing, whom this hitteth it hitteth. And it shall hit home.

And this which followeth, all whom it concerneth, by what name or title soever dignified or distinguished.

3 You mostly hate those (called Levellers) who (for ought you know) acted as they did, out of the sincerity, simplicity, and fidelity of their hearts; fearing least they should come under the notion of Covenant-breakers,[14] if they did not so act.

Which if so, then were they most barbarously, unnaturally, hellishly murdered; and they died Martyrs for God and their Countrey.

And their blood cries vengeance, vengeance, in mine ears, saith the Lord.

4 Well! let it be how it will; these * Levellers (so called) you mostly hated, though in outward declarations you owned their Tenents as your owne Principle.

So you mostly hate me (saith the Lord) though in outward declarations you professe me, and seeme to owne me, more then a thousand whom you despise, and account worse than your selves, who are nearer the Kingdome of Heaven then your selve.

You have killed Levellers (so called) you also (with wicked hands) have slain me the Lord of life, whom am now risen, and risen indeed, (and you shall know, and feele it with a witnesse) to Levell you in good earnest. And to lay low all high hils, and every mountaine that is high, and lifted up, &c.

* Once more know, that Sword-levelling is not my principle; I onely pronounce the righteous judgements of the Lord upon earth, as I durst.

5 Well! once more, read *Jam.* 5, 1. to 7——Ye have killed the just——Ye have killed, ye have killed, ye have killed the just.

The blood cryeth in mine eares, Vengeance, vengeance, vengeance, vengeance is mine, I will recompence.

Well! what will you do with *Bray*,[15] and the poore prisoners elsewhere? You know not what you do.

You little know what will become of you.

One of you had best remember your dream about your Fathers Moule[16]——

---

13   'Infected, stained' (*OED* v. 3).

14   Many collectively taken oaths and agreements, such as the Solemn League and Covenant (Sept. 1643–Jan. 1644) and the Leveller Agreements of the People were understood as covenants designed to enhance national and personal reformation.

15   Captain William Bray was the only senior officer to side with the Levellers at the Ware mutiny in 1647. He was subsequently imprisoned and discharged, due to the personal enmity of Col. Henry Lilburne. Coppe refers to Bray's imprisonment in 1649, along with other Leveller leaders. See also Bray's entry in *BDBRSC*.

16   A mole seen on someone's person in a dream betokened illness or a quarrel.

6 Neither do I forget the one hundred spent in superfluous dishes (at your late great *London* Feast,[17] for I know what——) when hundreds of poore wretches dyed with hunger.

I have heard a sound in mine eares, that no lesse then a hundred died in one week, pined, and starved with hunger.

Howle you great ones, for all that feast daies dole, &c. heare your doome.

CHAP. IV.

How the Judge of Heaven and Earth, who judgeth righteous judgement, passeth sentence against all those Great Ones, who (like Oakes and tall Cedars) will now bow. And how he intends to blow them up by the roots.

1 THus saith the Lord: All you tall Cedars, and sturdy Oakes, who bow not down, who bow not down—

This sentence is gone out of my mouth against you, M E N E, M E N E, T E K E L.[18]

Thou art weighed in the ballances, and art found wanting.

God hath numbred thy Kingdome, and finished it.

And thou, and all that joyne with thee, or are (in the least degree) accessary to thy former, or like intended pranks, shall most terribly and most strangely be plagued.

2 There is a little sparke lies under (that huge heap of ashes) all thine honour, pomp, pride, wealth, and riches, which shall utterly consume all that is uppermost, as it is written.

The Lord, the Lord of Hosts, shall send among his fat ones, leanenesse; and under his glory he shall kindle a burning, like the burning of a fire, and the light of *Israel* shall be for a fire, and his holy one for a flame, and it shall burne and devoure his thornes, and his briers in one day.

And shall consume the glory of his Forrest, and of his fruitfull field, both soule and body (*i.e.* this shall be done inwardly and outwardly, and shall be fulfilled both in the history and mystery) and the rest of the trees of his Forrest shall be few, that a childe may write them.

And the Lord, the Lord of Hoasts, shall lop the bough with terror, and the high ones of stature shall be hewen down, and the haughty shall be humbled, And he shall cut down the thickets of the Forrest with iron, and *Lebanon* shall fall by a mighty one, *Isa.* 10.

3 Behold, behold, I have told you.

Take it to heart, else you'l repent every veine of your heart.

For your own sakes take heed.

Its my last warning.

For the cryes of the poore, for the oppression of the needy. For the horrid insolency of proud man, who will dare to sit in my throne, and judge unrighteous judgement.

Who will dare to touch mine Annoynted, and do my Prophets harme.

For these things sake (now) am I arrisen, saith the Lord,

In Auxilium Patris כף[19]

17　Banquet at which City aldermen entertained Commonwealth officials and commanding officers after the decimation of the Levellers at Burford.
18　Dan. 5.26–27.　19　'Into the help of the Father.' See p. 75, n. 4.

CHAP. V.

1 **O***London, London*, my bowels are rolled together (in me) for thee, and my compassions within me, are kindled towards thee.

And now I onely tell thee, that it was not in vaine that this forme hath been brought so farre to thee, to proclaime the day of the Lord throughout thy streets, day and night, for twelve or thirteen dayes together.

And that I have been made such a signe, and a wonder before many of thine Inhabitants faces.

2 Many of them (among other strange exploits) beholding me, fall down flat at the feet of creeples, beggars, lazars, kissing their feet, and resigning up my money to them; being severall times over-emptied of money, that I have not had one penny left, and yet have recruited againe-

3 And now my hearts! you have been forwardly in all the appearances of God,

There is a strange one (now on foot) judge it not, least you be judged with a vengeance.

4 Turne not away your eyes from it, least you (to your torment) heare this voyce—*I was a Stranger, and ye tooke me not in.*[20]

Well I bow down before Eternall Majesty, who is universall love, bow down to equality, or free community, that no more of your blood be spilt; that pride, arrogance, covetuousnesse, malice, hypocrisie, self-seeking, &c. may live no longer. Else I tremble at whats comming upon you.

Remember you have been warned with a witnesse.

Deare hearts Farewell.

CHAP. VI.

A terrible word, and fatall blow from the Lord, upon the gathered Churches (so called) especially upon those that are stiled Anabaptists.

1 **H**E that hath an eare to heare, let him hear what the Spirit saith against the Churches.

Thus saith the Lord: Woe be to thee * *Bethaven*, who callest thy self by the name * *Bethel*, it shall be more tollerable (now in the day of judgement, for *Tyre* and *Sydon*⟨⟩), for those whom thou accountest, and callest Heathens, then for thee.

* The house of vanity.
* The house of God.

---

20   Matt. 25, 43.

2 And thou proud *Lucifer*, who exaltest thy self above all the Stars of God in heaven, shalt be brought down into hell; it shall be more tollerable for *Sodom* and *Gomorrah*, for drunkards and whoremongers, then for thee. Publicans and Harlots shall, Publicans and Harlots do sooner enter into the Kingdome of heaven, then you.

I'le give thee this fatall blow, and leave thee.

3 Thou hast affronted, and defied the Almighty, more then the vilest of men (upon the face of the earth) and that so much the more, by how much the more thou takest upon thee the name of Saint, and assumest it to thy self onely, damning all those that are not of thy Sect.

4 Wherefore be it knowne to all Tongues, Kin⟨d⟩reds, Nations, and languages upon earth, That my most Excellent Majesty, the King of glory, the Eternall God, who dwelleth in the forme of the Writer of this Roll (among many other strange and great exploits) hath i'th open streets, with his hand fiercely stretcht out, his hat cockt up, his eyes set as if they would sparkle out; and with a mighty loud voyce charged 100. of Coaches, 100. of men and women of the greater ranke, and many notorious, deboist,[21] swearing, roystering roaring Cavalliers (so called) and other wilde sparks of the Gentry: And have proclaimed the notable day of the Lord to them, and that through the streets of the great Citie, and in Southwark; Many times great multitudes following him up and down, and this for the space of 12. or 13. dayes: And yet (all this while) not one of them lifting up one finger, not touching one haire of his head, or laying one hand on his raiment.

But many, yea many notorious vile ones, in the esteeme of men (yea of great quality among men) trembling and bowing to the God of heaven, &c.

But when I came to proclaim (also) the great day of the Lord (among you) O ye carnall Gospellers.

The Devill (in you) roared out, who was tormented to some purpose, though not before his time.

He there shewed both his phangs and pawes, and would have torn me to pieces, and have eaten me up. Thy pride, envy, malice, arrogance, &c. was powred out like a river of Brimstone, crying out, a Blasphemer, a Blasphemer, away with him: At length threatning me, and being at last raving mad, some tooke hold of my Cloak on one side, some on another, endeavouring to throw me from the place where I stood (to proclaime his Majesties message) making a great uproar in a great congregation of people: Till at length I wrapt up my self in silence (for a season) for the welfavour'd harlots confusion, &c.

And to thine eternall shame and damnation (O mother of witchcrafts, who dwellest in gathered Churches) let this be told abroad: And let her F L E S H be burnt with F I R E.

Amen, Halelujah.

FINIS.

---

21   Debauched (*OED* adj. 1).

A SECOND
Fiery Flying Roule:
TO

All the Inhabitants of the earth; specially to the rich ones.

OR,

A sharp sickle, thrust in, to gather the clusters of the vines of the earth, because her grapes are (*now*) fully ripe. And the great, notable, terrible, (yet glorious and joyfull) day of the LORD is come; even the Day of the Lords Recovery and Discovery. Wherein the secrets of all hearts are ripped up; and the secret villanies of the holy Whore, the well-favoured Harlot (who scornes carnall Ordinances, and is mounted up into the notion of Spirtualls) is discovered: And even her flesh burning with unquenchable fire. And the pride of all glory staining.

Together with a narration of various, strange, yet true stories: And severall secret mysteries, and mysterious secrets, which never were afore written or printed.

As also, That most strange Appearance of eternall Wisdome, and unlimited Almightinesse, in choosing base things: And why, and how he chooseth them. And how (most miraculously) they (even base things) have been, are, and shall be made fiery Chariots, to mount up some into divine glory, and unspotted beauty and majesty. And the glory that ariseth up from under them is confounding both Heaven and Earth. With a word (by way of preface) dropping in as an in-let to the new Hierusalem.

These being some things of what are experimented.

Per AUXILIUM PATRIS כף[22]

Howle, rich men, for the miseries that are (just now) coming upon you, the rust of your silver is rising up in judgment against you, burning your flesh like fire, &c.

And now I am come to recover my corn, my wooll, and my flax, which thou hast (theevishly and hoggishly) detained from me, the Lord God Almighty, in the poore and needy.

Also howle thou holy Whore, thou well-favour'd Harlot: for God, and I, have chosen base things to confound thee, and things that are.

And the secrets of all hearts are now revealing by my Gospell, who am a stranger, and besides my selfe, to God, for your sakes. Wherefore receive me, &c. els expect that dismall doom, Depart from me ye cursed, I was a stranger, and ye took me not in.

Printed in the Yeer 1649.

---

22   See above, p. 75, n. 4.

Chap. I.

The Authors Commission to write, a terrible wo denounced against those that slight the Roule. The Lords claime to all things; together with a hint of a two-fold recovery, wherethrough the most hypocriticall heart shall be ript up.

1. THe Word of the Lord came expressely to me, saying, write, write, write.

2. And ONE stood by me, and pronounced all these words to me with his mouth, and I wrote them with ink in this paper.

3. Wherefore in the Name and Power of the eternall God, I charge thee burn it not, tear it not, for if thou dost, I will tear thee to peices (saith the Lord) and none shall be able to deliver thee; for (as I live) it is the day of my vengeance.

4. Read it through, and laugh not at it; if thou dost I'l destroy thee, and laugh at thy destruction.

5. Thus saith the Lord, though I have been a great while in coming, yet I am now come to recover my corn, and my wool, and my flax, &c. and to discover thy lewdnesse, *Hos. 2.*

Thou art cursed with a curse, for thou hast robbed me (saith the Lord) of my corn, my wool, my flax, &c. Thou hast robbed me of my Tythes, for the Tythes are mine, *Mal. 3.* And the beasts on a thousand hills, yea all thy baggs of money, hayricks, horses, yea all that thou callest thine own are mine.

6. And now I am come to recover them all at thy hands, saith the Lord, for it is the day of my recovery, and the day of my discovery, &c. And there is a two-fold recovery of two sorts of things, inward, and outward, or civil, and religious, and through both, a grand discovery of the secrets of the most hypocriticall heart, and a ripping up of the bowels of the wel-favoured Harlot, the holy Whore, who scorns that which is called prophanesse, wickednesse, loosenesse, or libertinisme, and yet her self is the mother of witchcrafts, and of all the abominations of the earth.

But more of this hereafter.

7. For the present, I say, Thus saith the Lord, I am come to recover all my outward, or civill rights, or goods, which thou callest thine own.

Chap. II.

How the Lord will recover his outward things [things of this life] as Money, Corn, &c. and for whom, and how they shall be plagued who detaine them as their owne. Wherein also are some mysticall hints concerning Michaelmasse day, and the Lords day following it this year, as also of the Dominicall letter D.²³ this year.

1. ANd the way that I will walk in (in this great notable and terrible day of the Lord) shall be thus, I will either (strangely, & terribly, to thy torment) inwardly, or els (in a way that I will not acquaint thee with) outwardly, demand all mine, and will say on this wise.

---

23   But Coppe will in fact discuss the 'Dominicall letter G.' (see below, p. 93).

2. Thou hast many baggs of money, and behold now I come as a thief in the night, with my sword drawn in my hand, and like a thief as I am,—I say deliver your purse, deliver sirrah! deliver or I'l cut thy throat!

3. Deliver M Y money to such as * poor despised *Maul* of Dedington in Oxonshire,[24] whom some devills incarnate (insolently and proudly, in way of disdaine) cry up for a fool, some for a knave, and mad-man, some for an idle fellow, and base rogue, and some (true lier then they are aware of) cry up for a Prophet, and some arrant fools (though exceeding wise) cry up for more knave then foole, &c. when as indeed, ther's pure royall blood runs through his veins, and he's no lesse then a Kings Son, though not one of you who are devills incarnate; & have your eyes blinded with the God of this world, know it.

For some speciall reason this poor wretch is here instanced.

4. I say (once more) deliver, deliver, my money which thou hast to him, and to poor creeples, lazars, yea to rogues, thieves, whores, and cut-purses, who are flesh of thy flesh, and every whit as good as thy self in mine eye, who are ready to starve in plaguy Goals, and nasty dungeons, or els by my selfe, saith the Lord, I will torment thee day and night, inwardly, or outwardly, or both waies, my little finger shall shortly be heavier on thee, especially on thee thou holy, righteous, religious *Appropriator*, then my loynes were on *Pharoah* and the Egyptians in time of old; you shall weep and howl for the miseries that are suddenly coming upon you; for your riches are corrupted, &c. and whilst impropriated, appropriated the plague of God is in them.

5. The plague of God is in your purses, barns, houses, horses, murrain will take your hogs, O (ye fat swine of the earth) who shall shortly go to the knife, and be hung up i'th roof, except—blasting, mill-dew, locusts, caterpillars, yea fire your houses and goods, take your corn and fruit, the moth your garments, and the rot your sheep, did you not see my hand, this last year, stretched out?

You did not see.

My hand is stretched out still.

Your gold and silver, though you can't see it, is cankered, the rust of them is a witnesse against you, and suddainly, suddainly, suddainly, because by the eternall God, my self, its the dreadful day of Judgement, saith the Lord, shall eat your flesh as it were fire, *Jam.* 5. 1. to 7.

The rust of your silver, I say, shall eat your flesh as it were fire.

6. As sure as it did mine the very next day after *Michael* the Arch-Angel's; that mighty Angel, who just now fights that terrible battell in heaven with the great Dragon.

And is come upon the earth also, to rip up the hearts of all bag-bearing Judases. On this day purses shall be cut, guts let out, men stabb'd to the heart, womens bellies ript up, specially gammer Demases,[25] who have forsaken us,

---

24 Deddington parish register records the burial of Roger Maule on 25 April 1648.
25 Gamesome, playful, merry. Coppe is also suggesting wantonness. The Biblical story here is from 2 Tim. 4.10–14.

and imbraced this wicked world, and married *Alexander* the Coppersmith, who hath done me much evill. The Lord reward him, I wish him hugely well, as he did me, on the next day after *Michael* the Arch-Angel.

Which was the Lords day I am sure on't, look in your Almanacks,[26] you shall find it was the Lords day, or els I would you could; when you must, when you see it, you will find the Dominicall letter to be G. and there are many words that begin with G. at this time [GIVE] begins with G. give, give, give, give up, give up your houses, horses, goods, gold, Lands, give up, account nothing your own, have ALL THINGS common, or els the plague of God will rot and consume all that you have.

By God, by my self, saith the Lord, its true.

Come! give all to the poore and follow me, and you shall have treasure in heaven. Follow me, who was numbred among transgressors, and whose visage was more marr'd then any mans, follow me.

CHAP. III.

A strange, yet most true story: under which is couched that Lion, whose roaring shall make all the beasts of the field tremble, and all the Kingdoms of the earth quake. Wherein also (in part) the subtilty of the wel-favoured Harlot is discovered, and her flesh burning with that fire, which shall burne down all Churches, except that of the first Born, &c.

1. FOllow me, who, last Lords day Septem. 30. 1649. met him in open field, a most strange deformed man, clad with patcht clouts:[27] who looking wishly[28] on me, mine eye pittied him; and my heart, or the day of the Lord, which burned as an oven in me, set my tongue on flame to speak to him, as followeth.

2. How now friend, art thou poore?

He answered, yea Master very poore.

Whereupon my bowels trembled within me, and quivering fell upon the worm-eaten chest, [my corps I mean] that I could not hold a joynt still.

And my great love within me, (who is the great God within that chest, or corps) was burning hot toward him; and made the lock-hole of the chest, to wit, the mouth of the corps, again to open: Thus.

Art poor?

Yea, very poor, said he.

Whereupon the strange woman who, flattereth with her lips, and is subtill of heart, said within me,

It's a poor wretch, give him two-pence.

But my EXCELLENCY and MAIESTY (in me) scorn'd her words, confounded her language; and kickt her out of his presence.

---

26   See p. 26.
27   Heavily-repaired clothing; a garment made of sewn-together rags.
28   'Intently' (*OED*, adv.).

3. But immediately the W EL-FAVOURED HARLOT [whom I carried not upon my horse behind me] but who rose up in me, said:

, Its a poor wretch give his 6.d. and that's enough for a Squire or Knight, to give to one , poor body.

, Besides [saith the holy Scripturian Whore] hee's worse then an Infidell that provides not , for his own Family.

, True love begins at home, &c.

, Thou, and thy Family are fed, as the young ravens strangely, though thou hast been , a constant Preacher, yet thou hast abhorred both tythes and hire; and thou knowest not , aforehand, who will give thee the worth of a penny.

, Have a care of the main chance.

4. And thus she flattereth with her lips, and her words being smoother then oile; and her lips dropping as the honey comb, I was fired to hasten my hand into my pocket; and pulling out a shilling, said to the poor wretch, give me six pence, heer's a shilling for thee.

He answered, I cannot, I have never a penny.

Whereupon I said, I would fain have given thee something if thou couldst have changed my money.

Then saith he, God blesse you.

Whereupon with much reluctancy, with much love, and with amazement [of the right stamp] I turned my horse head from him, riding away. But a while after I was turned back [being advised by my Demilance[29]] to wish him cal for six pence, which I would leave at the next Town at ones house, which I thought he might know [*Saphira* like] keeping back part.[30]

But [as God judged me] I, as she, was struck down dead.

And behold the plague of God fell into my pocket; and the rust of my silver rose up in judgement against me, and consumed my flesh as with fire: so that I, and my money perisht with me

I being cast into that lake of fire and brimstone.

And all the money I had about me to a penny [though I thought through the instigation of my *quondam Mistris* to have reserved some, having rode about 8. miles, not eating one mouth-full of bread that day, and had drunk but one small draught of drink; and had between 8. or 9. miles more to ride, ere I came to my journeys end: my horse being lame, the waies dirty, it raining all the way, and I not knowing what extra-ordinary occasion I might have for money.] Yet [I say] the rust of my silver did so rise up in judgement against me, and burnt my flesh like fire: and the 5. of *James* thundered such an alarm in mine ears, that I was fain to cast all I had into the hands of him, whose visage was more marr'd then any mans that ever I saw.

This is a true story, most true in the history.

Its true also in the mystery.

And there are deep ones coucht under it, for its a shadow of various, glorious, [though strange] good things to come.

---

29   Literally a light horseman; another name for the inner voice of the 'well-favoured harlot' who
       seems to Coppe to be a traveling companion.
30   See Acts 5.1–11.

7. Wel! to return—after I had thrown my rusty canker'd money into the poor wretches hands, I rode away from him, being filled with trembling, joy, and amazement, feeling the sparkles of a great glory arising up from under these ashes.

After this, I was made [by that divine power which dwelleth in this Ark, or chest] to turn my horse head—whereupon I beheld this poor deformed wretch, looking earnestly after me: and upon that, was made to put off my hat, and bow to him seven times, and was [at that strange posture] filled with trembling and amazement, some sparkles of glory arising up also from under this; as also from under these ashes, yet I rode back once more to the poor wretch, saying, because I am a King, I have done this, but you need not tell any one.

The day's our own.

This was done on the last L O R D S D A Y, Septem. 30. in the year 1649. which is the year of the Lords recompences for Zion, and the day of his vengeance, the dreadfull day of Judgement. But I have done [for the present] with this story, for it is the later end of the year 1649.

C H A P. IV.

How the Author hath been set as a signe and a wonder, as well as most of the Prophets formerly. As also what strange postures the divine Majesty that dwells in his forme, hath set the forme in, with the most strange and various effects thereof upon the Spectators. Also his Communion with the spirits of just men made perfect, and with God the Judge of all, hinted at.

1. IT is written in your Bibles, Behold I and the children whom the Lord hath given me, are for signs and for wonders in Israel, from the Lord of Hoasts, which dwelleth in Mount Sion, *Isa.* 8.18.

And amongst those who were set thus, *Ezekiel* seems to be higher then the rest by the shoulders upwards, and was more seraphicall then his Predecessors, yet he was the son of *Buzi* (*Ezek.* 1.) which being interpreted is the son of contempt; it pleases me [right well] that I am his brother, a sonne of *Buzi*.

2. He saw [and I in him see] various strange visions; and he was, and I am set in severall strange postures.

Amongst many of his pranks—this was one, he shaves all the hair off his head: and off his beard, then weighs them in a pair of scales; burns one part of them in the fire, another part hee smites about with a knife, another part thereof he scatters in the wind, and a few he binds up in his skirts, &c. and this not in a corner, or in a chamber, but in the midst of the streets of the great City Hierusalem, and the man all this while neither mad nor drunke, &c. *Ezek.* 5. 1. 2. 3, 4. &c. as also in severall other Chapt. amongst the rest, Chap. 12. 3. &c. Chap. 4. 3. Chap. 24. 3. to the end. This *Ezekiel* [to whose spirit I am come, and to an innumerable company of Angels, and to God the Judge of all.]

3. [I say] this great Courtier, in the high Court of the highest heavens, is the son of *Buzi*, a child of contempt on earth, and set as a sign and wonder (as was *Hosea*, who went in to a

whore, &c.) *Hos*. 2. when he (I say) was playing some of his pranks, the people said to him, wilt thou not tell us what these things are to us, that thou dost so, *Ezek*. 24.19. with the 3. verse and so forwards, when he was strangely acted by that omnipotency dwelling in him; and by that eternall, immortall, INVISIBLE (indeed) Majesty, the onely wise God, who dwells in this visible forme, the writer of this Roule, [who to his joy] is numbred amongst transgressors.

4. The same most excellent Majesty (in this forme) hath set the Forme in many strange Postures lately, to the joy and refreshment of some, both acquaintances and strangers, to the wonderment and amazement of others, to the terrour and affrightment of others; and to the great torment of the chiefest of the Sects of Professours; who have gone about to shake off their plagues if they could, some by crying out he's mad, he's drunk, he's faln from grace, and some by scandalising, &c. and onely one, whom I told of, by threats of caneing or cudgelling, who meeting me full with face, was ashamed and afraid to look on me, &c.

5. But to wave all this.

Because the Sun begins to peep out, and its a good while past day-break, I'l creep forth (a little) into the mystery of the former history, and into the in-side of that strange out-side businesse.

Chap. V.

The Authors strange and lofty carriage towards great ones, and his most lowly carriage towards Beggars, Rogues, and Gypseys: together with a large declaration what glory shall rise up from under all this ashes. The most strange, secret, terrible, yet most glorious design of God, in choosing base things to confound things that are. And how. A most terrible vial powred out upon the well-favour'd Harlot, and how the Lord is bringing into contempt not only honorable persons, with a vengeance, but all honorable, holy things also. Wholsome advice, with a terrible threat to the Formalists.[31] How base things have confounded base things; and how base things have been a fiery Chariot to mount the Author up into divine glory, &c. And how his wife is, and his life is in, that beauty which makes all visible beauty seem meer deformity.

1. ANd because I am found of those that sought me not. And because some say, wilt thou not tell us what these things are to us, that thou dost so?

Wherefore waving my charging so many Coaches, so many hundreds of men and women of the greater rank, in the open streets, with my hand stretched out, my hat cock't up, staring on them as if I would look thorough them, gnashing with my teeth at some of them, and day and night with a huge loud voice proclaiming the day of the Lord throughout London and Southwark, and leaving divers other exploits, &c. It is my good will and pleasure [only] to single out the former story with its Parallels.

2. [*Viz.*] in clipping, hugging, imbracing, kissing a poore deformed wretch in London, who

---

31   Those obsessed with forms of worship and church governance, to the detriment of the spirit (*OED* A. n. 3b).

had no more nose on his face, then I have on the back of my hand, [but only two little holes in the place where the nose uses to stand.]

And no more eyes to be seen then on the back of my hand, and afterwards running back to him in a strange manner, with my money giving it to him, to the joy of some, to the afrightment and wonderment of other Spectators.

3. As also in falling down flat upon the ground before rogues, beggars, cripples, halt, maimed; blind, &c. kissing the feet of many, rising up againe, and giving them money, &c. Besides that notorious businesse with the Gypseys and Goalbirds (mine own brethren and sisters, flesh of my flesh, and as good as the greatest Lord in England) at the prison in Southwark neer S. *Georges* Church.

Now that which rises up from under all this heap of ashes, will fire both heaven and earth; the one's ashamed, and blushes already, the other reels to and fro, like a drunken man.

4. Wherefore thus saith the Lord, Hear O heavens, and hearken O earth, Ile overturne, overturne, overturne, I am now ⟨sta⟩ining the pride of all glory, and bringing into contempt all the honourable of the earth, *Esa.* 23. 9. not only honourable persons, (who shall come down with a vengeance, if they bow not to universall love the eternall God, whose service is perfect freedome) but honorable things, as Elderships, Pastorships, Fellowships, Churches, Ordinances, Prayers, &c. Holinesses, Righteousnesses, Religions of all sorts, of the highest strains; yea, Mysterians, and Spirituallists, who scorne carnall Ordinances, &c.

I am about my act, my strange act, my worke, my strange work, that w⟨h⟩osoever hears of it, both his ears shall tingle.

5. I am confounding, plaguing, tormenting nice, demure, barren *Mical*,[32] with *Davids* unseemly carriage, by skipping, leaping, dancing, like one of the fools; vile, base fellowes, shamelessely, basely, and uncovered too, before handmaids,—

Which thing was S. *Pauls* Tutor, or else it prompted him to write, God hath chosen BASE things, and things that are despised, to confound—the things are.—

Well! family duties are no base things, they ar⟨e⟩ things that ARE: Churches, Ordinances, &c, are no BASE things, though ind⟨e⟩ed Presbyterian Churches begun to live i'th womb, but died there, and rot and stink there to the death of the mother and child. Amen. Not by the Devill, but [by * God] it's true.

* That's a base thing.

Grace before meat and after meat, are no BASE things; these are things that ARE. But how long Lord, holy and true, &c.

Fasting for strife and debate, and to smite with the fist of wickednesse,— (and not for taking off heavy burthens, breaking every yoke, *Esa.* 58.) and Thanksgiving daies for killing of men for money, are no BASE things, these are things that ARE.

☞ Starting up into the notion of spirituals, scorning History, speaking nothing but Mystery, crying down carnall ordinances, &c. is a fine thing among

---

32   Michal was David's wife — 2 Sam. 6.16–23; 1 Chr. 15.29.

many, it's no base thing (now adaies) though it be a cloak for covetousnesse, yea, though it be to maintain pride and pomp; these are no base things.

6. These are things that A R E, and must be confounded by B A S E things, which *S.Paul* saith, not God hath connived at, winked at, permitted, tolerated, but God hath C H O S E N &c. B A S E things.

What base things? Why *Mical* took *David* for a base fellow, and thought he had chosen B A S E things, in dancing shamelessly uncovered before handmaids.

And barren, demure *Mical* thinks (for I know her heart saith the Lord) that I chose base things when I sate downe, and eat and drank around on the ground with Gypseys, and clip't, hug'd and kiss'd them, putting my hand in their bosomes, loving the she-Gipsies dearly. O base*!* saith mincing *Mical*, the least spark of modesty would be as red as crimson or scarlet, to hear this.

I warrant me, *Mical* could better have borne this if I had done it to Ladies: so I can for a need, if it be my will, and that in the height of honor and majesty, without sin. But at that time when I was hugging the Gipsies, I abhorred the thoughts of Ladies, their beauty could not bewitch mine eyes, or snare my lips, or intangle my hands in their bosomes; yet I can if it be my will, kisse and hug Ladies, and love my neighbours wife as my selfe, without sin.

7. But thou Precisian,[33] by what name or title soever dignified, or distinguished, do but blow a kisse to thy neighbours wife, or dare to think of darting one glance of one of thine eyes towards her, if thou dar'st.

It's meat and drink to an Angel [who knows none evill, no sin] to sweare a full mouth'd oath, *Rev.* 10. 6. It's joy to *Nehemiah* to come in like a mad-man, and pluck folkes hair off their heads, and curse like a devill—and make them swear by *God,—Nehem.* 13. Do thou O holy man [who knowest evill] lift up thy finger against a Jew, a Church-member, cal thy brother fool, and with a peace-cods[34] on him; or swear I faith, if thou dar'st, if thou dost, thou shalt howl in hell for it, and I will laugh at thy calamity, &c.

8. But once more hear O heavens, hearken O earth, Thus saith the Lord, I have chosen such base things, to confound things that are, that the ears of those [who scorn to be below Independents, yea the ears of many who scorn to be so low as carnall Ordinances, &c.] that hear thereof shall tingle.

9. Hear one word more [whom it hitteth it hitteth] give over thy base nasty stinking, formall grace before meat, and after meat [I call it so, though thou hast rebaptized it—] give over thy stinking family duties, and thy Gospell Ordinances as thou callest them; for under them all there lies snapping, snarling, biting, besides covetousnesse, horrid hypocrisie, envy, malice, evill surmising.

10. Give over, give over, or if nothing els will do it, I'l at a time, when thou least of all thinkest of it, make thine own child the fruit of thy loines, in whom thy soul delighted, lie with a whore—before thine eyes: That that plaguy holinesse and righteousnesse of thine might be confounded by that base thing. And thou be plagued back again into thy mothers

---

33   One who rigidly observes rules and forms. In the seventeenth century the word was
      synonymous with Puritanism.
34   'A term of mockery' (*OED* n. 2).

womb, the womb of eternity: That thou maist become a little child, and let the mother *Eternity, Almightinesse,* who is universall love, and whose service is perfect freedome, dresse thee, and undresse thee, swadle, unswadle, bind, loose, lay thee down, take thee up, &c.

—And to such a little child, undressing is as good as dressing, foul cloaths, as good as fair cloaths—he knows no evill, &c.—And shall see evill no more,—but he must first lose all his righteousnesse, every bit of his holinesse, and every crum of his Religion, and be plagued, and confounded [by base things] into nothing.

By base things which God and I have chosen.

11. And yet I shew you a more excellent way, when you have past this.—In a word, my plaguy, filthy, nasty holinesse hath been confounded by base things. And then [behold I shew you a mystery, and put forth a riddle to you] by base things, base things so called have been confounded also; and thereby have I been confounded into eternall Majesty, unspeakable glory, my life, my self.

12. Ther's my riddle, but because neither all the Lords of the Philistins, no nor my Delilah her self can read it,

I'l read it my self, I'l [only] hint it thus.

Kisses are numbered amongst transgressors—base things[35]—well! by base hellish swearing, and cursing, [as I have accounted it in the time of my fleshly holinesse] and by base impudent kisses [as I then accounted them] my plaguy holinesse hath been confounded, and thrown into the lake of fire and brimstone.

And then again, by wanton kisses, kissing hath been confounded; and externall kisses, have been made the fiery chariots, to mount me swiftly into the bosom of him whom my soul loves, [his excellent Majesty, the King of glory.]

Where I have been, where I have been, where I have been, hug'd, imbrac't, and kist with the kisses of his mouth, whose loves are better then wine, and have been utterly overcome therewith, beyond expression, beyond admiration.

13. Again, Lust is numbered amongst transgressors—a base thing.—

Now faire objects attract Spectators eyes.

And beauty is the father of lust or love.

Well! I have gone along the streets impregnant with that child [lust] which a particular beauty had begot: but coming to the place, where I expected to have been delivered, I have providentially met there a company of devills in appearance, though Angels with golden vialls, in reality, powring out full vialls, of such odious abominable words, that are not lawfull to be uttered.

Words enough to deafen the ears of plaguy holinesse. And such horrid abominable actions, the sight whereof were enough to put out holy mans eyes, and to strike him stark dead, &c.

These base things (I say) words and actions, have confounded and plagued to death, the child in the womb that I was so big of.

14. And by, and through these B A S E things [as upon the wings of the wind] have I been carried up into the arms of my love, which is invisible glory, eternall Majesty, purity it self,

---

35   Latin for kisses is *basia.*

unspotted beauty, even that beauty which maketh all other beauty but meer uglinesse, when set against it, &c.

Yea, could you imagine that the quintessence of all visible beauty, should be extracted and made up into one huge beauty, it would appear to be meer deformity to that beauty, which through BASE things I have been lifted up into.

Which transcendent, unspeakable, unspotted beauty, is my crown and joy, my life and love: and though I have chosen, and cannot be without BASE things, to confound some in mercy, some in judgment, Though also I have concubines without number, which I cannot be without, yet this is my spouse, my love, my dove, my fair one.

Now I proceed to that which followes.

CHAP. VI.

Great ones must bow to the poorest peasants, or els they must rue for it.

No materiall sword, or humane power whatsoever, but the pure spirit of universall Love, which is the eternall God, can break the neck of tyranny, oppression, abominable pride, and cruell murder. A Catalogue of severall judgements recited—as so many warning-pieces to Appropriators, Impropriators, and anti-free-communicants, &c. The strongest, yea purest propriety that may plead most priviledge shall suddainly be confounded.

1. A Gain, thus saith the Lord, I in thee, who am eternall Majesty, bowed down thy form, to deformity.

And I in thee, who am durable riches, commanded thy perishable silver to the poore, &c. Thus saith the Lord,

Kings, Princes, Lords, great ones, must bow to the poorest Peasants; rich men must stoop to poor rogues, or else they'l rue for it.

This must be done two waies.

You shall have one short dark hint.

Wil.Sedgewick[36] [in me] bowed to that poor deformed ragged wretch, that he might inrich him, in impoverishing himself.

He shall gaine him, and be no great loser himself, &c.

2. Well! we must all bow, and bow, &c. And MEUM[37] must be converted.—It is but yet a very little while; and you shall not say that ought that you possesse is your own, &c. read *Act.* 2. towards the end, chap. 4. 31. to the end, with chap. 5. 1. 2. to the 12.

It's but yet a little while, and the strongest, yea, the seemingly purest propriety, which may mostly plead priviledge and Prerogative from Scripture, and carnall reason; shall be confounded and plagued into community and universality. And ther's a most glorious design

---

36   William Sedgwick (1609–1663/4), minister at Ely, fervent spiritualist who influenced Laurence Clarkson, criticized the New Model Army commanders for selfish politics, sympathized with Leveller franchise demands, but in *The Spiritual Madman* (1648) recommended a restoration of the king in a commonwealth where all property would be shared.

37   Latin for 'mine.'

in it: and equality, community, and universall love; shall be in request to the utter confounding of abominable pride, murther, hypocrisie, tyranny and oppression, &c. The necks whereof can never be chopt off, or these villaines ever hang'd up, or cut off by materiall sword, by humane might, power, or strength, but by the pure spirit of universall love, who is the God whom all the world [of Papists, Protestants, Presbyterians, Independents, Spirituall Notionists, &c.] ignorantly worship.

3. The time's coming, yea now is, that you shall not dare to say, your silver or gold is your owne.

It's the Lords.

You shall not say it is your own, least the rust thereof rise up in judgement against you, and burn your flesh as it were fire.

Neither shall you dare to say, your oxe, or your asse is your own.

It's the Lords.

And if the Lord have need of an asse he shall have him.

Or if two of his Disciples should come to unloose him, I wil not [for a 1000. worlds] call them thieves, least the asse should slat[38] my braines out, my bread is not mine own, it's the Lords.

* A rogo, to ask   And if a poor * Rogue should ask for it—the Lord hath need of it—he should have it, least it should stick in my throat and choak me one way or other.

4. Once more, Impropriators![39] Appropriators! go to, weep and howl, &c. *Jam.* 5. 1. to the 7. the rust of your silver shall rise (is rising up) against you, burning your flesh as it were fire, &c.

That is (in a word) a secret, yet sharp, terrible, unexpected, and unsupportable plague, is rising up from under all, that you call your own, when you go to count your money, you shall verily think the Devill stands behind you, to tear you in pieces: You shall not put bread in your mouthes, but the curse shall come along with it, and choke you one way or other. All your former sweets shall be mingled with gall and wormwood: I give you but a hint.

It's the last daies.

5. Well! do what you will or can, know you have been warned. It is not for nothing, that I the Lord with a strong wind cut off (as with a sickle) the fullest, fairest ears of corn this harvest, and drop't them on purpose for the poore, who had as much right to them, as those that (impudently and wickedly, theevishly and hoggishly) stile themselves the owners of the Land.

6. It's not for nothing that such various strange kinds of worms, grubs, and caterpillars (my strong host, saith the Lord of Hosts) have been sent into some graine: Neither is in vain, that I the Lord sent the rot among so many sheep this last yeer; if they had been resign'd to me, and you had kept a true communion, they had not been given up to that plague.

---

38   To knock forcefully, beat or strike.
39   One who receives the funds of a church benefice.

7. It's not in vain that so many towns and houses have been lately fired over the heads of the Inhabitants: Neither is it in vain, that I the Lord fired the barning and ricks of a Miser in Worcestershire (this yeer) the very same day that he brought in his own, as he accounted it.

On the very same day (I say) his barning and ricks were fired down to the very ground, though multitudes of very expert men in the imployment came to quench it.

Of this the writer of this Scroule was an eye-witnesse.

8. Impropriators! Appropriators! Misers! a fair warning: More of you shall be served with the same sawce.

Others of you I'le deal withall in another way more terrible then this, saith the Lord, till you resign.—

Misers! 'specially you holy Scripturian Misers, when you would say grace before and after meat, read *James* 5. 1. to 7. & *Hosea* 2. 8,9,10.

C H A P. VII.

A further discovery of the subtilty of the wel-favour'd Harlot, with a Parley
between her and the Spirit: As also the horrid villany (that lies hid under
her smooth words, in pleading against the Letter and History, and for the
Spirit and Mystery, and all for her owne ends) detected. Also upon what
account the spirit is put, and upon what account the Letter. Also what the
true Communion, and what the true breaking of bread is.

1. **B**Ut now me thinks (by this time) I see a brisk, spruce, neat, self-seeking, fine finiking fellow, (who scornes to be either Papist, Protestant, Presbyterian, Independent, or Anabaptist) I mean the Man of Sin, who worketh with all deceiveablenesse of unrighteousnesse, 2 *Thes.* 2.

Crying down * carnall ordinances, and crying up † the Spirit: cunningly seeking and setting up himself thereby.

I say, I see him, and have ript up the very secrets of his heart (saith the Lord) as also of that mother of mischief, that wel-favour'd Harlot, who both agree in one, and say on this wise to me.

2. 'Ah! poor deluded man, thou hast spoken of the Wisdome of God in a 'mystery, and thou hast seen all the history of the Bible mysteriz'd.

'O fool! who hath bewitcht thee, art thou so foolish as to begin in the 'spirit, and wilt thou now be made perfect in the flesh? keep thee to the spirit, 'go not back to the letter, keep thee to the mystery, go not back to the history.

'What? why dost talk so much of *James* 5. and *Hosea* 2. those words are 'to be taken in the Mystery, not in the History: They are to be taken in the 'Spirit, not as they ⟨li⟩e in the Letter.

* Downe
they must,
but no thanks
to him.
† Up it must,
but no thanks
to him.

Thus you have a hint of the neat young mans, and of the well-favour'd Harlots language.

3. But now behold I am filled with the Holy Ghost, and am resolv'd [*Acts* 13.8,9,&c.] to set mine eyes on her and him, (who are no more twaine, but one) and say:

'O full of all subtilty and mischief, thou child of the Devil, thou enemy of all righteousnesse, 'wilt thou not cease to pervert the right ways of the Lord?

'Be it known to thee, o thou deceitfull tongue, that I have begun in the spirit, and will 'end in the spirit: I am joyn'd to the Lord, and am one spirit. The spirit's my joy, my life, my 'strength; I will not let it go, it's my delight.

'The mystery is mine, [mostly] that which I most delight in, that's the Jewel. The historie's 'mine also, that's the Cabinet. For the Jewels sake I wil not leave the Cabinet, though indeed 'it's nothing to me, but when thou for thine own ends, stand'st in competition with me for it.

'Strength is mine, so is weaknesse also.

4. I came by water and blood, not by blood only, but by blood and water also.

The inwardnesse is mostly mine, my prime delight is there; the outwardnesse is mine also, when thou for thine own ends, standest in competition with me about it, or when I would confound thee by it.

5. I know there's no Communion to the Communion of Saints, to the inward communion, to communion with the spirits of just men made perfect, and with God the Judge of all.

No other Communion of Saints do I know.

And this is Blood-life-spirit-communion.

6. But another Communion also do I know, which is water, and but water, which I will not be without: My spirit dwells with God, the Judge of all, dwells in him, sups with him, in him, feeds on him, with him, in him. My humanity shall dwell with, sup with, eat with humanity; and why not [for a need] with Publicans and Harlots? Why should I turne away mine eyes from mine own flesh? Why should I not break my bread to the hungry, whoever they be? It is written, the Lord takes care of Oxen.

And when I am at home, I take a great care of my horse, to feed him, dresse him, water him and provide for him.

And is not poor *Maul* of Dedington, and the worst rogue in Newgate, or the arrantest thief or cut-purse farre better, then a 100. Oxen, or a 1000. such horses as mine?

7. Do I take care of my horse, and doth the Lord take care of oxen?

And shall I hear poor rogues in Newgate, Ludgate, cry *bread, bread, bread, for the Lords sake*; and shall I not pitty them, and relieve them?

Howl, howl, ye nobles, howl honourable, howl ye rich men for the miseries that are coming upon you.

For our parts, we that hear the APOSTLE preach, will also have all things common; neither will we call any thing that we have our own.

Do you [if you please] till the plague of God rot and consume what you have.

We will not, wee'l eat our bread together in singlenesse of heart, wee'l break bread from house to house.

C h a p. VIII.

The wel-favoured Harlots cloaths stript off, her nakednesse uncovered, her nose slit, her hunting after
the young man, void of understanding, from corner to corner, from Religion to Religion, and
the Spirit pursuing, overtaking, and destroying her, with a terrible thunder clap ith' close, &c.

1.   ANd we wil strip off thy cloaths, who hast bewitch't us, & slit thy nose thou wel-
favoured Harlot, who hast (as in many things, so in this) made the Nations of the
earth drunk, with the cup of thy for⟨n⟩ications: As thus.

Thou hast come to a poor irreligious wretch, and told him he must be of the same Religion
as his neighbours, he must go to Church, hear the Minister, &c. and at least once a year put
on his best cloaths, and receive the Communion—he must eat a bit of bread, and drink a sip
of wine—and then he hath received, &c. he hath been at the Communion.

2. But when he finds this Religion too course for him, and he would faine make after
another,

Then immediately thou huntest after him, following him from street to street, from corner
to corner, from grosse Protestantisme to Puritanisme, &c. at length from crosse in baptisme,
and Common-Prayer-Book to Presbyterianisme, where thou tellest him he may break bread,
with all such believers, who believe their horses and their cowes are their own; and with such
believers, who have received different light from, or greater light then themselves; branded
with the letter B. banished, or imprisoned fourteen weeks together, without bail or main-
prize.[40]

3. And here I could tell a large story, that would reach as far as between Oxonshire and
Coventrey.

But though it be in the original copy, yet it is my good will and pleasure, out of my great
wisdome, to wave the printing of it, and I will send the contents thereof, as a charge and secret
plague, secretly into their breasts, who must be plagued with a vengeance, for their villany
against the Lord.

Well! to return from this more then needful disgression, to the discovery, and uncovering
of the wel-favoured Harlot.

Thou hast hunted the young man void of understanding from corner to corner, from
religion to religion.

We left him at the Presbyterian—where such a believer, who believes his horses and
his cows are his own, may have his child christned, and may himself be admitted to the
Sacrament—and come to the communion.

And whats that?

Why after a consecration in a new forme, eating a bit of bread, and drinking a sip of wine
perhaps once a moneth, why mother of mischief is this Communion?

O thou flattering and deceitfull tongue, God shall root thee out of the Land of the living,
is this Communion? no, no, mother of witchcrafts!

---

40   'Action of procuring release of prisoner on someone's agreement to stand surety for their
     appearance in court at a later time' (*OED* n. 2).

5. The true Communion amongst men, is to have all things common, and to call nothing one hath, ones own.

And the true externall breaking of bread, is to eat bread together in singlenesse of heart, and to break thy bread to the hungry, and tell them its their own bread &c. els your Religion is in vain.

6. And by this time indeed thou seest this Religion is in vain.

And wilt therefore hie thee to another, to wit, to Independency, and from thence perhaps to Anabaptisme so called.

And thither the wel-favour'd Harlot will follow thee, and say thou must be very holy, very righteous, very religious.

All other Religions are vain.

And all in the Parish, all in the Countrey, yea all in the Kingdome, and all in the world [who are not of thine opinion] are without, are of the world.

Thou, and thy comrades are Saints.

[O proud devill! O devill of devills! O *Belzebub*!]

Well! [saith she] thou being a Saint must be very holy, and walk in Gospell-Ordinances [saith the wel favour'd Harlot] ay and in envy, malice, pride, covetousnesse, evill surmising, censoriousnesse, &c. also.

And on the first day of the week, when the Saints meet together, to break bread, do not thou omit it upon pain of damnation.

By no means omit it, because thou hast Gospell Ordinances in the purity of them.

—Papists—they give wafers.-

Protestants—give—to all ith' Parish tagg ragg, and his fellow if they come.

But we are called out of the world, none shall break bread with us, but our selves, [the Saints together, who are in Gospell Order.]

Besides the Priests of England cut their bread into little square bits, but we break our bread [according to the Apostolicall practise] and this is the right breaking of bread [saith the wel-favour'd Harlot.]

Who hath stept into this holy, righteous Gospell, religious way, [Gospel-Ordinances so called] on purpose to dash to pieces the right breaking of bread: and in the room thereof thrusting in this vain Religion.

7. A Religion wherein *Lucifer* reignes, more then in any.

And next to this in the Independents [so called] both which damn to the pit of hell, those that are a 100. times nearer the Kingdome of heaven then themselves: flattering themselves up in this their vain Religion.

But take this hint before I leave thee.

He that hath this worlds goods, and seeth his brother in want, and shutteth up the bowells of compassion from him, the love of God dwelleth not in him; this mans Religion is in vain.

His Religion is in vain, that seeth his brother in want, &c.

His brother——a beggar, a lazar, a cripple, yea a cut-purse, a thief ith' goal, &c.

He that seeth such a brother, flesh of his flesh [in want] and shutteth up the bowels of his compassion from him, the love of God dwelleth not in him, his Religion is in vain: and he never yet broke bread——that hath not forgot his [*meum.*]

The true breaking of bread——is from house to house, &c. Neighbours [in singlenesse of heart] saying if I have any bread, &c. it's thine, I will not call it mine own, it's common.

These are true Communicants, and this is the true breaking of bread among men.

10. And what the Lords Supper is, none know, but those that are continually [not weekly] but daily at it.

And what the true Communion is, those and those only know, who are come to the spirits of just men made perfect, and to God the Judge of all; all other Religion is vain.

Ay, saith the wel-favour'd Harlot [in the young man void of understanding] I see Protestantism, Presbytery, Independency, Anabaptism, are all vain. These coverings are too short, too narrow, too course for me, the finest of these are but harden sheets, and very narrow ones also.

I'l get me some flax, and make me both fine and large sheets, &c. I'l scorn carnall Ordinances, and walk in the Spirit.

Ay, do [saith the wel-favour'd Harlot] speak nothing but mystery, drink nothing but wine, but bloud, thou need'st not eat flesh, &c.

12. And so my young man starts up into the notion of spiritualls, and wraps up a deal of hipocrisie, malice, envy, deceit, dissimulation, covetousnesse, self-seeking in this fine linnen.

Being a hundred fold worse Devills then before.

But now thy villanie, hipocrisie, and self-seeking is discovering, yea discovered to many with a witnesse.

And though the true and pure levelling, is the eternall Gods levelling the Mountains, &c. in man. Which is the

Bloud-Life-Spirit levelling.

Yet the water, or weak levelling, which is base and foolish, shall confound thee.

And hereby, (as also by severall other strange waies, which thou art least of all acquainted withall⟨⟩). I'l discover thy lewdnesse, and shew the rottennesse of thy heart.

I'l call for all to a mite, to be cast into the outward treasury.

And wil bid thee lay down all at my feet, the Apostle, the Lord, And this is a way that I am now again setting up to try, judge, and damne the wel-favour'd Harlot by.

Cast all into the Treasury, &c. account nothing thine owne, have all things in common.

The young man goes away very sorrowfull,——&c.

The wel-favour'd Harlot shrugs at this.——

13. When this cometh to passe, a poore wretch whose very bones are gnawn with hunger, shall not go about 13. or 14. miles about thy businesse, and thou for a reward, when thou hast hundreds lying by thee.

I will give thee but one hint more, and so will leave thee.

The dreadful day of Judgement is stealing on thee, within these few hours. Thou hast secretly and cunningly lien in wait, thou hast craftily numbered me amongst transgressors, who to thy exceeding torment, am indeed a friend of Publicans and Harlots.[41]

---

41   Matt. 21.31–32.

Thou hast accounted me a devil, saith the Lord.

And I wil rot thy name, and make it stink above ground, and make thy folly manifest to all men.

And because thou hast judged me, I wil judge thee (with a witnesse) expect it suddainly, saith the Lord.

Per AUXILIUM PATRIS כף[42]

---

42 See above, p. 75, n. 4.

Letter from Coppe to Salmon and Wyke

MY Quintessence, my heart, and soule, my sal, and sol, my Wyke, (which being interpreted) is my Fort and strongehold⟨.⟩ how can I bee solitarie while sol shines uppon mee, and what weede I feare while I am in safetie in my Wyke, my Rocke & strongehold, wch can neither bee surprised or the walls thereof scaled, I live in yor. peace & freedome because I dwell in my self att Coventrie, Newgate (where I am) for suspition of Blasphemie and Treason agt the State) is noe prison to mee while I am inthroned in my Triple heart wch is but one & triangular, which is as firme as a stone, when I my selfe (‡ heere & there × and everywhere) raise uppe my selfe, the mighty shall bee afraid by reason of Breakings, they purifie themselves the sworde of him that layeth att mee cannot hold the speare, the dart, nor the Habergeon,[1] I esteeme iron as straw, & brasse as rotten woode, and (a halter as a spiders webb) I count darts as stubble, & laugh att the shaking of the speare. My deare salute all the saints in the Gaole. Haile from the Gen⟨er⟩all to the Peddee's,[2] with an holy Kisse. Love mee & love my dogge, I am soe backwards forever,

Alpha & omega ABC.

poore pure Ceney[3] & I can shake hands together when shee is in her's, and I in my Chamber, & hath sent you a thousand kisses. I have received the earnest penny I would have had some more, but in Newgate wee are poore, Noe more

To his dearest Mr Salmon
Mr Wike & Mr Butler[4]
in Goale Coventrie.

[Newgate, c. April–June 1650; Worcester College, Oxford, MS Clarke 18, fol. 24^r-v. Printed by permission of the Provost and Fellows of Worcester College, Oxford.]
1   Sleeveless coat or jacket of mail or scale armour.
2   Infantry.
3   Mrs. Seney, matron of the Savoy Hospital, carted through London for prostitution.
4   The gaoler at Coventry.

DIVINE FIRE-WORKS.

OR,

Some Sparkles from the Spirit of B U R N I N G in this dead Letter.

HINTING

What the Almighty Emanuel is doing in these W I P P I N G Times.

AND

In this H I S day which burns as an O V E N.

IN *A B H I A M*.

Can any good come out of⸺? Come and see.

THe LYON, who a long time sleeped,
Is (by the *Consuming* Fire) out of his Den fired.
Being rouzed,

	He roared,
	The Beasts of the Forrest trembled.
* *This was*	Were any of the children frighted?
the Lord	Have any of them stumbled?
knows where	Sure I am the Heathen raged.
the 29th. of	Have any of the P E O P L E (also) a vain
the last mon.	thing imagined?
An. BLVI &	

besides spectators and auditors.

	The Hell Hounds yelled.
By CRAV C-	The Dogs with open mouth gaped,
VR witnessed.	and greatly barked.

At length

The men of *Sodom* were (strangely) with blindness smitten.

The Dogs mouths which were so wide open, were (with a pure and heavenly cunning) stopped:

They also fawned, and their tails wagged, *&c.*

It's the earnest of good things to come.

And thus saith our Almighty Emanuel,

My wayes are unsearchable, and my Judgements past finding out, &c.

O the heights! and depths! and lengths! and breadths! how unsearchable? *&c.*

The rest is torn out,

Yet it's written

From

My joyous Fiery-fornace, where I am in the Spirit on the LORDS DAY.

Which burns as an Oven,
And where I am joyfully dwelling
With everlasting *Burnings.*

This first day of the $\begin{cases} BLVI. \\ BLVII. \quad A.B. \end{cases}$
New Year,

London printed in the beginning of the year, BLVII.

Felt, heard, and understood, manifested and Revealed at the end of—An.⸺BLVI.

Let none but Angels sing this round,
The end hath the *beginning* found.

And what and if one risen from the dead, *&c.*
And what and if a sleepy Lyon out of his Den fired, *&c.*

Should tell you the truth? could ye in any wise believe?

Hoc accidit dum vile fuit[1]

CHAP. II.

The sight, reception, and enjoyment of the TRUE BLV (which far surpasseth the Philosophers Stone, &c.()) Hinted at.

⸺ *Hoc accidet dum vile fui*

For wo is me, I am undone, I have seen the Lord the King.

I am undone. I am a fool.

Suffer fools gladly; if you may, if you can.

---

1 'And this happened, while it was of little worth.'

If I am a fool, it is for your sakes.

I am besides my self; and if I am—it is to God

I am not—for God hath took me.

I am undone, yet gloriously and joyfully undone.

I have seen the Lord. THE King;

Who appeared unto me

On [*Innocents Day*] the 28 of the last moneth.

He spake to me and with me, (as a friend speaketh to his friend) of things unspeakable and unutterable.

* *viz* 28 *Jan.* from ten at night til about 3 i'th' morning.

By * night (on my bed also) he whom my soul loveth, set before mine eye, both mental and corporal.

BLV

Exceeding glorious, most transparent and most transplendent.

And what I am now about (with fear & trembling, as also with high rejoycing) I can present to you, no more, no otherwise, then as part of the black, dark shadow of a man, against a sun-shine wall, &c.

At this strange, glorious, and unexpected sight,

The Spirit of Burning (by which the filth of the daughter of Sion is purged) did so surround me, and took such real possession of me,

That it not onely waxed hot within me;

But also (on a sudden) set my body on such a flame; that (at a distance) it would warm the stander by, as if they were warming their hands at a burning fire, &c.

Then was I raised to sit up in my bed (in my shirt) smoking like a furnace.

And with glorious holy fear and trembling, I bowed the Knees of my soul; as also my body

With all awful reverence before the dreadful, (yet to his friends) the glorious presence of the God of *Abraham*, the God of *Isaac*, the God of *Jacob*,

With my hands wringing, the Spirit groaning,

And at length saying,

I beseech thee, I beseech thee, I beseech thee

Tell me what is this?

● Then HE spake;

Whose voice once shook the earth; But now not onely the earth, but the heavens also. Saying,

Fear not, it is I BLV I.

Whereupon the Spirit within me (with exceeding joy) exceedingly groaned; & with a loud voice, out-sounded

O the BLV! O the BLV! O the BLV!

And the worm, and no man said, what BLV;

Lord

He, as a loving Father, gave me (as it were) a box 'ith' ear, saying,

Dost not remember, when thou was't a School-boy, thou heard'st this saying,

TRUE BLV wil never stain, will never fail,

White is the signal of Innocency. BLV, of Truth.——

And I that am incomprehensible, without colour, invisible,

Yet in (an unfathomable sense) * as visible,

And as I may, can, & wil so say; * *Heb.* 11. 27

I both have, can, wil, & do ap-pear in my COLOURS, at my pleasure.

The White—as Innocency, the BLV—as trueth.

TRUE BLVI, True BLVI I AM.

And though I am in heaven, earth, & hel, &c

Yet earth, hel & heaven, yea the heaven of heavens is not able to contain me, &c.

Now have I in an unspeakable eminent way bowed the heavens, & am come down upon the earth. And will shew my self,

As in my Coulors,——&c.

Whereupon he drew a sharp two edged flaming sword, &c.

(Another manner of Sword then that hee wore on Mount Sina)

Saying,

Bear thou the typical testimony thereof.

And in a dark, low, beggarly shadow, wear BLV,   With this Superscription,

TRUE BLV I will never fail,

TRUTH is great, and will prevail.

And (not conferring with flesh and blood) I was obedient to the heavenly commandment.

Whereupon with an exceeding holy fear and trembling, filled brim-ful [also] of joy and rejoycing,

I bowed down both soul and body, before the God of *Abraham*, *Isaac*, and *Jacob*.

And the Spirit within me sounded forth, O eternal spirit of TRUTH, which wil never fail

What am I, a worm, and no man?——

—— A Nazarite (By the Lord of Hosts, which

dwelleth in Mount Sion) made blacker then a cole——

——Not known in the streets——

Known at home Only.

Fear thou not, I am thine, & I am with thee and a wal of fire round about thee.

I will also tell thee what I am doing in *These whipping Times,*

And in this my Day

Which burns as an *OVEN.*

Hark!

Chap. III.

What the Lord *is doing these whipping Times? &c.*

Hark!

The noise of a whip, on top of the Mountains,

Whip and burn, whip and burn, whip & burn.

I, THE consuming fire in An. BLVII—have bowed the heavens, & am come down,

I am come to baptize with the Holy Ghost, and
* *Some have* with * *Fire.*
felt it with   My Fan is in my hand, and I
a witness.   will *throughly purge* my *Floor,* &c.
                                But,

The chaff I will burn up, with unquenchable Fire.

O chaff, chaff, hear the Word of the Lord.

To the unquenchable fire thou must, it is thy doom.

It's a whipping Time. The day burns as an Oven.

Wherein (II) all the proud, and all that do wickedly shall be stubble. And the day that cometh, and [NOW is] shall BURN them up.

It shal leave them neither root nor branch.

Mal.4.1. Learn what that meaneth,

Whom it hitteth, it hitteth.

It's a whipping time.

And he that's TRUTH, and no Lye, hath bowed the heavens, and is come down.

(III⟨⟩) TO whip the Thieves   † *Ye are the*
out of his own * Temple. And   *Temple of the*
amongst all the rabble that are   *living God, as*
there, he wil whip out that   *God hath said,*
old thief, that foul & unclean   *I will dwell in*
spirit that saith, Stand back, I   *them, &c.* I Cor.
                                         6. 2 Cor. 6. 10.

am holier then thou, &c.

That Thief also shall not scape his Lash, who saith, Lo *here, or lo there*, &c,

These are whipping time; and

The day *Burns* as an Oven.

And thus saith my God,

Who (to my exceeding, exceeding joy) is a consuming Fire, I have bowed the heavens, and am come down.

(IV) To try every mans work so as by *Fire;* and this consuming fire shall enter into the marrow and the bones, and search the heart and the reins:

And shall go on and do its work, as it hath begun:

And turn the IN-side outwards.

To the eternal fame of some; and to the everlasting shame of others.

Let the later expect what is upon them coming with a vengeance.

The day burns like an Oven.

For (V) He hath bowed the Heavens—and is coming down in flaming Fire,

To render vengeance to those that know him not; especially to those who talk much of him, yet call him, *Beelzebub, &c. &c. &c.*

These are whipping times.

For [VI) he hath bowed the heavens, and
                   is come down to whip

These froward foolish children who call their Father Rogue, if he appear in any other garb then what they have usually seen in him, &c.

And he will never give over whipping them, till they give over saying to him, What dost thou?

Till they give over Injoyning him his way, &c.

And their daring to be so arrogantly foolish, as

To JUDGE the things THEY know not—

He that hath an ear to hear let him hear.

And AL shall feel

It is a whipping time.

For (VII) He hath bowed the Heavens,
        and is come down to whip and burn,
                   whip and burn.—

None shall escape his lash,

No not his dearly beloved Daughter of *Sion.*

Among many other things he will soundly

scourge her for her haughtinesses, and outstretched-neckedness.

For holding her neck so high.

For her cursed Scorn, Hellish Pride and niceness.

For not remembring her Sister *Sodom* in the day of her pride, *&c.*

And the roaring ramping Lyon, with the sharp two-edged Sword, wil run her through and through.

And with unquenchable fire

Will burn up the bravery of their tinkling Ornaments.

The bracelets, *&c.* The changeable Suits of apparel, *&c.*

The Glasses, and fine Linnen. The Hoods and the Vails, *&c.*

And instead of sweet smelling there shall be a stink; and BURNING instead of Beauty.

And because she turneth away her eyes from her own Flesh, yea, and denies her own Spirit and Life;

Yea, her Father that begot her; and

Her eldest Brother, the Heir of all,

For this her haughtiness, and stretched-neckedness, she shall not onely be whipt, but also the crown of the head of the Daughter of *Sion* shall be smitten with a *Scab*.   And

The Lord wil discover her SECRET parts.

And this shall be done to the green Tree.

And if this be done to the green Tree,

[VII] What shall be done to the Dry Tree?

At present I will not tell them.

They shall feel with a witness, *&c.*

And Ile only here insert a Prophecie, which sparkled forth from the Spirit of Prophecy, before these whipping times were thought on or expected.

The Prophecy.

Sith that their wayes they do not mend,

Ile finde a Whip to scourge them by;

And with my Rod Ile make them bend,

and so divide them suddainly.

This is but the beginning of sorrows.

And this that is now (in this dead Letter hinted) is but the bare contents of some of those many things which the consuming fire is about to do

these whipping times; and in this day which BURNS as an Oven; and where in triumphs and joy I now live.

You shall have it more at large one way or other, one time or other.

The End

Is not yet.

London, Printed for the Author,

Jan. 20. An. $\begin{cases} \text{BLVI} \\ \text{BLVII.} \end{cases}$

Written *Jan*. I & 3. *An.* $\begin{cases} 56. \\ 57. \end{cases}$

True BLVI. will never fail;
TRUTH is great, & will prevail.

Laurence Clarkson

A
SINGLE EYE
All *Light*, no *Darkness*; or *Light* and *Darkness* One:

In which you have it purely Discussed,

1. The Original of *Darkness.*
2. What *Darkness* is.
3. Why it is called *Darkness.*

As also,

What God is *Within*, and what *Without*; how he is said
to be *One*, yet *Two*; when *Two* and not *One*, yet
then *One*, and not *Two*.

Likewise
*A Word from the Lord touching the onely Resurrection
of the Body, In, From, and To the* LORD.

With a certain parcel of *Quæries* to be answered from
Heaven or Hell,

This revealed in L. C. *one of the* UNIVERSALITY.

Imprinted at *LONDON*, in the Yeer that the
POWERS OF Heaven and Earth *Was, Is,*
and *Shall be* Shaken, yea Damned, till
they be no more for EVER.

B Ehold, the King of glory now is come
  T'reduce God, and Devil to their Doom;
For both of them are servants unto Me
That lives, and rules in perfect Majesty:
Though called God, yet that is not my Name,
True, I be both, yet am I not the same:
Therefore a wonder am I to you all,
So that to titul'd Gods ye pray and call.
Oh then my Creature, let me speak to thee;
Thy Worship, and thy God, shall dy truly.
Why dote ye Worldings? up and down being hurl'd,
As he is, so are we even in this World;
And so are all things perfect, just, and good;
Yea, all are sav'd by's Cross, his wounds, and blood.
Where else is heaven, but in our present peace
From him? or hell, but when that this doth cease?
Fie then for shame, look not above the Skies
For God, or Heaven; for here your Treasure lies
Even in these Forms, Eternall Will will reigne,
Through him are all things, onely One, not Twain:
Sure he's the Fountain from which every thing
Both good and ill (so term'd) appears to spring.
Unto this Single Eye, though Adams two
Cannot perceive, to Such, to All
                                                    Adieu.

Aving experience that his Majesty, the Being and Operation of all things, appeareth in and to the Creature under a two-fold Form or Visage, by which that becometh real with the Creature, which is but a shadow with this Infinite Being: So that from hence it ariseth, the Creature supposeth God to be that which is not, and that not to be, which is God.

Therefore hath his Majesty divulged his pleasure, that thereby he may take occasion to unfold himself in and to the Creature under such a prospect, that the Creature may know God, as he is known of God, that so from the clear appearance of God, the Creature may behold purely what God is, which as yet is manifest, the Creation in this Nation inhabiteth in no other Region then the Woman of Samaria: And therefore it is the cry of his Majesty is not fulfilled and obeyed, but by Churches, Saints, and Devils opposed and contemned: So that rare it is to find the Creature that is awaked out of his deep sleep, that hath shaked off the covering, so that he can from the clear Appearance of God say, the vail is taken away, and that he believeth the Truth as it is in his Majesty.

In answer to this, I have travelled from one end of England to another, and as yet could find very few that could define unto me the Object of their Worship, or give me a Character what that God is, so much professed by them; yet notwithstanding I could come into no City, Town, nor Village, but there I heard the name God under one Form or another, worshipped that for God, which I had experience was no God: So that in the period of my Pilgrimage, I concluded there was gods many, and lords many, although to me but one God: Therefore at my return, I was carried out by God to hold forth to the Creature, the God yesterday, to day, and for ever.

To that end, in the perusal of his Majesties pleasure, you may notice what is intended, or rather, in the ensuing Treatise recorded, having for the present but only presented to you a Map, in which you may take a full view what that God is thou pretends to Worship, whether he be Infinite, or Finite; whether he be subject to passion and affection, whether he behold the actions of the creature as the Creature esteem them, and whether he can be changed by thy prayers, so as to expiate a judgement, or produce a deliverance, yea whether he be all, and in all, or but all in part, that is to say, whether one act be good, another evil, one light, another darkness; and if so, reason from Scripture declareth, God is passionate, God is affectionate, and if either, then changeable.

But by forms and spiritual God like forms he is professed, and so worshipped as a God that beholds evil and good; so passionate with the one, and affectionate with the other, so that in conclusion they imagine him as themselves, not infinite, but finite, therefore it is, one Act in God is conceived two in themselves, to wit, one Act Adultry, another Honesty; when if Reason were admitted, and thereby Scripture interpreted, then should they observe in that Act they call Honesty, to be Adultry, and that Act so called Adultry, to have as much honesty as the other, for with God they are but one, and that one Act holy, just, and good as God; This to me by Reason is confirmed, and by Scripture declared, That to the pure all things are pure:[1] *So that for my part I know nothing unclean to me, no more then it is of it self, and therefore what Act soever I do, is acted by that Majesty in me, as in the ensuing Treatise will appear what Acts they are, the nature of Acting them; and in the period: how I esteem them: So that I weigh not how I am judged, in that I judge not my self. So to conclude, the censures of Scripture, Churches, Saints, and Devils, are no more to me than the cut⟨t⟩ing off of a Dogs neck,*

Vale.

---

1   Tit. 1.15.

Isaiah 42.16.
I will make Darkness Light before them.

He God of gods hath cast me on this Subject, to the end he may take occasion to unfold himself what he is in himself, and how he maketh out himself in his Appearance to the creature.

To that end, be pleased to peruse the precedent verses, and you will find what occasioned these terms in this Text; In brief, you may behold the Original thereof arise from the present state of the Gentiles, they being then as it were Prisoners, and in the state of darkness; So that in reference to their bondage, Christ called the Son of God was promised, to redeem them from the Region of Darkness; that notwithstanding they had worshipped that for God which was no god, yet now is the time come, now is the day that God will plunder them of their Idols, that God will enlighten their dark understandings, as in my Text, *God will make darkness light before them.*

Notwithstanding it may be supposed by some, that the connexion hereof doth only concern the Gentiles, yet let me tell thee, I find that God is not so limited in his pen, inke, and paper, but that he can and will make the darkness of the Jew light, as well as the Gentile; yea, the darkness of you as any other: for never was there more superstition, more darkness in the Churches than now, therefore never more need to have the light of God expel those dark mists that at this time is spread over all opinions in the Kingdom: So that now doth the time draw neer that the sayings in this Text shall appear in the unfoldings of the Spirit, *I will make darkness light before them.*

Being now ar⟨r⟩ived at the wished Haven, all the difficulty will be how to unload the Vessel fraughted with such hidden pearls, how to make merchandise of them, how to unfold this Subject to your capacity, how to give you the mind of God, in such terms as God appears in you.

And that the more, I find these unfoldings of God in this, seem to appear contrary to most that is quoted in the History; *I will make darkness light*; How is it possible, when there is no communion, no correspondency but enmity? Yea, so great, that they cannot dwell in one house, lodge in one bed, but devour one another; for where darkness is, light is not, and where light appeareth, darkness is gone; yet notwithstanding you hear, *he will make darkness light.*

So that the first thing I mind from hence is, *That he will not take darkness away, and in the room thereof place light, but that which in Scripture is called darkness, and by the Creature believed darkness, shall be made light.*

Secondly we shall enquire, *Whether that in Scripture, or by the Creature entituled darkness, be darkness with God or no?*

To this end you may read Light and Darkness are both alike to God. So then it appeareth but a darkness in the Creatures apprehension, so but an imagined darkness; for saith the Text, *God is light, and in him no darkness.* So that you see, whatsoever or howsoever it is called darkness in Scripture, yet it is none with God.   Then

Thirdly, I shall search, *Whether that in Scripture or by the Creature called God, admit of any other Title but* unus (*to wit*) One himself, *and if I find there is but one Being, one God, and that all that is be light with God, then shall I not cease till I find the Original of Darkness, what it is, and why it is called darkness*, &c.

First, I find in his Divine Being, in his Essence, there is but one God; the history declareth the same. *I am what I am: I am the Lord, and there is none else: There is no other God beside me:*[2] with varieties of Scriptures to this purpose. So then, it is cleer by the History, That the Being and Essence of God admits not of the plural but singular.

So that there is but one God, whose name is *Light*, so called God; for, that which God is, is God (*to wit*) God is light, then that light is God; for what God saith he is, that is himself, but God saith, He is light, therefore Light is God; so from the Scripture where God said *Let there be Light*, it is no more then if he had said, Let there be God, and there was God, for God is light.   For,

You have heard the Scripture holds forth but one God, which God is Light; yet the same Scripture holds forth not only light, but lights; as *verse* 14.[3] *Let there be Lights, and that Lights in the Firmament of the Heaven*: So that God made two great lights, that is to say, The light of the Sun, the light of the Moon, Stars, fire, and candle. From hence take notice, that though but one God, yet divers Lights, and that all made by God; for he that said *Let there be light*, said *Let there be Lights*; therefore he is called *The Father of Lights*, &c.

But then how shall we do with that place, *For God is light*, not lights; either he must be as well lights as light, or else, that all other lights but one hath a Being and Original besides God.

And if it appear that all lights, or that which is called light, though the light of the candle, be made by God, then the light of the candle is the light of God; but if all that is called light, to wit, the light of the Sun, Moon, Stars, Fire, and Candle, have not their being in God, then not made by God; So it will follow, that there is not onely one, but two gods.

But the Scripture saith, That *God made the Light*, and *God made the Lights*: So that both light and lights were made by God, then had they their being in God; for all that he made were in him, of him, and to him, as well the Sun as the Moon, the Stars, the Fire, and the Candle, as any of them; So that in making of these, he made nothing but himself; for God is light, as well the one as the other.

But then, If God be light, then lights; so that we may as well say *Gods*, as *God*; a God of the Sun, another of the Moon; for in that God is light, he must as well be the light of the Moon, as the light of the Sun, the light of the fire, the candle, as the stars.

Not denying but *God* is as well the light of the one, as the light of the other; yet notwithstanding that, God is but one light, and although called lights by God, yet they are but one light in God; to that end he is called *The Father of Lights*,[4] but one Father, though many lights. So that why they are but one light in God, or God one light, and yet by God called lights, are in reference to their distinct appearance in those several bodies (to wit) the body of the Sun, the body of the Moon; that as you see notwithstanding several beams from one Sun, yet in their rise from the Sun, they were but one in the Sun; nay indeed, they were nothing but the Sun, but after they are issued out of the Sun, one this way, another that way

---

2   Isa. 45.5.   3   Gen. 1.14.   4   Jam. 1.17.

from the Sun, then according to this divers appearance, it is no more called a Sun, but a Beam, not only Beam, but Beams, which when reduced to their being, they are no longer called a Beam, but a Sun.

So why they are called lights, and yet but one light with or in God, who is light, it is but according to its divers appearance, which in the being is but one appearance, because he that is the being of the light, is the appearance of the light, in what kind or degree whatsoever.

So that now you may take notice, and in some measure behold what God is, and what is to be understood by those terms, *God is light, and light is God*; which if it be that light is God, to wit, the light of the Sun, Moon, Stars, Fire, and Candle, which if the light appearing in these, and held forth by these, be the light of God, Why may not the whole Creation say with their brother *Jacob, Surely God were in these, and we knew it not?*[5]

But may be you will say, the light that is there recorded, is not to be understood the light of the Sun, Moon, &c. but a light that is quoted in these several Scriptures, to wit, a divine and Scriptural light, by which a creature beholds and enjoy⟨s⟩ God.

However God that is light appeareth in you, discovering to you that the light in the creature is not the same light of the Sun, yet the appearance of light in me, sheweth me (and that from Scripture declareth to me) that one is as much divine as the other; no more precious (simply in it self) then the other: for as you have heard, though Lights, yet but Light with God: so that all that is light, is nothing but God; for Light is Light, and God is light: this may be will in some measure be beleeved. But now to the matter in hand, *I will make darkness light, and crooked things straight*, &c.[6]

Whether it is intended the darknesse of the night to become the light of the day, or it is the Dark, as in several portions of Scripture is recorded: yea it is intended that you call the darknesse in the Creature, which darknesse is sin, hell, and misery: this darknesse he will make Light, Heaven, and Felicity; for in God is no darknesse, sin, nor misery; yet this will he make Light. So that now I am come to the place where I told you I would shew you the rise of Darknesse, what it is, and why it is called Darknesse.

To this end you shall find in Scripture a two-fold Power, to wit, more Powers than one, yet notwithstanding there is no Power but of God, and the Powers that be, are ordained of God. From hence you may observe the connexion hereof run in the plural, not Power, but Powers; a Power of darknesse, a Power of light, a Power in the wicked, a Power in the Godly; yet you have held forth in the same Scripture but one God.

So then, as it hath been proved, and I beleeve by you all will be granted, that the Power of Light, Life, and Salvation, cometh from God; the Power that acteth in the Godly, hath its rise from God; but then, What shall we say to the Power of darknesse, that Power in the wicked? for in them is a great Power, as saith the Prophet, *I have seen the wicked in great Power*,[7] (instance) the Power in *Esau*, in *Pharoah*, the Power in *Herod* and *Pilat*, by which they crucified Christ, from whom came this Power? the Scripture saith, from above, (to wit) from God: yet this was the Power of darknesse, of sin: was it not a sinfull act to crucifie Christ? that I know you will all conclude it was a wicked act; and yet this act was according to the will of

---

5   Isa. 45.14.   6   Isa. 42.16.   7   Ps. 37.35.

God, as saith the History, *By the Power of God the Kings of the earth stood up, and the Rulers were gathered together, against the Lord, and against his Christ.* &c.[8] What had they Power from God to destroy the Son of God? was this the will of God? so saith the Scripture, by the Power of God they gathered together: What to do? Nothing but what thy hand and thy Councel determined before to be done.

Well friends, consider this Power in *Pilate*, was a dark, sinful Power, yet it came from God; yea, it was the Power of God, as is recorded: *I form light, I create darknesse, I form Peace, I create evil.*[9] So that let it be a Power, whatsoever, in whomsoever, whether in Flesh or Spirit, wicked or Godly, it is the Power of God, yea, came from God. So that in time, he will make this Power of darknesse a Power of Light; that whereas you have called and condemned one Power for a dark sinfull Power; you shall have it appear to you, as now it is to me, that it is a Power of Light; for you heard this Power came from God, this Power of darknesse: yet God is Light, and in him is no darknesse.

So that consider, though two Powers, yet they have but one womb, one birth; to both Twins, both brethren, as *Esau* and *Iaakob*, then if Twins, if brethren, then one Flesh, one Nature, yea, of the self same Nature of God, from whom they came; as well *Esau* as *Iaakob*, *Pharoah* as *Moses*, *Pilate* as *Christ*: I say, although these be distinct, in reference to their several operations, as two streams runneth contrary ways, yet they are but of one Nature, and that from one Fountain: Herein it appeareth but a seeming opposition; instance the Tide, what striving for Victory; yet but one Water, yea and that from one Ocean. So is the case with these Powers, one opposite to the other, contending for Victory, till at last, one overcomes another, as the Tide the Stream.

Thus you may take notice from whence darknesse hath its rise, only from God.

Secondly, What Darknesse is; nothing but light with God.

Thirdly, Why it is called Darknesse, is but only in reference to the Creatures apprehension, to its appearance; so nothing but imagined Darknesse: therefore his meaning is, that which appeareth now under the form of Darknesse, shall ere long appear in a Visage of Light, as saith the Text, *I will make darknesse light before them.*[10]

Again, it may be granted by you, as it hath been by some, that the Power or Powers are of God; yea that Power by which *Pharoah* persecuted Israel; that Power by which *Pilate* crucified Christ, yet it will not be granted that God gave the Power so to do; neither was it the Power, but a corrupt thought, or sinful imagination arising from the Devil, and their own wicked inventions.

Answer.   Being now surrounded with the black Regiment, whose Commander is the Devil, and the whole legion consisting of the imaginations of the whole Creation, I have no way to escape this Camp and bottomlesse gulf, but by breaking through the Bulwark and strong hold fortified against me.

So that being armed with a weapon of Majesty, I doubt not but that God in me shall cast down those strong holds and imaginations, yea every thing that exalteth it self against the Power of the most high.

---

8   Acts 4.26.   9   Isa. 45.7.   10   Isa. 42.16.

To that end attend the nature of your objection, the sum thereof is to this effect, that a sinful act, or an act that is sinful, hath not its being in the Power of God, nor produced by the Power of God; no not that act of crucifying the Son of God, but from the Devil, and their sinful imaginations.

If thou by whom the Objection was raised, didst nakedly understand the truth therein contained, I should not in the least molest thee, but in that thou declarest Truth not knowing it, I am engaged to unfold the same, that thou maist know it, for whereas thou sayest a sinful act is not produced by the Power of God, its Truth: for that which is not in the Power, cannot be acted by the Power: but an act that is sinful is not in God, nor the Power of God, therefore hath not its being in God, nor acted by the Power of God, for God is light, and in him no darknesse: but sin is darknesse, therefore sin is not in God.

So that yet, notwithstanding that, I must tell you as before I have related, that as all Powers are of God, so all Acts, of what nature soever are produced by this Power, yea this Power of God: so that all those acts arising from the Power, are as Pure as the Power, and the Power as Pure as God.

So from hence it comes, there is no act whatsoever, that is impure in God, or sinful with or before God.

Yet say you, there is a sinful act, or acts that are sinful; so that if all that is an act be produced by the Power of God, then why not the act that is sinful arise from the same Power, so sinful in and with God.

As I have said, so I say again, that those acts, or what act soever, so far as by thee is esteemed or imagined to be sinfull, is not in God, nor from God, yet still, as I said, all acts that be are from God, yea as pure as God.

And yet, notwithstanding that act, or so much of the act that thou apprehendest sin is not in God, nor simply in thy self: for indeed sin hath its conception only in the imagination; therefore; so long as the act was in God, or nakedly produced by God, it was as holy as God: but after there is an appearance in thee, or apprehension to thee, that this act is good, and that act is evil, then hast thou with *Adam* eat of the forbidden Tree, of the Tree of knowledge of good and evil, then hast thou tasted of that fruit, which is not in God; for saith the Text, *Out of the mouth of the most High proceedeth not evil, and good*:[11] good but not evil; for God is good, and good is God: therefore it was he made all things good: yea that which by you is imagined evil, he made good: so that thou apprehending that from God which is not in God doth of all his Creatures most abuse God, in making God the author of that which is not in God, (to wit) Sin. But to the matter in hand, Thou hast heard all acts that are, had their being and birth from God, yea acted by God, to be plain those acts by thee called Swearing, Drunkenesse, Adultery, and Theft, &c.[12] These acts simply as acts, were produced by the Power of God, yea, perfected by the Wisdom of God.

What said I, a Swearer, a Drunkard, an Adulterer, a Theef, had these the power and wisdom of God, to Swear, Drink, Whore, and Steal? O dangerous Tenent! O blasphemy

---

11 Lam. 3.38.
12 Like Coppe, Clarkson refers to the printed edition of the Adultery Act: see above, p. 17.

of the highest nature! what make God the authour of Sin? so a sinful God! Well Friends, although the appearance of God in me be as terrible to you, as it were to *Moses* in the mount, yet notwithstanding, that what I have seen and heard, I do not in the least tremble, but rejoyce, that I have this opportunity to declare it unto you; however it may be received by you.

To that end consider what I said those acts called Swearing, Drunkennesse, Adultery and Theft, those acts, simply as acts, not as they are called (and by thee imagined) Drunkennesse, Adultery and Theft, that is in and from thy imagination; for there is no such act as Drunkennesse, Adultery, and Theft in God; though by his Power and Wisdom thou executest this act and that act, yet that appearance by which thou apprehendest and esteemest them to be acts of sin, that esteemation was not in God, though from God.

For indeed, it is but imagination, which is not, yea nothing in this, infinite being; for as I said before, so I say again, the very title Sin, it is only a name without substance, hath no being in God, nor in the Creature, but only by imagination; and therefore it is said, *the imaginations of your hearts are only evil continually.*[13] It is not the body, nor the life, but the imagination only, and that not at a time, or times, but continually. Herein sin admitting of no form in it self, is created a form in the estimation of the Creature; so that which is not to God, is found to be in a something creature; as you have it related, *One man esteemeth one day above another, another esteemeth every day alike:*[14] what to one is pure, to another is impure; herein it appeareth but a bare estimation.

To this end (saith *Paul*) *I know and am perswaded, by the Lord Iesus, that there is nothing unclean of it self, but to him that esteemeth any thing to be unclean, to him it is unclean.*[15]

So that the extent thereof is in reference to all things, as well as meats and drinks; let it be what act soever. Consider what act soever, yea though it be the act of Swearing, Drunkennesse, Adultery and Theft; yet these acts simply, yea nakedly, as acts are nothing distinct from the act of Prayer and Prayses. Why dost thou wonder? why art thou angry? they are all one in themselves; no more holynesse, no more puritie in one then the other.

But once the Creature esteemeth one act Adultery, the other honesty, the one pure, the other impure; yet to that man that so esteemeth one act unclean, to him it is unclean: (as saith the History) there is nothing unclean of it self, [but] but but to him that esteemeth it unclean: yea again and again it is recorded that to the pure all things, yea all things are pure, but to the defiled, all things are defiled: yea the Prayer and Prayses of the wicked are defiled, as saith the History, *The Prayers of the wicked are abomination to the Lord.*[16]

Observe not the act nakedly, as the act, for we find the Prayer and Prayses of some to be pure, though to others impure: impure to those acting, in relation to the title his apprehension, his Conscience in the improvement of them is defiled and condemned for a Swearer, a Drunkard, an Adulterer, and a theef.

When as a man in purity in light, acts the same acts, in relation to the act, and not the title: this man [no this man] doth not swear, whore, nor steal: so that for want of this light, of this single pure eye, there appeareth Devil and God, Hell and Heaven, Sin and holynesse,

---

13   Gen. 8.21.   14   Rom. 14.5.   15   Rom. 14.14.   16   Prov. 15.8.

Damnation and Salvation; only, yea only from the esteemation and dark apprehension of the Creature.

I will make darknesse light, rough ways smooth;[17] not half light and half darknesse, not part rough and part smooth; but as it is said, *Thou art all fair my Love, there is no spot in thee.*[18] Observe, all fair my Love; in thee only is beauty and purity, without, defilement: my love my dove is but one, thou one, not two, but only one, my love: Love is God, and God is Love; so all pure, all, light, no spot in thee.

So that consider what act soever is done by thee, in light and love, is light, and lovely; though it be that act called Adultery, in darknesse, it is so; but in light, honesty, in that light loveth it selfe, so cannot defile it self: for love in light is so pure, that a whore it cannot indure, but enstranges it self from darknesse from whence whoredom has its first original. Light is so pure, that it will not lodge with two; but treads the steps of the Apostle, saying, *Let every man have his own wife:*[19] when as darknesse is not ashamed to ly with his neighbours wife: for in light I declare that whoredom is the fruits of darknesse; therefore no companion for light, who scornes the society of a whore indeed. Light is like *Susanna*, that had rather dy, then be defiled with harlots. Yea, innocent *Susanna*, uncorrupted Light, must be accused, arraigned and condemned, for that her accusers are guilty of: Yet fear not *Susanna*, thou shalt be vindicated, and thy accusers condemned.

So that this is my Majesties pleasure to declare, again and again, that what acts soever is done by thee, according as thou esteemest it, yea according as thou beleevest it, so be it done unto thee; that is to say, if thou hast committed those acts in Scripture recorded for swearing, drunkenness, adultery and theft; and so acting apprehendest them, let me deal plainly with thee; to thee it is Sin: and for so sinning, thy imagination will pursue thee, arraign thee, and condemne thee for a Swearer, an adulterer and a theef.

When as on the contrary, thou are perswaded that those titles in Scripture, and thy apprehension recorded, for swearing, adultery, and theft, be no such acts with thee, but only titles without thee; neither dost thou apprehend them any other, but pure acts, without title: then I declare, according to thy esteemation so is the act to thee, and for so doing, thy imagination, will not, cannot condemne thee, but say with the Apostle, *We know that an Idol is nothing:*[20] what thou esteemeth Idolatry, to us is none: So that whatsoever I act, though it be that act you call swearing, adultery, and theft, yet to me there is no such title, but a pure act, for there is nothing that I do that is unclean to me, no more then it is unclean of it self.

And yet notwithstanding this, my priviledge doth not in the least approbate thee, yea thee that apprehendest the title to sweare, whore or steal, &c. because to thee it is unclean, therefore not lawfull for thee: neither canst thou upon the bare report hereof, say, Well, if it be but as man esteems it, then I will esteem it so too.

Alas friend, let me tell thee, whatever thy tongue saith, yet thy imagination in thee declares sad things against thee, in that thou esteemest them acts of sin, thy imagination will torment thee for this sin, in that thou condemnest thy self, thou art tormented in that condemnation; with endless misery: so that I say, Happy is the man that condemns not himself in those things he alloweth of.

---

17   Isa. 42.14; Luke 3.5.   18   Cant. 4.7.   19   1 Cor. 7.2.   20   1 Cor. 8.4.

No matter what Scripture, Saints, or Churches say, if that within thee do not condemn thee, thou shalt not be condemned; for saith the History, *Out of thine own mouth*, not anothers, *will I judge thee:*[21] Therefore, remember that if thou judge not thy self, let thy life be what it will, yea act what thou canst, yet if thou judge not thy self, thou shalt not be judged; For, *I came not into the World to condemn, but to save the World.*[22] But if the reproach and slander of Saints and Churches do cause thee to question thy self, then art thou ready to say within what they report without, I am guilty of what they accuse me: So that true is the saying, *O Adam,* thy destruction is of thy self.

But before I conclude touching how darkness is made light, sin holiness, and so all deformity converted into its own pure nature, it was my pleasure to treat somthing concerning the nature of this loss, that whether darkness in Scripture recorded, and by the creature believed, be cast out as distinct from light, and so said to be damned, in that it is not light, not pure, but defiled.

In answer to that, the Lord declares that those filthy abominable works of darkness (by thee so apprehended) shall be destroyed and damned; But how, or where they shall be damned? that is in the sayings of this Text, *I will make darkness light:* Oh that this were purely minded, then thou wouldst see that sin must not be thrown out, but cast within, there being in the Vat, it is dyed of the same colour of the liquor; as Saffron converts milk into its own colour, so doth the fountain of light convert sin, hell, and devil into its own nature and light as it self; *I will make rough waies smooth:* Now it is damm'd and ramm'd into its only Center, there to dwell eternal in the bosom of its only Father: This, and only this, is the damnation so much terrifying the Creature in its dark apprehension, that it shall be robbed and carried it knows not whither, cryeth out I am damned, I am damned, being carried out of its former knowledge, now knoweth not where it is, therefore lamenting, *Master, Save me, I perish,*[23] perished in its own Apprehension, yet saved in the essential. Thus much concerning *I will lead the blind by a way that they know not, and in paths they have not known: I will make darkness light, crooked things streight, &c.*[24]

A Word from the Lord touching Resurrection, there being reports not a few that I should deny the Resurrection of that body consisting of Flesh, Bloud and Bone. I answer, If I should not, Reason would arraigne me for a mad man, Scripture would declare me anti-Scripturist, in favouring such a palpable Tenent of Darkness, which if rightly understood, affirm no such thing as the Resurrection of this Body: both which affirm, that what the body is made of, that is the life, perfection, and happiness of the body; but thy body consisting of flesh and bone, is made of the dust of the earth, therefore when thy body is reduced to its center, then (and not till then) is thy body alive, perfected in its happiness; now for thee to raise this body, it would declare thee a Tyrant; for as it is destructive for the Fowl to live in the water, or the Fish in the Firmament, so to raise thy body to a local place called Heaven, would to thy body become a Hell; for as the earth would become a Hell to the Spirit, so that place called heaven, would become a hell to the Body, for after laid in the grave, it is buried in its heaven, glory, and happiness, where it shall rot and consume into its own nature for ever and ever.

21 Luke 19.22. 22 John 12.47. 23 Matt. 14.30. 24 Isa. 42.16.

Yet not denying but that body quoted in the History shall rise, which body hath several denominations, as *earthly, corruptible, dishonorable, weak, vile, and natural body*;[25] all which doth but make one cleer prospect, in which you may take a full view of what that body is made of that shall rise, whether a visible body consisting of flesh and bone, or invisible body, consisting of the Sensitive within this body; To this end the History speaketh on this wise, *That we our selves groan within our selves, waiting for the redemption*, to wit, *our Body*.[26]

So that in light I declare, that the corrupt senses must put on incorruption, thy mortal apprehension must put on immortality, that whereas before thou wast alive to five, and dead to one, now thou shalt be dead to five, and alive to one, that lovely pure one who beholds nothing but purity, wheresoever it goeth, and whatsoever it doth, all is sweet and lovely; let it be under what title soever, thou art risen from title to act, from act to power, from power to his name, and that only one name, pure and undefiled; so that now thou art of purer eys than to behold any iniquity, so that Devil is God, Hell is Heaven, Sin Holiness, Damnation Salvation, this and only this is the First Resurrection.

Yet here is no lodging, no safe inhabiting, in that thou art yet on the borders of Ægypt, only with *Moses* on Mount Hermon, only verbally, not practically, so short of the second Resurrection which is the life and power what thou saw, for till thou be delivered of that thou wast risen to, thou canst not say, *Death, where is thy sting? Grave, where is thy victory?*[27]

Wonder not at me, for without Act, without Birth, no powerful deliverance, not only the Talkers, but the Doers; not only your Spirit, but your Body must be a living and acceptable Sacrifice; therefore till acted that so called Sin, thou art not delivered from the power of sin, but ready upon all Alarums to tremble and fear the reproach of thy body.

Therefore my beloved ones, that supposeth your service is perfect Freedom, by having onely light into anothers life, know this, that if light without life, thy service will be perfect bondage; and therefore it is when a creature is drawn forth to act in anothers life, instead of tryumphing over sin, he will be conquered in sin; so that I say, till flesh be made Spirit, and Spirit flesh, so not two, but one, thou art in perfect bondage: for without vail, I declare that whosoever doth attempt to act from flesh, in flesh, to flesh, hath, is, and will commit Adultry: but to bring this to a period, for my part, till I acted that, so called sin, I could not predominate over sin; so that now whatsoever I act, is not in relation to the Title, to the Flesh, but that Eternity in me; So that with me, all Creatures are but one creature, and this in my form, the Representative of the whole Creation: So that see what I can, act what I will, all is but one most sweet and lovely. Therefore my deer ones consider, that without act, no life; without life, no perfection; and without perfection, no eternal peace and freedom indeed, in power, which is the everlasting Majesty, ruling, conquering, and dancing all into its self, without end, for ever.

---

25   Rom. 1.23–27.   26   Rom. 8.23.   27   1 Cor. 15.55.

The ensuing Queries.

What that God is so often recorded in Scripture, and by the Creature beleeved.

First, *Whether he admit of a Corporeal Substance (to wit) flesh, blood and bones; and if so (as by some of the Creation is beleeved) then the Question will be Where his habitation hath been, is and will be, to the end of the world? I say, if God admit of a corporal substance; whether then any other but a local place can contain that substance, or that he can be omnipresent in all places, and with all Creatures at one time, in that substance, &c?*

Secondly, *Whether God admit of any other but a Spirit, so invisible? and if so, (as by others of his Creation beleeved) the Query is then, where its Region hath been, is, and will be? I say, if God admit of no Corporal substance, form, nor image, but only a spirit, whether then any other but an invisible habitation, an infinite boundlesse region can contain an invisible infinite boundlesse spirit.*

Thirdly, *If God be a Spirit, then whether a Spirit can be confined from any thing? and if confined, then must we observe these two things,*

1. *What he is confined from, or confined in?*
2. *What it is that doth confine God?*

Fourthly, *If God be a Spirit, and cannot be confined, then whether God be not infinite and omni-present in all places, and in all things: as well Hell as Heaven, Devil as Angel, Sin as Holinesse, Darknesse as Light?*

Fifthly, *If God be infinite in all things: then whether all things are not finite in God? That if God be subject to nothing, then whether all things be not subjected to God, so as to do nothing without God, nor against God; but in the performance of the will of God, as well* Esau *as* Jacob, Pharoah *as* Moses, Pilat *as* Christ; *yea Sin, Devil, or any other instrument whatsoever?*

Sixtly, *Whether a creature living in God, so as to know God, as he is known of God, be not infinite with and in God; and so all things finite unto him, as unto God; subject unto him, as unto God whether Devil, Hell, Sin, Death, or any other thing whatsoever?*

Seventhly, *If God be in all things, then in all men, the wicked as the godly, wherein then is the state of the wicked worse then the godly? yea if God be in both, why have they not both one title, but one wicked, another godly?*

Eighthly, *If God be in all things, then in all Creatures that hath life whatsoever, so that wherein is man better than these, or hath any preheminence above these? yet if he have, by whom is it given: and the reason of so being given?*

Ninthly, *If God be in all, the wicked as the godly; why is not the wicked saved with the godly? but if not saved, what is that in the wicked more then the godly, that is damned? with the place where, and the nature of that damnation.*

Tenthly, *If God be in all, why are not all things one in God? and if they be all comprehended as one in God; how commeth it they are two distinct from God, yea so titled from the Scripture? now if Scripture were indicted by God the Question wil be, why it speaks not of things, as they are in God, but relates two distinct titles, two opposites; the one for God, the other against God?*

and whether that Scripture so contradictory be not the original or instrumental cause by which the Creation becomes blinded, divided, yea destroyed; in worshipping that for God, which in the Original is no God? I say, the Query will be, whether the contradiction in the Scripture, be not the contradictions in the Creation: and that so long as there is this Scripture, there will be Religions, not Religious forms, not Spirit; war, not Peace; envy, not Love; the teachings of men, not the teaching of God: yea in conclusion there will be gods, and not God: no not that God that is all in all, Alpha *and* Omega; *the God yesterday and to day, and for ever.*

F I N I S.

Letter from ?Clarkson
to William Rawlinson

My owne Deare,

With whome I now am, though I am not, in whome I live & love for ever.

Itt pleaseth mee exceeding well that I am in restraint & tied uppe from thy Companie & Societie of thy self together with those other of my freinds in whose veins runs my bloud, life, and in whose Rejoycing, I protest by the Almightie I die daily, how great my libertie & freedome is, in these seeming Bonds none but thy, my selfe knowes: I have crossed my Crowne, and Crowned my Crosse, I now know nott the one from the other, my glory is under my feete, and my shame is a shamelese Crowne uppon my head, my Beautie is defaced, my holy sanctuarie profaned, Judah is given to the Curse, and Israell to reproaches, dirt is become gold, the fine gold is become dimme, instead of my holy sanctuarie I have sett mee downe in the Tents of Egypt, and have made my grave with the wicked & (by Gods pretious woundes) I will in life & death bee willing to bee numbred amongst transgressors. Roll-in-Sun for that's thy name, my Light, and Solar Majestie is thy bed to tumble in, all the Beautie the world soe boaste of is but the lent reflecc⟨i⟩on of our glory⟨,⟩ when wee please wee will contract itt againe into our owne selfe, that soe all the glory of the world may become as an haire cloth, confounded & damn'd into ye blacknesse of Darknesse, and thy retrogradation of Glory is att hand thou knowest.

My deare, I wonder I yet heare nott from Mr. Salmon.[1] Remember mee to Mrs Rolinson, Brush, Mills, Leeke,[2] and the rest gather them uppe in one Bond of Love & lay them together with mee in Copp's[3] bosome where is our true & p⟨er⟩fect Center:

I am thy Soll.

I pray tell Mr Barker[4] I expect to heare from him my haste is great else I had writt to him.

To Mr Wm Rolinson.[5]

[No place or date recorded, but either Whitehall or New Bridewell, c. mid-July–October, 1650; Worcester College, Oxford, MS Clarke 18, fol. 23ʳ⁻ᵛ. Printed by permission of the Provost and Fellows of Worcester College, Oxford.]

1 Joseph Salmon.
2 The members of 'My One Flesh,' as recounted in *The Lost Sheep Found* (1660); see below, pp. 133–34, including Mary Lake and John Millis.
3 Abiezer Coppe.
4 Possibly the Dr. Barker mentioned in *The Lost Sheep Found*, p. 134.
5 William Rawlinson.

The Lost Sheep

F O U N D:

O R,

The Prodigal returned to his Fathers
house, after many a sad and weary
Journey through many Religious Countreys,

Where now, notwithstanding all his former Transgressions,and breach of his Fathers Commands,
he is received in an eternal Favor, and all the
righteous and wicked Sons that he hath left behinde, reserved for eternal misery;

As all along every Church or Dispensation may
read in his Travels, their Portion after
this Life.

Written by Laur. Claxton, *the onely true converted*
Messenger of Christ Jesus, Creator of
Heaven and Earth.

L O N D O N:

Printed for the Author. 1660.

... Sixthly, I took my journey into the society of those people called *Seekers*, who worshipped God onely by prayer and preaching, therefore to *Ely* I went, to look for *Sedgwick* and *Erbery*[1] but found them not, onely their people were assembled: with whom I had discourse, but found little satisfaction; so after that for *London* I went to finde *Seekers* there, which when I came, there was divers fallen from the Baptists as I had done, so coming to *Horn* in *Fleet lane*, and *Fleten* in *Seacoal-lane*, they informed me that several had left the Church of *Patience*,[2] in seeing the vanity of *Kiffin*[3] and others, how highly they took it upon them, and yet could not prove their Call successively; so glad was I there was a people to have society withal; then was I moved to put forth a book which was the first that ever I writ, bearing this Title, *The pilgrimage of Saints, by church cast out, in Christ found, seeking truth*,[4] this being a sutable peece of work in those days, that it wounded the Churches; which book *Randel*[5] owned, and sold many for me. Now as I was going over *London-bridge*, I met with *Thomas Gun*[6] a teacher of the Baptists, who was a man of a very humble, moderate spirit, who asked me if I own'd the *Pilgrimage of Saints?* I told him yea: then said he, you have writ against the church of Christ, and have discovered your self an enemy to Christ. Then I said, it is better be a hypocrite to man then to God, for I finde as much dissimulation, covetousness, back-biting and envy, yea as filthy wickednesse among some of them, as any people I know: and notwithstanding your heaven-like carriage, if all your faults were written in your forehead, for ought I know, you are a hypocrite as well as I; which afterwards it was found out he had lain with his Landlady many times; and that he might satisfie his Lust, upon slighty erands, he sent her husband into the country, that so he might lodge with his wife all night; which being found out, so smote his conscience, that he privately took a Pistol and shot himself to death in *Georges-fields*. As all along in this my travel I was subject to that sin, and yet as saint-like, as though sin were a burden to me, so that the fall of this *Gun* did so seize on my soul, that I concluded there was none could live without sin in this world; for notwithstanding I had great knowledge in the things of God, yet I found my heart was not right to what I pretended, but full of lust and vain-glory of this world, finding no truth in sincerity that I had gone through, but meerly the vain pride and conceit of Reasons imagination, finding my heart with the rest, seeking nothing but the praise of men in the heighth of my prayer and preaching, yet in my doctrine through all these opinions, pleading the contrary, yea abasing my self, and exalting a Christ that then

---

1   For William Sedgwick, see above, p. 100, n. 36; William Erbery (1604/5–54), influential and popular Welsh Independent, then Seeker; and Parliamentary army chaplain; known for his universalist and egalitarian sympathies, and his objections to visible churches.
2   Thomas Patient (d. 1666), Particular Baptist minister, glover and tailor, close associate of William Kiffin.
3   William Kiffin (1616–1701), key Particular Baptist minister and leader; prosperous leather merchant and funder of the Parliamentary cause.
4   This was Clarkson's first publication, in 1646; it adopted a Seeker stance.
5   As if Randall was a bookseller/publisher who owned the copyright to the book (there was a 1640s London bookseller called Thomas Randall), but it has been assumed that the Antinomian preacher and translator Giles Randall was selling copies of the book.
6   Thomas Gunne was another significant Baptist. He appears as representative of the fourth London Baptist Church in the 1644 *Confession* of the London Particular Baptists.

I knew not. Now after this I return'd to my wife in *Suffolk*,[7] and wholly bent my mind to travel up & down the country, preaching for monies, which then I intended for *London*, so coming to *Colchester* where I had *John Aplewhit*, *Purkis*, and some other friends, I preached in publick; so going for *London*, a mile from *Colchester*, I set my Cane upright upon the ground, and which way it fell, that way would I go; so falling towards *Kent*, I was at a stand what I should do there, having no acquaintance, and but little money, yet whatever hardship I met withal, I was resolved for *Gravesend*, so with much a do I got that night to a town called *Bilrekey*, it being in the height of Summer, and in that town then having no friends, and I think but six pence, I lodged in the Church porch all night, so when day appeared, I took my journey for *Gravesend*, and in the way I spent a groat of my six pence, and the other two pence carried me over the water; so being in the town, I enquired for some strange opinionated people in the town, not in the least owning of them, but seemingly to ensnare them, which they directed me to one *Rugg* a Victualler, so coming in, though having no monies, yet I called for a pot of Ale, so after a few words uttered by me, the man was greatly taken with my sayings, in so much that he brought me some bread and cheese, with which I was refreshed, and bid me take no care, for I should want for nothing, you being the man that writ *The Pilgrimage of Saints*, I have had a great desire to see you, with some soldiers and others, so for the present he left me, and informed Cornet *Lokier*[8] and the rest, that I was in town, who forthwith came to me, and kindly received me, and made way for me to preach in the *Blockhouse*;[9] so affecting my doctrine, they quatered me in the Officers lodging, and two days after they carried me to *Dartford*, where there I preached; so against the next Lords-day came for *Gravesend*, and there preached in the Market-place, which was such a wonder to the town and countrey, that some for love, and others for envy, came to hear, that the Priest of the town had almost none to hear him, that if the Magistrate durst, he would have apprehended me, for I boldly told them God dwelled not in the Temple made with hands, neither was any place more holy then another, proving by Scripture, that where two or three were gathered in his name, God was in the midst of them, and that every Believer was the Temple of God, as it is written, *God dwelleth with a humble and contrite spirit*;[10] So after this we went to *Maidston* and *Town-maulin*,[11] and there I preached up and down, so at last having given me about five pounds, I went to my wife and promised in two weekes to return again, which I did, but I found not *Lokier* nor the rest so affectionate as before, for he had a gift of preaching, & therein did seek honor, so suspicious of my blasting his reputation, slighted and persecuted me, so that I left them, and towards *Maidston* travelled, so one *Bulfinch* of *Town-maulin* having friends towards *Canterbury*, perswaded me to go with him, and so against the next Lords-day, having no steeple free, we had a Gentlemans barn free, where a great company was assembled: then for *Sandwich* I went, and up and down found friends, so coming to *Canterbury* there was some six of this way, amongst whom was a maid of pretty knowledge, who with my Doctrine

7   Frances, daughter of Robert Marchant of Weybread, Suffolk.
8   Cornet Nicholas Lockyer of Colonel Nathaniel Rich's horse regiment.
9   Small sixteenth-century fort built to defend river approaches to London.
10   Isa. 57.15.
11   East Malling, Kent.

was affected, and I affected to lye with her, so that night prevailed, and satisfied my lust, afterwards the mayd was highly in love with me, and as gladly would I have been shut of her, lest some danger had ensued, so not knowing I had a wife she was in hopes to marry me, and so would have me lodge with her again, which fain I would, but durst not, then she was afraid I would deceive her, and would travel with me, but by subtilty of reason I perswaded her to have patience, while I went into *Suffolk*, and setled my occasions, then I would come and marry her, so for the present we parted, and full glad was I that I was from her delivered, so to *Maidston* I came, and having got some six pounds, returned to my wife, which a while after I went for *Kent* again, but found none of the people so zealous as formerly, so that my journey was but a small advantage to me, and then I heard the maid had been in those parts to seek me, but not hearing of me, returned home again, and not long after was married to one of that sect, and so there was an end of any further progress into *Kent*. Then not long after I went for *London*, and some while remained preaching at *Bowe*[12] in Mr. *Sterry's*[13] place, and *London-stone*, but got nothing; so to *Suffolk* I went, and having but one childe, put it to nurse, intending to go to my Parents in *Lancashire*:[14] So leaving my Wife at my cousin *Andertons*, I hearing of *Seekers* in *Hartfordshire*, went thither, and at last was hired by Mr. *Hickman* to preach at *Peters*[15] in *St. Albans*, so being liked, I was hired for a moneth longer, so fetcht my Wife, and there continued till such time the Town of *Sanderidge* took me for their Minister, and setled me in the Vicaridge, where Sir *John Garret*, Colonel *Cox*,[16] and Justice *Robotom*[17] came constantly to hear me, and gave me several Gifts, so that in heaven I was again; for I had a high pitch of free Grace, and mightily flown in the sweet Discoveries of God, and yet not at all knowing what God was, onely an infinite Spirit, which when he pleased did glance into his people the sweet breathings of his Spirit; and therefore preached, it was not sufficient to be a professor, but a possessor of Christ, the possession of which would cause a profession of him, with many such high flown notions, which at that time I knew no better, nay, and in truth I speak it, there was few of the Clergy able to reach me in Doctrine or Prayer; yet notwithstanding, not being an University man, I was very often turned out of employment, that truly I speak it, I think there was not any poor soul so tossed in judgement, and for a poor livelihood, as then I was. Now in this my prosperity I continued not a year, but the Parson being a superstitious Cavelier, got an Order from the Assembly of Divines to call me in question for my Doctrine, and so put in a drunken fellow in my room: and thus was I displaced from my heaven upon earth, for I was dearly beloved of *Smiths* and *Thrales*, the chief of the Parish. Well there was no other way but for *London* again, and after a while sent my Goods for *Suffolk* by water: now at this I concluded all was a cheat, yea preaching it self, and so with this apprehension went up and down *Hartfordshire*, *Bedford*, and *Buckinghamshire*,

---

12   St. Mary-le-Bow, Cheapside, considered the second most important church in London after St. Paul's Cathedral; it was consumed in the Great Fire of London, 1666.

13   Probably Peter Sterry (1613–72), Independent minister, Cromwellian chaplain.

14   Clarkson was a native of Preston, Lancs.

15   St. Peter's Church, St. Peter's St., St. Albans. Clarkson follows the Puritan custom of dropping the 'St.'

16   Alban Coxe, col. of foot.

17   John Robotham, JP of St. Albans.

and by my subtilty of reason got monies more or less; as of one at *Barton*, I had twelve pounds
for the printing of a book[18] against the Commonalty of *England*, impeaching them for
traytors, for suffering the Parliament their servants, to usurp over them, judging the Commonwealth was to cut out the form, and shape of their grievances, and send it up to their servants
the Parliament to finish, shewing, as the Common-wealth gave the Parliament power, so they
were greater then the Parliament, with matter to the effect. And then being presented to a
small parish in *Lincolnshire*, thither I went, but finding no society to hear, I grew weary
thereof, and stayd with some friends at *Oford*, so with a little monies went home again, and
not long after going into *Lincolnshire*, I preached in several places, that at last Captain
Cambridge[19] hearing of me, and was much affected with me, and made me teacher to their
Company, and said I should have all necessaries provided me, and a man alowed me; then I
was well recruited and horsed, so that I judged it was the mercy of God to me, my distress
being great, and my care for my family. Now after a while our Regiment went for *London*, so
though I had preached in *Lincoln*, *Horncastle*, *Spilsby*, and many other places, yet they would
excuse me for two moneths, having no need of preaching at *London*, so with what monies I
had I went to my wife, and staid there a while, and so came for *London*: Now our Regiment
being *Twisltons*,[20] Quartered in *Smith-field*, but I Quartered in a private-house, who was a
former friend of mine, asked me if I heard not of a people called *My one flesh*? I said no, what
was their opinion, and how should I speak with any of them? Then she directed me to *Giles
Calvert*.[21] So that now friends, I am travelling further into the *Wilderness*, having now done
burning of Brick, I must still wander in the mountains and deserts; so coming to *Calvert*, and
making enquiry after such a people, he was afraid I came to betray them, but exchanging a
few words in the height of my language, he was much affected, and satisfied I was a friend of
theirs, so he writ me a Note to Mr. *Brush*, and the effect thereof was, the bearer hereof is a
man of the greatest light I ever yet heard speak, and for ought I know instead of receiving of
him you may receive an Angel, so to Mr. *Brush* I went, and presented this Note, which he
perused, so bid me come in, and told me if I had come a little sooner, I might have seen Mr.
Copp, who then had lately appeared in a most dreadful manner; so their being *Mary Lake*, we
had some discourse, but nothing to what was in me, however they told me, if next sunday I
would come to Mr. *Melis*[22] in *Trinity-lane*, there would that day some friends meet. Now
observe at this time my judgment was this, that there was no man could be free'd from sin,
till he had acted that so called sin, as no sin, this a certain time had been burning within me,
yet durst not reveal it to any, in that I thought none was able to receive it, and a great desire I
had to make trial, whether I should be troubled or satisfied therein: so that

Seventhly, I took my progress into the *Wilderness*, and according to the day appointed, I
found Mr. *Brush*, Mr. *Rawlinson*,[23] Mr. *Goldsmith*, with *Mary Lake*, and some four more: now

---

18 *A generall charge or, impeachment of high-treason, in the name of justice equity, against the
    communality of England; as was presented by experienced reason*, Anno 1647.
19 Captain Owen Cambridge in Colonel Philip Twisleton's horse regiment.
20 Philip Twisleton, col. of horse (d. 1701).
21 Giles Calvert (1612–63), influential networker and bookseller of radical Puritan material.
22 ?John Millis, baker.
23 William Rawlinson; probable correspondent of Clarkson.

Mary Lake was the chief speaker, which in her discourse was something agreeable, but not so high as was in me experienced, and what I then knew with boldness declared, in so much that *Mary Lake* being blind, asked who that was that spake? *Brush* said the man that *Giles Calvert* sent to us, so with many more words I affirmed that there was no sin, but as man esteemed it sin, and therefore none can be free from sin, till in purity it be acted as no sin, for I judged that pure to me, which to a dark understanding was impure, for to the pure all things, yea all acts were pure: thus making the Scripture a writing of wax, I pleaded the words of *Paul*, *That I know and am perswaded by the Lord Jesus, that there was nothing unclean, but as man esteemed it*,[24] unfolding that was intended all acts, as well as meats and drinks, and therefore till you can lie with all women as one woman, and not judge it sin, you can do nothing but sin: now in Scripture I found a perfection spoken of, so that I understood no man could attain perfection but this way, at which Mr. *Rawlinson* was much taken, and *Sarah Kullin* being then present, did invite me to make trial of what I had expressed, so as I take it, after we parted she invited me to Mr. *Wats* in *Rood-lane*, where was one or two more like her self, and as I take it, lay with me that night: now against next sunday it was noised abroad what a rare man of knowledge was to speak at Mr. *Brushes*; at which day there was a great company of men and women, both young and old; and so from day to day increased, that now I had choice of what before I aspired after, insomuch that it came to our Officers ears; but having got my pay I left them, and lodged in *Rood-lane*, where I had Clients many, that I was not able to answer all desires, yet none knew our actions but our selves; however I was careful with whom I had to do. This lustful principle encreased so much, that the Lord Mayor with his Officers came at midnight to take me, but knowing thereof, he was prevented. Now *Copp* was by himself with a company ranting and swearing, which I was seldom addicted to, onely proving by Scripture the truth of what I acted; and indeed *Solomons* Writings was the original of my filthy lust, supposing I might take the same liberty as he did, not then understanding his Writings was no Scripture, that I was moved to write to the world what my Principle was, so brought to publick view a Book called *The Single Eye*, so that men and women came from many parts to see my face, and hear my knowledge in these things, being restless till they were made free, as then we called it. Now I being as they said, *Captain of the Rant*, I had most of the principle women came to my lodging for knowledge, which then was called *The Head-quarters*. Now in the height of this ranting, I was made still careful for moneys for my Wife, onely my body was given to other women: so our Company encreasing, I wanted for nothing that heart could desire, but at last it became a trade so common, that all the froth and scum broke forth into the height of this wickedness, yea began to be a publick reproach, that I broke up my Quarters, and went into the countrey to my Wife, where I had by the way disciples plenty, which then Major *Rainsborough*,[25] and Doctor *Barker* was minded for Mr. *Walis* of *Elford*,[26] so there I met them, where was no small pleasure and delight in praising of a God that was

---

24 Rom. 14.14.
25 Major William Rainborowe (fl. 1639–73), Parliamentary army officer and Leveller; arrested by Parliament for financing *A Single Eye*.
26 Ilford, Essex.

an infinite nothing,[27] what great and glorious things the Lord had done, in bringing us out of bondage, to the perfect liberty of the sons of God, and yet then the very notion of my heart was to all manner of theft, cheat, wrong, or injury that privately could be acted, though in tongue I professed the contrary, not considering I brake the Law in all points (murther excepted:) and the ground of this my judgement was, God had made all things good,[28] so nothing evil but as man judged it; for I apprehended there was no such thing as theft, cheat, or a lie, but as man made it so: for if the creature had brought this world into no propriety, as *Mine* and *Thine*, there had been no such title as theft, cheat, or a lie; for the prevention hereof *Everard*[29] and *Gerrard Winstanley*[30] did dig up the Commons, that so all might have to live of themselves, then there had been no need of defrauding, but unity one with another, not then knowing this was the devils kingdom, and Reason lord thereof, and that Reason was naturally enclined to love it self above any other, and to gather to it self what riches and honor it could, that so it might bear sway over its fellow creature; for I made it appear to *Gerrard Winstanley* there was a self-love and vain-glory nursed in his heart, that if possible, by digging to have gained people to him, by which his name might become great among the poor Commonalty of the Nation, as afterwards in him appeared a most shameful retreat from *Georges-hill*,[31] with a spirit of pretended universality, to become a real Tithe-gatherer of propriety; so what by these things in others, and the experience of my own heart, I saw all that men spake or acted, was a lye and therefore my thought was, I had as good cheat for something among them, and that so I might live in prosperity with them, and not come under the lash of the Law; for here was the thought of my heart from that saying of *Solomon*, Eccles. 3.19. *For that which befalleth the sons of men, befalleth beasts, even one thing befalleth them; as the one dieth, so dieth the other, yea, they have all one breath, so that a man hath no preheminence above a beast; for all is vanity, all go into one place, all are of the dust, and all turn to dust again.* So that the 18th and 19th verses of *Ecclesiastes* was the rule and direction of my spirit, to eat and to drink, and to delight my soul in the labor of my minde all the days of my life, which I thought God gave me as my portion, yea to rejoyce in it as the gift of God, as said that wise Head-piece *Solomon*; for this then, and ever after, till I came to hear of a Commission, was the thought of my heart, that in the grave there was no more remembrance of either joy or sorrow after. For this I conceived, as I knew not what I was before I came in being, so for ever after I should know nothing after this my being was dissolved; but even as a stream from the Ocean was distinct in it self while it was a stream, but when returned to the Ocean, was therein swallowed and become one with the Ocean; so the spirit of man while in the body, was distinct from God, but when death came it returned to God, and so became one with God, yea God it self; yet notwithstanding this, I had sometimes a relenting light in my soul, fearing this should not be so, as indeed it was contrary; but however, then a cup of Wine would wash away this doubt.

But now to return to my progress, I came for *London* again, to visit my old society; which

---

27   See above, p. 126.
28   See above, p. 115.
29   William Everard (1602–?51), Digger.
30   Gerrard Winstanley (1609–76), chief theorist and leader of the Diggers.
31   St. George's Hill, Surrey, site of the main Digger commune.

then *Mary Midleton*[32] of *Chelsford*, and Mrs. *Star* was deeply in love with me, so having parted with Mrs. *Midleton*, Mrs. *Star* and I went up and down the countries as man and wife, spending our time in feasting and drinking, so that Tavernes I called the house of God; and the Drawers, Messengers; and Sack, Divinity; reading in *Solomons* writings it must be so, in that it made glad the heart of God; which before, and at that time, we had several meetings of great company, and that some, no mean ones neither, where then, and at that time, they improved their liberty, where Doctor *Pagets*[33] maid stripped her self naked, and skipped among them, but being in a Cooks shop, there was no hunger, so that I kept my self to Mrs. *Star*, pleading the lawfulness of our doings as aforesaid, concluding with *Solomon* all was vanity. In the interim the Parliament had issued forth several Warrants into the hands of Church-members, which knew me not by person, but by name, so could not take me, though several times met with me, that at last the Parliament to him that could bring me before them, would give a hundred pounds, so that one *Jones* for lucre of mony, knowing me, got a Warrant to apprehend me, who meeting me in the four swans within *Bishopsgate*, told me he had a Warrant from the High Court of Parliament to take me: Let me see it, said I, you have no power to serve it without an Officer, and so would have escaped, but could not the people so thronged about me, and a great tumult there was, some fighting with him for an Informer, but being a City Trooper, and some more of his Company with him, they carried me, as I take it, to Alderman *Andrews*,[34] where they searched my Pockets; but having dropped an Almanack that had the names of such as sold my books for me, they found it, and carried it to the Parliament, so informed the House I was taken, and likewise desired to know what they should do with me, who gave Order to bring me by water to *Whitehall*-staires, and deliver me to *Barkstead*'s[35] Soldiers, where after a while a messenger was sent to take me into custody, where I was lodged in *Whitehall* over against the *Dial*, and two souldiers guarded me night and day, for which I was to pay; but some being of my principle, they would guard me for nothing, and a Captain of theirs would give me moneys; so after two days I was sent for before the Committee of Parliament to be examined: so being called in, they asked me my Name, my Countrey, with many such frivolous things; so coming to the business in hand, Mr. *Weaver*[36] being the Chair-man, asked me if I lodged in *Rood-lane*? To which I answered, Once I did. Wherefore did you lodge there? Because I had a friend there of whom I hired a chamber. What company of men and women were those that came to you? To instance their names I cannot, but some came as they had business with me. Who were those women in black Bags[37] that came to you? As now I know not. But Mr. *Claxton*, we are informed, you have both wives

---

32   Mary Middleton; escaped arrest at a meeting of 'My One Flesh' at her husband's house on Moor Lane, St. Giles Cripplegate.

33   Nathan Paget (1615–79), physician to the Tower of London, member of the Independent and tolerationist John Goodwin's church; friend of Milton.

34   Sir Thomas Andrewes (d. 1659), financier and regicide.

35   John Barkstead (d. 1662), regicide and eventual major-general. In April 1650 his regiment was appointed to guard Parliament and the City of London.

36   John Weaver (d. 1685), M.P., pro-Commonwealth politician and government official.

37   Masks; often used to disguise marks of disease or dissolute living; drawn against the face by a bead held between the teeth.

and maids that lodgeth with you there? Those that informed you, let them appear face to face, for I never lay with any but my own wife. No: for you call every woman your wife? I say I lye with none but my wife, according to Law, though in the unity of the spirit, I lye with all the creation. That is your sophistication, but deal plainly before God and Man, did not you lye with none in *Rood lane*, and others places, besides your wife? I do deal plainly as you, but I being a free born subject ought not to accuse my self, in that you are to prove your charge. Mr. *Claxton* confess the truth⟨, it⟩ will be better for you: for we assure you shall suffer no wrong. What I know is trueth, I have, and shall speak. What did you at Mrs. *Croes* in *Rederiff*? I had conference with the people. As you were preaching, you took a pipe of Tobacco, and women came and saluted you, and others above was committing Adultery. This is more then I remembe⟨r⟩? No, you will not remember any thing against you: but surely you cannot but remember this *Almanack* is yours, and these mens names your own hand writing. Yea I did write them, was not these men your disciples? They were not mine, but their own. Did not Major *Rainsborough*, and the rest lye with other women? Not as I know. But Mr. *Claxton* do you remember this book is yours?[38] I never saw that before, but may be some of the like nature I have. Why did not you write this Book? That you are to prove. Here is the two first Letters of your name. What is that to me? it may serve for other names as well as mine. Did not Major *Rainsborough* and these men give you monies to print this Book? How should they give me monies to print that which neither I nor they knew of. This Book must be yours, for it speaks your language, suitable to your practise. I being but a stranger to you, how should you know my language or practise? Though you will confess nothing, yet we have witness to prove it. Let them be examined in my presence: So calling *Jones* ⟨t⟩hat betrayed me, did you never see Mr. *Claxton* lye with no woman? I have heard him talk of such things, but saw no act. Though you cannot, there is some will, therefore Mr. *Claxton* deal plainly, that though you lay with none, yet did not you alow it none others? I saw no evil in them to disalow; And Gentlemen let me speak freely to you, Suppose I were your servant, entrusted with your secrets, and knew that you were Traitors against this present Power, would you take it well for me to impeach you, and bear witness against you? At which, either the Earl of *Denby*,[39] or the Earl of *Salisbury*[40] said, No: Such a servant deserved to be hang'd; at which they laughed and said, this was a case of another nature. I say as it is in the one, so it is in the other. Well then, Mr. *Claxton*, you will not confess the trueth. You say you have witness to prove it. However the trueth I have confessed, and no more can be expected. Do not you know one *Copp*? Yea I know him, and that is all, for I have not seen him above two or three times. Then they said, this is a sad principle, which if not routed, all honest men will have their wives deluded. One of them said, he feared not his wife she was too old, so they dismissed me to the place from whence I came, and said we shall report it to the House, that so with speed you may have your trial, but I think it was about fourteen weeks before I received the Sentence of the House, which took up the House a day and half work, as *John Lilborn* said, stood the Nation

---

38   A copy of *A Single Eye* is held in front of Clarkson.
39   Basil Feilding, second earl of Denbigh (c.1608–75).
40   William Cecil, second earl of Salisbury (1591–1668).

in a Thousand pounds:[41] And thus they sate spending the Common-wealths monies, about friviolus things. Now having past some votes, at last they carried the day for my banishment, which vote that day was printed, and pasted upon many posts about the City of *London*, *That* Lawrence Claxton *should remain in* New bridwel *a moneth and a day, and then the High Sheriffe of* London *to conduct him to the High Sheriffe in* Kent, *and so to be banisht* England, Scotland *and* Ireland, *and the Territories thereof during life, and Major* Rainsborough *to be no longer Justice during his life*. Now when my moneth was expired, their Vote was not executed, so after a while I came forth of prison, and then took my journey with my wife to my house in *Stainfeild*, and from thence I took my progress into Cambrigdeshire, to the towns of *Foxen* and *Orwel* where still I continued my Ranting principle, with a high hand.

Now in the interim I attempted the art of Astrology and Physick, which in a short time I gained and therewith travelled up and down Cambridgeshire and *Essex*, as *Linton* and *Saffron-walden*, and other countrey towns, improving my skill to the utmost, that I had clients many, yet could not be therewith contended, but aspired to the art of Magick, so finding some of Doctor *Wards* and *Woolerds* Manuscripts,[42] I improved my genius to fetch Goods back that were stoln, yea to raise spirits, and fetch treasure out of the earth, with many such diabolical actions, as a woman of *Sudbury* in *Suffolk* assisted me, pretending she could do by her witch-craft whatever she pleased; now something was done, but nothing to what I pretended, however monies I gained, and was up and down looked upon as a dangerous man, that the ignorant and religious people was afraid to come near me, yet this I may say, and speak the truth, that I have cured many desperate Diseases, and one time brought from *Glenford* to a village town wide of *Lanham* to Doctor *Clark*, two women and one man that had bewitched his daughter, who came in a frosty cold night, tormented in what then *Clerk* was a doing, and so after that his daughter was in perfect health, with many such like things, that it puffed up my spirit, and made many fools believe in me, for at that time I looked upon all was good, and God the author of all, and therefore have several times attempted to raise the devil, that so I might see what he was, but all in vain, so that I judged all was a lie, and that there was no devil at all, nor indeed no God but onely nature, for when I have perused the Scriptures I have found so much contradiction as then I conceived, that I had no faith in it at all, no more then a history, though I would talk of it, and speak from it for my own advantage, but if I had really then related my thoughts, I neither believed that *Adam* was the first Creature, but that there was a Creation before him, which world I thought was eternal, judging that land of *Nod* where *Cain* took his wife, was inhabited a long time before *Cain*, not considering that *Moses* was the first Writer of Scripture, and that we were to look no further than what there was written; but I really believed no *Moses*, Prophets, Christ, or Apostles, nor no resurrection at all: for I understood that which was life in man, went into that infinite Bulk and Bigness, so called *God*, as a drop into the Ocean, and the body rotted in the grave, and for ever so to remain.

---

41   Lilburne often refers to finance in connection with his persecution. See, for instance, *The trial of Lieut. Collonell John Lilburne*, by Clement Walker (1649), 13, and Lilburne, *The Prisoners Mournfull Cry* (1648), 21–22.

42   Possibly Clarkson is referring to Samuel Ward of Cambridge, who wrote *Magnetis Reductorum Tropologium* (1637), which was translated in 1640.

In the interim came forth a people called *Quakers*, with whom I had some discourse, from whence I discerned that they were no further than burning brick in *Egypt*, though in a more purer way than their fathers before them; also their God, their devil, and their resurrection and mine, was all one, onely they had a righteousness of the Law which I had not; which righteousness I then judged was to be destroyed, as well as my unrighteousness, and so kept on my trade of Preaching, not minding any thing after death, but as aforesaid, as also that great cheat of Astrology and Physick I practised, which not long after I was beneficed in *Mersland*, at *Terington* and St. *Johns*, and from thence went to *Snetsham* in *Norfolk*, where I was by all the Town received, and had most of their hands for the Presentation, then for *London* I went, and going to visit *Chetwood* my former acquaintance, she, with the wife of *Middleton*, related to me the two Witnesses;[43] so having some conference with *Reeve* the prophet, and reading his Writings, I was in a trembling condition; the nature thereof you may read in the *Introduction* of that Book [*Look about you, for the devil that you fear is in you* ⟨1659⟩] considering how sadly I had these many years spent my time, and that in none of these seven Churches could I finde the true God, or right devil; for indeed that is not the least desired, onely to prate of him, and pray to him we knew not, though it is written, *It is life eternal to know the true God*,[44] yet that none of them mindes, but from education believeth him to be an eternal, infinite Spirit, here, there, and every where; which after I was fully perswaded, that there was to be three Commissions upon this earth, to bear record to the three Titles above, and that this was the last of those three: upon the belief of this I came to the knowledge of the two Seeds, by which I knew the nature and form of the true God, and the right devil, which in all my travels through the seven Chu⟨r⟩ches I could never finde, in that now I see, it was onely from the revelation of this Commission to make it known.

Now being at my Journeys end, as in point of notional worship, I came to see the vast difference of Faith from Reason, which before I conclude, you shall hear, and how that from Faiths royal Prerogative all its seed in *Adam* was saved, and all Reason in the fallen Angel was damned, from whence I came to know my election and pardon of all my former transgressions;[45] after which my revelation growing, moved me to publish to the world, what my Father was, where he liveth, and the glory of his house, as is confirmed by my writings now in publick; so that now I can say, of all my formal righteousness, and professed wickedness, I am stripped naked, and in room thereof clothed with innocency of life, perfect assurance, and seed of discerning with the spirit of revelation. I shall proceed to answer some Objections that may be raised, as unto what I have already asserted. ...

---

43   The two original leaders of the Muggletonian sect, John Reeve and Lodowick Muggleton, claimed to be the two witnesses named in Rev. 11.3.

44   John 17.3.

45   Unlike the Seekers, Ranters and the Quakers, the Muggletonians held a very strict view of election: accepting Reeve and Muggleton as the two witnesses.

A Jvstjfjcatjon of
the Mad Crew

A
JVSTJFJCATJON
OF THE
MAD CREW
IN THEIR WAIES AND PRINCIPLES.

Or
The Madnesse and Weaknesse of
GOD IN MAN
Proved Wisdom and Strength.

With a true Testimony of that sweet and unspeakable
Joy, and everlasting glory that dwels in and breaks out,
through this strange and unheard of appearance, and this in
many particulars declared; from that experiment the Author
of this Book hath made: and how wonderfully he hath been
wrought over, and led up to that life and Being which needs
not, is not, yea cannot be ashamed; being translated out
of that Kingdom that is, hath, and shall be shaken,
into that which neither is can or shall ever
be removed.

And all this dawned and sunned out in God the Son,
viz. God in the form: whom if ye crucifie, it is because you know him not.

*For whether we be besides our selves it is to God, or whether
we be sober, it is for your sake.* 2 Cor. 5. 13.

Printed in the day and year that mens hearts fail them for
fear, and for looking after those things that are coming, yea come upon the *Earth.* 1650.

To all, even to those that impatiently, as well as to
those that patiently read, and try the
things that followeth.

T*He Lord as in the latter ages of the World, darkens the glory of man, so he clears up his
own brightness that every eye may see it: and as he hath in the foregoing ages of the world,
limited himself and his appearances to a certain Election of things and persons: so in
these last days he extends himself to things and persons reprobated, and chooseth cast aways: and
this is the mystery (the non-knowing whereof) confounds and plagues the World. As for instance,
under the Law he elected the Temple as the place of his glory, the* Jews *as the people of his Portion
and Inheritance. Would you know God? to* Jerusalem *you must go, and to those people must
ye joyn, all other places and persons being accursed of God, as the withdrawings of his glory is a
curse: afterward as his glory further brake out, and as he came to be more plainly God the Son,
he leaves those people and their Temple, and joyns himself and his appearances to all Nations,
and makes every language know and hear him; and then a* Peter *a* Iew *can declare (though with
much wrastlings of spirit) that he is not to call any thing common or unclean, and that God is
no respecter of persons. And a* Paul *one of the strictest of that elected sect can say, there is nothing
unclean of it self, but to him that esteemeth it unclean, to him it is unclean, yet this was but a
bringing of them to Mount* Nebo, *and shewing them upon a hill, viz. a far off the land of* Canaan,
*but not letting them to enter in because of their unbelief, God having reserved some better things
for us, that they without us might not be made perfect; They having tasted of the tree of knowledge
of good and evil, and not seeing, enjoying, but waiting for the fulness of times, in which all things
both in Heaven and Earth, shall be gathered together in one, in Christ, and since that time for the
past ages, God hath parcelled out his glory, and spoken to us under the curtains, and withdrawn
himself from the greatest part of the Creation, even things and persons, cursing some, blessing
others, damning one, and saving another, but now he is risen to justifie himself in all, upon all,
both things and persons, and upon us is come the times of the restitution of all things which God
hath spoken by the mouth of all his holy Prophets since the world began. And the immutable God
(whom the Nations and Kin⟨d⟩reds of the Earth, Churches and societies, because they know him
not have not worshipped) is clearly manifesting the Earth to be his Foot-stool, and the Heavens his
Throne, that every creature that moves in the Earth and under the Earth, in the Sea and in the
Firmament above, is the seat of God, contains him, hugs him, embraces him, nay is really and truly
God, even the living God; that he is not affectionate or passionate, but that he loves all sweetly,
powring out himself in and upon all, making all at Peace with him, bowing and serving him, that
the devil and he are one, that the devil is but a part of Gods back sides, which terrifies because of
the curtain, that he sports and feasts himself in swearing, drinking, whoring, as when he is holy,
just and good: that the holliness of man and unholiness of man are both one to him; that he loves
and delights in one as well as the other: that the sons of God when they eat, eat God, and when
they drink, drink God: that they walk in God and tread upon God, and are covered with God:
That God lies with them every night and riseth up with them every morning, that he makes their
bed and dresses them, and puts on their apparel: that they see nothing but God, and behold the face*

of him in every thing: That they swear in God and abstaine from swearing in God, that they lye one with another in God, and are not ashamed, because God is in them: That they whore in God, that God is the Whore and the Whoremaster, & they depart not from him in any of their wais and now like little children they can play together, ly together, dance together, swear together, drink together, eat together; and yet think no evil, do no evil, knowing that if they swear not are they the better, or if they swear are they the worse: if they drink not are they the better or if they drink and are drunk are they the worse: the same if they whore, and the same if they whore not: their sins are forgiven them, and there is no guile found in these mens mouths. This is the time when the cast away Jew, and the cast away Gentile shall both be received in. The Lord is now receiving into one, making it as near himself, Whordom that hath bin a castaway, lying that hath bin a castaway, yea the Whoremonger and the Theif sweetly embracing, kissing huging these, shewing himself a new, a fresh and alive in and to the whole Creation: so that we may now truly say, Lord, whether shall we go from thy presence? Thou art in Hell, Heaven, the Sun, Moon, Stars, in the grass, in our outward dancing and sporting, there thou kissest us and there thou dandlest us upon thy knees. When we go to a Whore-house we meet thee, and when we come away thou comest away with us, and there thou takest us up into thy arms: so that now we see that thou electest and choosest reprobate things and persons; we now see that Esau hated and Jacob loved, was but in the days of our dimness, till having learned them in distinction, and as two, we might know them in one joyned and united, that Saint and sinner are all one, and that there in none good but one, that is God; and that whosoever calls any thing good unless God, and so hugs it as good, falls down to an Idol, and Worships a lie, that which his own fingers have made: and because the living God in me, and others, is condemned, as by you cast away, because of the twofold light and sight that dwells within you, I have justified my self in these poor, base, vile, sinful abominable things and persons, as by the sequel discourse appears, that I might thereby dam, ram and plague you into my self, who am,

Jesus the Son of God.

A
JVSTJFJCATJON
OF THE
MAD CREW
IN THEIR WAIES AND PRINCIPLES.

Or
The Madnesse and Weaknesse of
GOD IN MAN
Proved Wisdom and Strength.

Justified, *First in their Name.*

THey are named the mad crew: mad to the Heathen, mad to the Christian carnal, and seemingly spiritual, mad to the Gentile, mad to the Iew; mad, so was *David* accounted one of the mad men, one of the vain base fellows; so was *Lot* in his time, so was *Paul* a mad man, one that turn'd the world up-side down, so was Christ a Devil, yea the Prince of Devils. It is a common thing for God in the many and several appearances of himself to be called of men, mad, a fool, a drunkard, a vain person. It is true, the Lord in these acts madly as to you, vainly, cursedly, and profanely, as to you; it is the Lord in them, and you cannot see him, you cannot acknowledge and confesse that it is he, because you are blind and see him not; but he will arise and shew himself to their joy and your shame: I must confesse with you, this is strange un-heard of ways and principles, but entertain strangers, strange appearances; for in so doing, some have (you may if you do so) entertained Angels. And this I must further tell you, that these mad men have bin in your accompt, holy Godly men, brave teaching, preaching, praying men, such that you have loved and hugged, and they are not (though they act thus madly) a people bereaved of their senses, as you term it, that have lost their understandings; for they can if they please be as sober as any of you, speak as rationally, as judicially, act as civilly and discreetly as you, and depart not from this fleshly holiness, and outward civilities, these Tents of *Sodom* and *Gomorah*, but as the Lord by a mighty hand and out-stretched arm, acts them and carries them out; They are, I can truly say of them, a people that are as unwilling: but as they are made willing in the day of Gods power, to leave *Sodom* spiritually so called, as any of you, as opposite to that command of God, go and sell all that thou hast, as the young man in the Gospel, but that the Lords pleasure prospers in their hand. And this little Stone must (oppose it what you can) grow and become a Mountain that shall fill the whole earth. And thus you have them as they are named, by that name that shall perish and be damned; nay, is to them damned and plagued; But they have a new name, which the Lord their God shall, yea doth name, *viz*. I am eternity, Majesty, alive for evermore, the Creator, the maker of Heaven and Earth, brought up with him.

2. Justified in their Principles.

First, *That there is but one God.*

THis tenent of theirs, you all that hear or read this Discourse, will with them professedly hold and maintain; yet let me tell you, and that without offence, that thou Independent, thou Anabaptist so called, yea thou spiritual Notionist, that scornest carnal Ordinances, yet thou art a worshipper of many Gods: & dost not keep thy self to any one God purely. I could tell all of you, that money is your God, that all your care, industry, pains, is to get and keep this God money, You cannot though you can talk of it, trust God and live by Faith, if you have nothing for to morrow, but only for the present day, you are not contented, satisfied, your hearts then roars it out, and saith, what shall we do, we shall perish: and then cry out, why, because you have lost your God. I know it by the experiment I have made upon many of you, I see how ye can turn Seperatist Church men, baptise none but your holy fleshly seed, or none but such that believe, nay condemn all this as carnal, and talk of living holy in the Spirit, and all well enough till this voice sounds in your ears, Go and sell all thou hast, and come and follow me, who am numbered among the rogues, theeves, whore-masters, and base persons of the world, cast away your bags of mony, your riches, your substance, your trades, your wives, your children, be without a house & without a homet know not where in the morning to lay your heads at night; care not for to morrow, O then you storm and rage, you have lost your God, your Diana, and thus your God cannot save, nor deliver in the day of wrath. But this is but one of your Gods, there is another God, and that is such a one as ye call unchangeable, and yet you believe him, and make him to be in your imaginations one that hears, and answers prayers, moved by your speaking to him, and turning away from you, if you call not upon him; therefore, you cry and thunder it out, as if you would peirce his ears, and as if your zeal could move him to do you good, and thus you change God into a lie like your selves, sometimes gracious to you, and at other times cruel. There is another God you set up, and that is such a one that is in one, not in another, cursing one and blessing another, and so dam God as to the greatest part of the Creation, that he is onely in Saints, in a few, but he is not the God of all, and who is their God, who acts in the wicked, one called a Devil, another Spirit, and so they make something to be besides God; and if God be not the same, and only he, in one as in all, and all as in one, then there is another Being, another eternity. But now these men (that are male and female) hold one onely pure and individible, simple and uncompounded God, who is not withholden from any thing, who is in all as sweet and as glorious, acting as devinely and holily (though not to creature apprhensions) in the wicked, as in the godly, as in him that steals, lies, swears, and is drunk, as in him that swears and lies not: is no more in one then in another, is the same life, the same being, the same glory in one, as in another; in beasts, as in men, and in men as in beasts, the very same and no way different but in manifestation; and though he be in all, in every one, yet he is but one, and they are all one in him. That he is in *England, France* and *Turky*, and yet the very same in *France* as in *England*, and in *England* as in *France*: in Heaven as in Hell, and in Hell as in Heaven: in the Devils as in the Angels, and in the Angels as in the Devils: So that though there be to most of the Creation, Lords many, and Gods many, a God that takes care of the godly, some few, and they are his own, and forsakes all the rest as not his, *viz.* the wicked: And another God *viz.* the Devil that takes care of them, and feeds them, yet to these there is but one God, who feeds and cloths the wicked, causing his Sun to shine, and his rain to fall upon them; nay more, he that only leads them up, and takes them by the hand, and carries them up to the life of drinking, whoring, cursing, swearing, damning, so that there is to these men but one God, in them without them, and round about them.

---

2. PRINCIPLE.

That this one God is served, and gloriously worshipped
in all, both things and persons.

HEre glory lyeth, and is concealed to the most of men, it is coming forth to some, peeping through the lattis, and looking behind the wall; it is above board to others, well, what is it? Thus it is, the swearer serves God, the poor ignorant dark drunkard and Atheist serves God though he knows him not, the theif, the whoremonger serves God, all but he serves him ignorantly, as *Paul* said, *He whom ye ignorantly worship, shew I to you.* True, these poor men serve *God* ignorantly, yet this ignorant serving of *God*, is a sweet, devine and spiritual serving of him; they serve *God* in the spirit, these prophane persons serve *God* devinely; Ah! but how doth this appear? why they do in all these things act, as the most high acts them to, and it is the Lord that leads them up to this life, to this their so dark acting, as to the Creature, and he rejoyces in his own works and that which his own fingers have made, beholding drunkenness, swearing, lying, whoring, theeving, brought forth to light and open view, which he before acted in them; Thus they serve *God* and he serves them, the Lord serves them in moving, acting of them, and they him, in bringing forth those operations, and works of the Lord. And thus he hath made all things for himself, sin for himself, whoredom for himself, uncleanness for himself, yea the wicked to do his dark works, his wrathful furious works, to execute his anger, to cut off and destroy; and these he hath made for the day of wrath, to serve him in Hell, to worship him in the Tavern, in the Ale-house, in a Whore-house; and thus he is in these things served, and yet spiritually. There are others that serve him in these things drunkenness, swearing, lying, whoring, and yet knowingly in light in truth, some that do these things, yet do no evil, acting it in a holy way as holyness, swearing holily, and drinking holily, whoring holily, all is holy, righteous and good that they do, and they meet the Lord in these, and kiss the Lord in these. Nay further, he is served in unholy, beggerly, cursed praying and preaching, and Church societies; in all these whoredoms and Idolatries he is honored and obeyed, though but ignorantly and darkly: the Lord acts in these men, and they bring forth *God* as a praying *God*, as a *God* of the Churches and Societies, as a *God* of the separation of a few that thus worship him, and the Almighty is frollick and merry, and jocund in these foolish vain things, and the Lord clads himself with these fopperies and fooleries, and comes forth to the people in this gay apparel in this fools coat, and the people admire him and stare upon him, and fall down to him; and thus the Lord is every ways served in all things. The Beasts of the F⟨ie⟩ld, the Fishes of the Sea, the Birds they serve and fall down to this *God*, they feed and nourish man: because they are the living *God*, or the living *God* in them: and they refresh and glad man; the Fruits of the Earth they are all adorned with *God*, and Wine which as it is said 9. *Jud*. 13. glads the heart of *God* and Man.

---

3. PRINCIPLE.

That Good and Evil, are both one joyned hand in hand.

MAn, innocent, holy upright man, tasting of the tree of knowledg of good and evil, comes to divide and seperate that which *God* had joyned together, and thereby became accursed, calling one holy another unholy, this a good man that an evil man, and so hates the one and loves the other, joyns to the one and seperates from the other: But the holy innocent man knows not, owns not any such distinctions, from whose Throne flyes every unclean and corrupt thing, into which *Jerusalem* enters, nothing that is poluted, defiled, or any lie, any feigned thing, but what is really and truly the holy one, and he is at peace with all without him, with all within him: he is one with sin and sin one with him, sin is beloved of him and that for the Fathers sake; I mean those acts called sin, which are to him pure holy, as saith the History, *to the pure all things are pure*,[1] swearing, lying, whoring, these are pure things to him, he knows it not under these denominations or distinctions, he knows these acts as his life, as himself, as one with him; he is of purer eyes then to behold iniquity. These see no evil, all things to them hath the appearance of Cristall glory, transcendent excellency, in the dust doth purity and eternity lie, and thus their dead men shall live; and with this dead body shall arise, and all things shall become new. Oh my friends! my dear hearts all of you, the whole Crea⟨t⟩ion, my Life, my Being; this is the passing away of all old things, and all things becoming new. My dear ones, you wonder at it, you are amazed, no marvel, for these are terrible thundrings and lightnings, unheard of, Earth quakes and Heaven quakes; this shakes Houses, Families, Wives, Children: surely it is the day of Judgement; the Mountains are flying and the Hils skipping, for who is able to indure his presence. Purity and everlasting Glory shews it self, and who can bear it; the Lyon is eating straw with the Oxe, the Wolf is lying down with the Lamb, the clean hugs the unclean and the unclean the clean, and who can bear it.

---

1   Tit. 1.15.

4. PRINCIPLE.

That God is no respecter of Persons.

THe poor and the rich are both made by *God*, the Saint and the sinner they have both one Being, one fountain, one surse[2] and rise, they are al of one Family. They sit with him, in him at one table, eat the same meat, and drink the same drink one as the other: *God* as sweetly provides for the one as the other, as sweetly loves them, joys in them, delights in them: they are himself, they are not a part from him. The Lord in everlasting love and brightness, damns the Saint and saves the sinner, and again damns the sinner and saves the Saint: cares as little for the praying preaching man the *Pharisee*; *Peter* the Elect as *Judas* the Apostate, Loves *Judas* the Apostate, and *Alexander* the Coper-smith who did *Paul* much hurt, yea the cast aways as well every jot, for their is no distinction in him, as he loves the praying man the *Pharisee*, they are all alike to *God*; he beholds all things and persons, with the same and in the same purity, with and in the same glory, all perfect in him, compleat in him, righteous in him, children of pleasure in him. He sees dancing, lying with one another, kissing pure and perfect in him; He loves all with an everlasting love, the theif that goes to the Gallows as well as the Judg that condemns him, and the Judg with a love of and from eternity as well as the theif: He loves as dearly with an infinite unchangeable love the *Cavileer* as the *Round-head*, and the *Round-head* as the *Cavileer*: the *Army* as abundantly as the *Levellers*, and the *Levellers* as the *Army*: For with him is no distinction. He pulleth down the mighty from their Throne, and sets up men of low degree.

5. PRINCIPLE.

That the Righteous shall never be saved, that the Godly
shall go to Hell, the Wicked to Heaven.

THis may some say, if it can be made out to be a true Principle, is one of the strangest and most uncouth. You have it in your book, he came not to call the Righteous but Sinners to repentance, you have there a hint of it. Salvation is taken by the greatest part of the Creation, to be after death a going to Heaven a place above the skies; Now this I say, such a salvation that you all, or most men whatsoever exspect, the righteous shall never obtain. The truly righteous need not, yea cannot go thither; for they are, and alwaies were in Heaven, yea while they are upon Earth; The righteous that sin not, that are without fault, are ever really and truly before the throne in *God*, and *God* in them, singing for ever *Hallelujah* to the Lord, so that these holy ones enter not into such a vain, empty, foolish, imaginary Kingdom, know

2 Old spelling of 'source': origin of flowing water.

not such a Heaven. And the seemingly righteous that know good and evil, that choose the one and hate the other, they neither go to this Heaven and are not thus saved, for they are already in Heaven and know it not, it is with them as with *Jacob*, the Lord was here and I knew it not. There is no Heaven but God and they are in God and God in them, but they know him not, have no experience of him to be their perfection and glory, and therefore these righteous men are (through the ignorance in them) in Hell walking under vain imaginations under earthly fancies, building their hopes, salvation, and all upon the sands; their house is shaken and cannot stand, for it is not founded in God, but in a place above the skies. But the wicked (who to creature apprehensions are so) they that swear, ly, steal and whore, and all in the light of *God*, these go yea are already entred into Heaven, into the perfection of beauty, into eternity, singing to the Lord that liveth and reigneth for ever, while you righteous men are in Hell and at a distance from Heaven, and cannot by all your holiness, prayings, preachings reach this Heaven, this perfection, this joy, but these wi⟨c⟩ked men as you call them, are singing, rejoycing and feasted with the everlasting feast of fat things.

---

6. PRINCIPLE.

That they have overcome death, and mortallity is in
them swallowed up into imortallity.

NO marvell they are mad men for they are newly come out of their graves, and you are afraid to behold them; ye run away from them as from so many ghosts and spirits. They are passed from death to life, they can dy no more, they are he that was dead but is now alive for evermore, all mortal dying, perishing things are swallowed up in them, into a living immortal being, their earthliness dark and carnal apprehensions are not, but are drowned and lost in God, and in God are found a new. Horrors and fears of death they all fly before them, the tokens of death are all overcome in them. Sorrow is a token of death, they can weep no more, sorrow and sighing is in them past away. Sin is a forerunner to death; this is taken away, they can sin no more. Repentance is propper for dying men mortal Creatures, this is also taken away, repentance is hid from their eyes, they do not any thing worthy of repentance, they are past repentance. Shame that is propper to mortal Creatures, those that are under death and sin, this flyes before them, they are not ashamed of ought they do: they are naked as *Adam* and his wife was in Paradise and are not ashamed, they are past shame. They have overcome all things, and now inherit all things, all things are theirs: They one with every thing, and every thing one with them: destruction is their salvation, and damnation is their blessing: Hell their Heaven; and thus they plague death, play with death and laugh with death: and terrifie death that hath terrified the whole creation. These are the new creatures, they are past dying, perrishing or rotting, all things in them are rotted damned and plagued already, what ever thing it be that is under death, or borders upon it cannot come near their

Tabernacle. They are now nothing else but a blessing, a sweet savor, a sweet smell to all, in all, upon all: they are the life of all. All their garments smell of myrh, alloes and cassia, and their feet stand upon the Mount of *Olives*: They have trampled down every thing that was above them, and they are now ascended far above all Heavens. The resurrection though it was not in *Pauls* time; yet to these men it is past already, and they have hereby overthrown the faith of many, of all: and they live by sight, by a pure perfect enjoyment, and beholding of that eternal glory which is themselves, they purely wrapt up into it, and it into them: and upon these is brought to pass that saying is written, Death is swallowed up into victory: O death where is they sting? O grave where is thy victory.

---

7. PRINCIPLE.

That being in Heaven, (the light, glory, and perfection
of God) these neither marry nor are given in marriage.

YOu know upon what occasion this was spoken in the History; that when the people carnally questioned things in the resurrection, who should own her that had owned so many? the answer was, There was no such owning, marrying or giving in marriage in that world: observe the words, *Luk.* 20. 34, 35. *The children of this World, marry wives and are marrried.* The sons of darknesse, the sons of men of earthly low enjoyments, they that live in the twilight marry, take one woman, two or three or a few apart from the rest of the Creation, love them at a distance from others: those whom they have thus elected and chosen, have their hearts desires and affections, goods, body and all, but they are estranged to the other part of the world, who are really theirs, flesh of their flesh, and bone of their bone as they: but those who shall be accounted worthy to enjoy that world, the world to come, and the resurrection from the dead, *viz.* dead carnall cursed apprehensions and concernments, never marry, never joyn and disjoyn, never love one and hate another, never affect one dearly and the other overly, but have the same pure, perfect, entire love to one as the other. These mad Crew are come to the great Supper, to the great Feast, to the great marriage, and there is heard at this wedding, nothing but sweet melody, singing and dancing, no noise or confusion, but only the voice of the Bride and the Bridegroom, the Lamb and the Lambs wive, and yet but one, and one voice: There is here at this wedding many thousands, and yet but one: there are threescore Queens, and fourscore Concubines, and Virgins without number, yet my beloved is but one. These creatures are married all, to every woman is their wife, not one woman apart from another, but all in one, and one in all: There is not this voice heard at this feast, whose wife is this woman, and whose that? and whose husband is such a one? for there is but one Husband, and one Wife: and this man and wife, though made up of many thousands, ly with one another every night, the bed is large enough to hold them all; it is not such a bed that you have heard to be at Ware,[3] where twenty can ly in it, but a sweet bed made of Roses and Spices, large enough, where millions of millions can all stretch themselve on it, and yet it is but one stretching, one stretched, one loving, and one loved: the same kissing, and the same kissed, and all creatures are singing and dancing at this wedding; there is never a creature in heaven and earth but dances and leaps from that fulnesse of joy that is in him living in this house, and being made one of this family. These scorn the thoughts of Adultery, abhor and loath it as one of the abhominations that are spued out of their mouth. There is such a unity where there is this diversity, and such a diversity where there is this unity, that they cannot kisse one but they kisse all, and love one but they love all, and cannot take one into bed with them and leave out another, but they destroy this unity and diversity. They have attained the resurrection from the dead, yea from that death which saith, these twain, these two, such a one, and such a one, and they are come to this life that in power faith, they shall be no more twain, but one flesh; note the word, they were twain, a man and a woman, the marrying and the marryed before the resurrection, when God was locked up in some certain things, when Christ was in the Heavens, which must contain him for a time, but now they are risen from the dead they twain shall be one flesh, one body, one life, one spirit. The people in England shall not be one, and the people in France another, the people in Turky one, and the people in Christendom (as it is called) another: but the people in England France and Turkey, one people and one body, for where the one lives there liveth the other also. Therefore you that are the children of this world condemn not the children of the world to come as to you, but come already to these people. These people are ente⟨r⟩ed into heaven, attained this resurrection, are entered into this land of Canaan: you are yet in the wildernesse some of you, others of you come to the borders, envy not them that are entered in, but follow those who through faith and patience have attained the Crown, and speak not evil of the things you know not.

PRINCIPLE. VIII.

They hold all things common, and truly enjoy all things
in common.

THey on whom the sprinklings of the spirit fell, were (as saith the Scripture, which you professe to own) made to see and act in this Communitie, *Act.* 2. 44. nay, they called nothing they possessed their own: O you Independents, Anabaptists, so called, spiritual Notionists, that say you own and beleeve this to be true: you hypocrites why do you call any thing your own? why do ye say so much mony I have, so much land, so many children, such a woman is my wife, so many hundred pounds for such a childe, so many for such a childe?

---

3   The Great Bed of Ware, 3.38m x 3.26m, originally housed in the White Hart Inn in Ware,
     Hertfordshire was built c.1590. It could accommodate at least four couples. It is now in the
     Victoria and Albert Museum, London.

is this to make all things common? canst thou not yet see the earth to be the Lords, and the fulness thereof? then what hast thou? hast thou ever a childe that is not the Lords childe? or ever a wife that is not the Lords wife, or any land, or money that is not the Lords? then why is *Esau*'s voice heard among you? and why do you with him sell your birth-right for a mess of pottage? you sell your right to all things for some poor unworthy things? for some few poor unworthy things? why do ye rejoyce that you have so many hundreds, or so many thousands, if all be the Lords? and that you will now sit down and take no further care, for you have so much mony, and so much land that will maintain you and yours as long as you live, if all this land and mony be the Lords? you will say, Why we did never deny but that all we have is the Lords, and that to him we are beholden for every thing we have: well then saith the Lord, you have said, O that there were in you such a heart to do whatever you have said: you have well spoken, I wish it were as well practised. Well then, I your Lord and God, your Creator and Father, who am in all the Being, and Life of all, who am all that any man is, all that every man is: who have made man my Tabernacle and dwelling place, and in man am come forth, and do in them say, in the poor of the earth, in you out cast brethren and sisters, your own flesh, in these do I say, Come give me your mony, your land, your wives and children, let it be their land, mony, wives and children as well as yours, and yours as well as theirs; call it our mony, our wives, our children, our Table, our meat, our drink: let me the Lord, in such a rogue, theef and adulterer, sit at your Table, and eat your meat, and drink your wine, and say to them, All that I have is yours, keep not back part, remember *Lots* wife, remember the man and the woman that lyed to the Holy Ghost; you say that you have nothing but what is the Lords, and I the Lord come to you for my own, and ye keep it back: O ye hypocrites ye do but dissemble in all this; you honour me with your mouths, but your hearts are far from me. But these people whom ye call mad, have learned this Wisdom, yea this wisdom is theirs and lives in them, and saith, what is mine is every ones, and what is every ones is mine also: every woman is my wife, my joy and delight, the earth is mine, and the beasts on a thousand hills are mine: they have brought all they have, and have laid all down at the Lords feet, and if any keep back part he is accursed, they have not so learned Christ as to dis-own the Lord in any thing, in any poor dispised rogue. If any be in want an misery, let him be what he will be, he seeth his fathers name on him, the whole family of Heaven and earth is named of him and by him, therefore saith he come take thine own mony, thy own bread, thy own drink, thou shalt ly with me, and I will ly with thee, eat with me, and I will eat with thee: O there is meat enough in our fathers house, and shall we perish for hunger? it is a full house, a rich house, full of all fat things, why should we then dy by staying without, by living in a far country? we have lived in a country that hath been barren, dry, fruitless, that hath born fruit to some, to a few, but hath brought forth bryars and thorns to the rest; but we will arise and joyn our house to the fruitfull field, in whose earth there is no bryars nor thorns, but fruit enough for the whole family be it never so great. And to this Ierusalem and mount Syon are these people come, and in this land are these mens habitations found: These are they that have done the work of the Lord, and the will of the Lord, not because it is written without them, but because it is written within them, saying, Love not in word or in tongue, but in deed and in truth: there is that within them that will not suffer them to be at rest, untill they have slain all the Amalekites, and all the beasts and oxen, the fat ones as well as the lean ones, and this obedience (my friends) is better then Sacrifice. There are a people great Professors, that can say, I have done all the commandments of the Lord, and yet have not slain all as the Lord hath commanded, nor gon and sold all, but have reserved part to themselves, but from such have I this very day rent the Kingdom.

PRINCIPLE IX.

*That their Counsel shall stand, and they will do all their
pleasure.*

SWeet hearts, did my dear ones my brethren the Jews, that crucified Christ, think that he did whatsoever he was pleased to do, and do you my hearts of Gold that crucifie Christ now he is risen up, and come again in the clouds, even as he went from us, that he doth whatsoever he pleases to do. These men are so purely made one with God, and God one with them, they in God and God in them, that nothing stands but what is by them decreed to stand, and nothing fals but what is by them voted to fall. By this mad Crew do Kings reign, and Princes decree Justice. If the Lord in the ministry of Angels will preserve *Lot*, though the Sodomites would break open dores, and destroy *Lot*, yet shall his councel stand, and they shall be blinded, as to that work. If the Lord again in *Shimei*, will curse *David*, *David* shall not (though he hath thousands with him) go and destroy *Shimei*, but quietly submit, saying, Let the Lord do what he will. It is the pleasure of this mad Crew sometimes to give their back to the smiters, and their cheeks to those that pluck off the hair: and at another time to be in the fire and it shall not burn them, nor a hair of their head cinged. If you afflict and imprison their forms, they are well pleased, for their own arm hath done it: and if you lay not a hand on them, it is as well, for their power would not suffer it? if you be gathered together to crucifie the holy child Jesus, it is because their councel and hand hath determined it before to be done. Their will is become so much the Lords, and the Lords theirs, that they will what they will, and do what they will. And it is so decreed in Heaven, and in this great Councel, that you Independents, Anabaptists and Spiritual Notionists, must with men of all sorts and ranks, do the will of these Rogues, Theeves, Whore-masters and Drunkards, as you call them. And when you pray, Thy will be done, you pray (though ignorantly and unknown to your selves) Let the will of those we persecute, hate, and falsly call Drunkards, Swearers, Whore-masters, be done, and nothing else but their will. When you say, and that fervently, Father, glorifie thy will; you say, Father, gloryfie the will of these whore-masters, Drunkards and unclean persons: I tell you my friends, you know not what you say; but he whom ye ignorantly worship shew I to you: you know not the holy one, you pray to: would you see this as true without you, as these men do within them? read *Ioh.* 17. 24. Christ praying before that the will of God might be done, and that he would do so & so, as you may read at large in the chapter comes at last to this perfection & height of glory, I will that thou honourest these poor creatures I have prayed for, with the same honour as I have and had before the world began, and be where I am: and where was he but in God, in perfection? and as saith, *vers.* 2. That they may be one in us, I in them, and thou in me, that they may be made perfect in one, There is also no more twain, but one, no more two wills, but one. And this man Christ with his disciples was called, and that by the Church by the professors a wine-bibber, a drunkard, a devil. These men whom ye call mad, are Christ the anointed of God; they have the fulness of the Godhead bodily, in them is hid the treasures of all wisdom and knowledge, and these shall judge the world, yea Angels: these are they that shal (yea doth) condemne you and blesse you, that make you do their will, and give you power, as enabling you thereto.

And thus I have given you a discovery of the principles and ways of this mad Crew, and under these heads ly many others, of which you have a taste, which for brevities sake I have not singled out: but I have herein born testimony to them and their waies, and saved my self, and those that hear me. Now followeth a true testimony of that unspeakable joy that I have found in this appearance.

A true Testimony of that unspeakable and everlasting
joy that the Author of this book hath found in this
strange and unheard of appearance, and he hath hereby
made to passe over into the good land Canaan
that flows with milk and hony.

IT pleased the Lord who became a child in me, for certain seasons and times to train me up in childish things, where I was pleased with his back parts; and as his glory passed by me to stand in the cleft of the rocks: for it was enough being a child, that we played Bo-peep, I thought it then enough that in name and declaration my sinnes were all forgiven me, and cast into the sea, for counters were then to me as good as gold. And truly I must needs say that I had great joy and satisfaction in this estate, and I was very rich, especially in my own childish eyes; but I was at length brought to see that riches would not avail in the day of wrath: for a day since (one day being now with me as a thousand years, and a thousand years as one day) the day of Gods wrath and vengeance fell upon me, and burnt up all my childish things, and there was such an everlasting fire about my ears that I could keep nothing I had, but was burnt up both body and soul with all that I had, righteousness, holiness, preaching, teaching, prayers, wife, children and all that I had, by this fire I then (by God) began to be plagued with my holiness and my prayers became sin to me and all things else a burden, and whatever I kept back as I did for a time (until the fire burnt it all up) did torment and plague me: my former joyes became my sorrows and my pleasure torment, and I was a spectacle to my self and all about me. I wondered where I was and I fell down dead, and the power of God set me on my feet; I had a great mind to keep somewhat back, and would fain have clad my self with some outwardly holy garments, but so pure and fervent was the fire, that it would let nothing remain. My fleshly holiness and civil conversation me thought was such an ornament that I said with *Peter, Lord thou knowest that I have not to this day eaten any thing that is common or unclean*, I had never sworn, bin drunk, or given to any outward prophaness or loosness in all my life; and now Lord must I now joyn my self to these unholy things, but that within me said, call not thou any thing common or unclean, for I have made all things clean for thee, and the fire was so great that it burnt up all I had in these everlasting burnings, and divine purity, and then I looked and could see nothing but purity: I did then see purity and glory in all those things I formerly called impurity and prophanness, and I was made silent and obedient to the heavenly voice, and I had then but one eye and one pure sight given me, by which I saw all things pure to me, and the things I formerly washed my hands of could I now touch, and *I* could play with every thing as with my life and being, and saw all things reconsiled to me and *I* to it. *I* did then really see a Nation born at once, and the *Gentles* flowing in to behold this my glory and brightness. Then *Gentelisme* became to me as good as *Judisme* or *Christianisme*, *I* could then be feasted with the Lord wherever he appeared, and he was alwaies at my right hand, *I* was entred into the perfection of all things, of all happiness: my course was finished and *I* have obtained the Crown. *I* had many reasonings and disputings with my self, what should become of my self and of all that appertained to me, why *I* should thus leave all the credit and glory *I* had in the world, and why *I* might not keep it for a while and by means covertly to bring in others, and that by this great forsaking of all things, *I* might offend many and cause many to stumble; but the Sun went down upon all these reasonings, and they were all answered and found in everlasting glory and purity and whatever; yea a thousand times more that ever *I* have lost have *I* found in God. *I* futher reasoned age, but *I* might repent of these things when it is to⟨o⟩ late, and *I* were better to consider before hand what I did, then at last to repent, but I found that within me saying, repentance is hid from my eys, *I* can repent and weep no more, and from that time have I bin filled with the everlasting fulness of the Lord, and the Rivers of that pleasure have and do flow in upon me; The Sun hath bin ashamed and the Moon abashed in me, for he is reighning for evermore, nay in outward sporting, dancing, playing, and kissing and bodily embracing one of another have I clearly seen him that is invisible. There hath bin to me such a harmony, such a oneness, such a devine glory presented to me under all these, that I have wondred where I have bin, when I beheld eternity living in such vanity, blessedness in such cursing, (as it was once to me) and I have bin made to see a blessing in every thing. The earth hath ceased bringing forth Bryars and Thorns to me, and the curse to me is taken away. I have sometimes since then bin (as I have formerly called it) unclean, and yet never more clean, uncivil and yet never more civil, I have bin since then a great transgressor, and yet never a less transgressor; I have acted it in such purity in such a devine way, that I have not known it by its name of impurity or unholiness, it hath all bin risen in me to an immortal and incorruptible being: so that, though it was sowen in weakness, yet it was raised in power, sowen in corruption but it hath bin raised in incorruption. The time will fail me to tell you of the day that I live in that hath no night, of the glory that hath no end, of the Sun that never goes down, of the darkness that is with me as light, and sin that is with me as righteousness, how my soul hath bin and is feasted with these things, and how the vail and covering over my face hath bin rent in twain; I cannot utter it in words for it is unspeakable, I cannot clear it up to your apprehensions, for it passeth knowledg, it pleaseth me that I am in it, and it pleaseth me also that you are for a time out of it, (though were not wishing ceased in me) I could heartily wish you were in the same glory with me. It is enough at present that I give you to understand where I am, and where I am there shall ye be also, for in my Fathers house there are many Mansions. To draw to an end, I am endless, my glory is endless, my joy is endless, my life is endless, could I exchange it for all the world, pleasures, joys and delights thereof; yea for all the joys of childish lights and understandings, yet by Gods life I would not but I would scorn the thought of taking Brass for Silver and Iron for Gold, I am where I would be, and where I would be there I am, I have lost all things, and I have found all things, my loss hath bin my gain, and my death my life. I am come to the spirits of just men, made perfect, to *Abrahams* Spirit, to *Moses* Spirit, *Davids* Spirit, *Daniels, Pauls* and *Johns* Spirit, I familiarly talk with them and they with me; and therefore *Hallelujahs* to the Lord that liveth and reighneth for evermore.

F   I   N   I   S.

The POSTS⟨C⟩RIPT, directed to all Nations.

YOu the Nations of the World, though to me but one Nation, and one people, I have a long time been silent in Puritanisme, Presbyterianisme, Independensie, Anabaptisme, and spiritual Notionisme; but now in the last of these days am I made to stand upon my feet, and to curse and damn the inhabitants of the World, until there be but one inhabitant, and till there be but a man left in all the earth, who is, was, and shall be the glory of the Woman. I will now ly openly[4] before the Sun, with many women, and yet with my own Wife, and I will plague even bitterly, they that ly with any save their own Wives in the dark, in their thoughts and desires, in their words, I will make them gnaw their tongues, and gnash their teeth for pain, who pretend to be holy and not to touch a Woman, and yet can and sometimes have layen with Women in the dark: yea you that never did it actually, but in thought and desire, you have committed Adultery before me, and for it shall ye be damned. O you hypocrites you can spend your selves to the full, as oft as your lust carries you out, upon one Woman called your Wife, and there do as much as any Whore-master in the World upon many Women, and this is no sin, no pollution, ye hypocrites hath he not made of one blood all Nations? are they not one Flesh, one Body? what difference is there between your wife and another woman? O, you say you are married to your wife, and that is no evil: Why, what is marriage? is it any more but to gain the love and affections of a woman to be yours,[5]

---

4   a) naked b) publicly.
5   The printed text ends abruptly here.

Joseph Salmon

A Rout, A Rout;

Or some part of the
ARMIES QUARTERS
BEATEN UP,

By the DAY of the
L O R D

Stealing upon Them.

Wherein is briefly discovered
the present cloudy and dark Appearance
of God amongst them.

By JOSEPH SALMON, a present
Member of the *ARMY.*

He that hath an ear to hear, let him hear what the Spirit saith.
Arise ye, and depart, for this is not your rest; it is polluted, &c.
The weapons of our warfare are not carnal, but mighty through
God, to beat down strong holds, &c.

London, Printed for G. C. 1649.[1]

---

1   Another edition 'Printed by *T. N.* 1649' was collected by Thomason on 10 Feb. It is substantially identical to the Calvert edition, differing only in minor instances of punctuation, capitalization and spelling.

A
WORD
To the
Commanding Power
in the
A R M Y.

By your leave, Gentlemen,

Hope, in these days of Liberty, I may be free to speak a word to my fellow Souldiers: I shall not trouble *You* with much at the present, for I know you have more trouble already upon your spirits, then you can well tell how to be rid of. My speech is intended especially (as I said before) to my fellow-Souldiers, those of the inferior rank and quality; I have very little from the Lord to declare to You as yet: All that I have to say, is this; That you go on as fast as you can with the Work you have begun, for the time draws nigh that is allotted you: Make haste (I say;) yet not more haste then good speed: Make a short work; but cut it short in Righteousness; for the Day is at hand, wherein he that helpeth and they that are holpen shall fall together. Gentlemen, you are the Rod of God, yea, the Rod of the Lords anger in his own Hand, the Almighty Arm acts you; and so it appears; for no manly glory can encounter with you: in this Day of the LORDS Wrath you strike thorow King, Gentry, and Nobility, they all fall before you: You have a Commission from the LORD to scourge *ENGLAND'S* Oppressors; do it in the Name of God, do it (I say) fully, hotly, sharply; and the same measure you mete, shall be met to you again; for the Lord will ere long cast his Rod into the fire of burning and destruction: It will be a sweet destruction, wait for it.

Gentlemen,

Under an abrupt
form I sub-
scribe my self

Yours in life
and death,

JOSEPH SALMON.

TO
The Fellowship (of
SAINTS scattered)
in the A R M Y.

Dear Hearts,

I *Know it will be a wonder to some of you, to behold this Frontispiece faced with my Character; and truly it is as much my wonder as yours: I little thought that ever God would have called me hither.*

Friends, I am yet amongst you, I own you, I can say Amen *to your proceedings, although I cannot close with you in the managing of them. I have a fellowship with you in the Lord: but I am distant from your dark and fleshly enterprises.*

You are a scattered seed amongst tares, and it is your name that upholds the fame of the whole: You are that little Leaven hid in the meal, whose reputation seasons the whole lump; if it were not for you, this power of the sword, would vanish and be annihilated. Behold, I shew you a Mystery, it is yet hidden from many, yea most of you; Thus saith the Lord of Hostes, The Day is coming, and now is, when I will gather up my jewels in the Army (from under this dark and carnal form of the Sword) into my self; where I will be unto them Life, Liberty, Priviledg and Satisfaction, the fulness of Arrears, and plenty of Accommodation; when they shall no more contend with the world for outward Interest, but beholding all in Divine Fulness, shall in the enjoyment of it sit down contented. *And this I partly see fulfilled in my self and others.*

But now it may be you will wonder why I yet remain amongst you, seeing I am brought hither; I am sure many of your verdicts will pass upon me, I shall not want the censure of most. But it is no matter; Cast all your cruelty and malice upon me; the Lord in me is mighty to bear it: I will own it all, being willing to become sin for you, though the Lord in me knows no sin; that you, together with me, may be presented in the Lord an eternal righteousness.

I have but this at present to say: I am now with you, as Mary *at the Sepulchre, waiting to see the Lord: but he is risen. Your carnal affairs are the Sepulchre where the Lord is buried to me; he is not here, he is certainly risen, but where to see him in his next appearance, I wait: I must stand at the Sepulchre till the voyce be uttered behinde me, which I beleeve will be shortly, both to me and many others.* Till the day break, and the shadows flee away, *Farewel my Beloved,* be thou as a Roe, or a young Hart upon the mountains of *Bether.*

Sirs, I am yours,

J os: S al.

A ROUT,[2] *A ROUT,*

OR,

Some part of the Army's Quar-
ters beaten up, by the DAY of the
LORD stealing upon them.

Hat Power (or Mystery) which acts all things, and by which whole man (in his councels, actions and engagements) is led out and disposed according to divine will and pleasure; I say, this Power (which is God) comes forth and offers it self in a diversity of appearance, and still (by a divine progress in the affairs of the earth) moves from one power to another, from one dispensation to another, from one party to another; hereby accomplishing his eternal decreed design in and upon the Creature. This is manifest in all dispensations, civil and spiritual.

Time was, when God had faced the Jewish Ceremonies (those carnal manifestations) with a great beauty and splendor of divine Majesty: the Lord was there seen under that form to vail and hide his beauty and glory. In a time appointed he departed from them, went out of them, he would dwell there no longer; but he casts off that form or garment, and clothes himself with another, swallowed up that glory in another, the lesser in the greater; and then all the brightness and lustre of divine appearance resided in, and dwelt upon the flesh of the Son, as being a more true pattern, and exact resemblance of God the divine Power. But the Lord was not here in his appearance where he would be neither; and therefore having no resolution eternally here to tabernacle[3] or abide, in the fulness of time he lays this form aside also. Though he was the Son, the dear Son, the only begotten Son, a Son so like the Father, yet he must not be spared, he must be crucified, the Lord will move hence also: whence note, That this divine Power (or Mystery) admits of no eternal habitation in any thing below it self.

Now as this Power [God] hath a dayly motion out of one dispensation spiritual into another, so also it is in civil or outward dispensations.

This I have found in my own experience, (by tracing this divine Power, in its going forth amongst the sons of Men) that it sometimes owns this, sometimes that form; sometimes this, sometimes that party, dayly moving from one to another as it pleaseth: now the Lord lives in all these, though in some darkly, in others more purely; and all these motions are as so many footsteps of God, whereby he gradually ascends out of the creature, into a more compleat image or likeness of himself.

Time was, when God dwelt amongst us in the darkness of absolute and arbitrary Monarchy: the face and beauty of divine mystery lived in it, deny it who can, that sees God in all things.

In this form of Monarchy God hath vailed his beautiful presence with a thick cloud of darkness: He hath made darkness his secret place, and his pavilions round about him have been thick clouds of the Sky. Though the image and brightness of God have dwelt in it, yet under

---

2   Defeat; disordered, hurried retreat.
3   To dwell for a time; said of Christ's earthly life (*OED* v. 1).

such black darkness that man could never discern it. Tyranny, persecution, opposition, wil, nature and creature, hath been (as it were) that vail betwixt God and man in this dispensation; all this, and whatever you will call evil in Monarchy, the Lord was pleased to hide himself under, while resident in this carnal form. I know its difficult to see God in this darkness, the bright Sun under this black cloud: the naked and pure Spirit, under this foul habit and filthy attire; but he that cannot here discern God is blind, and sees not afar off.

God (having hitherto walked under this form) is now (and hath in these last days) come forth to rend this vail in pieces, to shake this form, to lay it waste, and clothe himself with another.

How God hath and does destroy Monarchy, and what it figures out to us.

The power and life of the King, and in him the very soul of Monarchy sunk into the Parliament, and here it lost its name barely, but not its nature; its form, but not its power; they making themselves as absolute and tyrannical as ever the King in his reign, dignity and supremacy; yet the Lord ascended a little nearer himself, by taking off this form (the Parliament) and hereby made way for his after-design.

We see in a short time, he lays aside that glorious shew and Idol (the Parliament) and clothes himself with the Army: And thus, both King, Monarchy and Parliament fell into the hands, and upon the swords of the Army: and thus the Army are to be the Executioners of that beast (Monarchy) which they had formerly wounded, and whose wound the Parliament had healed and salved over by a corrupt and rotten Treaty: all which doth figure out to me the stain of the glory of all flesh; as Monarchy (or arbitrary regal power) falls by the sword, so also shall that Kingly and Imperial power of all flesh be cut in sunder by the stroke of Divine Justice; for by his fire and by his sword will the Lord plead with all flesh, and the slain of the Lord shall be many: The Lord will kindle a burning under that glory wherein he hath formerly appear'd; God himself shall be the burning, the holy One shall be the flame, and all fleshly regality in us shall be the fuel which shall be burnt up and consumed. But we shall hence proceed to our former Discourse, and shall next in order consider

How God lives in the A R M Y.

Thus far we see God hath moved from party to party, and sits down at present in the Army; and here also God makes darkness his secret place, living under a poor, low, carnal form, and few can behold his beautiful presence under the power of the Sword. The Lord here besmears himself with blood and vengeance, deforms his own beauty, hides his aimable presence under a hideous and wrathful form.

And now in as much as God hath called me forth (from an impartial spirit) to declare my Light; I shall (from some clear experience of the Armies present condition) discover that dark and cloudy appearance of the supream Power [*God*] amongst them, whereby may be discerned how far below the pure appearance of the spirit, their present station renders them. And I am very confident, that which I shall say, the Lord will testifie and bear record the truth of the same upon the hearts of many amongst them. Friends! Look about you, for the Lord is now coming forth to rip up your bowels, to search your hearts, and try your reins;[4] yea, to let loose the imprisoned Light of himself in you; and if the Lord by this doth not shake many of you, then say, That I have prophesied Lyes in the name of the Lord. Then let him that hath an ear to hear, hear what the Lord, that Spirit saith.

Thus saith the Lord, yea the Lord saith it:

That the present condition of the Army, or the present appearance of the supream Power amongst them, renders them in darkness, and far below the pure Light and Life of God.

That it is so, I offer my appeal thus.

First, let them and all others (who are spiritually wise) consider, by and from what principles God acts these men; I mean you Heroes of valour in the Army, you Grandees of the present power in the Kingdome: In patience possesse ye your soules till I shall race your foundation, and discover your principles, which God hath hitherto and still does act you in: they are either publick or private, common or (more properly) peculiar; your common and publick principles, are the outward liberty and freedom of the Nation, the establishment of outward Lawes, Liberties, and Priviledges; and some outward form of Gover⟨n⟩ment; which may correspond with your sence of Justice: what no farther yet? This is poor earthly Tabernacle, which God at present hath taken up in you; I wish I might not have cause to say, It is a speckled pretence under which your private interests resides: For I know this is the main spur that drives you on, (self-preservation:) This is your *D⟨e⟩lilah*, you⟨r⟩ proper, private and peculiar principle: Resolved you are to save your Lives, and preserve your self-interest, though in this expedition you destroy all other powers and interests whatsoever: Herein, (though you walk, as men, very carnally) yet, Dear hearts I blame you not. I know God acts you in this cloud, he goes out with you in this darkness, and lets out his presence through this vail of self-preservation amongst you, he hath crowned you with fame, success and victory, while you have lived and acted in this earthly body of outward Liberty. But how far inferiour and below this is, to a Life in the purity of Divine light, (now God hath disclosed himself) I am in some measure able to discern.

You know not yet what it is to be dead to you⟨r⟩ own Interests, though you have professed a great deal of self-denyall, yet *I* profess many of you never knew what true self-denyall was; and what it is truly to be dissolved and dye out of your own carnal Interests: I know your honour and dignity is great in your hearts, your renowned enterprises call for merit: Your lives and safeties are also dear to you; it is so, so it must be, God will have it so: he lives in these low concernments, and yet your hearts cannot be imbittered or dis-ingaged from them: you hug them, you prize them, they are an object of your embraces. But I tell you (Sirs) God is going about to unbody himself in you, whiles you are embracing this body of self-safety and outward Liberty, he is dying and departing from it, though you see it not. And This know, That God will ere long leave you exceeding dark and dead in your enterprizes: I was alive once as well as you, and in my life I laboured amongst you (in my sphere) as much as another; but I am now dead with the Lord; I am at rest from my labour; Ah happy death! oh blessed loss! how far better is it O Lord to be dissolved and gathered up into thy rest, then to

---

4   Kidneys; understood to be the seat of the feelings or affections (*OED* n. I 1, 2).

live the life of a worldly and carnall labour? and I know also that the hour of Gods judgement is come upon many of you: some of you have received your mortall wound already; I see you gasp and strugle in your confused and dark enterprizes. Let this silver probe[5] but sink to the bottom of your wounded hearts, and something, without question, will speedily be discovered.

 Ah Friends,—

If you saw your Interests in the Lord, your Lives and Liberties in the Lord, if you saw all yours in the Lord, you would think it a beggarly thing to contend for any thing, or to plead Gods quarrel with any that shall demand them of you. Doubtlesse, it is a poor, low, base, earthly Spirit, that raises contests, and seeks after the ruine and blood of creatures, for the enjoyment of that which at best is but a bitter-sweet, a well-being subject to all manner of casualties. Lo, This is the principle that God at present acts you by: It is the Lord in you, inhabiting his secret place; and because I see it is the Lord, I can embrace it, I can tender you in my bosom-affections, while you are carried forth in this carnal dispensation. Nevertheless, I will in part discover to you how far some are dead to their own Interest, and whither shortly you must be brought.

Those that live in the more pure knowledge and Life of God, see themselves (their Lives, Liberties, and all outward enjoyments) not their own, but the Lords, and theirs in the Lord, not a jot below him, or at the least distance from him,

If we have the Lord, we have enough, because he is all to us, and we the same fulnesse in him: Lo, this is life, libertie, and satisfaction. Now no outward losse or misery can make us unhappy: we may be persecuted, yet not forsaken, cast down, yet not destroyed; dying, and behold we live, in bondage, yet free; because the Lord is all this, and more to us. *To live, to us is Christ, and to die is gain.* If we have a portion of outward safety amongst others, we see it is the Lord; if not, it is the Lord; and where the Lord is, there is Liberty: God is to us light in darkness, glory in shame, beauty in deformity, liberty in bondage, we possess nothing, yet enjoy all things; suffering is our crown, death our life; yea, we live upon death dayly, we cannot live without it.

Again, We are also contented with the dispose of providence in any thing that may be called ours: If any party or power command us, our lives, liberties, or interest, it is the pleasure of the Father in us to give up all to them: we see a divine call in it, and can with alacrity yeeld obedience. Oh, it is a sweet smelling sacrifice, acceptable with the Father, when we (the son) are thus drawn forth to offer up our dearest Interests for the world. It may be you cannot in this apprehend me: it is no matter, the Father willeth it should be a mystery.

 Yet farther:

Our Interest of Life and Liberty is at your service; if you call for it, take it; we are contented to be prodigal of it, to satisfie the blood-thirsty spirit of any man in the Kingdom.

While we are in the enjoyment of these outward things, we use them as if we used them not, being free to throw them off at the first demand: we are as free to suffer, to be trampled upon, to hang and burn, as to enjoy that outward liberty which you (so seriously and resolutely)

---

5 Long slender piece of silver used to find bullets in wounds.

press after. I tell you, Sirs, Suffering is our Conquest; While we are ground to pieces under any power whatsoever, all this while we trample upon them: debasing is our exalting; in that which you call misery and calamity, we are more then conquerors: We dare meet you (even you, whose courage hath excelled, whose fierce countenance makes the earth to tremble, you who are the present terror of the Nation) and appear in a naked posture before you; yea, throw your selves, lives, liberties, and all upon the edg of your cruelty; and we are sure, if you dare encounter with us here, we shall overcome you. Ah Sirs! When you see this way of conquest, you will throw your swords behind you in an holy despite and scorn; you shall lay all your honor in the dust, and by that sweet spirit of meekness shall destroy and subdue your enemies.

But secondly:

I wish you might be carried forth into a serious view of the manner of your present Actings. As your Principles are poor and beggarly, so also the manner of your Engagements[6] is dark and fleshly. This cloudy and vailed appearance of God amongst you, puts you upon preposterous designs, upon low and carnal Enterprizes: You have taken away *Charls* his life, because otherwise he would (it's likely) have taken yours. True, it is the good will of the Lord it should be so, I have nothing to say against it; the Lord in this cloud leads you forth to it, and in this you have plaid the parts of men acting under a fleshly discovery of things. You are led forth in a way of vengeance upon your adversaries; you sentence and shoot to death at your pleasure; it little moves you to trample upon the blood of your enemies; this is your Victory, Glory and Triumph. All this is well; you must tarry here till God moves higher amongst you.

I have only this to say to you:

Is it not a poor carnal thing for Saints, so high in profession as you have been, to stand brangling[7] with the world for a few carnal enjoyments? What, the sons of everlasting peace, and ingaged in a carnal combat? Well, it is the Lord; I am satisfied. But oh, that sweet and meek Spirit of Christ! Who, when he was reviled, reviled not again; was persecuted, but with patience under-went it, and committed himself to him that judged righteously. You cannot, you dare not commit your selves, your cause, your lives and liberties to the Lord, and nakedly, without any carnal opposition, surrender your Interest to a divine dispose: Nay rather, Shall not your swords soon be sheathed in the bowels of those who obstruct, or impede, your furious march in the road of self-preservation? Poor dear Hearts! It is the lowness, weakness and darkness of God by which you are led forth and acted. The Lord, ere long, will come forth in another appearance amongst you; he is coming out of darkness, his secret place, into a light and open view; he will let out a more pure glory upon you, when, in an holy shame, you will reflect upon your present Employments.

I tell you, dearly esteemed, it is a scorn to us, either to pick, or plead a Quarrel with any party, for an outward or carnal Interest; The Lord hath shewed us (and will shortly manifest to you) a more easie and sweet way of Victory; we can overcome by being conquered, we can lose all, and yet be savers in the conclusion.

---

6   a) formal agreements made within the New Model Army, such as the Solemn Engagement of 5 June, 1647, resolving not to disband until the Army's grievances were met (*OED* n. 2a); b) involvement (*OED*, n. 5).
7   Squabbling (*OED* v. 2).

Again, for I draw homewards.

The manner of your present Actings is in much fear, dread, darkness and confusion; it is your dayly thoughts and care how to complot your designs, and lay out your work so, as that you may save your selves, your honor and reputation, but all is too little, you must shortly part with all; your name, fame, success and victory must all be forgotten, yea, you your selves shall rejoyce at your own Overtures.

You are very fearful and jealous of your defamation; you are afraid to think of it: your spirits are involved in confusion and distraction, for fear lest your design should betray you. These are your imprisoned thoughts, I am very certain, but spiritual wisdom can discover them. The Lord knows that you lie under a sad weight of fear, terror and distraction: Fear, the pit, and a snare have taken hold on you, disorder and confusion abounds amongst you: You grope for the wall like the blind; you aim at Liberty and Priviledg, but you grope blindly after it, as knowing not which way to accomplish it; and thus many times you sit down weeping by the Rivers of *Babylon*; you are oft so over-whelmed in these troubled waters of Liberty and Priviledg, that you are constrained to sink under the waves of sorrow and darkness: I know the Lord judges many of you, and throws you down by the sad and serious consideration of your actings; He turns your hearts, ways and enterprises upside down before you, and I know you are under dayly convictions of spirit. Thus the dark presence of God shuts you up in fear, and keeps you under bondage: The thick cloud of horror and confusion vails that sweet presence, and bright splendor of Peace and Liberty from you; but in an appointed time the mystery of light will break out in you, and upon you, when in the shinings of Divine Majesty, you will clearly and purely behold things in a naked appearance, when you shall see no cause of fear or trouble in any thing.

Those that live in love to all, see no cause to fear any; for there is no fear in love, perfect Love casts out fear: If you were in Charity with all men, you would fear no man; for Charity thinks no evil, it knows none, it fears none: All things are not yet reconciled to you, earth and heaven are not yet agreed; but you labour under a body and bulk of cursed enmity, and hence is the spring of all your fear and jealousie: If you could see all men, all interests, all power in the Lord, you would be offended at none, you would not fear any, but would, with a sweet, patient, contented, and quiet spirit, lie down under any thing coming from a Divine dispose. We see and behold our selves (as in the Lord) without fear or jealousie, because we are really reconciled to all men, all designs, all interests; and all they that know us are carryed forth in a spirit of Love towards us. The reason why we are hated, despised, and trampled upon, is, because the world knoweth us not, they know not the Father in us.

In this state of ignorance we are the objects of scorn and contempt, and it is our Freedom and Liberty to be so: The Lord in us, and we in the Lord, and with him, travel together under the worlds infirmities, and because we see it the Fathers will, it is our meat and drink to do it; we love to sweat drops of blood under all mens offences: Throw all the wrath, malice, envy and scorn of man upon us, we fear it not, but in the Lord we are able to bear all, and suffer under it. Lo, thus we fill up behinde the measure of the sufferings of Christ in our flesh, the dyings of the Lord are manifested in us dayly: Here, O here's a way to bring forth peace and unity: the Lord is coming, (he is coming) to discover it: For by this death We ascend to a life, in all mens hearts and affections; after this cross of hatred, we are crowned (as most choyce and precious) in all mens love and esteem, when the spirit shall descend from on high, and be poured out upon them; they shall look upon us (whom in the Lord they have pierced) and mourn over us with a spirit of love and tenderness: Then shall we see of the travel of our souls, and be therewith satisfied.

Ah my dear Friends! my Soul travels again in birth with you, till the Lord be thus formed and brought forth in you: I know many of you are almost spent under your burthen; you are so lost in a wilderness of Confusion, That you desire and seek after a retired rest; you begin to loath your husks, and to have some desire after your Fathers table: I say no more, he that does come, will come, and will not tarry; behold, he comes with a recompence: you are afraid to lay down your Swords, lest you should lose your Liberties; but the Lord will recompence this seven-fold into your bosom, he is coming forth to make you free to suffer a blessed Freedom, a glorious Liberty, a sufficient recompence for the loss of all outward glories: Is it the loss of your Honor, Fame and Dignity that you are afraid of? The Lord is coming to make you glad to part with it, and with a holy rejoycing to throw it all behinde you: Ah friends! The Lord will honor you with meekness; you shall be the fame of the world, for true valor and spiritual courage; yea (now and not before) shall the desire of the Nations be towards you, their lamb-like spirits of meekness and innocency will be an enforceing invitation to the lion-hearted devourers of the world to feed together with you in your green pastures, and to drink of your quiet and still waters: when you are become children of this new birth, you shall be able to play upon the hole of the Asp, and to dwell with the Cockatrice in his den, oppression and tyranny shall be destroyed before you; the sons of your afflictors shall come bending to you: that sweet spirit of love and subjection, that God shall bring forth in you, shall attract the hearts of the world towards you, they shall throw down their crowns at your feet; and shall take hold of that skirt of Righteousness which is upon you, and say, We perceive of a truth, that the Lord is in you and amongst you. But in the mean time, you, together with the world, are shut up in darkness, and not truly discerning one another: you fear the world, and they are afraid of you; you are at a distance, involved in a bloody contest, an earthly, lustful, and carnal War-

————————farr.————————

Where Live *and* Lie, *and die together;*
Yet but a while, it's not for ever.   *Farewell.*

Post-script.

Friends,

BUt one word more, and I have done. I told you before, and now I say it again, That your reputation is the fame and glory of this present Army; you (I know) are the main supporting Pillars of it. I will tell you *what I see in this*, more plainly then I have hitherto declared. I see the Lord, *our spiritual Sampson*, hath laid his hands of almighty power upon (*You*) these Pillars of this woodden Fabrick, he will dis-joynt you, and shake you all to pieces, and in you the whole edifice of this swordlie Power shall be annihilated: the Lord will die with it,[8] in it (or rather out of it, and from it) and in this death he will destroy more then you have done all your lives time. The Lord will *here* take you napping, as you are eating and drinking, marrying, and giving in marriage to strange flesh, and the lake of divine burning shall consume you. Oh, it will be a glorious day; wait for it.

I have here offered a few things to a publique view, I know the wise ones amongst you will slight it, and dis-regard it; the form, method and language invites not the curious and nice spirit of anie man; it hath no beautie upon it, though a great deal in it, which the Princes of this world cannot discern. It is indeed the foolish language of the Spirit; if you do not like it, retorn it again, and I will carrie it where I had it; you are like yet to have no better from me. I was once wise as well as you, but I am now a fool, I care not who knows it: I once also enjoyed my self, but I am now carried out of my wits, a fool, a mad man, besides my self; if you think me any other, you are mistaken, and it is for your sakes that I am so.

And now Friends, *In him that was, is, and is to come,* I take my farewel of you: Remember what I say, (*is, was, and is to come.*) The Lord *was*, when you were lowest; he *is*, now you are highest; and he *is to come*, when you shall be nothing. *Even so, Come Lord Jesus, Come quickly.*

FINIS.

---

8   Christopher Hill (*The World Turned Upside Down*, 218) makes the point that this is one of only two places in seventeenth-century literature where he can find a reference to the death of God.

DIVINITY
Anatomized.

O R,

Truth nakedly appear-
ing out of its fleshly cloath-
ing, and Creature Attire

BY

JOSEPH SALMON,
A Member of the Army.

I thanke thee oh Father, Lord of Heaven and
*   earth, that thou hast hidden these thing*
*   from the wise and prudent, and hast re-*
*   vealed them unto Babes.*
Even so oh Father, because it seemes thee
*   good.*
The Spirit searches all things, yea, the deep
*   things of God.*

LONDON,
Printed for *Giles Calvert*, at the signe of
the *Black-Spread-Eagle*, at the West-end
of *Pauls*, 1649

TO ALL
Sions Off-Spring,
to whom these poor Labors
may be communicated.

Choicely esteemed in Jesus Christ; *Those ardent affe⟨c⟩tions of mine toward you all, have drawn me forth to salute you, in the presentation of this small* Treatise, *to your pious considerations.*

That which was my most solemn tye and engagement in this action, consisted chiefly in this; namely, The maner of Truths Discoveries amongst Saints, *considering how we are apt to live upon the shell of spiritual glory, as not relishing at all that spiritual kernel, and divine substance; to live upon the continual beholding of that carnal and fleshly habit that* Truth *oft-times walks in, and not upon that ravishing light of a naked Spirit, appearing out of its fleshly and carnal* Vesture. God *having through* Mercy *in manifold particulars, pulled off this Mantle, and made bare himself, (as being formerly hid in the clefts of the Rocks, and secret places of the Stairs) I say (having now disclosed that* lovely countenance *of himself to me,) whereby I more purely and fully* have apprehended *him in the center of his glory ; I have presumed to give you this brief account of my present* Discoveries, *desiring, that what I have written, may be offensive to none, but that all may so accept of it, as that present* station *which* God *hath placed me in. For my own part, I am preciously affected with all* Saints: *Where ever I can but see the Image of* Christ, *my love is drawn out upon it, as being that which most delights me in any creature: And this also I know, that* God *makes out himself sundry ways, and various maners to his people. That which is milk to some, is meat to others; but the true relish of pure* glory *is too strong for most : (as to their low and weak* discoveries,) *I force my light upon none, least those who are not able to digest it, should retort it upon me, as* blasphemy *and* heresie; *I therefore conclude, That my best and safest way (to avoid the censure of all) is to let all men know, That this present* discovery *is communicated to them, no otherwise, but as a true relation of that* light *and* truth *which is wrought in me; (for I dare not speak by any other principle, lest my sentences should flow from* notion, *and not real* apprehension.) *What I have seen, heard, tasted and handled of the* mystery of life, *that I have declared, to the intent that my speeches might not savor of any outward, but inward teachings. Let me therefore in tenderness beseech all* Saints, *not to censure that which they cannot judg or discern; but wait in the sincere practice of that which they know, till* God *shall exalt them too the more pure aspects of his presence, when they may better discern betwixt things that differ. In the mean time, I shall desire* God *to vindicate his* truth *from censure, in his own way and maner: And I am also confident, that the* glorious appearance *of* truth *in the hearts of Christians, shall destroy that rigor, and inveteracy that they have towards it; (till when and for ever) both to the weak and strong, to the high and low, the meek, and also the most rash and rigid. I shall be willing and ready to ingage my self a servant, in love, to you all; so far as* God *shall make me useful to you; and remain yours by* Interest *in the* Father *and* Son.

JOSEPH SALMON.

Divinity Anatomized.

Sect. I.
Of the Mysterie of Christ.

The glory of mysteries is Christ, and to that soul which sees him as he is a mysterie to him, he is indeed glorious. Know therefore Christian, first, that Christ is a mysterie. Secondly, learne how this mysterie revealeth, and in what manner it manifesteth it self. 3^{ly}. the operative effect of it, when known.

First, Christ is a mysterie, and here we shall see, that most in the world are mistaken as concerning Christ. Some men, they apprehend Christ to be flesh, and thats all; & others (though by what rule know not) apprehend him (as they confesse) to be God, and yet to be a distinct subsistance from the divine Essence; these certainly are too low, too carnal conceptions of Christ: my present discovery of Christ, gives me this sight of him, to be God in flesh, complete, infinit, eternall, invisible God; manifesting or discovering himselfe in our flesh and nature; hence Christ is termed *Isa*. 9. The mighty God, the everlasting father: and also in *Mat*. I. he is rendred to be Emanuell, which is God with us: So that there is no difference between Father, Sonne, and Spirit, as to their essence; but only distinction in terme: the Father (indeed) is not the Sonne nominally, neither the Sonne the Spirit, but the Father and sonne are one really and vertually, as Christ sufficiently testifies John 14.5,6. as also in sundry other places by that Evangelist.

Object. But what then needs distinction nominall, where there is none reall?

Sol. Although God be one pure beeing of spirit in himself, yet he is pleased to administer himself in divers wayes and manners, and so admits of diverse termes. If you look upon God as in reference to creation, you shall there see him admit of the terme Father, as being the author, and begetter of all things; if you look upon him in redemption, as manifest in the flesh, he will there admit of the terme Son; so that this great mysterie is thus to be considered, one pure substance of Spirit (operating in divers manners & appearing in plurality of dispensations, according to its divine pleasure) was pleased to assume our nature, and manifest it selfe in the flesh; yet still retaining its owne unmixed union, and uncompounded Deitie.

Ah deare friends, could we but thus behold God, how would all fleshly glosses (which the creature hath masked him withall) appear to be folly and vanity to us; we should then no longer be possessed with a plurality of persons, which the world dotes upon, (as if one God, a glorious single being of light, could admit of more then one into his divine union) O the darknesse of the sons of the faln *Adam*! and all for want of this experience, that plurality of dispensation (not of persons) is sutable to a simple beeing of divine glory: and certainly, without controversie, great is this mysterie, God manifest in flesh; In the spirituall aspect of which, the soule cannot but highly admire these two things in God.

First, his wisdome, in finding out a way so sutable to reconcile lost man to himselfe.

Secondly, his love, in pusuing man to the heeles (as it were) to familiarize himselfe with him. No sooner had man fallen, but the bosome of compassion of God was extended towards him, *Adam* (saith God) where art thou? Now the immediate voice of God to fallen creature, was so sad, and direfull, that he was ashamed to shew himself in his nakednesse, before a spirit clothed with glory; and afraid to heare that pure voice, which was then uttered: God looking upon his creature as lost from his presence, and communion, resolves in love and mercy to take some other course to acquaint himself with man; to this end this King of glory meetes man, (not in the height of glory, and divine splendor, whereby man might be justly afraid of that purity, which he had so unjustly defied formerly) but in his owne cloathing, or nature, he appeares to him, and would let him know that he was yet reconciled to him, though man so much transgressing: true indeed man thou hast lost thy selfe by thy sin, from my sight and presence, but I am now come downe to thee in thine owne nature as being conformable to thy weaknesse to informe thee, that I am the same towards thee as ever, my unchangeable love yet flowes out upon thee; It is only thy carnall, sinfull, weak apprehension of me, that begets that vast difference between us, and therefore now know O man, that thy mutabilitie hath not altered my immutability; thy sin hath not overcome my love; thy wickednesse hath not caused any cessation of my goodnesse; but I am now as ever towards thee; this is Gods sermon in his flesh to the creature; and had not God thus condescended, certainly lost man could never have attained to any glimpse of love, or discovery of grace and mercy; And now deare friends, take notice of a farther thing in this mysterie, as a consequence flowing from it: God seeing all mens natures declined from him, does daily make use of the mysteries of the flesh, to acquaint himself with us; hence all fleshly formes and ordinances are usefull, as being that flesh of Christ, wherein God meets those souls, which with *Adam*, are not able to behold him, in the more pure discoveries of his presence; God not ending hereby to suit the heart for more spirituall glory, and then to depart out of that fleshly vesture, and clothing; thus far of the mysterie of Christ, as to God.

Christ as a Mysterie to the Saints.

And as Christ is a mysterie in reference to God, so also in relation to the Saints God manifest in the flesh of Christ, is no more but a figure or resemblance of the farther progress of this work in every Christian; For as the father and sonne in mysterie are one, so also God and the Saint are really one, in that glorious union of the spirit: the mysterie of God manifest in the flesh, is not only extant in Christ, but also in every Christian, the one being as a figure of the other; all those mighty works accomplished in and by that flesh of the sonne (to me) are but a shadow of those miraculous, and powerfull workings of the spirit, in the hearts of Saints; in a word, whatsoever that flesh acted or suffered, was no more than a type, or resemblance of that which God will accomplish in every of his people: God in our flesh mortifying & subduing, changing and transforming, reviving and quickning, exalting and advancing, according to his divine pleasure. Ah Lord, what a glorious mysterie is this, whereby the soule comes to be so gloriously metamorphosed & changed, so wrought up by the power of the spirit, into a union with God! This was what that which Christ so much urged in his Petition, *John* 17. that they father may be one: How one? I am in thee, and thou in me, that they also may be one with us; I in them, and thou in me, that they also be made perfect in one, &c.

Wheresoever this mysterie inhabits, it works the creature out of it selfe, & brings it into a more neer union, and communion with God; and this is a preparative to the third thing considerable, as to the knowledge of this mysterie, and that is,

How this mysterie works, and in what manner it operates in the Creature.

The manner of the spirits work in the soule, is to consume and destroy all that is contrary to God, to comprehend the minde of the creature, and to empty it of all self and flesh, and transforme it into its own spirituall nature; shall I tell you my deare friends, it is the designe of God in you, to destroy all that is not himself, that so nothing but himself may be exalted; the Prophet *Isaiah* hath a passage to his purpose, in *Isa* 2. which shall be fulfilled in an appoynted time in all Saints: the haughtinesse of man shall be abased, and the loftynesse of man shall be brought low, and God alone shall be exalted in that day; this is the time when the seed of the bond woman shall be cast out, that so the seed of the free-woman (or free begettings of spirit) may enjoy the inheritance; & this, in my apprehension is that spiritual day, wherein two shall be found grinding in one Mill: the one taken, and the other left; flesh and spirit opposing and labouring together in one soule, the flesh taken, judged, & cast out, & the spirit left, or remaining to effect further glory.

Now is the time when our works are tryed, by the refining fire of the spirit, when all that will not abide the burning of divine mysterie, vanish away, and turne to nothing. Yea, this is the day when all flesh shall be but as grasse, and the goodlinesse, forme, and beauty of all creature-glory shall be but as the flowre of the field, the grass shall wither, yea, the flower shall fade and decay, because the breathings of spiritual mysterie shall dissolve it, but the word of mysterie, God in us, shall abide and indure for ever; when the other is taken, this shall be left; for the servant, or seed of bondage, the flesh, abides not in the house for ever; but the sonne or mysterie of God in us, remaineth eternally: In a word, this is that kingdome which cannot be shaken; Alas deare friends, whatsoever you live in, below this mysterie, it is shakable; heaven and earth shall passe away, but not one jot or title of the word in us, shall vanish away; all glories below spirituall glory shall consume, the heavens shall be rowled together as a scrowle, and the earth, or lower excellency shall be dissolved; but the immortality of the divine mysterie remaines unfading in the creature, glorifying it self in the soul, by making the soul glorious in its owne divine splendor. Behold then the manner of truth working in the heart, how it transports the minde beyond it self, how it consumes and devours in its spirituall progresse in thee: Spirit, or word, is therefore called and compared to fire in Scripture, and God is said, *Psalm* 50. to come with devouring fire before his face; that look how fire usually subdues its subject, and changes it into its owne genius, even so, when the flame of spirituall ardour comprehends the mind, they work it out of it self, out of its deadness, coldness, blindeness, and darkness, and transport it into the light, life, glory, and nature of God, and this is truly verified in so much of man, as God comprehends; the rest is as that seed of the Serpent, whose head (or power) in time, the seed of the woman (or God manifest in us) shall destroy, break, and dissipate.

We now proceed to the effects of this mysterie, when thus known and revealed in the creature.

Thirdly, the glorious effects of this mysterie, thus revealed in the creature are many: I will instance only in two, as the substance of all the rest. First, the knowledge of God manifest in us, it effects in the creature, a spirituall resignation to God, which before was altogether averse to him; the soule now is willing to owne himself to be nothing, that so God may be all; and the true cause of this effect lies in that transcendent glory and lustre, that it sees and beholds in God.

Beloved, doth not sometimes the discovery of the beauty, glory, and excellency, even of nature, so infatuate your affections, as that you could be willing with *Jacob*, to live a life of servitude, for the enjoyment of that which your desires streame after? Shall I tell you (or know yee not rather in your own experience) that this vehemency of affection, and heat of love, is far more vigorous, as to God, then to any outward glory.

Ah God! what divine infatuations, what spirituall inflamations of love is the soul of the Saint possessed withall, in whom this glorious mysterie is manifest? in so much, that now it is willing to deny his own wisdome, strength, and glorie, and to resigne it selfe up to the spirits disposings, as a passive servant, to its divine supremacy.

And now tell me, O Christian, that hast the least experience of the manifestation of this mysterie in thee, how hath this naked appearance of spirituall glory ravished thy soul, and led out thy affections in a holy discontent, (as it were) till thou hast in some measure been satisfied with an enjoyment of that which thy soul thirsted after? Nay, what spirituall amazements, and powerfull astonishments have violently many times fallen upon thee at the sight of that eternall beauty?

It was said of *Enoch*, (as in reference to his translation) that he walked with God, and he was not: Behold a pure resemblance of the powerful effect of the knowledge of God in the soul.

Where the soul lives in God, and walks with God by the pure translations of the spirit, while the creature walks in that love, light and beauty, and splendor of spirit, behold it is not, that is, it is not it self, but liveth in that divine sphear and center, which is far beyond all creature light and glory; for indeed there is no man did ever thus behold God in the purity and glory of himself, and lived before him. O friends, know assuredly, that when the beams of Divine mysterie begin to send forth their light and glory in you, that the Prince of darknesse shall the more be abolished and confounded, and self and flesh shall be more subdued, and brought under.

Can the dazling eye indure to behold the extremity of the Suns light and lustre. Can darknesse behold light, and yet abide? Can stubble encounter, and grapple with the flames of consuming light and glory? Even so, can self stand in its darknesse, where the excellency of Divine light is manifest? certainly, if the Queen of *Sheba* at the beholding of *Solomons* glory in I *Kings* 10.2 was so overcome, as that she had no spirit or life in her, how shall not then the soul, at the beholding of the beauty of Christ, that spiritual *Solomon*, be amazed, yea, confounded in it self? Beloved, though the heart of man have a long time lived (as a Queen) in its own honour and dignity, yea, although advanced to the heaven of creature-glory, yet when once it comes to behold *Solomon* in his throne, Christ Crowned with glory in the heart, it will die, and vanish at this Divine aspect: Go forth therefore, O ye daughters of Ierusalem, and behold King *Solomon* in the Crown wherewith he is Crowned in the day of his spiritual espousals, (or gladnesse of his heart) so shall you see, and know the powerfull effect of the revelation of Divine mysterie.

Secondly, and lastly, the knowledge or discovery of Christ in us, it doth, in short, produce a strange and suddain alteration in the creature; take but one evidence for this, and so we leave it: the Apostle having in 2 *Cor.* 3. been treating at large about the low, and carnall discovery of God in law, or letter, together with the effects of such discoveries, comes, toward the latter end, to speak of a more glorious administration, which was the ministration of the Spirit, and he thus describes it to us: now (saith he) we all with open face (as in a glasse) beholding the glory of God, are changed into the same Image, from glorie to glorie, as by the spirit.

First, here is considerable the discovering work of the spirit, and that is herein implyed [we all behold] joined with the last clause [as by the spirit.]

Secondly, here is the glorie of the spirits ministration, advanced above the Letter, that is implied in these words [with open face, as in a glasse].

Thirdly, here is the object discovered, or revealed, and that is [the glorie of God.]

Fourthly, here is the effect of this glorie thus revealed, and that is this [we are changed into the same image, from glorie to glorie, as by the spirit].

From all (therefore) that hath been spoken, I thus conclude, that is far better to know Christ in mysterie, then in hystorie; in spirit, then in flesh, in his divine and inward motion, then only in a bare and verball relation; Oh my deare ones my soule is almost uncessant in your behalfes, together with my self, till we are gathered up into the mysterie of God; how then should all janglings and contentions cease amongst us? Yea, how would love and union more increase, and abound in us each to other? Nay, what soule ravishing communion would all Saints (under all dispensations) enjoy each with other, daylie increasing in love, and growing up into the light and glorie of Christ? how then should we (under our severall formes and stations) judge of each other, not by the forme, but the power of godlinesse? But truly I must needs tell you, my deare ones (till such time as God brings you to look more at spirit then letter, more at power then forme, more at internal workings, then external worships) I never looke to see contentions cease amongst you.

I shall now commit my discoverie, as to the mysterie of Christ, to your serious consideration, and proceed to some other truth, as manifest in me.

Sect. II.

Of the Resurrection, & finall Judgement.

The Scripture (as in other things) doth set forth the mysterie of resurrection and final Judgement, to our capacities, in a corporall and carnall sence, and in this manner doth the apostle at large discourse, in I *Cor.* 15. In which doubtless is much mysterie and spirituall glory.

Some say that the resurrection consists in raising this carnall and fleshly body into a glorified estate and condition, and that this body, according to the deeds done in it, shall, together with the soule be admitted, either to eternall joy, or misery: others have a more spirituall discoverie, as to the resurrection, and they apprehend, that as Christ is the resurrection and the life, so to rise again, is to be made alive in that new and spirituall nature, that as the soul hath shared with Christ in the likeness of his death, so also in the likness of his resurrection, in wh^ch the soul shall be raised up out of its grave of earth and flesh, and be taken into a spirituall and heavenly glory, and this is to bear the Character, or Image of the second *Adam*, which is the Lord from heaven; this is that life after death, which is made over to the Saints, for if we be dead with him, we shall also live with him; they also say, that a fleshly and corporall resurrection is a discovery of the Letter, yet but allegoricall, whereby is shadowed out a spirituall and glorious life, and being with God; and also that flesh and blood cannot have communion with a spirituall beeing, and that God doth manifest himself in our flesh for a while, (as in the flesh of the son) and then laies it aside, on purpose to raise up the minde, or inward man into a compleat and full enjoyment of union with himself, which cannot be accomplished as to the flesh and blood. Loe! here is corruption putting on incorruption, and mortall clothed with immortality, death being swallowed up in victory; and this was that which *Paul* so earnestly pressed after, when he desires to attain to the resurrection of the dead. That I might know him (saith he) in the power of his resurrection, &c. And this is to be raised up together, and made sit together in heavenly places in CHRIST.

In a word they affirm, that the true resurrection is, for the spiritual nature to exalt it self above the carnall creature, and that it is the design of God to destroy, judge, and condemn all that is opponent to himself and so to enjoy himself in that which is himself, the minde spiritualized; this is our eternall fellowship, union and communion with God, which we shall be raised up to at the sound of the seventh Angell, or the last, and most glorious dispensation; now is the time finished, the end is come, now shall Christ deliver up the Kingdom to the Father, when all Rule and Dominion is subdued, when the flesh is totally destroyed now God is all in all, now also is that spiritual outcry of the Saints accomplished, Allelujah, for the Lord God omnipotent reigneth. I commit these discoveries of the resurrection to the diligent perusall, and serious debate of all Christians, and shall proceed.

Sect. III.

A word in brief, as to Election, and Reprobation

The discovery of some, as to Election and Reprobation, is this, that God doth in mercy elect and chuse some to life, and salvation, in whom he will magnifie the riches of love, as vessels of Honour, and doth set apart others as vessels of dishonour, in whom he will magnifie the glory of justice upon, as to their eternal ruin and destruction, and this proceeding from his own meer will and pleasure: others say that election and reprobation, though they are occasional, as in God, yet conditionall, as to the creature, and that although there be election and reprobation of persons, yet it is in reference to something foreseen in the creature, (as they thus amplifie it,) God foreknowing who those were that (in the improvement of that talent, or power bestowed upon them) should (or would) beleeve in Christ, and roul themselves upon mercy and free grace according to this foreknowledge, did so elect, and chuse such and such persons; not for any worth or merit he saw in them, but making Faith as that means whereby he doth elect: so that (say they) the cause of choosing remains yet untouched in that love and goodness of God, but onely God is pleased to elect through and by a means. This they say is election according to Gods foreknowledge, through sanctification of the Spirit, and belief of the Truth.

Some have farther and more spiritual discovery, as to election; and they say, That the Scriptures hold forth the Mystery of election in similitudes, and allegories, and so also of reprobation; minding election and reprobation not so much related to persons of men and women as to flesh and spirit; the one being the object which the choice of Divine love reflects upon, the other, as the subject reprobate, being excluded from any commerce, society and fellowship with God. This election and reprobation is shadowed out by that allegory of *Jacob* and *Esau*, *Rom.* 9. For we are not there to understand that Gods love or hatred is considerable as to the persons; for this is but a meer allegory, speaking in a mystery of the two seed of *Abraham*, as the scope of the chapter will testifie: Which two seeds the Apostle interprets, *Gal.* 4.19 to be the Law and Grace, Flesh and Spirit. God loves *Jacob*: why? because the promised seed: How the promised seed? because born of *Isaac*: For in *Isaac* shall thy seed be called. The effect is this, That immortal seed of the new-birth in us, that law or minde of the spirit; in a word, That part of the creature that is called or regenerated in Christ, is no less then that spiritual *Jacob* of Gods love and pleasure: and also that mystery of iniquity (being that seed of bondage) is that (working) *Esau*, or object of divine hatred, (for so the word *Esau* signifies.) It was told *Rebecca* from the Lord, That two nations were in her womb: These two nations were but shadows of flesh and spirit, and do resemble to us the spiritual predestination; How that God will have the elder to serve the younger: God hath appointed in eternal purpose, that *Esau* nation (or old world of flesh in us) shall be destroyed perpetually, from the least enjoyment or familiarity with him; and also hath decreed, that *Jacobs* nation, the young or new world of the spirit in us, shall for ever be magnified and advanced.

For truly (my precious ones) we have all these two seeds, or nations in us, yea, we travel with them. Ah Lord! what struglings, strivings, yea, pangs of contention is many times the poor Christian sensible of? And thus it will be, for the seed of the bond-woman will persecute the seed of the free-woman: But now these two are objects of divine choice and refusal. God he refuses the elder, and pitches electing love upon the younger. This elder brother is spiritually the flesh, as being that old faln earthly *Adam*. This *Paul* calls the old man, which must be put off: This is elder, or of longer standing in the creature then that young one which God chuses. For that is not first that is heavenly, but that which is earthly, and after that which is heavenly. The younger brother, or seed of love, is that new spiritual heavenly *Adam*, or immortal seed of the Spirit: to which the elder must submit, for the elder shall serve the younger. This is that seed, which if God had not created and begotten in us, we had for ever been a spiritual *Sodom*, deprived from the union and fellowship of God; yea, this is that remnant which remaineth, (and shall remain) according to the election of Grace.

The summe of all breifly, is this, God hath in eternal counsel ordained and decreed, that all darknesse and confusion shall be destroyed by that consuming violence of divine burnings. He hath also designed to glorifie himselfe in himself, in the utter confusion of all inferiour Excellencies and glories; and this is the highest heaven, and most superlative glory, when the new nature, or spiritual minde hath subdued all things to it self, and brought downe every exalting power to its own rule and dominion: Yea, this is our eternall fellowship, union, and communion with God.

Sect. IV

Of the six Witnesses.

And now deare friends, I shall yet farther presume to give you an account of the Saints record or testimony, which in their various attainments they accordingly enjoy.

For the better accomplishment of which, I shall consider what the Apostle saith in I *Iohn* 5. He there tells us, that there are three that bare record in heaven, and also three that bare record in earth.

In which I shall consider; First, the variety of spiritual testimony; here is father, word, spirit, water, and blood, where you may note, that God is not bound to any one maner of evidence but as (his incomprehensible being can be mixed with no limitable quality) so he is not tied to any way, forme, or maner whatsoever; to appear in, or give evidence of himself to his people.

And certainly, were but all Christians really informed of this truth, they would not so rigidly contend for their present ways and worships, as if God were therein only wrapped up, and no where else to be discovered.

Ah friends! That you once could but know that God will not, cannot be bound up in any form whatsoever. Doth God give in the evidence of love to thee, in thy present way and station? And is he not able also to make out himself to others, who cannot see him where thou dost? or shall thy eye be evil to thy poor weak brother, because God is so unspeakable good to him in his weakness and infancy? is not the bruised reed and smoaking flax very tenderly esteemed by God? and shall it not also by thee? This is but the fruit of the flesh amongst Christians. What means therefore all that bitterness, strife, and contention among Saints? what is the reason of those revilings and reproaches, slanders, and ignominies cast upon many precious ones, who walk above the customary Religion of the world? why cannot the strong bear with the weak? and why shall the weak envy the strong? ariseth it not from hence, because Christians are so carnal, and have such low fleshly thoughts of God, as that they imagine him to be like themselves, confined to some particular way or form; and that God testifies of himself, but in one way and maner? yea , is it not from that ignorance that resides in our hearts, we not knowing that God makes out, and testifies of himself, (as I shall afterwards declare) in diversity of dispensations to his people? To some, the day-star is but newly risen, to others the day is dawning, upon others the morning light of glory appears, and to some (though few) the heat and bright splendor of the sun of Righteousness is broken out: And now to all these dispensations, there is a suitable and proportionable testimony.

But I know the carnal and ignorant will thus object.

Quest. Why, can there be any more then one true way for the sons of men to walk in?

Answ. No; for Christ is the way, the truth, and the life: But yet, although Christ be the way, yea, the onely way to the Father; yet it pleaseth God to dispence himself through this way, in various maners, and in a diversity of spiritual Record. All men walk not in one path in this high road to glory; but as they have received from the Father, so they walk: All sit not in one place, but in heavenly places in Christ; for in the Fathers house (which is Christ) there are many Mansions; every Christian hath his place or mansion in Christ: some sit in more glorious discoveries of divine presence then others; others, under glimmerings of spiritual light; some sit high, others more low; but all sit in heavenly places: the lowest saint sits as high as heaven, being satisfied with those spiritual aspects of God, and sweet evidences of the Spirit, which are proper to his present discovery. And so much in brief, as to the variety of divine testimony.

Of the place where these Witnesses bare record

The next thing considerable, as to these Witnesses, is, where they give in their evidence; for all do not bear witness in one place of dispensation.

The former three bare record in heaven, and the latter three bare record in earth; the substance of all is this, That according to the present attainment of saints, God hath a suitable and proportionable evidence of himself for them; for to me heaven and earth are no more (here considered) then the high and low, (strong and weak, spiritual and more carnal) discoveries of God to the Christian: For what is heaven, but a vision of divine presence, a sweet enjoyment of commerce, society and familiarity with the Spirit? Why then (dear souls) have we such carnal thoughts of heaven, as thinking it either to be some local paradise, where God resides, or else, at least to be very far from us, and not to be attained while we are cloathed with this body? Give me leave then, with an ingenuous and free spirit, to press but these few queries upon your consideration.

Whether an unlimited, and unbounded spirit, that hath its divine current and motion, in and through all places can be comprised in any one place whatsoever? And whether eternal union and communion with God (so incomprehensible) can have reference to any imagined place, as more peculiar then another?

Whether heaven is any where more local, then in the saints, where God is daily discovering himself in the brightness of his glory, refreshing and warming the soul with the powerful influence of his spiritual presence? Our *Saviour*, being demanded of the Pharisees, when the Kingdom of God should come, (they conceiving that it should come in some carnal, sensual, and visible maner) He thus answers, The Kingdom of Heaven comes not with observation, as to say, Lo here is Christ, or, Lo there is Christ; but the Kingdom of Heaven is within you.

Truly my deare friends (we with the *Pharisees*) have had very strange, and alienated thoughts of heaven, looking for some outward observatorie appearance of God; and while these bare dreames of heaven have possessed our thoughts, we have lost the glorious and unspeakable vision of divine presence: how hath carnall and outward expectations deprived us of our inward, and more spirituall apprehensions of glory?

I have thus farre taken Libertie to deviate from the matter intended: considering heaven therefore thus spiritually, and not carnally in us, not from us, we returne to the Substance: Heaven and Earth, they are but figures, or representations of the Saints superiour, or inferiour discoveries: now in both these, there is divine testimony, and spiritual record apparent; Some they live in the earth, (or more earthly, and carnall representations of God) they have a discoverie of Christ, as he was only the substance of that first *Adam*, and so he is indeed the first man of the earth, earthly, they see God only in the flesh (or carnall figures of his presence) now it pleases God to beare record to his people in these inferiour dispensations, by Spirit, water, and bloud; that is, the Spirit (by water and bloud, together with such carnall and fleshly figures) doth testifie and seale over to the Saints, abundance of spirituall sweetnesse, love, and mercie. Oh how precious is God in the most low and carnall discoveries of himselfe to the Christians! Yea, what testimonies of love, and sealings of the spirit doth the weakest Christian enjoy in his present station? Finally, what a heaven in earth is the Christian wrapt up in, that enjoyes God, though in never so weak or earthly dispensations? for although the Christian live in earth, as to his dispensation, yet heaven in earth is manifested, as God lets out his spirituall presence through earthly and carnall similitudes: Christ in the flesh, although but a figure or shadow, yet how glorious was God manifest in that flesh to the Disciples? insomuch that at its remove, the Disciples were in much sorrow and sadnesse: and yet the highest glory of that flesh was but the image, or substance of the first earthly or fleshly *Adam*: and truly alike precious doth God appeare to his people who live in the fleshly manifestations of his presence; I meane all you (my deare ones) who live in, or under the carnall figures of God, as your water, and your bloud, your several forms and carnal worships; I know God appears very sweet and precious to you in them; but yet I must tell you, (in the love and tendernesse of the spirit) that you live but in the earth, your tabernacle is but the mysterie of the flesh, and accordingly the spirit evidences to you in fleshly and carnall things: this is but that tabernacle that must be dissolved, and God will cloath you upon with a more spirituall house, or dispensation; and then you shall also enjoy a more glorious, and single testimonie; and this leads me to what followes.

As God hath a people living in the earth (or earthly representations of himselfe) so also he hath a people living in heaven, or more heavenly visions of glory; that is, under a more spirituall and glorious dispensation: for although the lowest Saint enjoyes heaven, because he sees God, and is with him in the fellowship of the spirit in some measure; yet he may not be said so to live in heaven as the more spirituall Christian; because the low, carnall, or weak Saint sees God but in the flesh, and so his heaven is discovered by earth; this is but *Sinai*, and must be removed, this heaven must passe away, yea, be rowled together as a scroll; it must be swallowed up in a more excelling light and glorie: but now the more spirituall Christian beholds God after a more naked, and uncloathed manner, he sees him out of his fleshly robes in the more pure glory of the spirit; he lives in the Mount *Sion*, or in the exceedings of divine appearance, and this (in me) is the heaven which is here spoken of: in which there is also a threefold witnesse, but its only nominall, not reall; the Father, word, and spirit, though three by name, yet all one in essence; the father is the word, the word is the spirit, the spirit is both Father and word: now herein differs the Record in heaven, from the Record in earth. The three that bare record in earth (or earthly dispensation of the S^t) they are not all one, but they are all said to agree in one; but now the three that bare record in heaven, they are all simply one, without distinction in being or qualitie; they are only called three, to discover how that one, pure God may dispence himselfe (as I said before) in various and divers manners: the summe of all is this: in the Saints low, weake, and earthly station, God is pleased to testifie of himself to them by fleshly and carnall things, as water, and bloud, which are of a different nature from the Spirit; but now in heaven (or more heavenly attainments of others) he there testifies of himself by no other but by himself to the soul; the Spirit by flesh, forme, letter, &c. bears witness to the Christian, while yet living in the earth; but when God hath translated a soul from earth to heaven, the glorious sight of divine presence is (not only a sufficient, but) far more transcendent witness: for truly, (though I could wish my light might not offend no one Saint) I must tell you, that I apprehend all outward things that God manifests himself through (as letter, forme, water, bloud, &c.) to be but as signes given to Christians, who being yet weak, cannot beleeve without them: and here (my dear ones) give me leave a little to dive into your closet thoughts, and secret meditations: Is it not often thus with you? Can you judge anything to be of God that suits not with your signe? Nay, though God move by his Spirit, yet can you assent to any thing, till you can apprehend it will correspond with your outward signes and evidences, as letter, forme, outward order, and the like? though things are more spirituall in themselves, then possibly the Letter can declare them; yet can you give up your hearts to embrace this inward glory, without an outward verball testimony? I blame you not (deare souls) for I know without these signes you dare not, you cannot beleeve: But to go farther; Can you judge any (almost) to be declared Saints, but those who walke in your evidence and testimony (I meane your forme, and way of worship?) neither do I herein blame you, because I know your present discovery will not admit you to judge otherwise: you cannot believe without your signe, you must have some other witness besides God, while you tabernacle in this earthly mansion; hence it is that Saints living in the flesh, judge only after the flesh; what meanes all those carnall thoughts of God; his wayes, his attributes, his essence, his residence, and his sundry appearances? is it not because people judge of things according to the letter and forme? yet I say not, but these outward signes do sweetly testifie of God according to the present, low, and carnall dispensation of the creature: for the soul living in the earth, God is pleased to condescend to its weakness, and so appears to it by creature and carnall things: and according to this appearance, so the Christian judgeth of God, his people, his wayes, attributes, and essences; but I must also tell you, that the soul that lives in heaven, needs none of these things; because he living in the more full enjoyment of God, is enabled to beleeve without them, and so these low, outward, and carnall signes to him are not usefull: God beares witness to him by no other testimony but himself: this soul thus spiritualized (walking with God in the more pure translations of the Spirit) he is enabled to beleeve, because the Spirit speaks inwardly, and not because the letter speaks outwardly; he looks not at outward evidences and carnall testimonies, but at that inward witness, and spirituall record; and if God speakes within, it sufficeth him, though all outward signes are silent, because God hath laid these aside to him; and what ever he now communicates to the Saint, he testifies the same by the inward Dictates of the Spirit.

This is that (dearly beloved) that causeth the soul to lie down under providence, satisfied and contented with its measure of light and knowledge, because it comes with a witness within, that is able to perswade and convince to purpose: whereas the poor, carnall, weake Christian, that walks more by Letter then Spirit, more by outward signe, then inward testimonie; alas, how unstable and wavering, how full of perplexities and tossings? his spirit wandering from one outward signe to another, from means to men, and from men to meanes againe, and still rests unsatisfied, because it enjoyes no evidence so infallibly powerfull, as to convince and fully perswade the heart; for indeed this is the alone work of that one witnesser, the Spirit. Consider (my beloved) what I shall now say, and see if I do not hit just upon your thoughts and inward motions: Is it not often matter of wonder to you, to see how your witnesses faile you? How are you troubled and perplexed when you see not that correspondency in that one evidence of letter as you would? how are you daily inventing this way and that way to reconcile Scripture and Scripture, running from one translation to another; if that will not suffice, from one mans judgement to another, and still heres no satisfaction in all this to be found: all these prove but empty, yea, broken cisternes? are you not often troubled, yea, amazed at that various discovery of God and the truths of God by the letter? I know I speake your thoughts, the secret of your hearts; now truely the spirituall man, he that lives in heavenly witness and evidence, he sees no matter of trouble in all this, what ever the letter saith, or however outward things discover God in an outward maner, & after a creature fashion, yet he rest co⟨n⟩tented in what evidence and testimony the Spirit gives in; it never disturbs that spirituall, and sweetly enjoyed peace that harbours in his breast, to think of the contrariety of opinions, & variety of judgements that are abroad in the world; he lives in God, as God lives in him, being really satisfied with an inward assurance, and herein resolves to acquiesce. In brief, this heavenly witness cleares all doubts and ambiguities in the creature, wch neither the letter, nor any earthly testator can resolve: the spirituall man, he discernes and judgeth the letter by the Spirit; he knows that God is not changeable, though the letter sayes he repented, he knows that God is not subject to passion, though the Scripture renders him sometimes Anger, sometimes Love; he is very well ascertained, that God is not such a thing in beeing as the creature, though the letter very frequently describes him after a creature fashion; finally, God in him by the pure disclosings of the Spirit is that evidence in which he walkes, that light in which he lives; that assurance that all uncertainties can never daunt or discourage; and this is Gods way, to witness by himself, to the soul that lives in heaven; which is the more superlative enjoyment of gods presence, and likewise to the Saints living in the earth (or low discoveries of God) he is pleased herein to manifest himself gracious, in not leaving them destitute & desolate without a testimony of himself; if meat be too strong, then God will provide milke for his young ones; for he will not break the bruised reed, nor quench the smoaking flax; but he will gather the Lambs with his arm, he will carry them in his bosome, and will gently drive those that are with young, &c.

Upon the consideration of the premises, I am imboldned to speak a word of Caution to all Saints. And first, to you (my beloved) who live in Forms, Ordinances, and earthly or carnal Representations of God: Although I know your forms are but earth, yet I also know that much heavenly comfort is made out to you, through these earthly signes and evidences. But (seeing its possible for Saints to behold God in a more spiritual and naked maner, then your present dispensation can discover,) I earnestly press these two things upon your consideration.

First, I would you might know, that your present dispensation is but movable, and that God doth but appear to you in your fleshly forms and ordinances, to fit and suit your hearts for more high discoveries of his presence; when your diversity of earthly testimony (as water, blood, form, letter and the like) must be swallowed up in that one eternal, glorious, and satisfying evidence of the Spirit. But ah Lord! how hardly is this entertained and received by you? I know some of your hearts are up in arms, by this time, against this supposed heresie; poor souls! Your present enjoyments I know are sweet and precious; you are loath to move out of your stations: Well, be contented, you shall not stir till God move; and when you see a motion of divine appearance, your spirits I hope will be willing to pursue it. Far be it from any of you, to have a thought of abiding, and taking up your continued dwellings in your so low, weak and earthly discoveries. I know some of you enjoy Christ in a more transfigured appearance then others: Of this sort I conceive you, under the evidence of water and blood, are included; I mean you (my Brethren) who are congregated by baptism, and enjoy society in shadows of Christs blood and body: These are but fleshly transfigurations of Christ to you; whereby you behold him more clearly in the flesh (or outward elements) then the rest of the dark world: But I hope you will not here build your tabernacles, and (with a resolution to move no higher) say, Its good for us to be here; no, my comfort of you rather is, That God will give you such sweet tastes of a more excelling glory, that your constant expectations shall be after the motions of divine presence. If thus thy heart is fixed, know, that he that cometh will come, and will not tarry: Behold he comes with a witness, yea, such an evidence, as shall more establish thy soul in divine assurance.

But secondly, my desire is, that you might be cautious in casting a rash censure upon those truths or persons, who live above your judgment, or discernance. O that all that spiritual heat and choller were subdued in the Saints! with which, they are apt to censure and condemn those ways and truths, which indeed are above their carnal reach. Consider therefore (my Jewels) that all truth harbors not in your brest, (I mean as to your measure of discoveries) all light (nay, it may be the more glorious and excelling light) doth not center in your Horizon. The inundations of spiritual light, and knowledge, are not so few, as to run onely in your slender chanel. All the beams of that Sun of Righteousness reflect not upon your present station. All heavenly testimony is not evidenced in your cause. I say no more, but wish that this temerity and bitterness of spirit were subdued amongst you.

And now let me conclude with a word to you also (my beloved) who live above all these earthly discoveries, and carnal evidences, in a more naked and pure sight of God. I must needs tell you, I see something worthy of reproof in you also: I mean, that slight esteem you are apt to have of weak Christians, judging them to be carnal, as not enjoying God in their earthly mansion, or dispensation. O consider, shall God own weak ones, and will not you, because you have a more glorious discovery of God? shall you have mean thoughts of them that live below? do all sit in one place and mansion? doth not God fill earth as well as heaven with his presence? I must tell you, this God will destroy in you. There is yet a farther work to accomplish then you are aware of: Therefore henceforth know, that God is preciously enjoyed by his weak ones; even those that scarce know what meat is; while they are yet sucklings, yea, babes in Christ, yet God nourisheth them by the daily refreshings of his Spirit: beware then of censuring those who walk not in your evidence and testimony.

I shall now proceed to some other particular.

Sect. V.

Of the holy Anoyntings.

The glorie and excellencie of the holy anointings is very sweetly set forth to us in that sentence of the Spouse, in *Cant.* I. 3.

Where the Spouse being affected with the sweetnesse and fulnesse of Christ, thus describes his glorie.

Because (saith she) of the savour of thy good ointments, thy name is as ointment poured forth, therefore the Virgins love thee: She here compares the name (or nature of Christ, for so the word here imports) to ointment.

Secondly, to ointment poured forth.

First, to oyntment, which heales, and refreshes: this ointment is the Spirit flowing out, and expending it selfe, upon the soule, in which dispensation, all the sores, wounds, and breaches of the creature are salved and cured: this is the balme or balsome of *Gilead*, whose nature is excellent, for the cure of all the sick soules distempers: God in the sweet exchanges of dispensations, is said to administer the oyle of joy for mourning; Its oyntment, yea, joyfull oyntment, it expends it selfe upon the soules maladie, distemper, and sorrow: hereby expelling those grosse apprehensions of the flesh, which have disturbed the Saints peace and comfort; God who formerly kindled hell in the Saint, whose breath, or life did blow up the coales of indignation into a flame of confused burnings; yet now hath exchanged his appearance, and lets out himselfe in a healing, saving, refreshing presence to the soule.

Secondly, thy name is as oyntment poured forth: And why oyntment? Oyntment is usually applied to supple, mollifie, and lithen the stiffenesse of the joynts. This betokens that spirituall freedome, and libertie that the soule enjoyes under the influences of this spirituall unction; this it is that causeth the lame man to leap as a hart, and the tongue of the dumbe to singe, and waters to break out of the wildernesse: this proclaimes libertie to the Captives, and freedome to spirits that are bound up and straitned.

Ah Lord! how dead and indisposed is the creature to the receiving of any thing, when God hands it out, till God poures this oyle of freedome upon it; and then behold what libertie! yea, what freedome and cheerfulnesse hath this effected? This makes the soule like the Chariots of *Aminadab*, so swift and speedie in its goings out towards God, which before was captivated, yea, bound up in the chaines of darke and dismall apprehensions,

Thirdly, as oyntment poured forth.

A briefe touch of this shall suffice, and then we proceed to some effects hereby produced in the soule.

This expression bears a great Emphasis upon it, wherein is contained a saints excellencie and glorie.

It saith not, as oyntment dropping downe, but (poured forth) it resembles the fulnesse of the Christian in God, by the power of that spirituall union: Christ is not the only soules sweetnesse; but also fulnesse; for we are made perfect in one with him, yea, we are compleat in him who is the head of all principalitie and power. The pouring out of this spirituall unction doth dictate Gods fulnesse in us, and ours in him. God hereby being represented as the light, life, glorie, excellencie, happinesse, and fulnesse of himselfe to us. My beloved, Christ is not only your hope of glorie (but the fulnesse of heavens glorie) in you. Is he Camphire? and is he not also a Cluster? or is he Mirrhe? and is he not also a Bundle? yea, he is as Mirrhe, Camphire, and oyntment for spirituall sweetnesse; and also as clusters, fountaines, and bundles, for divine fulnesse and plentie to the soule: hence it is, that the Saints, which are the body, are said to be the fulnesse of him, who fils all in all: yea, as touching *Sion*, the *Psalmist* saith, out of *Sion* [the perfection of beautie] God hath shined. Loe, heres the Saints glorie! as they are perfected, compleated, and united in God, by that fulnesse of God communicated to them.

Ah that all Christians could behold their fulnesse in Christ! how then would they see the vacancie, and emptinesse of all things below Christ? and hereby become dead to all inferiour excellencies and glories.

Most men imagine of a future perfection, and conceive that they are not, neither can be perfect in this life: not knowing that the Kingdome, with the fulnesse and glorie therof lives in them; this is the Saints nonnage, is infantiall weaknesse; he hath a portion, but doth not possesse it. He is full, glorious, and perfect in the son, but he doth not know it; he is an heir, but though an heire, yet a servant, because in bondage: now I shall easily grant, that a farther manifestation of our fulnesse, union and glorie is essentiall to a future condition: but yet know, that your measure of glorie, I meane your fulnesse in God is already effected: you are now sanctified, justified, saved, glorified and compleated; only you remaine ignorant of this, as being under a vaile with *Moses*: God in flesh, or in the carnall outlets of his presence is this vaile, or darknesse, which produces that slender and small glimpse of divine presence to the soule; and when God shall take away this vaile; I meane those low and carnall discoveries of himselfe; when he that now comes in cloudes and darknesse, shall come in light and glorie in you, then shall you see your fulnesse, enjoy your inheritance, possesse your portion, and appeare glorious in the fulnesse and splendor of Christ.

As oyntment [*poured forth.*]

This expression corresponds with that of *David*, when he would set forth the glory and excellencie of the Saints union, and amitie; he thus resembles it, It is like (saith he) the precious oyntment upon the head, even *Aarons* head, that ranne downe to his beard, and descended to the skirts of his garment. This oyntment is those sweet anoyntings, that precious unction of the Spirit, here called [precious] oyntment, in regard of that choyce of vertue, and power contained in it, as it is no lesse then those sweet impartings, and glorious influences of the divine nature.

Oyntment upon the head of Aaron

This *Aaron* spiritually is Christ who is called, or anoynted of God, after the order of *Aaron*, who is all our spirituall head and power, who is anoynted with the oyle of gladnesse above all his fellowes, namely, those high Priests, appertaining to the Law; now upon this head the anoyntings are placed.

The divine nature is essentially in Christ, as being one, in whom the fulnesse of the God-head dwelt bodily; in whom was contained the treasures of wisdome and knowledge: God setting him out as an exact patterne, and full compendium of all the glorie and happinesse of the Christian.

And ran downe upon the Beard, &c.

The spirituall unction, or fulnesse of God, although poured upon the head; yet centers not only in the head, but it hath a sweet influence upon the rest of the members; it ran downe upon the beard, and descended to the skirts of the garment: the fulnesse of God dwelling in the Sonne, is no more but a patterne or figure of the same fulnesse in us; God in the Sonne being but a resemblance of God in the Saint; for we all eat the same spirituall meat, and drinke the same spirituall drinke: being made partakers of the same divine nature: God manifest in our flesh, is Christ anoynted, the fulnesse of the Father; the like excellency and glory of Divine glory.

The same fulnes, purity, and glory that was given to Christ, hath a sweet influence, and spiritual descension upon every Saint. The two olive branches in *Zechariahs* vision, were seen to empty golden oyl out of themselves: These two olive trees are said to be the two anointed ones, which stand continually before the Lord of the whole earth. These two anointed ones, are two Witnesses, or Dispensations, which God daily makes out himself in; (namely, his appearances in flesh, and spirit,) both which dispensations are as olive branches, filled with golden oyl, or sweet vertue: God in one very precious, although in the other more glorious. And as they are full, so they are free; for they are said to empty the golden oyl out of themselves.

My beloved, every dispensation of God to you, is as an Olive branch, or anointed Witness, which empties out the fulness and glory of God upon you. God (after a maner) expending, or unloading his fulness upon the Saint, though still retaining the immensity of divine glory.

We proceed to some effects, which these anointings produce in the soule; and I shall give you a taste of all, by the mention onely of two or three.

First, The partaking of this spiritual Unction, it begets a knowledg of God in the Creature: When ye have received of this holy unction, ye need not that any man teach you; for the same anointing teaches you; it is truth, it is no lye; but it truly discovers God to you; all other discoveries of God besides, they are but signes, and lying wonders, they are but like the Magicians art of *Egypt*; they can counterfeit God, but not really discover him. Antichrist can come with signes and wonders, but they are lying and deceitful. My beloved, while you look upon some for their admirable parts; others, for their great learning; others, for their outward knowledge of Christ, in letter, form, and outward appearance; All this while you gaze after vanity, and are led by a false fire, whose flashings, though never so glorious, yet are but fading, and vanishing. Nothing but the anointings, or spiritual nature can truly teach or declare God to the soul: The Spirit, that searches all things, yea, the deep things of God: that that eye hath not seen, ear hath not heard, neither hath entred into mans heart to conceive; even this glory God reveals by his Spirit. O the worth and excellency of the Spirits teachings! Did poor souls but know the value of it, how would they dis-esteem all things below it?

Truly Friends, I must needs tell you. Since I found God in those teachings of the Spirit, and in the power of the anointings, I have exceedingly lamented my own former estate, and the present condition of many, who are apt, to look more at outward, then inward teachings. Poor man is very apt to set something up as his rule and guide, which indeed is not the Spirit: One exalts men for their learning and wisdom; and he that scapes this snare, runs upon another, and he it may be exalts means above God; looking upon the Letter, and such outward things, as the onely fountain of truth and knowledg: and alas, what are all these? when weighed in the ballance of the sanctuary, they prove too light and invalid. What is the man in the height of carnal wisdom, creature excellency, and glory? Truly all this is but the perfection of the first *Adam*, which must all fall before the glory of Christ; neither indeed is there any discovery of God here attainable, for Gods wisdom is folly to carnal wisdom;

light, is darkness to a carnal eye: The natural man perceiveth not these things; so also it may be said (as to all outward means which the world so much dotes upon) what are they, but as so many weak, and carnal glimpses, watery shinings of Divine glory? What's the Letter it self, any more then a dispensation of God, suitable to a low, lost, and carnal creature, wherein God shews himself, as to our weak and low apprehensions? And what are all Forms and Ordinances, but wordly Elements, and carnal Resemblances of God; which the heir, whilest a childe, is in bondage under? All these are but shadows of glory; when the substance is revealed, by the anointings in us, the form of these things shall vanish and be annihilated.

Now the effects which the anointings produce in the soul, is a true and real knowledg of God. This is to know the truth as it is in Jesus, not to know the truth as it is in man, or as it is literally declared to us in a dark shadow, and in a cloudy form; (for truth living in any outward thing is clouded and darkned by the fogs and mists of the flesh;) but to know truth as it is in Jesus, clearly and purely; to discern it appearing in its radient brightness and splendor, out of those litteral clouds, formal and carnal shadows. This is onely by the power of divine Unction.

Secondly, A second effect produced by the power of the Anointings.

They work the soul out of love with it self, and by a spiritual power carry out the minde and affections towards God. However glorious and excellent the creature hath formely appeared to it self, yet now beholding Christ in the power of the anointings, it becomes dead to all its own excellency: it now lowly esteems of it self, of its own righteouness, and glory; and with *Paul*, counts all but loss and dung, in comparison of the fulness and beauty of Christ.

Ah beloved! how hath the power and efficacy of the Spirit transformed you many times, from your creature and carnal discoveries of God, and translated your hearts above your selves, beyond your own wisdom and glory? yea, how hath the rayes and splendor of the Spirit drowned your sparkling light, which you have formerly walked out by? yet further, how hath those beautiful disclosing of Divine presence darkned your shinings, and deformed those amiable representations of the creature? in a word, how hath the power of these anointings stoln your hearts from you, and plundered you of all your own worth and treasure? nay, how willing and free (under the powerful operations of the Spirit) have you been to deny your selves and to suffer your own powers and principalities to be spoyled before you? rejoycing in your own destruction, yea, exalting over your own debasings.

Truly, its a wonder to consider how the power of the Spirit, the vertue of this Divine Unction, overcomes the soul; gathering up its love, delight and affection from all self interests, and forcing the soul to lay it self in the dust, before the glory of Divine presence. The expression of the Spouse in our present Text, is hereto very pertinent.

Therefore do the Virgins love thee.

Here's two things considerable, and that is, a cause, with its effect; the effect bearing in it an answerable proportion to the excellency of the cause.

The cause is inserted in the former words, *Because of the savor of thy good oyntments.*

The effect produced by the cause, included in the future expression, *Therefore do the virgins love thee.*

[*Therefore*]

The soul here sees it but reason that she should love Christ: Men delighted with the majesty and beauty of nature shall not want Reasons and Grounds thence produced, to ingage them to give up their fancies and affections to it.

Even so the sweetness and glory of these anointings, give out a binding ground and convincing Reason, whereby the soul is (as it were) perswaded by the force of divine Argument, to throw it self down before God, to be nothing in it self, but to exalt Christ as the onely supream in its affection.

When the natural eye is fixed upon the beauty and form of outward things the minde begins to argue, What reason it is that I should now expend my delight upon this excellency and glory.

Even so the anoyntings in the heart (revealing the fulness, amiableness, and beauty of Christ) do represent to the soul a sufficient cause, why it should surrender in desires, together with its delight and affection to the Lord.

The soul is now perswaded, that it is but reason that she should expend the stength of her heart upon this object, so choice and glorious; and also, that she should deny her self, throw down her crown, and lay her honor in the dust; before that beauty, whose transcendent lustre hath so powerfully surprized her affections.

The virgins [*Love thee*]

The soul now is possessed with a spiritual passion: and (as men in passion are most vigorous and ardent) so the soul in the heat and fervor of the Spirit spends it self upon God; answering those sweet aspects of glory, with the earnest returns of her choice and most vehement love: It is now (as it were) in a holy conflict of joy, being (after a maner) troubled, or disquieted, till it hath discharged the violency of its love upon Christ, always thinking it can no way sufficiently ease its love, burthened spirit upon him: ever conceiving, it can never enough prize, affect, and esteeme such a choyce and precious object: still earnestly desiring, and daily pressing after a farther compleating in (and more full enjoyment of) that pure and divine presence: when the Spouse thereof had apprehended Christ to be her Bundle of Mirrhe, (that is) her fulnesse, and sweetnesse, she thus resolves, he shall lie all night between my breasts.

[*Between my Breasts*]

The soule desires to have Christ neare her heart, that so her choycest bosome love may streame out upon him.

The eye is never satisfied, the minde never contented, while the object of its delight is absent; but when present, theres satisfaction, because nature enjoyes its desired object: Behold the wisdome of divine love! how it embraces the sweet presence of God! oh what satisfaction unspeakable, what joy unutterable is here, when God lies downe in the sweet embraces, and refreshing bosome of his own love! yea, what sweet ravishings, and holy raptures is the soule carried up in, when it can thus spend its love, and delight upon these sweet anoyntings! those things which men love most, they desire to have most neare to them. Divine love layes Christ in its heart, the presence of the Spirit in its bosome, yea, betwixt her breasts, that so affection may be the more fervent, and love the more stirred up, and awakened.

[*Between my Breasts*]

It is a Metaphoricall espression, borrowed from the naturall delight, which we usually take to weare sweet flowers in our breasts, or bosomes, delighting in them for their sweet smell and savour.

Oh! how precious is the sweet odour, and spirituall savour of the holy anoyntings to the soul? yea, how freely welcome, and gladly entertained is the precious perfumes of the Spirit, into the warme and refreshing bosome of divine affection? Behold! this is the rose of *Sharon*, and the Lillie of the garden; which for its beautie and glorie is so much prized, and esteemed: this is that attractive, which drawes out of the hear⟨t⟩ in a holy expence of spirituall love; this love is a love of complacencie, the soule is well pleased with it; great is the pleasure and spiritual repast which the Saint enjoyes under the sweet exchangings of spirituall love.

This love is a powerfull love, a vehement, fervent love, it is strong as death, many waters cannot quench it, &c.

Strong as Death.

Death seizes violently upon the creature and against all meanes and helps it prevailes, its greedie and not satisfied, but in the subduing and conquering of natures powers.

Behold a true character of spiritual love: in its operation, its strong, and prevalent, it overpowers all carnall shifts and props whatsoever, and carries out the heart against all opposition after God.

Many Waters cannot quench it.

It is also like fire in its operation, yet unquenchable fire, fire not to be extinguished: all carnall inundations, the overflowings of false apprehensions, are not able to extinguish this fire, to quench this fervour and heat of Love: Divine love sets the heart on fire, it inflames the Spirit; these burning flames are impossible to be subdued, but are continually ascending towards their center of light and glorie.

Againe, spirituall love is a jealous love.

Jealousie is cruell as the grave.

True love is wonderful jealous over any creature, excellencie, or glory which might endeavour to rob God of his honour and supremacy; and when once love spies any thing but Christ supreame, the flames of its jealousie surprises that object; and (like the grave which

Solomon saith is always unsatisfied) swallowes it up in the height of its crueltie, devouring that which would exalt it selfe supreame in the soule, above the excellency and glory of the pure anoyntings.

Lastly, [*The Virgins*] *love thee*:
[*The virgins.*]

The love of God begotten, and produced by the power of the anoyntings, its a pure love, a chaste, an undefiled love, its the love of virginity, the soule regenerated by the power of the anoyntings: it gives up its heart, minde, will, and affections to God, as its alone husband and spirituall lover: Divine love in this hath responsion[1] to its object, God, who is the object, or cause of love, he is holy, pure, cleare, just, and righteous; the anoyntings they are clean, pure, bright and glorious: so also that love which proceeds from hence is honest, pure, chaste, cleane, free from all defilement. Indeed true love beholds nothing worthy of love but God; all seeming glories, and creature excellencies are represented as ugly, deformed, and loathsome to the pure eye of Divine love; wherefore, passing by all sublimary glories, and carnall excellencies, she entertaines the pure anoyntings into her bosome, and thus returning whence she came, and reflecting upon her naturall object, she sits downe satisfied in the same enjoyment, not affording the least smile of affection to any but God only.

These briefly are the effects produced by the holy *Anoyntings*.

Sect. VI.

Some briefe Touches of Good and Evill

Herein, deare friends, I shall desire your patience and charity towards me, while I shall afford some tasts and relishes of my present Discoveries: I shall not (cannot, I dare not) unbosome my thoughts too apparently, lest I should be offensive: I doubt not but I shall speak enough to incur the displeasure of many, and the rash censure of most: however, my comfort is, I speak that I have seen, and testifie that I have heard.

Then to proceed: I finde, that in the world there is that which men call good, and also that which men call evill; these two are contraries, as to the creature, but all one in God: I finde that there is but one power acting all things, this power is God; appearing now in darkness, then in light; sometimes in shame, otherwise in glory: God is darkness as well as light, they are indeed alike to him, he being all things, working and acting all things by the power of his owne will: if God say, let there be darkness, behold, it is presently accomplished; let there be light, and it shall be so: and God lookes upon darkness, and behold it is very good; hell, heaven, light, darkness, good and evill, they are all one in God; darkness is light before him, evill is good, he lookes upon all things, and behold they are very good; Gods eye is so singly pure, and his actions so equally just, that all things are pure before him, because all thinges are done by him, for in him we live, move, and have our being.

---

1   Reply, response (*OED* n. 2).

Nothing workes against God, but all works for him, and therefore good.

The lowest and most carnall action of man, tends to the high advancement of Gods glory; all things concurring together to advance the glory and majesty of their supream power.

Beloved, it is our happieness to see good advanced in evill; light magnified in darkness; God exalted in all the workings of the creature.

We finde that nothing can dishonour God, nothing can hurt God, nothing can molest or trouble God, but all things reach out themselves to the advancing of that chiefest good, & most supream glory.

Adams fall was no more but Gods weakness, (pardon my expression) but this weakness of God was stronger then man, for hereby God accomplished a future designe of glory.

We finde that all things are perfectly reconciled to God (for he hath reconciled all things to himself by the death of the Son) not that God then (and not before) did actually accomplished this reconciliation, but did then and by that meanes remonstrate, and manifest the same to mankinde.

This reconciliation is generall, it appertaines to things in earth, as well as heaven; earth, and heaven, light, and darkness, good and evill, are all concerned in this reconciliation. And thus we finde good and evil, as it concernes God, considered as he injoyes and possesses himself.

Of good and evill, as it concerns the creatures apprehension.

But though good and evill be all one as to God, yet not so as to the creature: and the reason is, because the manifestations of God to the creature are various, according to our present dispensations, so we judge of good and evill.

That is clear to me, that what ever the soul apprehends can suite and correspond with its discovery or knowledge, this it calls good, holy, just, and pure: and also whatsoever doth cross its dispensation and not concord with its light and knowledge, this is called sin, evill, and darkness: this is looked upon as Gods opposite: thus behold every man judges according to the measure of light received; that which is evill to one, is good to another, one mans light is anothe⟨r⟩s darkness; one man accounts it sin not to observe dayes, another apprehends an evill in all such observations, a third is free to both: now all these correspond in God, though contradictive to us, because as men have received, so they walke, and all is sin and evill, that opposes their light: we clearly see that sin is no more but a transgression of the Law.

Now all men have a law, which being obeyed, it excuseth, but being broken it accuseth; my light is my law, if I offend my light I sin, I do evill, (not against God considered as in himself, but) against my law (or measure of light) received.

This also I see, that men walke towards God according to their severall apprehensions of him: and when men offend their own light, and transgress their law, then they imagine they offend God: When *Adam* had (by the will and counsell of Providence) eaten of the tree, and so transgressed his law, he presently conceives that God was angry, and therefore he hides himself in the garden: now this is only mans false apprehension of God, as conceiving him offended, when it is only an apprehension of sin, terrifying and amazing the creature.

I also perceive, that God sees not as man sees, apprehendeth not as man apprehendeth, judgeth not as man judgeth: God seeth all good, because nothing is contrary to him, neither can any thing move the Eyes of his glory to anger, or provoke his goodness to wrath; but the creature under his law, or carnall representation of God, apprehends that every thing crossing, or opposing his law is Gods enemie. Thus, I see, and behold the Law to be the strength of sin: My beloved, let me tell you, that your severall laws, dispensations, or carnall apprehensions of God, are the very fomenters, and authors of a carnall conceivance of sin in you; the one being as a proper effect of the other: sin is nothing without your law strengthen it, but when your law (or carnall dispensation) appears, sin revives, and you die before it: now this is hell, death, and destruction, when the soul consumes and spends it self in the confused burnings, and scorching flames of false apprehensions:

To conclude all then in a few words, There is nothing but what is good in the pure sight of divine presence: but to man (that thinketh and apprehendeth evil) to him there is evill, in regard of his carnall and low discernance of God.

But if all be good, as in God, and nothing evill, as in his presence: you may demand what that is that must be destroyed by the power of the Spirit?

To this I shall thus answer, that which must be destroyed in us, is our carnall and false apprehensions of good and evill; those carnall dispensations which we live under, which render God, sin, good, and evil to us, after a low and carnal maner; for while we have God thus darkly represented to us, we call light darkness, and darkness light, sweet bitter, and bitter sweet, calling that evill which indeed is good, though falsly discerned and apprehended.

This false apprehension is Antichrist and must be destroyed by the pure breathings, and sweet disclosings of Divine presence.

I tell you friends, all your carnall discoveries of God, they are to be destroyed, what ever God makes use of now to convey himself to you thorow: yet all these must perish, because these are but such things as wherein God lets out a fleshly sight of Divine presence. This is God in weakness, God in flesh, God representing himself to be what he is not.

This is that which must be destroyed by the sweet exchanges of Divine appearance: When God lets out the fulness of his beauty and excellency upon us, then our former, low, and carnal apprehensions will be swallowed up in the immensity of Divine glory.

Behold! now all enmity is nailed to the cross; we behold a perfect reconciliation between all things and God; we see as God seeth; we pass a righteous and equal sentence upon all things, and actions, beholding God (in all the actings of the creature) advancing his own glory, exalting his own wisdom, and effecting his own eternal counsel and purpose.

Behold, an embleme of true happiness: Here's true satisfaction; this is indeed pure rest and refreshment, when the soul can see evil good in God; darkness light in God; trouble and sorrow to be joy and peace in God; all things and actions to be pure and righteous in God; and to see a thorow reconcilement between God and the Creature.

But we proceed.

Sect. VII.

Of the Law.

Among⟨st⟩ the many Contests that are at this day about the Law, I presume to offer a breif declaration of my present knowledg concerning it.

To me (then) it appears, that there are divers Laws that Christians walk under, some more spiritual, some more temporal and carnal; all men walk not by one rule, but God dispences himself to the sons of men according to his divine will and pleasure.

I also see, that the diversity of Gods dispensations may be comprised under these two notions, Either outward or inward, carnal or spiritual, earthly or heavenly: There are outward, earthly, and carnal Laws; and there is one inward, spiritual and heavenly Law. The former is a Law wherein the Creature beholds God after and outward carnal an earthly maner, the latter represents him after an inward and spiritual maner: The outward Law consists in outward things; as Letter, Form, outward Ordinances, and carnal Resemblances of God; the inward is more in Spirit then Letter, more in power then form, more in inward discoveries then outward resemblances. God living in one, is but a figure or shadow of the surest residence of Divine presence in the other. For the glory of Gods presence in the one, surmounts the glory of his presence in the other; the last house is more glorious then the first: God in the Temple or Tabernacle of his Spirit, more glorious then in the flesh, or outward Temple.

It shall be our work herein to pass by the shadow, and fix the strength of our souls aspect upon the substance.

In this our progression, we shall briefly discover these two things.

First, What this true, pure, and spiritual Law is.

Secondly, How it differs in its nature and quality, from all others.

I. *What this true Law is?*

It appears evidently, That the substance, end, and scope of the Law, is God himself, in the pure and naked disclosings of his pure and glorious nature. God giving himself as the Law, Rule, and Power of a Christian. All mens discoveries (be they never so high or seraphical) that are below a naked sight, and uncloathed vision of divine presence, they are but shadows of this substance: no more but *Sinai*, flesh, and bondage. *Sion* is above, and beyond all these.

God himself made out in us, our Law, Direction, and Guidance, is the Law coming out of *Sion*, which that appearance in the flesh of the Son did very lively prefigure. The Law proceeding from *Sion*, and the Word coming from *Jerusalem*, is God flowing out, and pouring forth the brightness and glory of his spiritual nature. This is *Sion*, not *Sinai*; this is peace, rest, and refreshment, not blackness, darkness, and confusion; this is the voyce (not a trumpet, or any creature language, or stammering tongue, but) of the Spirit, sweet, still, yet powerful and glorious. This is the Word from *Jerusalem*; not fleshly *Jerusalem*, not Letter, Form, or any outward glory, but heavenly *Jerusalem*, which is above; its free, and the mother of all the free born of the Spirit. This Law, (or God administring in this dispensation) is light without darkness, love without hatred peace without distraction, freedom and liberty without bondage. Now all other discoveries of the Law render God in a mixed and compounded maner; sometimes love, sometimes hatred, sometimes spiritual, sometimes fleshly; but God (out of all other forms) thus offering himself, and disclosing his pure presence to the soul, is a Law free from all such various testimonies.

Thus you see then what the true Law is; we now proceed to the second thing, as relating to the Law, and that is;

How this Law (or administration) differs from all others.

First then, this Law is God in power and substance; all others is but God in weakness, shadow, and darkness. God in Letter, Form, and all outward discoveries, is but God in darkness, administring not as to himself, but as to the darkness of the creature: God in all such fleshly representations, is but expending himself upon the lowness and carnality of men; but God (out of all these, beheld in a naked purity) is (in this) power, strength, and substance. And thus God, swallows up one dispensation in another, till at last the soul lies down in the overflowings of Divine presence.

Look how light swallows up darkness, so God in these sweet exchanges, devoures one glory in another; the lesser in the greater. I leave the inlargement of these things to divine workings.

Secondly, all other Laws, or dispensations are killing and condemning, this only is saving and justifying.

The reason is, because in all inferiour dispensations, God is (or appears to be) what he is not, but here he appears as he is: in this Law (or spirituall administration) we with open face behold God as in a glasse, we have here a familiar discoverie of God.

Now God appearing in all other things (which the creature cals meanes) is but under a vaile, dwelling in clouds, and darknesse, as to the creatures discoverie; God in *Moses* is a vaile, at *Sinai*, is obscurity; in *John*, is but a figure, in Christ is but a shadow, in Letter, is but darknesse, in formes and ordinances here is but weaknesse; heres no true or naked appearance of God in all these, these sights or aspects are dreadfull and fearfull, killing and condemning. *Moses* feares, and quakes at this appearance; the *Israelites* tremble at this administration, *Adam* hides himselfe from divine presence, while possessed with these carnall apprehensions; but now God in the Law, or administration of the Spirit, is salvavation, justification, peace and refreshment: the violence of spirituall death can now take no hold upon the soule; *Oh death, where is thy sting? oh grave, where is thy victorie?* Sinne which is deaths sting, and the carnall Law, which is sins strength are now both swallowed up in the excellings of divine light: *Thankes be to God, who hath given us the victory through Jesus Christ our Lord. We are more then Conquerours through him that loves us.* The Law carnall cannot terrifie, the Letter cannot condemne, nothing can now charge the soule: Who shall lay any thing to the charge of Gods Elect? its God that justifies, who shall condemne?

Thirdly, This Law, or covenant is new: all others are old, and failable.[2]

All outward Lawes, or administrations are old, they relate to the old man or carnall nature; but the inward Law, or spirituall administration is new; as relating only to that new and spiritual nature.

The soule also under this dispensation becomes new and spirituall; it now knowes Christ no longer after the flesh (or image of that old, earthly, fleshly nature) but in the Spirit, which is the image (or power) of God.

All old things passe away at the appearance of Spirit, glory, and all things become new. A new heaven, a new earth, a new light, a new Law; a new nature, a new creature. We are now come from old *Sinai*, to new *Jerusalem*; from bondage to freedome; from flesh to Spirit; from death to life; f⟨ro⟩m *Egypt* to *Canaan*; from a servant to a sonne; f⟨ro⟩m a fleshly sight, to a new and spirituall discoverie of God: this is *Canaan*, that new land, that extends peace like a river, and abounds with divine satisfaction, this is a Law that was from the beginning, and yet new, because it retaines its splendor, strength and beauty: It was, is, and shall be; it was the first, and shall be the last; it is *Alpha* and *Omega*, and yet alwayes the same, in its glory and excellencie; all other Lawes or administrations are old, they decay, and lose their beauty, because they are but flesh: God, who is the glory of all outward things, at his departure out of them, leaves them as a desolate land, a barren wildernesse, a house not inhabited, as grasse withered, and a flower faded but the word in us, or new Law remaines eternally.

Sect, VIII.

The Sonnes freedome exalted above carnall Libertie

There is (I see) amongst men a fleshly, and also a spirituall liberty.

When Christ told the *Jewes* they should know the truth, and the truth should make them free, the *Jews* stumbled at this saying, they thought they had freedome enough, they were *Abrahams* seed and were never yet in bondage to any: thus they were ignorant of true freedome. We perceive that most men delight in outward freedome, they boast of their outward priviledges, and fleshly Prerogatives; they see no farther then *Abraham* after the flesh: outward discipline, carnall forme and order is the freedome that most men live in, and whosoever shall tell them of another freedome must be sure to undergoe their cruell censures. This was once *Pauls* freedome, he was, touching the Law, a *Pharisee*; this liberty was but bondage, losse and dung in comparison of the sonnes freedom.

The highest freedome, as appertaining to flesh, is indeed meer slavery, it is but meere *Egypt* and *Babylon*.

The true Libertine, is one that walks in the Spirit, is led by the Spirit, and so from under these carnal laws of bondage; he is free in all his actions, and in every performance; he is a son, not a servant, he acts towards God, not from duty, but liberty; he is meerly passive, under the power of the Spirit, being led out according to divine motion; the new nature act as in God,

---

2   Unreliable (*OED* adj.).

and from God, and therefore free; its the seed (or conception) of the free woman; it proceeds not from *Sinai*, but *Sion*; its not borne after the flesh, it lives not in the flesh, its comes from *Egypt*, it lives in *Canaan*, or spiritual freedome and liberty.

While we live in servitude, we are in bondage to all outward things, and worldly elements, accounting this the greatest liberty; here we serve, here we feare, as being overawed by a carnall discovery.

In our sonship we are free, we serve no more, we fear no longer; we love our freedome, and we are free to love, we act not because we are bound to act but because we are lead out by a power of freedom.

The true libertine is free to all things, he is free in all things, yet wil be brought under the power of nothing; he is free to eat, he is free not to eate; he is free to the lowest forme or worship, as by way of brotherly condiscention, but not bound as by way of duty; he can walk in anothers light, he can speake in anothers language, he can be a Jew to the Jew, as one without law, to him that is without law, he can be all to all in their low and carnall attainments; he can observe a day, with them that observe a day, he can refraine with them that observe not, he lives in the highest attainment, yet can sit down in the lowest of Christs mansions.

A brief Conclusion

These (though brief) yet are real Touches of my present Discoveries: What I have spoken, hath been through a clear testimony, and from a sincere Evidence of the Spirit, by which I walk, and the light in which I live: how it will be accepted, I know not; but this I know and am certain of, That what is here inserted, is the interest of every Christian. This Truth is in you, it lives in you, although you know it not.

I am yours, my Discoveries are your interest, though you own neither me, nor my light.

Thus Truth comes to its own, and its own received it not.

While you spurn at this, you kick at your own portion, you slight your inheritance, you trample upon your crown and dignity.

If you shall censure me in this behalf, it shall not trouble me, because I know I am one with you, while you apprehend at a distance.

You shall not, you cannot dis-ingage me from you, God hath given you up to my affections, he hath thrown you in my bosom, and my affection your temerity cannot dissipate: I will go with you whether you please; before I will lose you, I will be as you are, do as you do; I will become any thing, that I may enjoy you: I am given up to you, you cannot throw me ⟨a⟩way, or reject me, because I can subject my self to your will in all things.

If in this my Discovery any thing have offended you, blame it not, it is a rock of offence to you; its a snare to intrap you, a stone to stumble at, and I am sure you must fall upon it, and be broken; you will be offended, and you shall be taken; yet all this shall conduce to your benefit and comfort. A little one shall become a thousand, the small one a strong Nation, the Lord will hasten it in his time.

FINIS

Letter from Salmon to Thomas Webbe

My own heart bloud, from whom I daily receive life and being, in whom my eternall freedom is perfected, to whom is ascribed now and forever, *Amen*.

Thou art the *Webb* of my own spinning, I have laboured to bring thee forth in this glorious form that thou now livest; let me cloath my self with the *Webb* of my own travel. My dear thou art to me as a garment of Needlework,[1] I wear thee as my choicest robes of Royalty; because thou art as a vesture upon me, winde nor weather affright me not; the Northren gales and Borean blasts of cruelty, I know cannot pierce through thee, my garment of salvation. Well, to be brief, I know, my heart, thou art not altogether unascertained of my present estate as appears by yours lately received. My love, thy patheticall lines, I did with much tendernesse accept, and I shall never forget thy love therein manifested. *Cop*, my, thy own hart is gone to *London*; No other note from the Vulgar but hanging at least for him. The last week save one a Souldier was burnt through the tongue for a businesse of the same nature.[2] The glory of these things possesseth multitudes both in City and Country, notwithstanding all their cruelty. For my own part I finde my Genius much elevated and heghtened, to look the worst of casualties in the face, that can succeed these things: My condition outwardly is very poor, when lying here at great expences, yet am I made not to care for the future, although sometimes I scarce know over night how I shall be provided for on the morrow. Well, what my Titular Angel, the Gardian Genius will do with this handfull of earth, I know not, neither am at all troubled, but that if I live, my love to thee; if I die, I die to thee: So that whether living or dying I am thy

Jo. Salmon.

Ten thousand salutes, *alias* holy kisses to thy dear wife, with whom is my heart; my tender respects to thy Uncle, my Father, his Spouse, my beloved, my dear love to *Mary* your maid: Eternal plagues consume you all, rot, sink and damn your bodies and souls into devouring fire, where none but those that walk uprightly can enter. Sirs, I wish you damnable well, because I dearly love you; the Lord grant we may know the worth of hell, that we may forever scorn heaven: For my own part I am ascended far above all heavens, yet I fill all things, and laugh in my sleeve to think whats coming: well I say no more, but farewel.

From my Pallace of Royall Majesty, in the last year of the reign of the beast, and in the day wherein the ⟨l⟩east of all hearts are ripening as fast as possible may be.

Coventry, *April* 3. 1650.

[Printed from E. Stokes, *The Wiltshire Rant* (1652), pp. 13–14.]

1   Ps. 45.14; 'raiment' for 'garment' in the Geneva and King James Bibles. ?A reference to Joshua Garment (see above, pp. 11–12).

2   This was Jacob Bauthumley; the punishment for blasphemy took place on 14 March, 1650.

Heights in *Depths*

AND

Depths in *Heights.*

O R

TRVTH

no less *Secretly* then *Sweetly*
sparkling out its G L O R Y
from under a *Cloud* of

O B L O Q U I E.

Wherein is discovered the various *Motions* of
an *Experienced Soul,* in and through the
manifold dispensations of G O D.

And how the Author hath been acted in, and
redeemed from the unknown paths of darkness;
wherein, as in a wilderness, he hath wan-
dered without the clear vision of
a *Divine Presence.*

Together with a sincere abdication of certain
Tenents, either formerly vented by him,
or now charged upon him.

Per me J O . S A L M O N .

Are they Hebrews? So am I. Are they Israelites? So am I.
Are they the seed of Abraham? So am I.
The God and Father of our Lord Jesus Christ knows that
I lie not.

London, Printed by *Tho. Newcomb,* 1651.

AN
Apologeticall Hint
to the ensuing Discourse.

READER,

His little Piece comes to thy view as a poore Pilgrim, void of that large accommodation which happily it may finde at its own home. I have here dressed it in a homely Language, and formed it as like my self as possible I could; if thou canst see so much w⟨o⟩rth in it, as to give it entertainment, I am bold to say (ere it part from thee) it will return thee satisfaction. It steales like a Thiefe upon the benighted world: However, bee not shy of it; for it shal take nothing from thee but what thou shalt bee made willing to part withall.

Lastly, *I* send it into the World, to discharge some debts which in my late Travels through Egypt land *I* left unsatisfied.

As more plainly thus:

It is not long since wherein that eminent appearance of light, which dawned out its glory upon my Spirit, and from thence gave a sweet and powerfull reflexe upon the World, did shroud it selfe under a most sable and enigmaticall cloud of darknesse, and withdrew for a season, behinde the dark Canopies of Earth and Flesh; in which state the Hemispheare of my spirit was so bespread with obscurity, that *I* knew not whither *I* walked, or what *I* did.

Thus was *I* led into paths that *I* had not known, and turned from a King to become a * Beast, and fed upon huskes for a season.

* Like Nebuchad-nezzar.

After a while posting most furiously in a burning zeal towards an unattainable end: my manner of walking being adjudged by those in power contrary to the peace and civill order of the * Commonwealth) *I* was justly apprehended as an offender: who never before had demerited any thing from them, except love and respect for my faithfull service, which upon all occasions I was ever free to offer as a due homage to the justness of their Cause.

* *Which indeed were no lesse, according to the present state of things.*

I suffered above halfe a yeares imprisonment under the notion of a blaspheamer; which through want of air, and many other conveniences, became very irksome and tedious to my outward man.

Being now retired from the noyse of the world, and cloystered up from the usuall society of my friends, having my grates on the one side for a defence, and my doore fast bolted on the other, I had time enough afforded me to ponder my state and condition.

Upon which I summoned my heart to an appearance before the throne of divine Justice, where after a scrutinous and serious debate, I found that *I* had in many things, been led out and acted in the most undoing and destroying paths of darknesse.

Upon which *I* was for a reason deeply, yea intolerably sensible of these things; and multitudes of armed thoughts all at once beleaguered my soule, as if they had agreed with one consent to devour me.

In the middest of this trouble and distraction, *I* was led to consider that certainly Providence had some end in leading (or suffering me to bee led) into these appearances.

This stayed me, and got by degrees more ground upon my Spirit; in which to this day I can rejoyce and lift up my head above the most insulting and daring Fury: insomuch as I know the Lord had a speciall end to accomplish through all these declinings.

The rage of man shall turn to the praise of God, & for ever blessed be that *Grace* & *Love* which hath taught me to say from an inward experience of light, I thank God that I was made a servant of * sin. But to return: Having this clear conviction upon my spirits, I forthwith addressed my selfe to those who had been the causers of my then present confinement: and truly I will speak it to their everlasting praise, (especially some of them) they were as willing to embrace me & my desires (upon such faire termes propounded) as I could be to offer my selfe to them.

> * All things shal work together for the best to them that love God

Major *Beak*[1] (a man much honored in my thoughts, though once a professed enemy to me) upon the discovery of my mind to him, seemed to be much affected with my condition, & withall informed me of divers blasphemous expressions, which were vented in certain letters of mine which had lately been intercepted; which (after my humble request) hee offered to my view one or more of them: I drew out from them those expressions which most deserved my severest censure, arraigned them and condemned them as guilty.

I offered what *I* had done to Major *Beak*, together with a Petition to the Councel of State for my liberty. Who according to my desires, being in himselfe perswaded of my hearty and penitentiall remorse, did with all care and speed present the same in my behalfe, and so next under God became the onely means of my Release.

Not long after the Right Honorable Colonel *Purefoy*[2] came down to *Coventry* wth my discharge from the Councell, who after strict examination (and finding himselfe with the rest satisfied) presented my Discharge to the Mayor and Aldermen then present, which accordingly was received, and *I* set at liberty, ingaging to his Honour and the rest, that *I* would with all convenient speed declare my selfe in Print against those things which I was then charged withall, and still am by many.

This then is one and not the least end of my exposing these lines to a

---

1   Robert Beake (d. 1708), Warwickshire Independent and Parliamentarian army officer; governor of Coventry in 1650.
2   William Purefoy (c. 1580–1659), Presbyterian, Parliamentary colonel, M.P. for Warwick, regicide.

publick view, that I may appeare to bee no worse then my word to them whose indulgencie in a time of need was sufficiently manifested towards me.

And truly had not this with some other weighty reasons prevailed with me, I should not have troubled the world with things of this nature. Onely. Therefore Reader take notice that my main ends in this business are,

1. To give a faithful account of the dealings of the most High towards me, as he hath led me along through manifold dispensations of himselfe.

2. To declare to all men what I now am, onely in what *I* am not: if thou (Reader) art so wise as to discover my spirit by what *I* shall here declaim, thou wilt spare me the labour of making an after profession of my Faith, which *I* confesse *I* shall hardly be drawn to declare to * any man.

* Hast thou Faith, have it to thy selfe.

3. *I* now am made to speak, because *I* am almost weary of speaking, and to informe the world that silence hath taken hold of my spirit. The thunderstrokes of the Almighty have to purpose uttered their voices in me, heaven and earth have trembled at their dreadfull sounds: the Alarm being over, ther's silence now in heaven; for how long *I* know not.

I lie quietly secure in the Lord while *I* see the whole world consuming in the fire of envie one against another. I heare much noyse about me, but it serves onely to deafen me into the still slumbers of Divine rest. The formall world is much affrighted, & every form is up in Arms to proclaim open wars against it selfe: The Almighty power is dashing one thing against another, and confounding that which hee hath formerly faced with the glory of his own presence: Hee setteth up and casteth down, and who shal say, *What doest thou?* Come then, O my Soule, enter thou into thy Chamber, shut thy doores about thee, hide thy selfe in silence for a season till the indignation bee blown over.

Reader, I heartily bid thee farewel, commending thee into that bosome of love, where *I* rest,

Thine in silence.

Heights in Depths,
AND
Depths in Heights.
O R
T R V T H
no less secretly then sweetly
sparkling out its GLORY
from under a *Cloud* of
O B L O Q U I E.

Anitie of Vanities, All is Vanitie saith the Preacher.

The highest piece of wisdom, is to see wisdom it self but Vanity.

The whole world is a Circle, including nothing but emptiness.

*Wisdom it self is but a womb of Wind, whose wringing Pangs, pretend the
* Worldly. birth of pure Substance, but in times revealing Order it amits[3] nothing, except travel for sorrow, whose high aspires, do cursorily expire into an airy notion, even while it appears to be something, it proves nothing.

Man walketh in a vain shew, he shews to be a man, and thats all.

* Below.   * Here is nothing that truly is, because it * abides not; things onely appear to
* What God
doth he doth be, and so vanish.
for ever.   I am satisfied in nothing so much, as in knowing that * nothing can satisfie me.
* In the world   We seem to live in the State of variety, wherein we are not truely living, but onely in appearance: in Unity is our life: in one we are, from one divided, we are no longer.

While we perambulate variety, we walk but as so many Ghosts or Shadows in it, that it self being but the Umbrage of the Unity.

To descend from the oneness or Eternity, into the multiplicity, is to lose our selves in an endlesse Labyrinth.

To ascend from variety into uniformity, is to contract our scattered spirits into their original center and to finde our selves where we * were, before we * were.

* In Eternity
Certainly, when a man looks upon the face of things and with a serious by Gods
inspection eyes the shaken Frame of them, he must conclude that there is decree.
* As to
somthing above and beyond all appearances, which can onely and alone satisfie. outward

If we look upon the Tempora⟨r⟩y, or more outward state of things; good appearance.
Lord how subject is it to revolutions and vicissitudes? what is it that we can call certain, but onely uncertainty.

---

3   From Latin *amittere*; to send away, to let go or slip.

Behold the Lord maketh the earth empty and voyd; he layeth it waste: it reels to and fro like a drunkard: all its Foundations are out of course: one change succeeds another, while the earth is become subject to a constant inconstancie.

The world travels perpetually, and every one is swoln full big with particularity of interest; thus travelling together in pain, and groaning under enmity: labouring to bring forth some one thing, some another, and all bring forth nothing but wind and confusion: this is certainly a great evil that God hath given men to be exercised withall under the sun.

If further we cast our eye upon these things which promise greater Stabillitie, (*viz:* formes of righteousnes and Religion) alas how doth experience daily informe us, of the violent turnings and overturnings which are incident to these also?

Doth not the Almighty power blast those things daily, which have been most in request amongst us? is he not dashing one forme against another as potters Vessels? what lively Characters of sudden mortalitie may we runn and read upon all * outward formes? what meanes this great noyse, and stir, that alarmes the world continually? the bitter contention, that intermixes it selfe with mens wayes *So farr as they are bare form.* and worships? the perpetuall clashings of one forme against another? The heaven of forme is passing away, which goes not without much clamour, strife and contention. Thus is it the Lords will that people shal labour in the fire, and weary themselves for very vanitie.

The farther a man * reaches beyond himselfe to contemplate an incomprehensible glory, though his labour may be delightfull, yet his loss will prove very * extensive. *As Adam, who desired to be as God, to know good and evill.*

While with a swift winged ambition, we are transported into the sublimity of notion; the Scorching influences of the heavenly Splendor, meets us (as it were) with an untimely check; Singes the golden *plumes* of our soring fancies; & down we fal into unconceivable depths of darknes. *I speak by deep experience.*

Ob. How then shall a man attaine to a onenes, and communion with this inaccessible glory?

Sol. Seeing there is no way probable for us, (by our most lofty aspires) to interesse our selves in that

We must patiently expect its seasonable descenscion upon us; whose nature it is to * consume us into it selfe, and to melt us into the same nature and likenes: *Out of al our dross & tinn: for he is a refiners fire.* And truly till this come, and thus manifest it selfe, all that man can doe to acquire satisfaction, does but multiply his sorrow upon his head, and augment cares upon his spirit. Vanitie, vanitie, all is vanitie.

It is but vanitie for me to write, vanitie for you to read. Words are but wind; you read you know not what, and perhaps I write I know not what: and so let it be till God will have it otherwise.

There is a set time for ever⟨y⟩ purpose under heaven; vanity hath its time also; nay time it selfe is but a lengthened threed of vanitie; there's no reallity but in eternitie:

When time shall be no longer then things will appeare in their proper and perfect substance.

Well; to every thing there is a season; a time to * cast away stones, and a time *A vaine thing.*

to gather stones together, I know not very well which of these times I am now under, while I am thus busied:

It may be I am now casting stones against the wind, [that is but vanity] However, (if so) methinks the wise reader might find some better employment, then to stand as a spectator of such folly and madnes.

Truly I would very willingly say nothing, & yet at present I am forced into a freedom to speak my mind:

If I speak any thing more then my reason dictates to me as truth; I am become a foole;

And yet I have not so much reason in me, as to make what I say appear reasonable to others: this is also vanity, and a sore travell. But to draw near to what I intend:

I have lived to see an end of all perfections; that which I now long for, is to see perfection it selfe perfected.

I have bin led out to seek the Lord in manifold appearances, I must now (by himselfe) be found in himselfe, who is the good it selfe, and nothing but this can satisfie: Take only this br⟨ie⟩f hint, for information.

How the Author hath beene acted
in, and carried thorough va-
rious and manifold ap-
pearances.

NO sooner had I attained to any maturity in a natural understanding, of common principles of morality, but I found in my selfe a secret longing to sore in a more celestiall orbe; (being partly convicted of a higher life than that of nature.)

This desire being kindled, and supplied with the timely breath of the Almighty, it soone begann to warme and afterwards to set my whole heart of a flame, which to this day could never be extinct; but hath ever since (like the ambitious sparke) made its constant ascensions, and earnest aspires, towards this heavenly center.

Receiving (after my nocturnal slumbers in nature's grave) some quicknings of a divine principle within me; I presently arose and (as it were) shooke of my night dresses, and appeared to my selfe, like the sunn, dawning out its refulgent splendor, from behind the darke canopies of the earth: I was now adorned in another hue, and devoutly resolved to tread the paths of a more princely dignity.

I presently set forth for heaven, the whole powers and faculties of my soule being infinitely ingaged thereunto, by some taste of the fruits of that good land, which I received as pledges of divine love, and as the earnest of that more glorious inheritance, which I now waited for.

I now forsooke my owne kindred and my fathers house, withdrew my selfe from my former vanities, and willingly exposed my selfe to all the contempt and reproach of the world, that I might owne Christ, his cause, and people.

By this time (the honest presbyterian party) were looked most upon, as owners of, and sufferers for, the cause of God;

These, being newly crept out of the shell of Episcopacy, were hatched into a more pure and refined forme; and (after a small time) did seeme to hover gently, and sore sweetly, in a more sublimer region than the former.

With these I now joyned, and became a Zealous hearer and a very great affecter of them; and truly did enjoy much of God in this station while the Lord appeared to me in it.

After a while, the notion of Independency offred it selfe upon the stage, to which I was willing to lend my audience (at least) and make proofe of its plausible proposalls. I understood they were a people, much decryed by the vulgaritie, which made me imagine that there was something of God amongst them;

I saw they were a people farr excelling others in the strictnes of their forme; and (which most affected me) were gathered out of the world, and knit one to another in a more close, and comfortable bond of love, than any;

The more excelling lustre of this forme, (to me) darkned the beauty, and dim'd the glory of the other: my affections (upon the illumination of the understanding) were soone commanded and forth they runn with a great deale, of delight, to wel-com this newly received glory; in this forme I was concluded and shutt up for a season: wherein I also enjoyed much satisfaction:

Soone after, the doctrine of beleivers baptisme was much pressed by many: and this (though it were a much despised forme) I was yet free to make triall of it, and owne it so farr as I could see it hold a correspondencie with truth.

I (after some serious debate) was convinced that it was my duty to obey God in my subjection to that ordinance of water baptisme: I hereupon tendered my willing and chearful submission, and consulted not with flesh and blood in this business. In the hottest time of Persecution: I was made one eminent both in holding forth this way to the world, and also in an open suffering for the same.

By this time I began to think it was high time to settle, and not to expose my minde to such changes and alterations in things of this nature: Whereupon I here built me a Tabernacle, and was fixed in a peremptory resolve, That this and no other could lawfully be adjudged the way of God.

Then came that voice from the throne of the heavenly Almightiness: Arise and depart for this is not your rest.

I was made as truly sensible of this inwardly, as the eye is sensible of the light, or the ear of the outward sound.

I was certainly struck dead to all my wonted enjoyments.

Stript I was of my glory, and my Crown taken from my head, & I could see nothing but Vanity (and that legibly written) upon all my former travels.

I then had a clear discovery in my spirit, how far all my former enjoyments came short of that true rest which my soul had all along aimed at.

Here I stood for a season weeping with *Mary* at the Sepulcher: fain I would have found Christ where I left him, but alas he was risen: I found nothing in form but a few * signals of Mortality; as for Jesus, he was risen and departed.

* A few grave clothes, or such like stuff

Thus have I followed Christ from his babe-ship, or infancy, to his Grave of mortality, running through the life of Form in a bare knowledge of Christ after the flesh, till

I expired with him * into his death, and was sealed up in the Grave of most darke, and somnolent retires for a season.

Loath, full loath I was thus to shake hands with form, & to leave the terrestrial image of Iesus Christ; yet so it was designed that hee must goe to his father, and (although * I were ignorant of it) prepare a higher mansion in himself for me.

* Like the disciples, who were ignorant of the promise of the Spirit.

When my 3. dayes (or set time) was expired, I begann to feele some quickning comfort within me; the grave stone was rolled away, and I set at libertie, from these deep and darke retires; out I came with a most serene and chearfull countenance, and (as one inspired with a supernaturall life) sprang up farr above my earthly center, into a most heavenly and divine enjoyment: Wrapt up in the embraces of such pure love and peace, as that I knew not oft times, whether I were in or out of this fading forme.

Here I saw heaven opened upon me and the new Ierusalem (in its divine brightnes and corruscant beauty) greeting my Soule by its humble and gentle descensions:

Now I certainely enjoyed that substance, which all this while I had groped after in the shadow.

My water was turned into wine-form, into power; and all my former enjoyments being nothing in appearnce to that glory which now rested on my spirit.

Time would faile to tell, what joy unspeakable, peace unconceiveable; what soul ravishing delights, and most divinely infatuating pleasures my soul was here possest with.

I could cast my eye no where, but that presence of love presented it selfe to me, whose beatificall vision, oftimes dazeled me into a sweet astonishment:

In a word, I can give you no perfect account of that glory which then covered me; the lisps and slipps of my tongue will but render that imperfect, whose pure perfection surmounts the reach of the most strenuous and high flown expression.

I appeared to my selfe as one confounded into the abyss of eternitie, nonentitized into the being of beings; my soule spilt, and emptied into the fountaine and ocean of divine fulness: expired into the aspires of pure life:

*Viz: the carnal self.

In breife the Lord so much appeared that * I was little or nothing seene; but walked at an orderly distance from my self, treading and tripping over the pleasant mountaines of the Heavenly land, where I walked with the Lord and was not:

I shall be esteemed a foole, by the wise world, thorough an over much boasting: otherwise I could tell you how I have been exalted into the bosome of the eternall Allmightines, where I have seene and heard, things unlawfull, (I say * unlawfull) to be uttered amongst men; but I shall at present spare my self the labour, and prevent the worlds inconsiderate censure.

*As to the weakness of many.

The proud and imperious Nature of flesh, would willingly claim a share in this glorious work, for which cause happened a suddain, certain, terrible, dreadfull revolution, a most strange vicissitude.

God sent a Thorn immediatly; hid himself from me by a sudden departure, and gives a speedy Commission to a Messenger of Satan to assault me.

The Lord being thus withdrawn, & having carried away (in the bundle of his Treasures) the heart and life of that * new seed in me, there now remained nought behind but the man of sinne, who (for his pride) being wounded with the thorn of Divine vengeance, began by degrees to act its part.

* Note wel what I say, that was reserved pure in the life of Christ, while the flesh acted its part.

This Thorn, I say was in the flesh (or fleshly principle) the spirit (or new man) that was preserved still in the heart of eternal love, and became a life occult, hid with Christ in God.

Angry flesh being struck at heart with the piercing dart of vengeance, begins to swell, and contracting all the evil humors of the body of death into one lump, to grapple with this thorne of wrath, at last violently breaks out, and lets forth the very heart and coar of its pride and enmity.

The rankor and venom of this subtil serpent, now discovers it self, and being sore sick with a cup of pure wrath, disgorges its foul stomack upon the very face, and appearance of Truth.

I was now sent into a strange land, and made to eat unclean things in *Assyria*; walked in unknown paths, and became a mad man, a fool amongst men.

Thus tumbling in my own Vomit, I became a derision to all, and even loathed by those by whom I had been beloved: being made drunk with a Cup of vengeance, every one begins to cast a squint eye towards me.

O the deep drunken bewitching, besotting draughts of the wine of astonishment that hath been forced upon me.

Well, my folly being discovered, and the bowels of corrupt flesh being let out, I lay as a spectacle of scorn and contempt to every eye; yea my mothers children were angry with me, and even those were apt to censure me for a firebrand of hell, an hypocrite, a cast away, into whose hands when the Cup of the Lord shall come, they may appear as bad, if not worse then my self.

But most true it is, he that slippeth with his feet, is as a Lamp despised in the heart of him that is at ease.

Certainly if the Lord would but let loose the reins of mens hearts, they should soon discover as bad, or worse in themselves, as they hate and despise in others.

The time of many is now at hand; yea, its come upon them, wherein the baseness and rottenness of their hearts are discovered; they walk with their insides outwards, and shew their nakedness and shame.

They are turned and tossed as a ball in a large countrey: reel, stagger, stumble and fall with the desperate intoxicating draughts of wrath and madness: tumble up and down in their own filthiness and beastiality; and are become signs and wonders amongst men: yea, those that have been Rivals to the chiefest and most eminent in knowledge and enjoyment, have been puld down from the Throne, and set as mirrors of amazement in the world: Judged with a witness both by God and man: judged in themselves, the damnation of whose flesh sleepeth not: Judged, censured, stripped, persecuted, imprisoned by others.

The hand of the Lord meets them continually, and the world knows not, considers not, their most heavy and sad pressures.

O God, that men could a little consider the several disposings of the eternal wisdom!

I would gladly offer one silent whisper in the ears of the world, and leave it to the wise, and ponderous judgement of every Christian.

Hark then—

Think ye that those eighteen upon whom the Tower of *Siloam* fell, were greater sinners then others? I tel you, nay.

Are their impieties on their foreheads? and are not yours in your hearts? is there not the same spring of enmity, root of bitterness, den of Darkness, and spawn of folly and madness in you as in them.

What if the Lord should tear off your large Phylacteries of religion and righteousness, and instead thereof stamp the foul image of that hidden enormity, which harbors secretly in your breast.

What if God should uncloke you, and strip you of your lovely garbes of pretended holiness, and should let that appear which is hidden under this pleasing vesture?

Consider, is there not in the best of you a body of death?

Is not the root of rebellion planted in your natures?

Is there not also a time for this wicked one to be revealed?

Do you think that God will not one time or other, one way or another discover and judge that flesh, which now seems to sleep securely under the specious pretences of righteousness.

You little think, and less know, how soon the cup of fury may be put into your hands: my self, with many others have been made stark drunk with that wine of wrath, the dregs whereof (for ought I know) may fall to your share suddenly.

I speak not this either to extenuate my own evil, or to cast approbries[4] in the face of those who have (to the utmost) censured me; but rather to mittigate the severity of peoples spirits, and to give a by-hint of that doom and judgement, that is at hand upon the world.

For my own part, I do most ingeniously and candidly confess, that the worst of men cannot out-vie my iniquity. Hell it self cannot hatch that mischiefe, which my heart hath not been a receptable to imbrace; and if ever a proud Pharisee in the world dare stept up and plead his own innocency, let him cast the first stone at me: If every man be found guilty, and there is none that doth good, why should we so unseemly envy, and not rather pitty (and lament over) each others miseries.

But to return: being thus clouded from the presence of the Lord, I was violently posted through most dark paths, where I ever and anon stumbled and fell into the snare of open error and profaneness, led and hurried, (by what power let the wise judg) in a principle of mad Zeal, to tear and rend the very appearances of God, which I had formerly cherished in my brest.

Delighting my self in nothing but in that which rendred me most vile and ugly in the sight of all men, and glorying in nought, but my own shame.

I could not have imagined that such deadly poyson had lodged within me, had not the dreadful piercing lance of vengeance, let it out before my face, and made it palpably manifest to all men.

---

4   'Opprobries': insults, reproaches (*OED* n. 2a).

I was indeed full sick of wrath, a vial of wrath was given me to drink; the heavenly pleasure would not excuse me a drop of it; which no sooner had flesh received, but it burst in sunder, polluted and defiled my wayes and actions, with its filthy poysonous nature;

Well——drink I must, but mark the riddle.

'Twas given me, that I might drink, I drank, that I might stumble, I stumbled, that I might fall; I fell, and through my fall was made happy.

It is strange to think, how the hidden and secret presence of God in me, did silently rejoyce while flesh was thus manifested;

Spiritual I, or the new man

I had a sweet rest and refuge in the Lord, even while my flesh was frying and scorching in the flames of ireful fury.

I was ark'd up in the eternal bosome, while the flesh was tumbling in the foaming surges of its own vanity:

And although the beast ascended out of the bottomless pit, and cast out a flood of envy against me, yet I was preserved in the Lord from its insulting

Jesus Christ.

fury: and this I know is a riddle to many, which none but the true Nazarite can expound; and til he is pleased to unfold it, it pleases me it should lie dark.

But to conclude—

Thus have I been forc't into the strange paths of obscurity, driven up and down in a tempestuous storm of wrath, and split upon the rocks of dreadful astonishment; All the waves and billows of the Almighty have gone over me.

I am now at rest in the silent deeps of eternity, sunk into the abysse of silence, and (having shot this perilous gulf) am safely arrived into the bosome of love; the land of rest.

I sometimes hear from the world, which I have now forsaken; I see its Diurnals are fraught with the tydings of the same clamor, strife, and contention, which abounded in it when I left it; I give it the hearing, and that's all.

I meddle with none of them; though they are daily censuring me at their pleasure.

My lovely silence contributes to large a parcel of Peace to me, as that I would gladly be at Peace with all men: but yet such is the restless fury of the disturbed world, that it will not upon any terms enter into a league of concord with me.

I cannot inveigh against any form, party, or religious interest: it becomes not my sweet silence, to bawl and brawl with the unquiet spirits of men, who are therefore swoln with madness; and frenzy against me, because they cannot by their bitter emulation, either disturb the peace and rest of my spirit, or provoke me to a contest with them, upon such poor base and beggerly terms.

I see there is nought that can satisfie under the Sun.

And certainly were men possessed of that true enjoyment which they pretend to, they would be better satisfied, and more at peace in their spirits.

My great desire (and that wherein I most delight) is to see and say nothing.

I have run round the world of variety, and am now centered in eternity; that is the womb out of which I was taken, and to which my desires are now reduced.

My mind is wholly bent to contemplate that.

There is nothing in the world of so great amplitude, as to comprehend or contain my spirit within its measurable orb; something that is more durable, then any thing that is extant in the world, is that which my souls press after.

And in the interim I find my self mostly comprehended, and best satisfied in my still and silent reserves.

I am, or would bee, very little, or nothing in shew, yet I am indeed, both what I would be, or may desire to be.

I am drawne, from off the stage of outward appearances, on which (of late) I have acted a most sad and Tragicall part: I am bound in the close Galleries with my beloved, where (under the sweet verge of his Love, and shadow of his wing) I am wooed to refresh my selfe with most mellifluous delights.

I am as the Lords Lillie amongst Thornes; I stand in a very fertile soyl: though it be a valley, yet its both fat, rich, and pleasant.

I cannot envy the Thornes that are about me, neither can they hurt mee; I grow quietly by them, stand peaceably amongst them, and they are made (against their wills) a defensive hedge about me.

In summ,

While I view with a serious inspection the state of things about mee; I clearly perceive how every thing prides it self in a momentary state; when (alasse!) after it hath shewed it self, it suddenly is swallowed up by that being whence it first came.

Every thing beares a constant and greedy motion towards the center; and when once we are wearied in the prolixity of variety, wee revolve into silence, where we are as if we had never been.

Every one stands up, *Vi & armis*,[5] to plead the prerogative of his own interest; the World is so filled with Verbosity, that I am gladly constrained into silence, till I have time and opportunity to offer my minde amongst them.

I see partly what the end will be, but I must not declare, neither will the world hear it.

I have stept out of my silent Mansions, to offer these few words to the Vulgar view: how hardly I was perswaded to it, my own heart can evidence, and many in my behalf can testifie: some engagements urged me to it, more then any desire of mine to become publick.

I am quite a weary of popular applause, and I little value a vulgar censure;

5   See above, p. 67, n. 3.

the benefit of the one, cannot at all affect me, nor the prejudice of the other much molest me:

I enjoy greater treasures in my happy silence, then all their cruelty can make me capable of the want of.

'Tis true I have lost a good name, and honorable esteem in the world.

I have also another name, which is a new one, which none can read, but he that hath it; none can blast with the least blot of infamy.

I can cheerfully bear the indignation of the Lord, for I have sinned:

It is not for me to reply against the dealings of the Eternal Wisdome: it is rather good for mee to bear the yoke in my youth, with a Christian silence and gravity.

* In any christian contest.

I am made willing to give my * cheek to the smiter, to sit alone, (keeping silence) and put my mouth in the dust: any thing with the Lord, it is to mee very acceptable; nothing (without God) dares approach my quiet and still Mansions.

In a word: I am able both to doe and to suffer all things thorow an Eternall Almightinesse: And resolved I am to gaine a conquest over the World, by prostrating my self a subject to their weakness.

I must submit to them, that I may raign over them; and even then I trample them underneath my feet, when I am most subdued to their will and pleasure.

Well——to draw neer to my chamber, (for it's bad standing without doors, while a storm is impending) I am to this day set upon the account of a blasphemer, a seducer: what not.

I will not say but I have given some former ground of suspition, both by my unwary walking, and heedless expressions.

Especially the book intituled divinity anatomized.

Somewhat I have formerly vented in certain papers, which the weak stomacks of many can hardly digest: and truely I could heartily wish, that some expressions had been better pondered; and not so untimely exposed to a publick view: though I also beleeve, that if they were well chewed (and not so suddenly swallowed without relishing the nature of them) they would be better digested then they are.

'Tis a vanity and sore travail, for a man to unbosom his life in the face of a confused multitide; and to offer it up to the rude censure of the (no less mercylesse then) ignorant world.

I clearly see that the understandings of men (for the most part) are too gross and corpulent, to turn and winde in the nice, and narrow criticismes of truth; their spirits too dull and plumbous[6] to mount above their wonted notorious, and thread bare principles.

Whatsoever stands out of their Sphear, or bears, no proximity to their

---

6   Resembling lead; leaden (*OED* adj. 1; Salmon's usage is cited in *OED* and is the earliest).

commonly received maximes; must presently be deemed as blasphemy, and sentenced to the infernal lake, as most odious and abominable.

That which men call truth to day, they proclaim error to morrow: and that which now is adjudged and condemned as error, anon is embraced and extolled as truth. That man certainly is not otherwise, that will regard the uncertain censures of men.

Truely for my part, as I sit still and behold how the over-busie world is acted; so I can quietly let them alone, to roul in their confused labyrinth: but because in many things I have offended; and the froward spirits of men are not easily courted to a pardon: I have here thought meet, to cite a small parcel of the most crying errors of the times; and (before I withdraw into my sweet and safe retires) spend a little time in sweeping them from my door; that so the evil of error, may not lie in the porch, to disquiet my blessed rest, and disturb the sweet slumbers of my silent mansions. Which done, I shall then as well resolvedly, as quietly bid adeue to the wretched world; and wrap my self up in my mantle of silence, where I shall refresh my defessed[7] spirit with the pure naps of divine pleasure, while the beloved is pleased to awaken me into a more active state.

Briefly then in one word.

I shall linck the most capital errors now extant, in one chain; and expulse them by a free vote, f⟨ro⟩m having any future commerce with me, or claiming the least propinquity to my reformed jugement.

---

7   From Latin *defessus*, part. of *defetiscor*; weary, exhausted.

A sincere Abdication of cer-
tain Tenents, either for-
merly vented by, or now
charged upon the
Author.

I Am daily accused as one that holds these horrid opinions. *Viz.* That there is no God; no Devil; no Heaven; no Hell; as one that denies the Scripture, and the blessed Trinity of the God-head; that saith there is no Sin; or otherwise that God is the author of Sin; these (among others of less consequence) are chiefly alledged against me: to all which I reply, as followeth—.

And first, of God.

Ps. 14.1.

THE fool hath said in his heart, there is no God. 'Tis the greatest folly and madness in the world to assert or give credit to it.

The wise man, whose eyes are in his head, cannot harbor such a motion in his heart.

Act. 17.
25, 26,
27, 28.

I wholly banish such conceits from my minde; and on the contrary assert,

That God is that pure and perfect being in whom we all are, move and live; that secret blood, breath, & life, that silently courseth through the hidden veins and close arteries of the whole creation.

Col. 1.16, 17.
Isa. 45.8.
Ps. 65.8, 9,
10,&c.
Col. 3.11
Isa. 54.16

Every thing both visible and invisible is fraught with his presence, & brim'd up wth the plentiful distils of a divine life: he is both all and in all, he truly is, and there is nothing besides him that derives not power from him.

He hath but a weak eye, that sees not the sparkling beams of eternity, darting out their refulgent beauty in and through variety.

What madman or fool will then deny a divine and eternal being.

Ps. 19.1, 2,
3, 4.
If I descend
into Hell, thou
art there,

Where can we go, what can we do without him? heaven, hel, earth, sea, sun, moon, stars, al that you see, all that you possess, is sweetly replenished with the glory of this pure majesty: every thing receives from him, and gives up to him.

More might be said but I hope this is sufficient to inform any reasonable man, that I wholly abjure this conceit, or rather deceit of the world.

Now to the next.

Of the Divell.

THe Divel is understood variously amongst men: either grosly, or corpulently by some, or more subtilly and mistically by others.

I am not now either to advance my own, or to fly in the face of any mans judgement. I am one under censure; it becomes not me to be over-busie in judging others, till I have cleared my self.

They say, I hold no Divel——

Truly if any thing ever was vented by me, that is infected with the least tang or tincture of such a principle; I shall heartily deplore my own weakness in it, and shall be ready to disown it, as the bastard brat of a vain and empty notion.

And on the contrary doe affirm.

That the Divel, * who was once an Angel of light, yet not keeping his first state, became a Denne, and receptacle of darkness; reserved in chains from the presence of the Lord til the great day.

> * A true history and pure mistery Ep. Jude: v. 6, Pet. 2.2. 4. 2. Thes. 2. v. 3. 4. 7. 8. I Sa. ch. 19. ve. 9. Job. 1. 12. 2. cor. 12. 7. Ep. 2. 2. 2 Thes. 2. 9.

He is that spirit or Mystery of Iniquity, which continually envies God in his pure ways and workings.

That dark Angel, or Messenger employed by the Almighty, to effect the purposes of his wrath and vengeance.

The Prince of the powers of the air; an airy fashionist,[8] that can assume any form: That can form, * conform, reform, and deform at his pleasure: one that chiefly rules in the hearts of the children of disobedience.

> * Transform him self into an Angel of light.

Let the wise judge, and the righteous, gently smite me, if I deserve censure in what I have spoken.

I proceed—

Of Heaven.

Heaven is the center of the souls bliss and happiness.

I can in no wise deny it, because my conversation is in it.

If there be no heaven, wheres our present enjoyment? Or what shal become of that future happiness which we all expect?

> Phil. 3. 20.
> 1 Cor. 15 19.
> Rev. 14. 13.

Heaven is the Christians rest, his divine Sabboth, where he keeps holy day to the Lord.

Did I ever insinuate a deniall of heaven? certainly it was because the

---

8   One who flamboyantly follows popular (religious) modes (*OED* n. 1).

darkness of hel covered my understanding.

John 17.
24.
Eph. 2. 6.

To live with, and in God, to be raised up into the nature and life of Christ out of the somnolencie of flesh, is to live in the heavenly place; this we enjoy partly here, more fully hereafter.

Of Hell.

THat there is no Hell, I in no wise can imagine, but contrarywise say,—

That Hell is the appoynted portion of the * sinner, where in sinfull man is for ever to be tormented from the presence of the Lord: the inhabitants of whose dark mansions are ever weeping, wailing, and gnashing of teeth.

* The
wicked shall
be turned
into hel,
and all the
Nations that
forget God.
Mat. 24. 51.
Tophet is
prepared.

Hell is a * Tophet of scorching displeasure; a fire kindled and maintained by the continued breath of the Almighty, whereby it becomes a dying life, or rather, a living death. The * breath or life of Eternity augments and increases this death and misery, which death and hell hath a greedy Lake to receive it.

I hope malice it self will consent, that I am not guilty of this blasphemy.

I therefore proceed for my sweet invitations, to my silent feast, solemnize my devotions thitherward.

Of the Scripture.

CHrist is the Eternall word of the Father, the saving, teaching, enlightening Oracle of heaven, to whom the Scriptures ascribe all honor and dignitie.

I do not remember that in any thing which I have written, or declared, I have given the captious world the least ground to render me guilty of denying the Scriptures.

Yet because I am charged with it through weakness and mistake in some, malice and impudence in others, *I* give this satisfactory hint.

I own the Scriptures as the inspirations of the Holy Ghost; to holy men of old: a history, or map of truth, wherein (if our learned Translators have not deceived us) is contained a true discovery of the dealings of God with his people in former times, and ages of the world: wherein the life of many a precious promise is lockt up. They are known to be the word of God to those in whom the spirit declares them; others do but call them, not knowing them to be so.

Joh. 5.
38. 39.
40.
2 Tim. 1
13.

They bare Testimony to the great Oracle of Life and Salvation (Christ Jesus.) They are the letter, & sound of truth. The form (and but the form) of sound words where they are not corrupted with the false glosses of the learned.

I must embrace them, own them, honour them; yea, I cannot but delight in them, because they bear the image and feature of that pure word which was from the beginning, and is so everlasting.

Joh. 1. 1. 2.

Of sin, or God being the Author of sin.

THe vulgar censure, is, a many headed ill favoured monster, it lookes many waies; it favourably entertains, and smoothly invites, and eagerly gapes after all reports whatsoever.

Some say I hold no sinn, and with the same mouth will be apt to conclude that I make God the author of sinn: Here must needs be a gross mistake on the one hand or other certainely.

I humbly acknowledg my over readiness to present some notions of this nature to a publique view: If any things that I have written, will claime relation to these, I here recede them, and leave them to the mercy, or rather judgement of those to whom their nakednesse and folly are palpably evident: and further say concerning sin,

In Divinity anatomized.

That sin is that contagious leprosie, which hath Epidemically spread it self over the whole earth.

Neither the * righteous nor the wicked are free from it.

Ps. 14.2, 3. Rom. 3. 10. Prov. 20. 9 * The righteous sinneth seven times a day.

Sin is a transgression of the Law: unity was once the Law of man, he brake the Unity, run into the wilie intangles of devision and distance, and did plunge himself into the gulfe of sin, the abyss of misery.

The Law or Command of Unity, was to knowe one, and only one (God.) Man will know more then one; know himself in a state of division; here creeps in sin, and brings down man from his uprightness, and a state of obliquity.

Exod. 20 ver. 3. Gen 3, 5, 6.

Man, as man growing from the root of the first *Adam* (the Earthly-fallen principle) is nothing else but a massie heap of sin, a cursed lump of foul impiety, and must certainly expect to receive the wages of iniquitie.

1 John, 1 8. 10.

Sin makes every thing a curse and bitterness to us.

Were it not for this sin (or breach of the Law of Unity) all things would be sweetned with blessing, yea, blest with a Divine sweetness.

Death it self, the bitterest potion of sorrow, would be nectarized with a pleasant dulcitude, which (through sin) brings with it, (and bears in it) an unpleasing mordacity.

1 Cor: 15, 56.

In fine, tis sin that corrups our judgements, stains our natures, burthens our spirits, and betrays our souls into the snares of endless, and easless Torment.

Again,

This being the lothsome nature of sin, who will dare to be so impudent as to affirm, That God is the Author of it? tis true, the Scripture in many places seem to countenance such a thing, if not wisely and soberly interpreted.

But it is not my work, as I said before, to condemn any, before I have cleared my selfe: it is enough for me to exonerat my spirit of that load which is laid upon me by a fair recession of the Error I stand charged with.

1 Ioh: 1: 5. 6.

Let all therefore know, That I look upon God to be a single object of pure light, whose glorious nature cannot be touched with the least tincture of darkness; evill or sin may not, cannot * approach his perfectly pure presence.

* He is of more pure eyes than to behold iniquitie.

Mat. 19: 17.

He is good (the good it self) he doth good, nothing but good, al good: good is God, there's nothing good but himself.

Men, the best of men, things, the most excellent of things, they are all vanity & a lye, worse then vanity, vexation of Spirit.

God, the Unity is good: all vertue, and true worth is bundled up in it. Contrarywise—The Divel, division, distance, sin, they are naught, stark naught; evil, nothing but evil, continually evil.

The Divel is a lye, believe him not; sin is a lye; all that you see below besides God, it is a lie, froth, emptiness, winde and confusion.

God hath nothing to do with any thing that existeth not in himself, or is divided from himself: he is not the Author of division: he is all one in all variety: the divider is the Divel, God knows him not: the division is sin, God owns it not.

Col. 3. 11.

I say not then that God is the Author of sin.

Lastly, Of the Trinity.

GOD is one simple, single; uncompounded glory: nothing lives in him or flows from him, but what is his pure individual self.

Unity is the Father, the Author and begetter of all things; or (if you will) the Grandmother in whose intrinsecal womb, variety lies occult, till time orderly brings it forth.

Ion. 14. 9.

1 Ioh. 5. 7.

Christ sayes of himself, I and the Father am one: and the Apostle saith, there are three that bare record in Heaven; the Father, the Word, and Spirit, and these three are one. Without controversie, great is the mystery.

In the multiplicity or variety they are three, but in the unity or primary state, all one, but one.

The Father is not the Son, the Son is not the Spirit, as multiplied into form and distance; I may lawfully and must necessarily maintain three:——but then again trace them by their lineal discent into the womb of eternity, revolve to the center, and where is the difference?

The unity or Father in it self, is a massy heap of an undiscovered glory, which branches out it self into an orderly variety, and so admits of various names and titles: Father, Son, Spirit, three in name, but all one in nature.

Unity without variety, is like the * man in the Garden, solitarily slumbering in its owne profound retires; having nothing to delight in but it self.

The Father will not therfore be without the Son, without the Spirit: It is not fit the Man should be alone.

But then again to contemplate variety without Unity, is to bee over-much expensive upon the weakness, and to set up the woman without the man, which are not indeed two, but one in Christ.

I love the Unity, as it orderly discovers it self in the Trinity: I prize the Trinity, as it beares correspondency with the Unity; Let the skilfull *Oedipus*⁹ unfold this.

Gen. 2. 21.

Gen. 2. 18.

F I N I S.

---

9   Oedipus solved the riddle of the sphinx (Q. Which creature has one voice and yet becomes four-footed and two-footed and three-footed? A. Man): Apollodorus, *Library*, 3.5.8.

Jacob Bauthumley

The Light and Dark sides of

G O D

Or a plain and brief

D I S C O U R S E,

OF

The light side $\left\{ \begin{array}{l} \textit{God, Hea-} \\ \textit{ven} \text{ and} \\ \textit{Angels.}^{1} \end{array} \right\}$ The dark side $\left. \begin{array}{l} \\ \\ \\ \end{array} \right\}$ $\begin{array}{l} \textit{Devill,} \\ \textit{Sin,} \text{ and} \\ \textit{Hell.} \end{array}$

As also of the Resurrection and Scripture.

All which are set forth in their

Severall Natures and Beings, according to the spirituality of
the Scripture.

Written by *Jacob Bauthumley.*

---

*I thank thee O Father, Lord of Heaven and Earth, that
thou hast hid these things from the wise and prudent, and
hast revealed them to Babes, even so it is thy pleasure.*
*The spirituall man judgeth all things, and he himself is
judged of none.*

LONDON, Printed for *William Learner*
at the *Black-more* in *Bishopsgate-streete.* 1650.

---

1   The text follows the second edition, which differs only in minor details of punctuation, spelling, capitalization and paragraph division, except in three instances. On the title page of the first edition, dated 20 November by Thomason, 'Earth' is incorrectly in place of 'Angels' and '1650' is omitted.

THE
EPISTLE
TO THE
READER.

Have onely directed my discourse to thee, though I know the most unto whose hand it may come cannot read it; But that it will be a Barbarian to them, and they to It. However, if I be beside them; yet I am not beside my selfe. (If I be it is to God) The reason why I have not directed it to any particular man, or sort of men what ever: as is usuall in things of this nature, is, because I desire not any mans approbation of it, as knowing I am not subject to mans judgement: neither would I have any man to subject himself to mine: neither shall I be ashamed to own what I have writ for the present, or to cast it away for the future, if God shall lead me thereunto. I have cast up my accounts what all will amount unto, upon either of the former considerations, and so have sweet peace in my spirit, in my present thoughts and apprehensions, leaving the issue of all to the wise disposing providence. All I desire is, that those to whom these few lines may come, would (if they can) be so charitable of me, as to conceive and judge, that I have not writ any thing with any spirit of opposition to any sort of men, under what forme of godlinesse soever, as knowing, that there is a sweet appearance of God in them All. And however my person, and parts be meane in the Worlds Eye, and so may cast an odium upon the things that I hold forth; yet I shall runne the hazard in that kinde, and leave the Lord to gaine his own Honour and Glory in it; as seeing by sweet experience, it is one of his greatest designes in the World, to confound the high and mighty things thereof, by the most meane and contemptible; And so though men be not satisfied, yet herein I shall receive sweet content in my own spirit, that my worke shall either burne and consume, or else abide the fiery tryall of mens indignation; And as I shall wish no man to embrace it, or condemne me: So I shall neither thank them that do the one, or condemne them that do the other.

For the subject matter of the Discourse, I must confesse they are things of that nature, that are not obvious to every capacity, and so lye obnoxious unto their censure; and when time was, I should have been as ready to have sat in Judgement against the Maintainer of such Principles; yet to me they are such as wherein the Mystery of godlynesse mainly consists, and so are not to be slighted.

And however, I do not looke that I, or any man else shall receive much by this, or any other Booke; which had almost perswaded me, to have been silent in this kind; yet was I inwardly enforced thereunto, to ease the burden that lay upon my spirit; which was one great motive to me, to act my part so publickly.

Besides, having converst with men under severall formes and administrations, not to speake of those of the inferiour sort, as Papists, Episcoparians[2] and Presbyterians; But those that are got

---

2   Earlier form of 'Episcopalians'; those who accept church government by bishops; the established Church of England before 1642 and after 1660.

to the highest: as Independents *and* Anabaptists, *commonly so called; and seriously viewing the carnall apprehention of things in themselves, and there mis-apprehention of the minde of God held forth by others, condemning them as Heriticall and Blasphemous, in whom the Mysteryes of the Kingdome are most clearly revealed, and they themselves placing Religion, and the Mystery of godlinesse in outward Ordinances, and administrations of which they are all but Shaddowes; Having a strong conceite of a Creature happynesse, and selfe injoyment; and so are acted to attaine to the End. In all these respects, I could not but gratifie them so farre, as to set forth what is held out by a certaine Generation of Men and Woemen in the World; That if it may be, there may be such a favourable opinion of us from them, that we neither deny there is a G O D,* Heaven or Hell, Resurrection or Scripture, *as the World is made to believe we do; And I thinke they are all as plainly, and briefly made out, as they themselves could desire.*

And further, I know by experience, that there are some with whom my spirit sweetly closed in the Unity thereof, and that travell with me in the same birth; yet are not able to bring forth their conceptions, for so much as many times, the Truth suffers by a weake delivery; and for their sakes have I held this Glasse before them, that so they may be the better able to describe themselves to others; and to help them to bring forth that out of their mouths, which perhaps may lye in the bottome of their hearts.

For these Reasons have I taken the boldnesse to set pen to Paper, though otherwise I was unwilling, desiring that, and no more of others then what I would do to them; which is, to let every man stand and fall to his own Master.

One thing I thought fit to premise, onely to satisfie any that shall be so weake, as to make it a matter of offence to them. In that I have not set downe the chapter and verse, of many places of Scripture, which I do hint upon all along the Discourse. To answer them, and so to salve up that pretended soare; I found things of such a Mysterious nature as they are, that while I was looking for them in the Letter of the Scripture, I was at a great losse, in the present delivery of my selfe, of those things which I found spiritually and secretly conveyed to me in the Spirit; and so rather then I would loose, or let passe what was spiritually discovered in me, I was willing to omit the outward viewing of them in a chapter or verse. Besides, there is nothing laide downe by me by way of Argument, or formall dispute, which might ingage me to an outward proofe of things, as men usually do in matters of controversie; and what is positively affirmed, there is punctually Scripture for. But my designe was mainly, to deliver my private Meditations, and apprehension of such things which are most carnally conceived of. I thought it not therefore necessary, to trouble my self or the Reader, with multiplicity of places of Scripture, to prove those things of which I hed so reall and spirituall a Testimony of in my own spirit; and which I am confident, that the most spirituall man can set his seale unto. And yet I dare affirme to the most rigid spirit that workes in any man at this day against the things asserted, That there is not any thing positively affirmed; but I could with more ease prove the truth of them, by divers Testimonies of Scripture and reason, then he could with any truth or Scripture oppose them; and any man that shall impartially weigh things, may see that there is nothing in the Treatise then the very Language, and correspondency of Scripture in the Letter of it: will easily speake, and sweetly comply with: in a spirituall sence. So much I thought good to premise by way of Preface *to the* Discourse: *All that G O D aimes at in such things as are of this nature, is but to make out his owne Honour and Glory before men, and to gaine esteeme from them; And all I aime at, is, that we might resolve all the Comforts, Glory, and future felicity into G O D againe; and so to make G O D All, and the Creature nothing, and if in the* Discourse, *I shall detract or prevaricate from either of the Ends, I am much mistaken, and shall willingly confesse with that Prophet,* O Lord thou hast deceived me, and I was deceived.[3]

And so I leave the Discourse, and thee
together; and if you happyly agree, it
is all the fruite of my labour that I
expect to Reape; If not, I shall
willingly waite an opportu-
nity, to make you
both Friends,

As I am to every man.

J. B.

---

3   Jer. 20.7.

THE
Light and dark sides
OF
G O D.

Concerning God.

God, what shall I say thou art, when thou canst not be named? what shall I speak of thee, when in speaking of thee, I speak nothing but contradiction? For if I say I see thee, it is nothing but thy seeing of thy selfe; for there is nothing in me capable of seeing thee but thy self: If I say I know thee, that is no other but the knowledge of thy self; for I am rather known of thee, then know thee: If I say I love thee, it is nothing so, for there is nothing in me can love thee but thy self; and therefore thou dost but love thy self: My seeking of thee is no other but thy seeking of thy selfe: My delighting enjoying thee, is no other but thy delighting in thy selfe, and enjoying of thy selfe after a most unconceivable manner.

If I say I prayse thee, blesse or magnifie thee; it is no other but thy praysing, blessing, and magnifying of thy self.

I say thou art infinite, but what that is I cannot tell, because I am finite. And therefore I am led to believe, that whatsoever thy Scripture or any man else speaks of thee, it is but thy meer condescention to speak to us in the language of men, and so we speak of thee to one another.

For this I know, that whatsoever the Scripture or any man else speakes what thou art, I know thou art not that, because no man can say what thou art. And therefore when the Scripture saith thou art a spirit: It is because a spirit is the highest thing or tearme that men can give or apprehend: For thou art beyond any expression, and therefore thou art pleased to cloathe thy self with such Titles and Expressions of spirit, love, mercy, power, strength, or whatsoever is amiable or high in esteeme among men, to honour thy self, and beget an high esteeme and lawfull respect of thy self from men.

And therefore whatsoever I speak or write of thee, it is from thy writing and speaking in me; for I really see, that thou dost not speek to men, but in men; because there is nothing in man capable of thy speaking or hearing, but thy self, onely this man declares outwardly what he hath heard and seen inwardly, and yet that outward Declaration is of God also; for thou being the life and substance of all Creatures, they speak and move, yea live in thee; and whatever any Creature is, it is that as it is in thee: And therefore thou art pleased to give thy self that Title, *I Am*. This therefore I can say of thee, That thou onely art, and there is none beside thee: But what thou art I cannot tell. Onely this I see, that there is nothing hath a Being, but thy Being is in it, and it is thy Being in it that gives it a Being: and so I am ready to say with thy Servant: Lord whither shall I go from thy presence? for it is thy presence and Being, that is the subsistance and Being of all Creatures and things, and fills Heaven and Earth, and all other places.

And therefore I cannot as I have carnally conceived, and as men generally do, that God hath his personall being, and presence in one place more then another, or that he hath a simple, pure, glorious, and intire being circumscribed or confined in a place above the Starres and Firmament, which the men of the World call Heaven: And that all Creatures here below, are the products of that Being, and had their Being of him, and yet distinct from him: But the spirit in me speakes otherwise, and saith, I must not ascend up to Heaven to fetch Christ thence, nor descend into the depth to fetch him from thence; for the Word is even in you, which Word is God, and God is the Word.

Nay, I see that God is in all Creatures, Man and Beast, Fish and Fowle, and every green thing, from the highest Cedar to the Ivey on the wall; and that God is the life and being of them all, and that God doth really dwell, and if you will personally; if he may admit so low an expression in them all, and hath his Being no where else out of the Creatures.

Further, I see that all the Beings in the World are but that our Being, and so he may well be said, to be every where as he is, and so I cannot exclude him from Man or Beast, or any other Creature: Every Creature and thing having that Being living in it, and there is no difference betwixt Man and Beast; but as Man carries a more lively Image of the divine Being then any other Creature: For I see the Power, Wisdom, and Glory of God in one, as well as another, onely in that Creature called Man, God appeares more gloriously in then the rest.

And truly, I find by experience, the grand reason why I have, and many others do now use set times of prayer, and run to formall duties, and other outward and low services of God: the reason hath been, and is, because men look upon a God, as being without them, and remote from them at a great distance, as if he were locally in Heaven, and sitting there onely, and would not let down any blessing or good things, but by such and such a way and meanes.

But Lord, how carnall was I thus to fancie thee? Nay I am confident, that there is never a man under the Sun that lookes upon God in such a forme; but must be a grosse Idolator, and fancie some corporall shape of him, though they may call it spiritual.

Did men see that that God was in them, and framing all their thoughts, and working all their works, and that he was with them in all conditions: what carnall spirit would reach out to that by an outward way, which spiritually is in him, and which he stands really possest of? and which divine wisdom sees the best, and that things can be no otherwise with him. I shall speak my own experience herein, that I have made God mutable as my self, and therefore as things and conditions have changed, I thought that God was angry or pleased, and to have faln a humbling my self; or otherwise in thankfulness, never looking or considering that God is one intire perfect and immutable Being, and that all things were according to the Councel of his own will, and did serve the designe of his own glory: but thought that my sins or holy walking did cause him to alter his purpose of good or evill to me.

But now I cannot looke upon any condition or action, but methinks there appears a sweet concurrance of the supreame will in it nothing comes short of it, or goes beyond it, nor any man shall doe or be any thing, but what shall fall in a sweet compliance with it; It being the wombe wherein all things are conceived, and in which all creatures were formed and brought fourth.

Yea further, there is not the least Flower or Herbe in the Field but there is the Divine being by which it is, that which it is; and as that that departs out of it, so it comes to nothing, and so it is to day clothed by God, & to morow cast into the Oven: when God ceases to live in it then it comes to nothing, and so all the visible Creatures are lively resemblances of the Divine being. But if this be so, some may say: Then look how many Creatures there are in the world, there is so many Gods, and when they dye and perrish, then must God also die with them, which can be no lesse then blasphemy to affirm.

To which I answer, and it is apparent to me, that all the Creatures in the world; they are not so many distinct Beings, but they are but one intire Being, though they be distinguished in respect of their formes; yet their Being is but one and the same Being, made out in so many formes of flesh, as Men and Beast, Fish and Fowle, Trees and Herbes: For though these two last Trees and Herbes have not the life so sensibly or lively; yet it is certain there is a Life and Being in them, by which they grow to that maturity and perfection, that they become serviceable for the use of Man, as other Creatures are; and yet I must not exclude God from them; for as God is pleased to dwel in flesh, and to dwel with and in man, yet is he not flesh, nor doth the flesh partake of the divine Being. Onely this, God is pleased to live in flesh, and as the Scripture saith, he is made flesh; and he appears in severall formes of flesh, in the forme of Man and Beast, and other Creatures, and when these have performed the designe and will of God, that then as the flesh of Man and other Creatures, came from the Earth, and are not capable of knowing God, or partaking of the divine nature, and God ceasing to live in them, and being gone out of them, that then they all shall return to their first principle of dust, and God shall as he did from all eternity, live in himself, before there was a World or Creatures: so he shall to all eternity live and enjoy himself in himself, in such a way as no man can utter: and so I see him yesterday, and to day, and the same for ever: The *Alpha* and the *Omega*, the beginning and end of all things.

Yea further, as God shall cease to live in flesh, and so all things shall come to nothing that are below him: Then shall he live in spirit, he will cease to live in the humane nature, and live in the divine, and so he is that eternall and everlasting life, in whom all the glory, beauty and excellency of Creatures are wrapt up; for as all things were let out of God: so shall they all give up their Being, life and happiness into God again; and so we may say truly, that God or the divine Being never dies; though the Clothing dissolve, and come to nothing, yet the inward man still lives; though the shadow dies, yet the soule or substance which is God, lives to all eternity. Further, to me it is cleare, that there is nothing that partakes of the divine nature, or is of God, but it is God. The reason is, because there are no distinctions in God, he Being one individed essence: however Man out of a simple ignorance, distinguish of his Will, and of his love, of his justice and mercy, of common guifts, and of spirituall, as they call them; yet I cannot see any such things in God, or that he is capable of any degrees of more or lesse, or that he loves one man more then another, or hates one man more then another. However the Scripture saith, *Jacob* have I loved, and *Esau* have I hated; it is but after the manner of men:

for I cannot see that there is love or hatred in God, or any such passions: that which admits of degrees is not perfect.

Indeed in respect of men as they imagine God is angry and he is pleased, he threatens and he promises, he Commands and he punishes; but in God there is no such things, he being that *I Am*, which changes not; but all things are according to the Councel of his own will: And God loves the Being of all Creatures, yea, all men are alike to him, and have received lively impressions of the divine nature, though they be not so gloriously and purely manifested in some as in others, some live in the light side of God, and some in the dark side; But in respect of God, light and darkness are all one to him; for there is nothing contrary to God, but onely to our apprehension. And for the proud selfish Being which is the *Esau*, is contrary to the sincere and pure divine Being, which is the *Jacob*: But the being of both serve the designe of God as we shall in the sequell of the discourse shew. But to speak a little more of the present subject; I wonder how that Divinity came into the world, and which is still maintained and used by those that call them selves Divines; who doe still hould and teach others, that there are three persons in the God-head, and yet but one God.

Surely it is a mystery to mee; But I rather thinke it is a mystery of Iniquity, for I suppose a person cannot be without an essence, so that it plainly appeares there must be three essences in God, and yet these three must be but one; But I suppose the most of them have received so much new Light that they are ashamed of such a Tenent, there being nothing in Scripture or reason to countenance such a grosse and carnall conceit of God: But I shall not enter upon any thing controvertall: onely I shall give you what is made out in me, and I conceive no other what the Scripture holds out in the letter, and so it is true, that there are three that bear record in *H*eaven, and yet these three but one. He doth not speak three persons, but three, and that thus, as farre as I conceive: The Father is God from all eternity, who's Being was in himself, having all Beings wrapt up in himself; This God letting himself and his Being in severall formes of flesh is God the Son: For I do not apprehend that God was onely manifest in the flesh of Christ, or the man called Christ; but that he as really and substantially dwells in the flesh of other men and Creatures, as well as in the man Christ, though as the Scripture speaks, he was the most express Image, and that the fulnesse of the God-head dwelt bodily in him; that is, in respect of manifestation: but otherwise I conceive that God who cannot admit of degrees, can be said to dwell in him more then another, and I might shew that his Being in spirit, is much more glorious then his Being in flesh; the one being but a shadow and Type of the other.

But I forbear, because it may afford another discourse of it self, and returne to what we have in hand; and that is, that God the Sonne is God manifest in flesh: Now that we call Holy Ghost, is God living in Spirit, and all these are not three distinct Beings, onely one Being made out in three severall tearmes. To make it a little plainer, the Scripture saith; *God is Love;*[4] and yet it tells us of a threefold Love: The first is Gods Love to us, the second is our Love to God, the third is our Love to one another.

Now it is plaine, these are not three, but one: For by the same Love that God loves us, by the same Love we love him; we love him, because he loves us, and it is the same Love by which

---

4   1 John 4.8.

we love one another; and therefore the Apostle saith, *He that loves not his brother, loves not God:*[5] And so we have communion with God, when we have communion with one another: So that Gods Love to us, and our Love to him, and to one another; are not three loves but one: so in like manner: Love is the Father; this Love manifested in Flesh is the Sonne; this Love loving the loved, is the Holy Ghost, and these three are one.

The Father is God forming all things; the Son is God, who is formed and manifested in Flesh; the Holy Ghost is God, manifesting or revealing the manifested: thus the Father, Son and Holy Ghost, are not three persons. but one intire Being, made out in severall expressions.

And thus I have done with this subject concerning God, being willing to loose my self in the thoughts of him, as knowing, that he cannot be known; and that all words, or expressions of Scripture or man come short of Him, and do but confound and darken the glory of that great Creator; who hath done all things according to reason, and is himself the reason and ground of all things; for in him they live, and move, and have their Being; and therefore to Him be the Glory for evermore.

Concerning Heaven.

NOw for that which we call Heaven, I cannot conceive it any locall place, because God is not confined, or hath his Being or station in our setled compasse; and therefore I see that true which the Letter speakes, *The Kingdom of Heaven is within you:*[6] and so I see Heaven to be there, where God displaies his own glory and excellency; For Heaven is nothing but God at large, or God making out himself in Spirit and Glory. And so I really see, that then men are in Heaven, or Heaven in men, when God appeares in his glorious and pure manifestations of himself, in Love and Grace, in Peace and rest in the Spirit; when God shewes himself to be all the happiness, comfort and reward, and so this Heaven is not outward, or a place of any outward or carnall bodily happines as men dream of; but it consists in righteousness, joy & peace in the Holy Ghost; all which are spirituall and terminated in God alone. I do not, as I have carnally conceived, that when *Paul* was rapt up into the third Heaven, and heard and saw things unutterable, that he was bodily taken up, or heard God with an audible voice; No, but I rather conceive it some extraordinary appearance of God, filling the Spirit with glorious amazements and admirations of its own excellency. So that, when God doth gloriously appeare to the silencing of flesh, and over-powering the selfish Being in man, and fils the spirit with its own glory, then is God and his Heaven come in the spirit, and such an estate some may be & have bin sensible of, that they have so felt the over-powering of God in their spirits, that they could not tell whether they were in the body, or out of the body: as was *Pauls* condition.

And this Heaven the Land of *Canaan* was a lively Type of, wherein God after he had by a strong hand, brought the Children of *Israel* from the bondage of *Egypt*, and through many dangers of the Wildernesse and red Sea, God at last brought them to a Land of rest, in which this is really made out to me; that it is the over-ruling power of God in us, that takes us from

---

5   1 John 4.20.   6   Luke 17.21.

the *Egyptian* bondage of self and flesh, and through the Wildernesse and Sea; much toyling and tossing up and downe in selfe-Workes and hard duties, outward and carnall services; the Law still beating us to Workes of prayer, humiliation; making us to make Brick without Straw, and setting hard and cruell Task-masters over us. ⟨S⟩o that we may say, through many tribulations we must enter into the Kingdom of Heaven; but when Gods power is destroying these enemies of our Peace, and bring us into that Land of rest, that spirituall *Canaan*, which we speak of, then do we cease from these labours. But truly, this I speake from experience, so long as men are under *Moses*, they cannot enjoy neither must they come into this Land.

And therefore, I do not wonder that the Scripture speaks, *Many shall seek to enter and not be able: and straight and narrow is the gate, and few there be that finde it.*[7] I would not speak to discourage any; but I really apprehend the greatest pretenders to Heaven scarce know what it is, or will ever enjoy it; but shall with *Moses* onely see it a farre off, God not being willing to do any great workes in their spirits: because of their unbelief; but what happyness and comfort they do enjoy, to whom God appeares thus spiritually in, none know but themselves. This is that heavenly *Jerusalem* spoken of in the *Hebrewes*, into which the souls of just men made perfect are come into.[8]

The text doth not say, we shall come to it hereafter; but that we are come unto it, and that we have full and actuall possession of it, and so saith the Apostle, *Our conversation is in Heaven,*[9] which is nothing but the glorious appearance of God in our spirits, when of naturall we are made spirituall: we shall see the Scripture speaks of no other Heaven but what is spirituall, and not consisting of any corporall or bodily felicity, as men conceive God, being all the glory and happiness of the creature; and so he that believeth hath everlasting life within him, and abiding in him; because God there gloriously makes out himself to be the Life and happiness. To look for a carnall and sensible enjoyment of God, distinct from that pure and divine Being of God, savours to me of a carnall spirit; because it sets up something beside God, when there is nothing that lives and is glorious to all eternity, but God. For as I said before, there is nothing in the creature capable of God, or to enjoy his glory, nor nothing is of God, but is God: because God cannot be devided, nor none can share with him in his Glory, he having not given any glory to any creature out of himself; but what ever the creature apprehends to be its own glory, it is truly and spiritually no other but Gods one Being and glory.

But the truth is, as men fancy a high God though yet very carnally: so they fancy a high place for him above the Starrs, I know not where; & herein indeed God condescends to the weaknesse of men in the Scripture, to set himself and his glorious presence out to us, as if they were properly in one place more then another, when as we know, a Spirit is not any where confined, but the God of Spirits is in all and through you all. And so Heaven is his Throne & the Earth his Foot-stool; That is, God is in low and dark appearances, as well as in the most glorious: God is the high and lofty one that inhabits eternity, and not any circumscribed place, and so he is in low Spirits.

And the truth is, where God is highest in the Spirit, he is so low in that Spirit, that they do not desire any glory out of himself; but are willing to be nothing that he may be all. It

---

7   Luke 13.24.   8   Heb. 12.22–23.   9   Phil. 3.20.

is very true that the Scripture saith, *We looke for new Heaven, and new Earth wherein dwells Righteousnesse.*[10] And truly, I find that where God dwells, and is come, and hath taken men up, and wrapt them up into the Spirit; there is a new Heaven and a new Earth, & all the Heaven I look ever to enjoy is to have my earthly and dark apprehensions of God to cease, and to live no other life then what Christ spiritually lives in me

The Scripture speakes likewise of a Kingdom, and a City, and Mantions, and that Christ went to prepare a place for the Saints, all which are true in the Spirit; For when God raigns in the Spirit, he brings all into subjection under him, and so he is King and Kingdom himself; and Christ went to prepare and to make out himself in Spirit, and so he left the flesh to live in the Spirit, and his spirituall coming, was much more glorious then his carnall and visible presence with them. And the truth is, the one was but a pre⟨p⟩arative, and fore-runner of the other; so it is spiritually true, that he that was least in the kingdom of Heaven was greater then *John* the *Baptist*; where note that those carnall and outward observations of Baptisme, and other administrations that *John* was in, they were but the preparatives & fore-runners of a more spirituall condition, the Kingdom of Heaven not consisting in them. And therefore it was reasoned, *Why do the Disciples of* John *Fast and Pray, Luke 9.*[11] *and thy Disciples Fast not?* and Christ gives them the reason

It was his presence, which is not to be understood of his carnall presence with them; but of his spirituall presence, which he promised to appear in them; and therefore the Baptisme of the Holy Ghost and fire, was the substance of which the water Baptisme was but a shadow; and so he that was least in the spiritual Kingdom, and had a spiritual enjoyment of him, was greater then he that was the greatest, and most strictest in the Observation of the outward Duties and Ordinances, that *John* was under; so that it is plain to me, that the spiritual presence of Christ, or God in the spirit, is the Kingdom of Heaven, into which whomsoever is entered, he ceases from the outward and formal use of outward Administrations and Ordinances, and so sits down spiritually in the Kingdom of the Father, and is as the Apostle saith, allready set down in the heavenly places; and when God thus spiritually appears in you, then you will be content with me, to sit down and enter with me into an eternall nothingness, and be willing to let God advance himself, glorifie himself unto all eternity, and so cast down your Crownes at his feet, in everlasting silence: Into which condition when you are brought, you shall not need to expect any other Heaven; for then shall you enter into that rest wherein you shall cease from that labour and toile of outward and formall duties: as seeing God to be that in you, which you expected in self.

If any shall say these things are true, but these conditions and this estate is reserved for another life: We cannot expect to be perfect here while we are in the flesh.

I answer, that it is true we shall not; that is, there is nothing of us that is capable of this spirituall enjoyment, and therefore we must know that our perfection lies not in any thing that the Creature is, but it lies in God, and in that respect, unless you will say God is not so perfect here as he will be; we are as perfect as ever we shall be, so that though this spirituall condition be not of us, yet it is in us, and what Heaven or Estate God will be in, when he ceases to live in the flesh, I think is as vain for us to imagine, as impossible to apprehend.

---

10   2 Pet. 3.13.   11   In fact Luke 5.33.

Yet if any man can tell me how he was before there was a World, I shall with as much ease tell him how he will be when the World ceases to be, and however men are so carnal, & women-like, that they dream of a Heaven, wherein they shall sit one at the Right hand of God and another at the left, and hope to have much outward felicity and glory, when they have glorified bodies, as they imagine; yet for my part I look for no such condition, and I see nothing in the Scripture to strengthen me in such a conceit.

For however, it speakes of a City that hath twelve gates and streetes paved with Gold, and yet I suppose all do but point out the glorious condition that God will appear in upon Earth; and therefore I mind that there was a *Jerusalem*, that it is said came down from God out of Heaven: In which there was no Temple, nor needed any Sun or Moon; which as I apprehend, was but that there should be such glorious and spiritual dispensations and discoveries of God in the Saints; and that they should enjoy such a life as that they should not worship in any outward external way or forme. And should not need to be taught by men or meanes, or of any outward Administrations or Ordinances; But that the Lord God and the Lamb should be their light, and they should be immediatly taught by him; and therefore it is said there was no Temple in it, the Lord and the Lamb, being the light, glory, Temple and all: which condition is glorious, and cannot but be Heaven to him that doth enjoy it, and into which I know some are brought, and have received the accomplishment of all those promises and Prophesies which are spoken of in Scripture, and have received that new name, which none know but they that have it.

And thus have I shewed you Heaven, as it appeares in my spirit, and for my part I see no otherwise of it, however men judge, I am willing to let fall any carnall apprehension of a visible or corporeal enjoyment of God, or any expectation of a happy condition out of God after this life and dayes are ended, being willing to resigne and give up to God what he is in me in flesh, that so God may be all, and advanced above all in the spirit. And for my part, I see the Lord so framing my spirit, that I am content to be nothing, that he may be all, though I must confess, when I think seriously of it, there is nothing so grievous to flesh and blood in me, as to think that all the glory and happiness that I expected to have had in a corporal and sensible enjoyment must be terminated in God onely.

This I am sure of, that if there be any such thing, I shall have my share among the rest, which for the present I think ridiculous to looke for; onely this, I wait what the Lord will do in my spirit for the present. And being sweetly refreshed in the spirituall Discovery of himself in me, which is to me *Heaven.*

Concerning the Angels.

FOr the Angels I see the world as much mistaken in them as in the former, for I really see that man lives in the Angelicall nature, and that the Angels are also Spirituall and in man, and herein man is honoured in that God, tooke humane nature and not the Angelicall. For had he confined his own glory in himself, he had missed one of his opportunities of magnifying himself, and therefore he took the humane nature, and so was God manifest in flesh, as well as seen of Angels; and as the divine nature is in man, so is the Angelicall;

and as the one acts, so doth the other; for may we not see the Angels of God ascending and discending in man? Are not the motions of mans spirit here and there in a moment? cannot man ascend into the hights, and discend into the depths? Are not the motions of a mans spirit at one end of the World at one time, and at another end of it instantly again? Doth not God make his Angels spirits, and his Ministers a flame of fire. Is not every spirit of illumination? and spirituall discovery of God? an Angell of God to convey some light and influence to the Creature whence is it, that all those sweet and spiritual assistances and consolations are flowing in the spirit; but by the power and presence of these Angels? It is said the Devill left Christ, and Angels came and ministred to him, and comforted him. In which I really see, every spirituall support and comfortable appearance of God, is an Angel of God. How do the Angels pitch their Tents about them that fear the Lord? which is no other, but that all providences and passages watch about them, and administer comfort unto them. I do not as I have conceived, that they are created spirituall substances distinct from God, and waiting upon God, as serving men about their Lord, to see what his pleasure is; and yet this I know, all accidents that are good or evill, crosse or pleasing, are of God, and are his Angels, and do his will. These are the Angels on which God rides in triumph, by which he plagues the World and doth great things in Heaven and Earth; and therefore I looke upon every glorious manifestation of the power and wisdom of God to be an Angell, when I read of Gods coming with thousands of his Angels. It refreshes my spirit to think that there will be times of more pure and spirituall glory manifested. Now there is here and there an Angel of spiritual discovery of God; then will the world be full of his glory, and all flesh shall see the salvation of God, I cannot conceive they have any fleshly forme or shape, though it is said, *Lot* received two Angels which is spiritually true, for there was something more then ordinary, of Gods mind discovered to him: And when I read of the Angel of the Lord smiting the Campe of the *Assyrians*, that there fell so many thousands in one night; I do not believe there was any visible appearance, but that there was an extraordinary appearance of Gods power which is called an Angell. And so whereever we read of Angels appearing to this or that Servant of God, I cannot look upon them otherwise then some more glorious appearance or manifestation of God, and his will and pleasure concerning things or persons. And whereas the Scripture speaks of good and bad Angels, I see onely this in them, that the one is pure discovery of God, the other the more impure & dark; for where as man had a glorious enjoyment of God, and lived in Gods light, when he left that & went to live in a self-being out of God; There were Angels, Hell, and his discoveries of God, became dark and confused, and so brought him into bondage; so that the dark and carnall knowing of God is the evill Angel, and the glorious and pure manifestation of God is the good Angel: So likewise the providences that fall out in the world, that tend to the comfort or well-being of Creatures, they are the good Angels, & the crosse providences & occurrences that do afflict and grieve a people or person, they are the evill Angells or Angels of wrath and displeasure, not that they are so indeed, but because the Creature doth misapprehend the mind of God in them; for all things, whether Angels good or evill, principalities, powers, life or death, things present, or to come, are for good to them that are called of God. When I read of *Michael* and his Angels, and the *Dragon* and his Angels, fighting against one another; I see nothing there but the fleshly and dark apprehensions of God against the pure and spirituall: and as *Michael* overcame the *Dragon*; so the more pure and spiritual dispensations of God shall overpower the dark and carnall, and so those Angels of darkness shall be cast into their lake, and there be reserved to the great judgement day of the Lord within us, when he shall sit as a refiner in our spirits, then shall the chaffe be burnt up & consumed by the brightnes, and fire of these Angelicall appearances of God; & this was an Angel of God comforting me against all the aspersions of heresie & blasphemy, that the people of God lye under at this day; and so you see what I thinke of the Angels, and what they are.

And thus have I done with that which I call *The light side of God*. I come now to the dark, and shall begin with that first which is called Devill.

Concerning the Devill.

I See; that which we call the Devill is also in man; and yet I cannot apprehend him to be a creature, as men generally do; For then I must give him a Being, and there is nothing hath a Being but God; (that is formally and properly) yet as men speake, though improperly, there is such a thing as we call Devill; which I conceive to be nothing but the fleshly Being; or, as men commonly speak, the corruption of nature; or, as the Scripture calls it, *the old Man*,[12] and this also moves, and acts in all those things which we call sinfull. So that so far as a man lives in a sinfull being, so farre the Devill in him; and therefore when *Mary Magdelen* had 7 Devils cast out of her, it gives me to conceive, that every sin is a Devill and so far as a man is led aside of his own lusts, so far he is led by the Devill; and therefore he is called Satan, Tempter and Deceiver, with divers other expressions. And hence it is, that whatsoever is hatefull or hurtfull to man, we use to say, the Devill is in it: and so every thing that doth hinder or darken our spirituall comfort and peace, that is a Devill in us. God is Light, and in him there is no darkness; and it is as true, the Devill is darknesse, and in him there is no light at all: And so farre as ⟨a⟩ny man is in that darknesse, so farre he is in the Devill, so much the nearer he comes to him: and therefore it is said, *You are of your Father the Devill, and his workes you do:*[13] God is the Way, Truth, and Life, and the Devill is falsehood, his wayes tend to darknesse and end in death and destruction. This is the deceiver that would perswade us of a happyness of our own, and a glory out of God; He is that Mystery of iniquity, that man of sinne whom the Lord is continually destroying, and for whose destruction God is man'd in our flesh; and as the Devill the deciever hath led us from God to live a life of our own: so God in us is reducing us againe to live in himself, and so the spirituall seed is breaking the head and power of the carnall; this Devill is the spirit of envy, malice, cruelty, ever seeking to devoure and rob us of that which is most precious to us. Men fear a Devill without them, and so fancy him to be terrible in their apprehensions, never considering that he is in them; and therefore it is said, *The Devill entered into Judas*,[14] not but that he was in him before; but then was there a more then ordinary appearance of him, and so he is that *Judas* indeed, which is ever betraying the

12   Rom. 6.6; Eph. 4.22; Col. 3.9.   13   John 8.44.   14   Luke 22.3.

spirituall Christ into the hands of self and flesh, and is continually crucifying the Lord of life, and putting him to open shame, and vailing his glory under shadowes, making men to take them for substances, and so is transforming himself into an Angell of light: and so makes men put light for darknesse, and darknesse for light: exalting himself, and perswading self and flesh to have high thoughts of himself: and seeking to put out all that spirituall light and glory, wherever it appeares in the spirits of men. So that, however men ascribe a Being and person, a Him to him; yet there is nothing so, neither would I call him any thing, but as it is the language of men to expresse our selves to one another about that which wee call Devill.

And so I shall leave the Devill, and speak something of Sinne: because that is most like him, being of the nearest Kindred to him.

Concerning Sinne.

FOr Sin, I cannot tell how to call it any thing, because it is nothing; I cannot give it a name, because it is no substance or creature; It is rather Primitive then Positive, we call it and give it a Being, though indeed in it self it hath none. It is no act, for then it were visible; but Sin is inward and spirituall, as that is which we call Grace and Holinesse; it is therefore called spirituall wickednesse, it is rather the defect of Grace and a deficiency in the Creature, then any act as visible to the outward view.

Further, Sin as Sin admits of no degrees for that which we call a great sinne, is no more then that which we call the least; but because we would not be thought to lessen it while we speake of it, we shall give you our thoughts of it in the language of Scripture; And therefore we see, the Apostle describes it to our hands, where he saith, *We have all sinned, and are deprived of the Glory of God.*[15] So hence I conclude, that Sinne is a coming short, or a deprivation of the Glory of God; and so farre as a man is short of that glory, or doth not live and act in that divine Being: so farre he sins, so farre as he is in darknesse, and hath this glory vailed in him: so far he is sinfull.

In brief, sin is a living out of the will of God; for God being the Supream will, and having ordered all things and persons to be in such and such a condition; this self and carnall Being wills something of its own below Gods Will, and so prevaricates from that, and centers in his own will; and so sins. Hence it is, that Nations and perticular persons, are grieved and discontented with their condition, and set dayes & times a part, as if they could alter the Supreme Will; not considering, that the Supreme will must be subjected unto, and that they must receive evill from the hands of God as well as good; and not knowing, that all is in the ordering of the Supreme will, and so run to this and that outward and formall duty, and so are carnall and sinfull while they think they do God good service, and yet I do not condemn them in so doing; for to them it is their light, though they be truely and spiritually in darkness; and though men act in darknesse, yet God is there vailing his glory, and so they must needs sin; for sin is properly the dark side of God which is a meere privation of light.

Further, we must consider, that God gives not any Law or Rule out of himselfe, or beyond his own glory: And as himself and his own glory are the ultimate end of all actions, and the

15   Rom. 3.23.

ground of them; and as they are spirituall & inward: so those spirituall and inward acts or motions that fall below, or tend to the crossing of this design of God, they are unlawfull: and yet, in some respect these also tend to the glory of God, and sin it self doth as well fall in compliance with the glory of God, as well as that which we call grace and goodnesse; for *sinne abounds that grace may abound much more.*[16]

And however men speak of offending God by sin, and the Scripture speaks of provoking God to wrath by the sins of a people; yet indeed to me it is apparent, that God is no more provoked by sin to wrath, then he is allured to blessing by any holiness of a people or person: And therefore *Jeremiah* saith, *The Lords* hand is not shortned, that he cannot save, or his eares heavy that he cannot heare; but it is their sins that hide his face from them:[17] In which I really see, that it is not as men generally take it, that sin causes God actually to withdraw himself, or to alter his porpose of good to the Creature; but the truth lies in this, that there is that people are as near and ready to be helpt and saved of God when they sin as when they do good. But onely this there is, that in the nature of sin, that guilt and condemnation to it, & that accusing power it is of in the Conscience, that men mis-apprehend and do misconceive the face or countenance of God to them, and sin it is, that is that vaile or covering over the face & glory of God, that hinders the shining of it in the spirit. For the Sun doth shine as clearly when the Cloudes interpose betwixt us and it, as when it is a clear day, onely it doth not so appear to us: and so it is with God, the sin is the Cloud that interposes betwixt God and us, though God be the same and all one to us when we sin, yet we do not so see it, so that it is not a peoples sinning or doing good that is any cause in God, of good or evill to the Creature; for what absurdity would follow if God should hide his face, and let out his love upon the Creatures sinning, or doing that which we call good: how mutable should we make God to be, whereas we know that all accidents and occurrences are the manifestations of that supream Will and Power which is immutable and unalterable, whether the Creature sin or do well:

And whereas some may say, then men may live as they list, because God is the same, and all tends to his glory, if we sin, or if we do well:

I answer them in the words of the Apostle: Men should not sin because grace abounds; but yet[18] if they do sin, that shall turn to the prayse of God, as well as when they do wel. And so the wrath of man praises God as well as his love and meekness, and God glorified in the one as well as the other. And however this may seeme to countenance that God is the Authour of sin, and wills sin; yet to me it is plain, that there is nothing that hath a Being but God, and sin being a nullity, God cannot be the Author of it, and so falles not within the decree of God; for so far as God was in man, and made him, so far he is God; but it was the man, the self-being that found out many Inventions. And all things that God made were very good when he lookt upon them; But sinne God could not behold, because it was not.

Herein is God glorified in sinne, as contraries set together illustrate one another: and God is glorious and powerful in the destroying that fleshly Being, which is exalting it self against the divine. And therefore is God manifest in our flesh to destroy the workes of flesh in us;

---

16   Rom. 5.20, 6.1.   17   In fact this is Isaiah: Isa. 59.1-2.
18   'but yet': here Bauthumley decidedly departs from St. Paul's sense.

and he is plucking down those principalities and powers, and destroying that old man with his deceiveable lusts, and forming the new man which is himself, or the devine Being, and new man in us.

Further, I see that the reason why we cal some men wicked and some godly, is not any thing in the men; but as the divine Being appears more gloriously in one then in another: so we say, the one is a Saint and godly, and the other is wicked and profane; and yet the one acts as he is carried forth by the Supreme power, and so doth the other: And if there be any difference it is not in respect of the creature, of what it is, or doth; for the same divine Being, is in the one as well as the other; but onely it doth not so manifest it self in the one as the other. And therefore, as I dare call no man good because there is none good but God: so I dare call no man wicked or ungodly, because it is God only that makes the difference, and who am I to judge another mans Servant?

And I see also that the same power that inables a man to do good, the same power prevents a man from evill. For neither the evill act or the good act are evill or good, as they are acts; and men can no more do evill then they can do good, as they call it: which may answer that common Objection that men make.

That if this be so, men may drink, swear, and be profane, and live as they list.

And I answer further, the sin lies not in these outward acts, for a man may do the self-same act, and yet not sin: that is, that a man drinks to excess, there is the sin, that a man drinks for necessity or delight, the same act and posture of body is put out in the one, as the other: And so I might instance in the rest, so that the sin is from within: The lust within, and an inward lusting after the Creature, beyond that end for which God hath designed it.

And further, this I affirm, that a man as man hath no more power or freedom of will to do evill then he hath to do good. I think *Joseph* had as many opportunities to commit folly as any man could have; and yet saith he; *How can I do this and sinne against God?*[19] So that it was the power within which kept him, though questionlesse, he might have had a naturall inclination to have done the act as other men.

And I believe *Esau* had as much will and power as a man, to do his brother *Jacob* a mischief, and to take away his life; but when God once appeared to him, then instead of killing him he imbraces him & so might be instance in divers other examples. So that, hence I conclude, it is onely the powerfull presence of God in one man more then another, that one man acts not as vilely as another.

Again I apprehend further, that there is not two wills in God, as men generally teach and affirm; that is to say, an active will and a permissive will, and so a power to make a man to do good, and another kind of power to restraine a man from evill, and so men confound the power and will of God, when as indeed: they are not distinct in God; for Gods power and will are all one: his will is his power, and his power is his will: and by the self same act that he wills things, by the selfe same act he doth things. and it is our weakenesse otherwise to apprehend; for God being one and intire, admitting of no distinction or division in himself, he admits of no variations, but all things are as that supreme will acts, and brings them forth;

---

19   Gen. 33.9.

And I see according to the Councell of his will, they did no more that crucified Christ, then they that did imbrace him.

These things I write, not to countenance any unseemly act or evill in any man; And I know, God being purity it self, cannot behold uncleannesse, and his Spirit in me doth condemn it wherever I see it, and I cannot but reprove it where ever it is found; Neither can I so close in society or fellowship with those that are in darkness, or walk unbeseemingly not becoming the Gospel; and yet I know, that if the grace of God appeared in them, it would as well teach them, to deny ungodlinesse and worldly lusts: as to live righteously and soberly in the World: Onely, I desire to open the nature of that which we call sin, and to make it as spiritually vile as I can: For I see my self to have been mistaken, and I see others are in sin, as well as in that we call grace & goodnes; For as I have made the formall and outward performance of a Duty, the onely thing wherein grace and godliness did consist so: have I made the outward doing or not doing of an act to be the sin; But I really see, that neither the one or the other, as an act is either good or evill: But as godliness is a mystery and inward, and is within us: so is sin likewise a mystery and also within us; and therefore it is called, a mystery of iniquity, from whence proceeds murders, adulteries, and are they not from the lust within? The inward lust and acting, is the sin which is contrary or below God; the outward acting or putting forth of that inward lust, is the sin against man, and is below a man: and whether the thing or sinne be acted outwardly, or no, there is sin; And therefore, the spirituality of the Gospel is above the Letter, the Letter onely forbiding the outward act of adultery, but the spirituality forbids the very lust within; and therefore, he that looks on a woman with a secret and inward lust, hath committed the sin in the Spirit and heart: as if he had done the outward act, and is in Gods account an adulterer: And all the use I can make of the premisses, duely considered, it rather aggravates the nature of sin, then extinuates or lessens it; for I can seriously reflect upon my own spirit, and see more sin within, then all the world can do without; I see that I have framed and fancied a God without me, and have given him an outward Worship while I have seem'd to be very spirituall, and so have been very far from that spirituall worship of him which is like himself, and consists onely in Spirit and Truth; for what a vaine thing is it to me for a man to put off his Hat, or kneele and show an outward reverence to an invisible God: and how carnall have I been, and men are in setting dayes and times a part to expresse an outward humiliation for an inward and spirituall sacrifice, whereas there is no humility but in the Spirit; and there is no spirituall exaltation of God; but when the Creature ceases from being, or doing any thing, and makes God All; whereas men think to get pardon and peace from God by a self-humiliation, prayers and duties, and I know not what: and so give that to a duty and a prayer, which is the onely proper worke of God, who subdues our sinnes, and pardons them for his own Names sake.

And so I have done with that which we call sinne, which we call a privation of God, or the living below God; you see we have made it something and nothing, in respect of God it is nothing; for he knowes no defect, neither is he in darknesse; but is all glory and light.

Again, it is something in respect of the creature; because it is in darknesse and lives not in the light and glory of that God; and there is that in the Creature, which as a vaile covers and hides the glory of God, and so it is sinfull: and yet here is God in all this; for should the Creature share in the Deity, God would not be so glorious; and should the Deity partake of the Humanity, and be one with it, there would be no sin, and therefore is God manifest in flesh, but not to flesh; and therefore doth the Divine Nature and Being live in the Humane, but is not the Humane, nor is the Humane capable of any conjunction or union with the Divine; and therefore the Divine lives in it self, and the Humane or fleshly Being lives in it self; and as the fleshly Being is below the Divine: so men living in it are sinfull; and as that acts: so they act sin, which is all at present I see of that we call Sinne.

Concerning Hell.

HAving spoken of the Devill and Sin, Hell must needes follow; for no sooner did Man leave to live in the Divine Being, and so lived in himself; but he was turned out of *Paradise* to digg for his living, and to worke, labour and toyle, to maintaine a self-Being, and to procure a self-happinesse, and so presently he came to shame and misery; he eating of the forbidden fruite, which was his own holinesse, righteousnesse, all is cursed to him, and so the man is in Hell: so that our ceasing to live in God, and living in the self-Being, is the Hell; For that Angelicall life in us, being vailed and covered, we live in the Diabolicall; whence it is we are in Hell. As soone as man ceast to live in the light, but he would be knowing something, and doing something: so soone did he fall into a *Chaos*, and all was darknesse: and so that develish and self nature is in man, and he is reserved in chaines of darknesse till the judgement of the great day of Gods appearing in his Spirit, and till then he is in Hell, untill God Judge and burne up that flesh, and carnall knowing of him; and reduce him to his first Being, to live in God till then, he suffers the fire of Hel in himself: so that the Hell in a mans selfe and the condemnation is, that a man is condemned of himself.

What adoe there is in the world to find Hell where it is, how many have puzled and beat their braines to find it out, as if it were a locall place? and therefore some because they would make it contrary to Heaven; and as they fancie that the highest place, so they will be sure to make Hell the lowest, and therefore being as carnall in the one as the other, make it to be the lowest part of the Earth. Others, because they find a place speaking of the Devill, calling him the Prince of the Aire, they will make Hell in the Ayre I know not where. But as the Devill rules onely in Aierie and light spirits, so I look upon this to be a Aierie fancy: For as the Devill is, and hath his Throne and Seat in every man, so is his Hell; & truly for my part I think they cannot be separated, and therefore I conceive any man that is in bondage to his own lust; nay further he that is under the Law or in any formal or outward duty, & is so possessed with a spirit of bondage, that he must be so and so, do so and so, or else he must be damned, and in the doing of such and such things he shall be saved: this man is in Hell, and Hell in him, and needes no other Devill to torment him, but his own false and carnall apprehension of God; for as the spirituall appearance of God doth necessarily and formally make Heaven, and cause joy and peace in the spirit: So the dark and carnall conceit or knowledge of God must needes cause sorrow and lamentation, and makes Hell.

I do not much wonder at the carnall Papist, no more then at the carnall Protestant, the one fancying a carnall purgatory, the other a carnall Hell.

And I think the one gets as much money for frighting men with the one, and making them believe they can show them the way to avoid it, and bring them to Heaven, as the other doth in frighting them with purgatory, and making the poor people believe they can keep them from that. But I let that passe.

And however, the Scripture speaks of Hell, and expresses it by fire and brimstone, and the worme dying not, and many other expressions. It speakes as in other cases, after the manner of men, not that there is such visible and material formes of punishment: But that as fire and brimstone are the most fearful things to the nature of man; so doth the Scripture set out the miserable and fearfull Estate of a carnall condition, and what miseries and torments do accompany such an Estate. And what consequences have followed the outward man from being in such darkness, and what the absence of God hath caused in the spirit, the Scriptures and many daily examples do abundantly testifie: whose terrors and distractions in their spirits have been such as have been easeless and remediless, and made them willing to become their own Butchers, and all this hath been from a misapprehension and confused knowledge of God. The truth is, I shall speak from my own experience, so long as I was in bondage, to dayes, times, and set times, that I must pray so often, and do so much, frequent such Ordinances, so long I was in trouble and sorrow; for I really saw there was this and that failing, and miscarriage in every duty that I suffered torment in my spirit, for fear I should never attain my end, which was a carnall and sensible enjoyment of some happiness which I called Heaven, and when I was inlarged in this and that duty, I thought then all was well, and that I should go to Heaven: And so I was continually suffering the torment of Hell, and tossed up and down, being condemned of my self. And this is all the condemnation that I see is come into the World, that men love darkness rather then light, because their deeds are evill, That men live in love, the dark and fleshly Being, and not in the light, in the divine being; this is the condemnation not causally but formally: And this is that I found til God appeared spiritually, and shewed me that he was all the glory and happiness himself, and that flesh was nothing, and should enjoy nothing, and then I could not but cease from my former fleshly actings which caused nothing but fear and trouble, and saw God, or rather God made out himself in me joy and peace, and brought me into the glorious liberty of the Sons of God, whereas I was before in bondage to sin, law, an accusing Conscience which is Hell. And yet I cannot exclude God in all this, for if we descend into Hell he is there: He is in the dark, though we see it not as well as in the light that we see: He is in wrath and severity, and we are wisht to behold him in both; let there be never such confusions of spirit, never such terrors and Hell, let there be darkness and no light: yet there God is, there is some glimps of himself, in as much as there is a secret going out of the spirit towards God, and all the distractions the Creature lies under, is because it cannot enjoy the presence & love of God, & yet God is there amidst all that darkness and raignes in the midst of his enemies, and so he descends into Hell, and returnes with a glorious tryumph, rising with abundance of joy and peace in the spirit: So that though the Earth be moved, and the great mountains which the Creature had made to it self, be tumbled up and down, and the Creature have no rest, but is easeless and restless, yet God is there as a Rock unshaken of any storme, but is sweetly refreshing and delighting himself with himself, and so enters into the strong mans house, and disarmes him, and bindes him hand and foote, and casts him into utter darkness.

And to summe up all, if there be any that think this is not Hell enough to be inwardly and spiritually tormented. Let them but consult with those that have been under spirituall desertions as they are called, and have cryed out as if their bones had been broken, and would have chosen death rather then life, and thought they could have indured many burnings to have been rid of such a condition.

And I think they will tell them there is no other or need be no other Hell, and all this comes from a dark and carnall knowledg, or rather ignorance of God, for certain it is, God condemns none. But the condemnation is of a mans self, and in a mans self.

If any shall say, all this is nothing; I care not, if this be all the Hell, and that it lasts no longer then this life; But is there not a Hell hereafter, that is, the Hell to think of Eternity, and that the Creature shall be everlastingly tormented, and indure the wrath of God to all Eternity?

For answer hereunto, I must professe, I do not know of any such thing, nor do I conceive what should be thus tormented; for that which men call a soule, I had thought to have made it a particular of the present discourse; but I shall referr it to further consideration, onely to stay any mans appetite that desires my opinion of it, I shall onely give him this morsell to chew upon, and that is this:

I do wonder how any man can make it to be capable of any torment, when as it is well known, it came immediately from God, and is no other but of God, and if I may say further without offence, it is God; for that which is of God is God, because God cannot be divided. All men grant it is immortall, and came from God pure and undefiled: And how then it should be impure, I know not; for this I really see, that though it was infused into the body, yet I am sure it was not of the body, nor could the flesh be capable of such a thing as we call union with the spirit, and so the soule is in the body; but is not of the body or the body, but really distinct; and so it is in flesh but not flesh, and so it is God manifest in flesh: But not in union or conjunction with flesh, but hath a distinct and formall difference, both here and hereafter, the one returning to nothing, the other living to all Eternity.

And further, how this soule, as men speak of, should be impure and sinfull, I know not; for how flesh should defile a spirit I cannot Imagine, being that I am sure, and as every man will grant, That no effect can be produced beyond its cause; but every effect hath its rise and originall from its proper cause: And so hath God laid in nature the body proper to the seed, and to every seed its own body. And a man may as well gather Grapes of Thornes, and Figs of Thistles, as to conceive, it can be that a visible or fleshly substance can corrupt a spirituall and invisible substance: But then you will say, where is the sin all this while? you will say then, sin is nothing, or that there is no sin. To which I have partly answered in the foregoing Subject spoken of, which because it is so faln in my way, I shall speak a little further in answer to you.

First, I shall grant, and I think it is no lesse then blasphemy to affirm otherwise, that God is not the Authour of sin, or that any sin can be in him, he being light, and in him is no darkness at all, and so the soule being of him, it must needes be pure and holy, not admitting any mixture of flesh, or that which we call corrupted nature. And yet againe

Secondly, I cannot conceive there should be sin, untill God was pleased to let out himself in flesh: But for before he lived in himself, and so there could be no sin, there being nothing but God.

Thirdly, Inasmuch as this flesh is a vaile or covering, wherein this soule or divine Being lives: this God, soule, or divine nature, (call it what you will) the glory and beauty, the purity and excellency thereof being darkened and obscured, there is the sin: For whatever men conceive of things, this I really apprehend, That that which we call the soule, that is as men generally make it:

The understanding, reason, judgement, will, and affections are not positively or actually infected with sin; but onely are obscured, and cannot be so gloriously manifested, by reason of the flesh or fleshly Being: and so God tooke flesh upon him, and through the vaile that is the flesh, did destroy, and doth condemn sin in the flesh: So that whosoever prays or prophesies with a vaile or covering upon his head: Christ which is God in the Spirit, such a one dishonoureth his head, which is Christ, because he suffers something to come betwixt God and him. So that by this time, I suppose you see what I conceive of sin, and where it lies, and what I conceive of that we call soul, and of the body or fleshly part of man, wherein I have been forced to make a little digression, because things are mysterious.

And to come to the point in hand, concerning a Hell hereafter, what it should be, or what should be tormented in it, I do not as yet apprehend; for the soul came pure, and is of the essence of God, could not be corrupted, and the body not capable of any impressions of God, and returns to its first principle, of earth: so that unlesse you will imagine a Hell in God, which you would account Blasphemy to speak: I cannot fancy or imagine any such Hell hereafter as men dreame off.

The truth is, there is nothing lives to all eternity but God: every thing below God perisheth and comes to nothing: and as all things had their subsistance and Being in God, before they were ever manifested in the world or Creatures: so in the end, whatsoever is of God, or God in the world at the end of it, they shall all be rapt up into God againe. And so as God from all eternity lived in himself and all things in him: so when he shall cease to live in flesh and creatures, he will then live in himself unto all eternity, and will gloriously triumph over Sin, Hell and death; and all Creatures shall give up their Power and Glory unto God backe againe, from whence it Originally came, and so God shall be All.

However, if any man can imagine, that there will be any dark appearance of God hereafter, or unto all eternity, then may he conclude a Hell; for as sin is the dark appearance of God: so is Hell an inseperable companion of it; but to imagine the one or the other hereafter, or to all eternity, would render me in my owne apprehension one of those whose property it is to believe every thing; but I know whom I have believed.

Thus have I done with that part of my discourse, which I call the dark side of God, which I divide into three parts which we call *Devill*, *Sin*, and *Hell*: In all which I have indeavoured to clear God, and to make the Devill and sin as vile as I can; but am far short of the one or the other, wanting words to express my self in either, onely what was upon my spirit thou hast in the Letter.

Concerning the Resurrection.

NOw let us come to deliver our selves about that which we call Resurrection, and to express it as it is in me. I see it also to be spirituall and inward, and is also of that which is the inward man: For though I know the inward man which is God or the divine Being, admits of no degrees, either is more or lesse; but yet in as much as this God is more gloriously manifested at one time more then another in man.

Hence it is that we give this Title of resurrection of the Creature after this life is ended? But truly, for my part, I am fully satisfied in my own spirit with those words of Christ, where he saith, *I am the Resurrection and the life*:[20] and I see it fully made out in me, that Christ spiritually is that resurrection, which I thought should be of the creature. And I cannot tell what in the creature should rise or be capable of such glory and happinesse beside God, and so I see that which I did expect to enjoy hereafter onely proper and peculiar to God, for I really see that after God is manifest in flesh, and seen of Angels, preached in the world, and believed in, that then he shall after all this be received up into glory, and that flesh and bloud cannot inherit the Kingdome of God: and that nothing lives to all eternity, but pure Divine glory. I cannot conceive any other resurrection then of carnall to be made spirituall, and that is no other then the spirituall appearance of God: so that when I would find out what the resurrection is, I reflect upon my own spirit, and trace the goings of God there, and there I can find God rising from one degree of glory to another, and changing me into his image by his spirit: and so I see how he hath led me from one dispensation to another, and from one ordinance to another, till at last he appears so spiritually that he over-powers all flesh and formes which I admired in my carnall condition, and appears to be that temple, glory and light himselfe, which I had thought to have had in a sensible and carnall enjoyment hereafter, so that I am led to believe that there is no such outward felicity to be enjoyed in this resurrection: but that it is God arising in the spirit, and shining brighter and brighter, till the perfect day; & making all the creature-apprehensions, and knowledge of God to cease, and this resurrection I clearly finde in my owne spirit, that the most glorious and inlarged parts and abilities in prayer, speaking, or otherwise, in which I have delighted, and no question but I did enjoy God in them, though in a darke and low estate: these I say, the glory and beauty of them are all withered and vanished before the bright and glorious appearances of God in the spirit; for the Son in me having delivered up his Kingdome, and those fleshly and formall manifestations, and outward bodily worships ceasing, God is all in all, so that I can neither in *Jerusalem*, or in the Mount, or in any outward form or duty worship God, knowing that he is only to be worshipped in spirit & truth, and that though God was with me in my former carnall and dark condition, and did lead me in it gently, yet all was but to raise up himselfe,

---

20   John 11.25.

and to be that spiritually in me in another way then that which I expected, and so of naturall he hath made me spirituall, which is the spirituall resurrection that we are speaking of.

And further I really see that the flesh of man, and of all other creatures differ not any thing in the nature of them indeed, in respect of the kind and manner, some flesh is of men, some of Beasts, and some of fishes: but as flesh none of them are capable of any more glory then one another, all being of the same mould, and comming to the same end, and though the spirit in them, or whatsoever is God in them, return to their originall, which is God, and so lives in him again, yet the fleshly part returns to dust from whence it came: and as the man dies, so dies the beast; as dies the wise man so dies the foole, one end is to them all as *Solomon* speaks:[21] and whereas men imagine that there is a fleshly resurrection, and that the same body flesh and bones shall rise and remain a corporall and visible substance: how this should be I am sure they do not know themselves: for however men speak that the corporall body shall be made a spirituall, to me it is ridiculous, because the Scripture saith, *That which is borne of flesh is flesh,*[22] and can remaine in no other capacity. And besides, I hope no man will deny, that a spirituall thing can be seen of a fleshly, or that an externall organ of the body can see an internall and invisible thing, the Apostle makes it plaine, that the things which are seen are temporall, and the things that are not seen are eternall. Now how it can stand or consist with reason or Scripture, Logick or Rhetorick, that men should hold and maintaine that men should visibly see one another in heaven as they call it, and know one another, and see their visible shape as they lived in on the earth, & yet they maintaine on the other side this is a spirituall body: I cannot see if this be divinity, then I am not in the humanity; but indeed I am willing to give way to their weaknesse, because I have been as childish my selfe, only I cannot but take notice of the *Babell* and confusion that men are in, and yet thinke themselves the only Embassadours of peace, and as if all knowledge and spirituall learning were confined to them, but laying my hand gently on their sore, I let them passe, and go on to that in hand.

And whereas the Scripture speaks of a spirituall body, I conceived that there is a spirituall body, and that this body must be raised: which spirituall body I apprehend to be nothing but the divine Being, or God in spirit: termed a Body for these two reasons as I conceive: First, because God is the body and substance of all things, and so it is said, that this God dwelt bodily or substantially in the man Christ, he being that person in whose flesh God did more gloriously appear then in any other, so he was the most expresse Image of his Fathers person, and in this respect God may be termed a spirituall Body, though for my part I dare not imagine him to have either person or body. Secondly, God may be stiled a spirituall body; because this body or divine Being is, and hath its Being in many Members. And so God is stiled the head of the body, and Christ is the head of the Church, which is his body, wherein I really apprehend that all the apperances of God in the Saints as they are called, & all the manifestation of God in flesh, or in any fleshly or outward dispensation or form; they are but the Carkes[23] and shadow of God who is the body or substance of them all, and all these dying and vanishing as they shall: God shall onely live and raise himself a spiritual body, and therein

---

21   Eccl. 2.16.   22   John 3.6.
23   'Carcass': the outer shell or corpse without the living essence (*OED* n. 4).

live to all eternity; so that it is spiritually true, that the body which is fleshly shall perish, and the spirituall body shall be raised, as we shall have occasion in the sequel of the discourse to make out; but because men are still poring upon a Scripture without them to prove a carnall Resurrection, and will believe nothing but what they think the Scripture speaks in the letter, though indeed they erre, not knowing it or the power of God: I shall a little condescend to their weakness in this kind: though for my part, if there were not a letter in all the Bible to strengthen me in my opinion of the Resurrection I should not much care, nor need I the testimony of it as to my self; for I have a surer word within, to which I take heed: yet I say for other mens sakes, I shall take the most principall places of Scripture that men look upon, which speak of the Resurrection, and in the spiritual discoveries of them; if there be any thing to strengthen them in their opinion, I shall and must give way.

And we shall begin with that which is the prime piller of their Faith, and that is the I. of the *Corinths* 15. from the beginning to the end of it. It being the whole subject of the discourse therein to treat of the Resurrection: The drift of the Apostle is to prove the spiritual Resurrection of Christ to be as sure and certain as his fleshly; and by the same Argument that he proves the one, by the same he also proves the other, in a spiritual sense. And the comparison lies not betwixt the fleshly rising of Christ, and the fleshly rising of men, as most men imagine; but betwixt the fleshly rising of Christ in the humanity, and his spiritual rising in the divinity, and so all along, you shall see the comparison holds betwixt the naturall and the spirituall, and not betwixt the naturall and the naturall. And that we may see plainly it appears in the 47. verse, *The first man is of the Earth earthly; the second man is from Heaven who is the Lord*: so that we see, he compares the outward earthly man, and the Lord from Heaven which is the spiritual, and shewes evidently, that it is not the earthly man that is raised, but the spirituall, and so Christ after the flesh was but of the earthly man, and so must be destroyed and subdued, as wel as other things and formes, which did accompany that earthly being, and as the one vanished out of sight before the Apostles; so must the other, and that this may not seeme strange to any man, that the flesh of Christ must be destroyed, as well as other things. It is plain in the 28. verse.

So that it is apparent, that the Sonne of man being of the first *Adam* after the flesh, must as well be subdued and perish with the fleshly forms and administrations that did accompany him: For certain I am, that as he was God or the divine being in him, he could not be subdued, so that it is very clear, that it was the fleshly appearance that must needes come to nothing as well as the fleshly forme in other Creatures; and so Christ did cease to live in the flesh, that he might more transcendently live in the spirit, and so he laid down his humanity to live in the Divinity: and so it is true what the Apostle saith in the 20. *v.* That as Christ is risen from the dead, and is become the first fruits of them that sleep and are dead in him, so such as are dead in him shall surely rise. That is, they shall as surely rise to a spirituall condition as they have been spiritually dead in him. And so he goes on in the 22. verse. As in *Adam* all dyed, so in Christ shall all be made alive: Here is still the comparison betwixt the natural and the spirituall: that is, as sure as the fleshly *Adam*, and outward visible forme dies, so it is as certain, they that are in Christ or the spiritual man, shall be made alive and quickened, and

God shall rise and appear in more power and glory in that life of the spirit then ever he did in the fleshly forme or shape. But to go on, The first fruits is Christ, and then they that are Christs at his coming: which is thus, that as Christ herein was the first fruits of them that did live in the spirit; as he saith, a little while, and you shall see me, and a little while, and you shall not see me, because I go to the Father: that is, he was to lay down the flesh to live in the divine and spiritual life, in which he appeared after his ascension, and so was as good as his word, and did come in spirit; so it should be as spiritually true, that they should partake of the same spiritual life, and live in the same spiritual Resurrection as he, and live in the Father as he did; and therefore he comforted them, and told them, I ascend to my Father and your Father, to my God and your God: But yet in the mean time, till the Son of man and all fleshly formes were subdued to the Father, till men were brought to live in the Father, and to live in a spiritual life: till then Christ must raigne, till then there must be outward formes of Christs death, and there must be manifestations of God in flesh, and outward Ordinances. But when these are subdued, then men must rise, or rather God will appear to be that spiritually which they before enjoyed, onely in an outward manner as is argued by the Apostle in the 25. verse: And the last enemy is death: And certain it is, this death must be destroyed; and the dead must rise, or else death cannot be destroyed:

Now this must needes be a little opened, that so we may see what the Resurrection is; for certainly, the dead must arise, or else Christ cannot be risen.

For the opening of which death we shall take the same method as the Apostle doth here, to compare the natural with the spiritual. Then we say a man is dead, when a man is void of all visible sence and motion, when he ceases to act or move, when the life is departed, when the life is departed, when the being ceases to live in the flesh, that he cannot move to any outward or naturall act.

And so a man is spiritually dead, or dead in Christ, when a man ceases to be or act any thing in the things of God; but is moved and acted, as God is in him: when there is nothing of the self-being appearing; in a word, when to the world he appears to act nothing, do nothing in an outward and formall way, so that men think there is no spiritual life in him.

Then doth he die in the Lord, when he wholly resignes up all his grace, abilities, knowledge of God into God, and knowes not what he doth, or is or should know ceasing from his own reachings forth after God, living and being to any self-enjoyment, or expectation of any future felicity, life or comfort out of God: For it is certain so long as the Creature thinks that he must act or do something to attain salvation, or be any thing distinct from God, so long he is alive without Gods life, and so must needes be miserable, and therefore the Apostle saith, if in this life our hope was, we were most miserable:[24] which life is not to be understood of the fleshly Being: But in this life that is, if our happinesse comforts did depend upon our owne self-actings, and on our own being any thing, were we most miserable.

But our hope is, that all our felicity and comfort is terminated and centred in God onely. And so Christ spiritually in us is the hope of glory, which is a mystery; and so being dead in Christ, when Christ rises, we shall be sure to rise with him: so that there is a sweet truth in

---

24   1 Cor. 15.19.

that Scripture, where it is said, That the day of a mans death is better then the day that a man is borne: For better it is for a man to die spiritually, then to live naturally.

And so none of us liveth to himself, or dyes to himself; but whether we live or dye, all is in the Lord: and he is glorified in the death, as well as in the life: for our life is hid with God in Christ, as the Apostle saith to the *Collossians*:[25] though we be dead as he saith, and nothing appeares of life to our selves or others, yet we need not fear; for the life is hid with God in Christ: And when Christ our life shall appear: and so appear as to be our life and happinesse, then shall we appear glorious, but it is in him; when Christ rises so spiritually and gloriously, to subdue and destroy the fleshly being, which is the death and causes death; for no sooner did sin enter, but death entered with it, then doth Christ the spirituall being and life triumph. And then is death swallowed up of life, and mortality of immortality; That is, flesh is swallowed up of spirit, and death the fleshly being is swallowed up of life, the spirituall being. And then shall be brought to passe that saying, O Death where is thy sting! O grave where is thy victory![26] But thanks to God, for it is he that gets the victory: again as it is in the naturall, so it is in the spirituall.

This Resurrection is set forth by the resemblance of the graine of Corne, and it holds out a lively resemblance of the spirituall life and death, and of the spirituall Resurrection of the naturall; for as the graine of Corn dyes before it lives, and in this death there is life hid: so in this spirituall death there is spirituall life, though it be hid and lye buried in the grave of earthly and carnall apprehensions: as God gives the one a Body, and is himself the substance and Body, and the life: so doth the spirituall Body, the inward and spirituall life which is God, rise to more glory then ever he did appear in in the earthly and outward forme; and as the fleshly appearance dyes and ceases, and as in the death there is life: so God when he ceases to live in flesh, he lives and rises with much more glory in the Spirit: And yet it is true, till the fleshly and outward form or formall Being suffers the Divine cannot reigne; and therefore in the midst of death there is life, and God doth but dye in weaknesse to rise in power: Not that God is weak, but he is buried and hid in the carnall sense and life, to rise with more strong and glorious appearances of himself, which is the spirituall Resurrection; which is further illustrated, by the terrestriall Bodies, and the heavenly Bodies which doth but further confirm the spirituall rising of Christ; For though there be a glory in the terestriall and outward dispensations and manifestations of God in them, so when God is pleased to uncloath himself, and to let out himself in pure and heavenly dispensations, when these come and appear, and that God puts on the heavenly clothing, then is the corruptible swalled[27] up of the incorruptible; For it is true, that flesh and blood cannot inherit the Kingdom of God, nor corruption put on incorruption: but when there shall be a change, and of naturall we become spirituall: and when the last Trump shall blow, that is, when God shall gloriously sound forth his one praise & nothing but spirituall power appears; Then shall the dead hear the voice of the Sonne of God and live, and the dark and carnall appearances of God shall give way to the more pure and spirituall; and then shall God gloriously triumph over Sin, Death

25   Col. 3.3.   26   1 Cor. 15.55.
27   Swallowed, engulfed, made to vanish (*OED* v. 3a, 4).

and Hell, and live without any vaile, in his own pure and divine glory. The consideration of which is sufficient, to perswade me to be stedfast and to abound in the work of the Lord; knowing that though my labour be in vaine, as to self, or flesh, yet it is not in vaine in the Lord: he being the end and summe of all.

Thus have I as briefly and plainly as I could gone over the substance of the whole Chapter, though much more might be spoken; being conscious to my own spirit, that I have not hid or concealed any clause, which might serve to speak for a carnall Resurrection: or for a rising of the body after its dissolution here in any visible form or shape; But that as the light is in me: so have I manifested it out to others; and do onely referre my self for tryall, to that light which manifests all things, leaving other men to their own darke and carnall apprehensions of a carnall Resurrection; and conclude, that the Resurrection is from the carnall to the fleshly Christ: from Christ living in the flesh, to his living in the Spirit, which is that I call the Resurrection; and if time and mens patience would suffer, I could easily prove, that whatsoever Christ as man was, or did from his Birth to his ascension, in his life and death in the flesh; they were but all Types and shadowes of what he would be, and work in his glorious coming in the Spirit, and so they are applyed all along, if men wil let the Scripture speak in the very Letter; but I let it passe at present.

And further, to gratifie mens weakness, I shall proceed to another Scripture, which is as carnally urged as the former, to prove a carnall Resurrection; and that is in *Matthew*, concerning Christs reasoning with the *Sadduces*,[28] they denying the Resurrection: And Christ proving it to them, by saying, That he was the God of the living and not of the dead: and so, that though *Abraham*, *Isaack* and *Jacob* were dead long agoe; yet they lived: But to open this Scripture, we must know what Resurrection the *Sadduces* denyed, and what Resurrection Christ proved; I affirm, that it was the spiritual Resurrection which they denyed and that appeares plainly, by that in the 23 of *Acts* 8. where it is said, that the *Sadduces* deny the Resurrection or Angell or Spirit; but there is no mention of the Resurrection of the Body. And so it is clear, that Christs argument to them was to prove a spirituall Resurrection, and so it holds a full proof of what we affirme, and a full answer to the *Sadduces*; For God is not the God of the dead, but of the living: not of flesh, but of Spirit: And so *Abraham*, *Isaack* and *Jacob*, they did really and spiritually live in God, though they were dead in the flesh; So that I conceive, and it is clear to me, that a spirituall and Angelical appearance of God, is that Resurrection which is held forth and which should be; and they are the *Sadduces* that deny this spirituall Resurrection.

Another Scripture which is alledged to as little purpose, is that in *Iob.* 19.[29] I know my Redeemer lives, and that I shall see him with these eyes; I do wonder, what a God men fancy to be seen with a fleshly eye: I always took God to be a Spirit & invisible, and that no created fleshly things was able to see him. I cannot imagine then how *Jobs* eyes, which were and should be in a visible form and shape, should be capable of such a Divine invisible vision:

---

28   Mark 12.18–27. The Sadducees denied the resurrection of the dead, and the existence of angels and spirits. They were not so much a sect or school as a political party, formed essentially of the nobility.

29   Job. 19.25.

But yet if *Job* was so carnall to conceive, that his fleshly eyes should see a spirituall God: yet I am not.

And if any man shall say, that Christ hath a Body in heaven which he lived in when he was upon the earth: and that may be seen being visible and corporall; for that when any man shall prove heaven a locall place, and that God the Fathour sits there, and receives petitions from his Son Christ, as men do visibly here on earth: then I shall give him an answer, neither have I so learned Christ to make him to consist of flesh and bloud, or bodily shape in heaven (as men call it) for though it be said, that *Steven* saw the heaven opened, and Christ sitting at the right hand of God,[30] yet am I not so carnall to believe, That *Stevens* fleshly eyes might see up above the stars, and skies, and that the house top might be open where he was, and so he bodily saw Christ sitting in a bodily shape at the right hand of God in heaven. As a Divine of *Leicestershire* did affirm to me, in a private conference that he thought it might be so. But his divinity being as little as his person I leave him, as knowing that the man Christ left his fleshly being to live in the divine, which is void of all forme and shape, or to be seen visibly by any outward or corporeall substance, and that no light can see him, but his own, and when men live in this light, then they will agree with me, till then, I must leave men to their dark and carnall apprehensions, In the meane time I am content to be nothing that God may be all, and to let fall my thoughts of any glory or excellency hereafter, as a creature; as knowing that the fleshly man dies, that the spirituall may be raised, and that all creature or sensible enjoyment of God shall cease in eternall silence: and it is fruit and joy enough in my spirit, that God hath so discovered himself in me that I can willingly resolve all my comforts, joy and peace into God, who is that endlesse and infinite Ocean, and rather desire to be comprehended of it, then to comprehend it: so that by all that hath bin alleadged, I cannot see that there is any thing in that called Scripture to prove any fleshly living of the body after this life, but that all things and Creatures below God perish and die, and God onely lives, and rises in more power, and glorious appearance then ever he was in when he lived in the flesh: which is that resurrection which is spirituall, and which we have endeavoured to make out, and so I leave it, and come to the last Subject of my discourse, which is that we call *Scripture*: and because men are as carnall about that as any of the former, and because the ground of all the mistakes in the former is onely the mis-apprehension of the Scripture we shal insist upon that a little the more larger, and so conclude.

Concerning the Scripture.

I F you take Scripture as it was written by the Prophets and Apostles: It is a forme of wholesome words, a perfect rule, for all outward actions, a true Guide for a mans outward conversation among men: The liveliest expression of the mind of God, of all other books; setting forth all conditions, estates and enjoyments of all men in the world, it is the word in flesh, *The word was made flesh*,[31] it is the highest discovery of God in flesh, the truest testimony of God in the world: I do verily believe, that what pitch soever any man hath or

---

30   Acts 7.56.   31   John 1.14.

can attain unto, but it is able to speak to him in it thus, it is in the letter, and the out-side of it.

But if you ask me what I make Scripture? I look upon it to be spiritual, and so it is the Law written in the heart, and so it is spirit and life, as Christ saith, *The words that I speak are spirit and life:*[32] so that what Christ speaks spiritually, that is Scripture, and so it is the power of God; for take Scripture as it is in the History, it hath no more power in the inward man, then any other writings of good men, nor is it in that sense a discerner of the secrets, as it is in the History, so it is to be believed above all other writings in the world; but as it is a mystery, and God being the substance of it, so I must believe it as God makes it out in me: I must not build my Faith upon it, or any saying of it, because such and such men writ or speak so and so, But from that divine manifestation in my own spirit; for the Scripture, as it is written outwardly, is but an outward witnesse of that which is within; and the spirituality of it wherein the life and being of it doth consist, is made out by a spiritual discovery. I do not go to the letter of Scripture, to know the mind of God; but I having the mind of God within, I am able to see it witnessed, and made out in the Letter; for if I do a thing lawfull from the Letter; yet if I be perswaded in my own spirit I should not do it, I sinne. Yea further, that power and authority which the Scripture hath, is not because such and such men writ it; but from that divine manifestation in them: And so indeed, if I have the same discovery that they had; then I can say, it is the word of God, otherwise I lie; for it is one thing to believe the Scripture, because such and such write it, as most men do: and it is another thing to believe it because God saith so in me; and so it is the spirituall speaking of God that is the Scripture, and so that is true. They that are of God hear Gods Word: Now no man can hear God, but as God speaks: And it is as true, that as God speaks spiritually: so no man hears him but in a spirituall manner, and so we hear Gods word. And therefore it is said often in the I. *Rev. He that hath an eare, let him hear what the spirit saith to the Churches;*[33] Which cannot be understood of a carnall eare, because every man hath that; but as the Spirit speaks spiritually: so it is the spirituall eare that hears the Spirit: For all the outward speaking or hearing of men or Scripture, cannot reach the Spirit. Further, the Scripture I do apprehend, as it is written outwardly, is God clothed in fleshly tearmes and expressions, and speaks in the language of men, as when he speaks of himself; and he uses such expressions as are highest in mens esteem, and his commands, threatnings and promises, admonitions, exhortations, they are all as men speak to one another; for I dare not believe God is this or that, or can be named by any title, or that he ever threatned any people or Nation; or promised any, that upon such and such terms they should have this or that, or upon neglect of him they should suffer this or that; for to me it plainly appears, that there is neither wrath or anger, love or hatred in God, or that God was any thing more or lesse to a people, upon their sinning or doing any good; For then a thousand absurdities would follow. But the truth is, because men apprehend anger when they sin, and God pleased when they do well; therefore men speak as one to another, and God so far condescends, as to speak to men in their own language; But that he is so in himselfe, I should think blasphemy to affirme; for I am confident there is never an error or tenent in the world as men maintaine; but if men take that for Scripture, which they call the Bible, it doth fully and literally countenance and

---

32   John 6.63.   33   Rev. 2.29.

uphold: and I know no other way in the world, to uphold the authority of Scripture, than to make it spirituall. And whereas men speak that we deny Scripture: I must confesse for my part, that I know no greater door opened to the denying it, then for men to presse, and urge men to do such and such things, because the outward word saith so and so: indeed, so far I shall deny it as the Letter is inferiour to the Spirit: so far I conceive, the letter doth vaile and shadow the spirituality of it. And if men have the Law in their hearts, and be taught of God, they need not run so often to a great Bible, to relieve themselves in straights and doubts as men generally do, never reflecting upon their spirits, to see what God speaks there; I do not speak it to condemn the practise, neither is the fault in the Book, but in mens carnall conceits of it; and seeing men make an Idoll of it, and think the reading and perusing the outward word, is enough to cure all their wounds, and to resolve their doubts; so that as men look upon God outwardly and carnally: so do they have recourse to an outward word, to strengthen their carnall apprehensions. Truly, I must confesse ingeniously, that as to my own spiritual enjoyment, I see nothing of any concernment in it, or in looking upon it, but onely this I see, and so it is some comfort to me to read, that God hath discovered himself in others as well as in me, and that the spirit speaks the same in me, as it did in them. But for any thing of God that I look to attaine unto by reading or looking upon it, I do not care whether ever I look upon one again or no: And yet this is no detracting from the glory or authority of Scripture; because the Scripture is within and spirituall, and the Law being writ in my spirit, I care not much for beholding it in the Letter; but as to the ends aforesaid. And the truth is, it is the Law in the spirit that is the true Bible, the other is but a shadow or counterpart of it; and therefore I do not expect to be taught by Bibles, or Books, but by God: nay further, I do not do any thing, or abstain from any thing, because the outward letter commands or forbids it: but by reason of that commanding power which is God in me, and his speaking is the power of God to salvation, and it is in that by which I live, and by which I act: and so the Apostle speaks of the law outward, that it was not made for the righteous, but for whoremongers, and such and such.

And so I see, that if men were acted & guided by that inward law of righteousnesse within, there need be no laws of men, to compel or restrain men, and I could wish that such a spirit of righteousnesse would appear, that men did not act or do things from externall rules, but from an internall law within: Again to speak a little further, concerning the Scripture, men generally speak, that we must do nothing but what we have a rule for, and are asking, what warrant have you to do such a thing? shew a rule from Scripture, and then we will believe you, or else it is but a whimsey, and I know not what; Truly, it is true, and I would those that talk most of a rule, did see that rule; for the safest and prime rule that I know for any man, is that pure spirituall law and rule of righteousnesse which is within, and so far as any man doth any thing beneath or beyond that, so far he doth that which he hath no warrant for: but who must judge of this rule, whether this or that be according to the mind of God or no? To this I answer, in the words of Scripture, because men will soonest believe me: That it is the spirit which searches all things, even the deep things of God: and there is no knowing the spirit but in its own light which is spiritual, & therefore I think it not so safe to go to the Bible to see what others have spoken and writ of the mind of God, as to see what God speaks within me, and to follow the ducture and leading of it in me, I shall sooner, and so others shall sooner, mis-apprehend the mind of God in other men, then in my self, and the same law and rule being in me which was in those that writ the Bible, and to which internall and spiritual rule within, I must take a measure and scantling of all my actions, I had rather measure them from or by a rule within, then by any outward rule or word whatsoever; for the one, that is to say, the Bible without, is but a shadow of that Bible which is within, which is the Law spiritual, the safest and onely rule.

If any man shall say, that I may be deceived, and take that for a discovery of God which is but a fancie of my own Brain: I answer, I may mis-interpret the outward Scripture, and so run as great a hazard that way, and as soon fall into errour, because it speakes of and to men in variety of Estates and conditions, and so if I take that part of it, which doth not speak to my condition, I shall then make a false construction of it, so that I conceive the safest and surest rule to walk by, is that law of the spirit, and as many as walk according to that spirituall rule, peace shall be upon them, and on the *Israel* which is of God; but as many as walk according to a rule without them and so look for a God and Scripture without, they shall be but at a losse, and live in continuall trouble and disquietment: and if I may speak my own experience without offence, so long as I lived and looked upon the outward scripture, outward commands and duties, set times of humiliation, prayer, & I know not what, I was always tost to and fro like the waves of the sea. But when God appeared and shewed me that there was no scrip⟨t⟩ure God commands worships, but what were spirituall like himselfe, and within men, and what he was the authour and end of, and that all things else were but shadowes; what sweet, peace and comfort, I then did, and do now enjoy, I might tell you if I could; for the truth is they are unspeakable: and so it is the spirituall discovery of God that is the Scripture I look upon: and if so, then I must needs inferre, that those in whom Christ is spiritually discovered, and that live in a spirituall enjoyment of him, they must needs be best able to speak the language of the Scripture, and to give the sense and meaning of it, and are best acquainted with the originall: for God being the Authour of it, they in whom he is most spiritually discovered must needs know the mind of it, and what Scripture is; which may exclude all outward parts of learning, arts, and other qualifications, which men boast of; for though they may serve to speak scripture outwardly, and help to expresse men to one another, and to read it in the severall translations of it, from one Nation to another; yet they all come short of the spirituall discovery of God, and so are not essential to the knowledge of him; he being onely known and seen in his own light. And which may likewise condemne the *Romane* Clergy, I think the *English* Divines may take their part herein; That having attain'd a little skil in the several languages of several countrys, and received ordination (as they call it) they think themselves so invested with power above their brethren, that none must be infallible or authentick in the interpretation of Scripture, but themselves and men of their order; and unlesse they will say themselves that private men (as they call them) cannot have the same, or more spirituall discovery of God then themselves, I do wonder that they should so advance themselves, and undervalue or despise others.

But we shall let them passe and return to what we have in hand, and we shall see both the Authority and end of Scripture, laid down by the Apostle in the 2. of *Tim*. 3. 16. where he saith all Scripture is given by inspiration of God, and is profitable to teach, *&c.* that the man of God may be made perfect; where we see plainly what I have spoken all along, That the inspiration which is spiritual and of God, is the true & proper ground why men are taught, and no man can be taught, but it must be by a spiritual inspiration, or else it is not of God: and so the Scripture is not of any private interpretation; but holy men speak as they were inspired: so that, that which gives the rise & ground of Scripture is Gods speaking in men, or inspiring men, and they best know what is Scripture, in whom God most powerfully speaks. And it is as true that God speaks spiritually in man, and not in any audible voice or forme of words; for I do not conceive he ever spoke so to any, he being void of all shape and form, or bodily Organs. And when God so speakes that from naturall, they are made spiritual, then is it indeed they are spiritually taught. And to this sweetly falls in that of *David*: thou hast taught me truth in the secret parts;[34] then indeed men come to be convinced of their former weak and carnall condition, when God spiritually discovers himself in them: So that it is not the reading or perusing of the Scripture in the letter of it: for so a man may read all his life-time, and be never the better that teaches men spiritually: But when the Scripture is spiritually made out, and interpreted in them, then they are taught: And then it is, that the man of God is made perfect; then doth the inward fleshly Being, or carnall man appeare dark and carnall, and the spirituall or the man of God, comes to be perfect: and this spirituall man is able to judge all things as the Apostle saith, then can he spiritually discern the Scripture in him, and so can read it true in the outward letter; For I really see, that all the knowledge of the Scripture in the letter of it, reaches no further but to a historicall and fleshly knowledge of God, and indeed to this kind of knowledge, which many do boast of, the Scripture is very helpfull. But he that knows no further then the outward letter, knowes but Christ after the flesh. And though so I have known Christ, Scripture and God, yet henceforth know I them so no more; they being spirituall. Again, this I conceive, that all the whole story and letter of the Scripture, doth but set out and speak but of two estates and conditions of men or in men: that is the fleshly Being and the Divine; the naturall and the spirituall man: And all these are presented to us in their several degrees and actings in each state, and personated in severall persons from the beginning to the end of the Bible. And so *Cain* and *Abel*, *Isaac* and *Ishmael*, *Jacob* and *Esau*, *David* and *Saul*; and so the good Kings and the bad, the good Prophets and the wicked, the true Apostles and the false; they do but all expresse both Estates, and are not so much to be lookt upon in their severall persons; but are really fulfilled and appliable to every man in each Estate, Degree, and Condition whatsoever. As to instance, it tels us of the Man Christ, who lived and died at *Jerusalem*, and that he rose from the dead, and ascended and past through all conditions: But alas, how farre is this from reaching the spirit, a man may read it, and believe it, and yet be never the better, do him no more good then any other History which we call prophane. But the spirituality and Comfort, and that which is spirit and life, lies in this to see him found[35] in the spirit, to die in him, and to rise with him, to ascend and sit down with him

---

34   A loose allusion to Ps. 51.6: 'thou desirest truth in the inward parts.'
35   'formd' in first edn.

in the heavenly places, being made conformable to him in the spirit to have the everlasting Gospel preacht in the spirit. All which the History and Person of Christ and the outward Gospel, are but shadows: the other is the sealed Book which none can read, till God open himself to be the Scripture: Then indeed can we understand what Scripture is, and then are we guided by that inward life and spirit of truth, more then by the outward letter, and teachings in the World. So that is not the History of Scripture that is the Scripture, or that is the word of God, but it is the spiritual speaking of *God*, which is the word of *God*, and is spirit & life. But some may say, doth not the word say, Hear and your souls shall live; and faith comes by hearing, and hearing by the word of God?[36] Is not the Scripture and outward letter a meanes to convey the knowledge of God, and meanes to get Faith? To which I answer, it is true; but what living is it to which hearing is annexed. If an outward and carnall living and knowing of God, then the outward Scripture contributes to it; but if it be a spiritual living, which is a living in God, then that life must be enjoyed by a spirituall hearing: for all the outward hearing in the world cannot reach to that, so that to me it is plain, that then men spiritually live, when God spiritually speakes, and so this spiritual life is attained by a spirituall speaking of God; and when men heare that spiritual speaking, then their soules live spiritually in that, and so the word of Christ is verefied; That man lives not by bread onely, but by every word which proceedes out of the mouth of God,[37] that is, it is not any outward or external way or meanes that supports the Spirit, but it is the divine and spiritual food, that the divine and spiritual man lives upon, and on that he feedes spiritually with sweet content and satisfaction: it being sutable to him; and such are the onely blessed that eat bread in the Kingdom of Heaven: for they never hunger or thirst after any externall or outward teaching or speaking of men; and so it is true, that faith comes by hearing. But what do you make of Faith? If it be a spiritual thing, as it is, then it must needes come by a spiritual meanes, which is a spiritual hearing, and so the following words explain it, That hearing comes by the word of God: Now it is apparent, that God speakes spiritually, and so he is heard and believed spiritually; and men cannot heare God speak, but it must be by a spiritual hearing, sutable to the speaking. But men are still objecting and say, did not Christ and the Apostles convince men of the truth of things by the Scripture, shewing things must needs be so. I answer, it is true, but the reasons plain which was, that because men were not able to bear Christs spiritual speaking, it being mysticall: therefore he speaks to them in parables, and in such a way as they could apprehend, and so did condescend to their weaknesse, and so Christ speakes of himself, that he needed not Iohns Testimony, he had a sufficient proofe with himself, and needed not any mans Testimony of him.[38] And besides, as men did hasten their belief of things upon an outward letter: therefore Christ and the Apostle brought Scripture to prove things, that he might beat them with their own weapons. And so alleadged Scripture to the Devill, to answer him in his own way. And the Apostles brought Scripture to prove a Christ in the flesh which some went about to deny. And whereas some alleadge that to the Law and the Testimony, if any man speak not according to that, it is because there is no truth in him. It is also true, if any man speak not from that spirituall Law in himself, and hath not the inward Testimony of

---

36   Isa. 55.3; Rom. 10.17.   37   Matt. 4.4.   38   John 5.33–36.

the spirit within: in such a man there is no truth, let him speak what he will, and this is the grand cause why men do dispute and jangle about things, because men speak not from the inward experience and spiritual teaching, but from tradition and the outward letter. Nay I verily believe most of the Religion in the world is borne up, because others had held and done so before them, and they think it sufficient to walk in an outward conformity, in duties and Ordinances, and never eye the goings of God in their own Spirits: But this by the way, and all I drive at in this, and I hope no body will be offended, that I would make Scripture as it is to be spiritual, and not subject to the gross and carnall apprehensions and interpretations of any sort of men whatever; neither do I lessen the Authority of it in so doing: for the reason of all the mistakes in and about the Scripture, is not in the Scripture, but in mens carnall apprehensions of it. For if men were spiritual, they might judge it also to be spiritual as God himself is. And I would have men settle it upon a sure foundation, which is God and that Divine Law within us, which is pure and Divine Scripture.

F I N I S.

Index

*Note: documents reprinted are indicated in **bold** type. References to notes are in the form 12n1 (note 1 on page 12). Documents with named authors are indexed under the author's name.*

Index of Biblical References

Printed and bound by CPI Group (UK) Ltd, Croydon, CR0 4YY

09/06/2025

14685875-0001